RAPE AND
SEXUAL POWER
IN
EARLY AMERICA

Rape *and*

Published

for the

OMOHUNDRO

INSTITUTE

OF EARLY

AMERICAN

HISTORY AND

CULTURE,

Williamsburg,

Virginia, by the

UNIVERSITY

OF NORTH

CAROLINA

PRESS, *Chapel*

Hill

SHARON BLOCK

Sexual Power

in EARLY AMERICA

The Omohundro Institute of Early American History and Culture is sponsored jointly by the College of William and Mary and the Colonial Williamsburg Foundation. On November 15, 1996, the Institute adopted the present name in honor of a bequest from Malvern H. Omohundro, Jr.

Set in Carter Cone Galliard
by Keystone Typesetting, Inc.
Manufactured in the United States of America
Library of Congress Cataloging-in-Publication Data
Block, Sharon, 1968–
Rape and sexual power in early America / Sharon Block.
p. cm.
"Published for the Omohundro Institute of Early
American History and Culture, Williamsburg,
Virginia."
Includes bibliographical references and index.
ISBN-13: 978-0-8078-3045-1 (cloth: alk. paper)
ISBN-10: 0-8078-3045-3 (cloth: alk. paper)
ISBN-13: 978-0-8078-5761-8 (pbk.: alk. paper)
ISBN-10: 0-8078-5761-0 (pbk.: alk. paper)
1. Rape — United States — History. 2. Sex crimes —
United States — History. 3. United States — History
18th century. 4. United States — History 19th century.
I. Title.
HV6561.B56 2006
364.15′32097309033 — dc22
2005035320

The paper in this book meets the guidelines for permanence and durability of the Committee on Production Guidelines for Book Longevity of the Council on Library Resources.

cloth   10 09 08 07 06   5 4 3 2 1
paper   10 09 08 07 06   5 4 3 2 1

This volume received indirect support from an unrestricted book publications grant awarded to the Institute by the L. J. Skaggs and Mary C. Skaggs Foundation of Oakland, California.

FOR DAVE

ACKNOWLEDGMENTS

For years I've thought about writing the perfect acknowledgments to this book—engaging and heartfelt thanks to the institutions and people who have been instrumental to my research on rape in early America. Now that I'm putting these thanks on paper, I find myself short on clever repartee but do hope that I can convey how deeply appreciative I am of the generous support I have received over the years.

The Andrew W. Mellon Foundation, Princeton University, the John Nicholas Brown Center for the Study of American Civilization, a Woodrow Wilson National Fellowship Foundation Dissertation Fellowship in Women's Studies, and an American Historical Association Littleton-Griswold Research Grant all supported my original dissertation research. My supplemental research and revisions have been generously supported by the Omohundro Institute of Early American History and Culture, the Henry E. Huntington Library, the University of Iowa, and the University of California, Irvine. I also thank the *Journal of American History, Common-Place: The Interactive Journal of Early American Life, Journalism History,* the University of Pennsylvania Press, and the New York University Press for allowing me to present in their publications paragraphs and sections that appear here in different form.

John Murrin, Christine Stansell, Hendrik Hartog, and Kathleen M. Brown originally shepherded this project through the dissertation stages. The two official OIEAHC readers of the original dissertation manuscript, Cornelia Hughes Dayton and John Demos, provided excellent advice on expanding and refining the project. The readers of the final book manuscript, Norma Basch and Daniel Cohen, offered thoughtful comments that greatly improved the manuscript. Dozens of scholars have sent me citations about rape over the years (you can all stop sending them now!), and Nina Dayton, Kirsten Fischer, Timothy Gilfoyle, Philip J. Schwarz, and John Wood Sweet generously shared chunks of their own research. Thanks to Birte Pfleger and Jason Sellers for outstanding research and manuscript assistance.

I owe thanks to everyone at OIEAHC who has had input on this project. Fredrika J. Teute gave important and insightful comments on the dissertation that was the start of this book. I have the uncommon opportunity to thank four copy-editors. Emily Moore gave this manuscript OIEAHC-quality copyediting under increasingly difficult circumstances. Thanks also to Gil Kelly's copy-editing supervision; any "funny-looking" editing choices are mine alone.

Kathy Burdette stepped in with good cheer at beyond the last minute to take over substantial editing duties, and Meg Tilley arrived just in time to finalize the copy-edited manuscript. I greatly appreciate Ron Hoffman's extensive and good-natured efforts at getting my finished manuscript into production.

I have been blessed with multiple communities of supportive scholars, beginning with my brief tenures at OIEAHC at the College of William and Mary and in the Department of History at the University of Iowa. My current department at the University of California, Irvine, has an array of great colleagues who are also good friends, including Sarah Farmer, Douglas Haynes, Laura Mitchell, Rachel O'Toole, Ulrike Strasser, Heidi Tinsman, Charles Wheeler, and Jon Wiener. Multiple senior scholars have been particularly wonderful mentors to me, freely offering professional and personal advice. Alice Fahs, Lynn Mally, Bob Moeller, and Vicki Ruiz have gone beyond the call of duty, reading chapters, answering frantic e-mails, and sharing their hard-earned wisdom.

My friends in the UCI community, Linda Bauer, Natalka Freeland, Candace Hsieh, Bill Landis, Glenn and Ursula Levine, and Danielle McClellan, have made daily life that much sweeter by their presence. Many of my colonial history sex-gender-race compatriots, Jennifer Baszile, Kirsten Fischer, Ann Little, Jennifer Morgan, Elizabeth Reis, and Jennifer Spear, have enriched the field with their work and made me proud to do colonial history alongside them. Kathy Brown, Nina Dayton, and Ruth Bloch have provided invaluable mentorship and intellectual advice at crucial moments along the way.

This book manuscript would never have been finished without the outstanding childcare provided by the UCI's Infant/Toddler Center and Children's Center. Their skilled teachers meant that I didn't have to choose between two loves: academia and my children. I can't say that having two children on the tenure clock is an easy road, but the University of California's parental leave policy along with the support of family and friends made it possible.

My grandparents, Louis and Sylvia Block, have been unswerving in their love and support—and my grandfather has let nary a phone call go by without asking "whether that book is finished yet?" My sister, Heidi Block Barishman, has generously offered her home, her heart, and her energy. She has tendered legal advice, filled our freezer with dinners, and even taken my son on a cross-country trip so that I could get my work done. My parents, Anne and Alan Block, have been the best supporters anyone could ask for. They have enriched my life in thousands of ways and put up with my continued attempts to throw off patriarchy with good humor and respect.

Casey N. Block and Ripley B. Newman have provided comic (and not-so-comic) relief from this manuscript. They have taught me to work more efficiently, to survive on less sleep, and have shown me a different production from the publishable kind. Friends have joked that I birthed them at home with midwives to get a taste of the colonial experience. I'm not that dedicated to my profession. But their births did remind me of my own powers and give me perspective on cranking out a few hundred typed pages.

I hope that David J. Newman already knows the place he holds in my heart. I want publicly to thank him for the many choices he made that allowed us to have a two-career family. I could not begin to detail the ways he has enriched my professional and personal life. He has been my biggest booster and best sounding board. He has taught me to laugh more and stress (a little) less. He has washed more dishes and changed more diapers than any husband I know. And that doesn't even scratch the surface. To paraphrase the poignant lyrics of Jason Robert Brown, he has always offered me the stars and the moon. I am a far better person for having him in my life and am grateful for every day we share together.

CONTENTS

LIST OF ILLUSTRATIONS

ABBREVIATIONS

AAS	American Antiquarian Society, Worcester, Mass.
APS	American Philosophical Society Library, Philadelphia
CCA	Chester County Archives, West Chester, Pa.
CSL	Connecticut State Library, Hartford
DPA	Delaware Public Archives, Dover
GA	Georgia Archives, Morrow
HHR	Hunterdon Hall of Records, Flemington, N.J.
HL	Henry E. Huntington Library, San Marino, Calif.
HSP	Historical Society of Pennsylvania, Philadelphia
KLA	Kentucky Department for Libraries and Archives, Frankfort
LCHS	Lancaster County Historical Society, Lancaster, Pa.
LOV	Library of Virginia, Richmond
MA	Massachusetts Archives, Boston
MdHS	Maryland Historical Society, Baltimore
MdSA	Maryland State Archives, Annapolis
MHS	Massachusetts Historical Society, Boston
NAC	National Archives of Canada, Ottawa, Ontario
NCSA	North Carolina State Archives, Raleigh
NHA	New Hampshire Division of Archives and Records Management, Concord
NJSL	New Jersey State Library, Trenton
NYHR	New York Hall of Records, New York
NYHS	New-York Historical Society, New York
NYMA	New York Municipal Archives, New York
PSA	Pennsylvania State Archives, Harrisburg
PUL	Princeton University Library, Rare Books and Special Collections
RIHS	Rhode Island Historical Society, Providence
RIJRC	Rhode Island Supreme Court Judicial Records Center, Pawtucket
SCDAH	South Carolina Department of Archives and History, Columbia
TNA:PRO	The National Archives of the UK: Public Record Office, London

RAPE AND
SEXUAL POWER
IN
EARLY AMERICA

INTRODUCTION

John Adams. Olaudah Equiano. Benjamin Franklin.
Thomas Jefferson. Cotton Mather. Thomas Paine.
Mercy Otis Warren. George Washington.

Elizabeth Allen. Nancy Cobb. Sabina Cole. Sarah Langly.
Amy London. Ann Mitchell. Hester Osborn. Dolly Walden.

What does a list of well-known historical figures have in common
with a collection of unfamiliar names? All of these early Americans left records
about rape. The textbook figures usually wrote about rapes in which they were
rather tangentially involved. They were lawyers or witnesses, condemned a
criminal or a crime, and used rape as metaphor or humor. In contrast, the
figures on the nondescript list experienced rape more intimately. They were
women and girls who each accused a man of a sexual assault.

These divergent lists highlight a central incongruity: rape in early America
was both pervasive and invisible. On the one hand, early Americans spoke
authoritatively about rape in public and private settings alike. In the abstract,
they agreed that rape was a heinous act unworthy of civilized society and
worthy of serious punishment. For assaulted women and girls, however, rape
was the most intimate of violations, a private trauma that often did not translate into a believable public wrong.

I originally chose the topic of rape because it had the potential to provide
me with roughly equal numbers of male and female historical actors, but I
quickly learned that a body count does not equal a body of evidence. I may be
able to recite the names of as many women as men involved in recorded instances of sexual coercion, but I can offer little information about the thoughts
of these individuals. We know nothing of what nine-year-old Elizabeth Allen
thought of rape or of the man who sexually assaulted her. And we do not even
know the name of the woman who accused Robert Holeman of a sexual assault
in New Jersey in 1752, or of the slave who was sentenced to death for raping
Sabina Cole in early-nineteenth-century Georgia. Yet outside commentators
regularly recorded their views of rape. Cotton Mather associated fornication
with rape and worried about the threat of African American rapists. Thomas

Jefferson thought castration was a reasonable sentence for rape, believed that women would file false rape charges against men who rejected them, and did not think that Indians would rape war captives.[1]

Such holes in extant records are a fact of a historian's life, but the preservation of certain kinds of records regarding sexual coercion is not mere happenstance. Ideologies of race, gender, class, and social standing shaped whose words were taken down and preserved for posterity and, ultimately, whose perspectives on rape have become representative of early American society. The challenge for a historian of rape (as for sexuality scholars more generally) is to recreate the complex meanings of intimate sexual relations without reinscribing a time period's singular hegemonic view onto the subject of study.[2]

By employing a conceptual framework that analyzes the gap between the personal coercion of sex and the public classification of rape, my work identifies early American systems of power without replicating the perspective of those systems. I use the term "rape" to signify legal judgments (whether in terms of indictment or conviction) of forced heterosexual intercourse. When a North Carolina court charged a man named Jem with raping Sarah Langly in

1. John Ward indicted, Mar. 11, 1766, Massachusetts Superior Court of Judicature Records, Suffolk Files, nos. 100811, 100815, MA; *State v Major*, Nov. 16, 1812, Baldwin County Trial of Slaves, Inferior Court Minutes, 1812–1826, microfilm 199–25, GA; *King v Robert Holeman*, October 1752, New Jersey Court of Oyer and Terminer and Gaol Delivery, 1749–1762, PUL; [Cotton Mather], *Pillars of Salt . . .* (Boston, 1699), 69–71; [Cotton Mather], *Advice from the Watch Tower . . .* (Boston, 1713), 29; Thomas Jefferson to Edmund Pendleton, Aug. 26, 1776, http://www.yale.edu/lawweb/avalon/jefflett/let9.htm; Jefferson to James Madison, Dec. 16, 1786, in Julian P. Boyd, ed., *The Papers of Thomas Jefferson*, X (Princeton, N.J., 1950), 604; Jefferson, *Notes on the State of Virginia*, ed. William Peden (Chapel Hill, N.C., 1955), 200.

2. On the difficulties of balancing authoritative discourses and subjective experiences of sexuality, see Estelle B. Freedman, "'The Burning of Letters Continues': Elusive Identities and the Historical Construction of Sexuality," *Journal of Women's History*, IX, no. 4 (Winter 1998), 181–200. On critiquing hegemony without reproducing it, see Ann DuCille, "'Othered' Matters: Reconceptualizing Dominance and Difference in the History of Sexuality in America," *Journal of the History of Sexuality*, I (1990), 102–130, and response by Estelle Freedman and John D'Emilio (129–130); DuCille, "The Occult of True Black Womanhood: Critical Demeanor and Black Feminist Studies," *Signs*, XIX (1994), 591–629; Judith E. Grbich, "The Body in Legal Theory," in Martha Albertson Fineman and Nancy Sweet Thomadsen, eds., *At the Boundaries of Law: Feminism and Legal Theory* (New York, 1991), 63. On re-presenting outrages such as rape without prurience or numbed indifference, see Saidiya V. Hartman, *Scenes of Subjection: Terror, Slavery, and Self-Making in Nineteenth-Century America* (New York, 1997), 4.

1775, at least some community members and court officials thought that this was an act of potentially unacceptable sexual force. I apply the category of "coerced sex" to acts not necessarily identified as rape in early America that nevertheless contained some degree of extorted or forced sexual relations. So when a Creek leader complained to British officials in 1764 that "many white men are very impudent" to female Indian traders and asked the officials to ensure that the white men just "pay her and let her go again," he was likely complaining about white men's sexual coercion of Indian women. But we have no evidence that any legal or political official condemned such acts as rape, let alone statements of Native American women's perspectives on white men's exploits. I argue that the very absence of recorded categorization of such acts as rape was crucial to early American systems of sexual and social power.[3]

This two-tiered conceptualization (with "coerced sex" on one level and "rape" on the other) reveals that social and economic relations underwrote sexual power, both through the act and through a community's reaction. The identities and relationships of the participants, not the quality of a sexual interaction (which was largely unknowable to all but the participants) most easily defined rape. Matrices of gender, ethnicity, race, and socioeconomic status were inseparable from early Americans' sexual practices and ideologies. I

3. *Crown v Jem,* Apr. 27, 1775, New Bern District Superior Court Miscellaneous Records, 1758–1806, "Slave Records 1766, 1778, 1775" folder, NCSA; Oakchoy King, speech [to Gov. Boone and John Stuart], Little Halsey, Apr. 10, 1764, enclosed in John Stuart to Thomas Gage, May 20, 1764, Thomas Gage Papers, American Ser., XVIII, Clements Library, Ann Arbor, Mich. Scholars have found that rates of rape or attempted rape prosecutions rarely top more than 3 percent of serious crimes in any region but agree that these recorded cases probably represent just the tip of a very large iceberg of sexual coercion. See Garry P. Secor, "Crime and Criminals in Westmoreland County, VA, 1710–1764," unpublished MS at LOV; Michael Stephen Hindus, *Prison and Plantation: Crime, Justice, and Authority in Massachusetts and South Carolina, 1767–1878* (Chapel Hill, N.C., 1980), 64, 65; Jack Marietta and G. S. Rowe, "Rape, Law, Courts, and Custom in Pennsylvania, 1682–1800," in Merril D. Smith, ed., *Sex without Consent: Rape and Sexual Coercion in America* (New York, 2001), 81; James D. Rice, "Crime and Punishment in Frederick County and Maryland, 1748–1837: A Study in Culture, Society, and Law" (Ph.D. diss., University of Maryland at College Park, 1994), 251, 286, 339. For comparable prosecutorial rates outside of British America, see Derek Noel Kerr, "Petty Felony, Slave Defiance, and Frontier Villainy: Crime and Criminal Justice in Spanish Louisiana, 1770–1803" (Ph.D. diss., Tulane University, 1983), 142–144; J. M. Beattie, *Crime and the Courts in England, 1660–1800* (Princeton, N.J., 1986), 126, 131; C. K. Talbot, *Justice in Early Ontario, 1791–1840* (Ottawa, 1983), 149.

expand my study beyond the legally adjudged cases of possible sexual force, thereby questioning specifically how definitions of rape created and reflected technologies of power. This study examines evidence and ideologies related to coerced heterosexual sex in British North America from 1700 through 1820 to analyze early American sexual norms and boundaries. Normative practices of consensual sex are understood only when we know where the category of consensual sex ended and that of rape began.

To comprehend the intersections of social and sexual practices, I focus on the slew of individual and cultural negotiations that preceded an endpoint legal classification of rape. Recreating the process of sexual coercion reveals that community definitions of rape did not just categorize sexual encounters after they occurred. Men's racial and class identities largely determined whether they could coerce sex undetected and unpunished, just as women's identities determined their vulnerability to men's sexual force. Such identities did not exist independent of life experiences but could be generated through these very sexual interactions. Elite white masculinity did not just allow powerful men to possibly avoid criminal prosecution for rape; it also helped such men re-shape coercion into the appearance of consent before, during, and after a sexual attack.

Unraveling the power dynamics reflected in sexual coercion also requires that we attempt to understand individual women's perspectives beyond the public classification of rape. White women had an undeniable advantage over women of color in every aspect of sexual coercion. For white women, patriarchy held out the possibility of providing protection from or remedy for sexual assaults. For nonwhite and other marginalized women, protective patriarchs were, at best, absent figures or, at worst, able to use their status to sexually oppress with impunity. Placing these erased women back into the story of sexual coercion reveals that the exclusion of women of color from the status of rape victim was a crucial feature of American racialization of rape through not only legal prosecution, but also the privileges afforded to whiteness. Moreover, racial dividing lines were not absolute: black and white women's economic dependency could link more than distinguish their experiences of sexual coercion.[4]

4. On the silencing of rape victims, see Cathy Winkler, "Rape as Social Murder," *Anthropology Today*, VII (1991), 12–14. On the silencing of African American women's history and sexuality more generally, see Darlene Clark Hine, "Lifting the Veil, Shattering the Silence: Black Women's History in Slavery and Freedom," in Hine, ed., *The State of Afro-American History: Past, Present, and Future* (Baton Rouge, La., 1986), 223–249; Barbara

To successfully move between individuals' experiences of sexual violence and institutional handlings of rape, I decided, early on, that this would be a large-scale project. Geographically, I set my study in all of mainland British North America and the later states and territories of the new United States. Such an extensive regional base allows me to draw broad conclusions that move beyond the localism that can accompany sexuality studies. Despite scholars' productive efforts to define colonial America by its regional cultures, my study of rape reveals an American culture that shared many commonalities. Sexual beliefs, racial ideologies, legal practices, and public discourses united colonial Americans long before they became a politically unified nation.[5]

I made a similarly expansive choice of temporal limitations. This study spans from the beginning of the eighteenth century, when most colonies had begun to evolve into solid surviving entities, to 1820, when Americans had successfully defended their nation from its former colonial parent. Three major shifts suggested 1700 as a starting point for a study of rape. First, British colonies' criminal justice systems became more formalized as close-knit community courts gave way to growing legal professionalization and as increasingly specific statutes limited local justices' individualized application of the law. Second, the declining influence of Puritan religious ideologies meant that an early focus on sexual morality crimes was being replaced with an emphasis on the secular and social costs of sexual misbehavior. Finally, racial ideologies underwent significant shifts in the seventeenth century, and, by 1700, both southern and northern colonies began to institutionalize race-based slavery.[6]

Omolade, "Hearts of Darkness," in Ann Snitow, Christine Stansell, and Sharon Thompson, eds., *Powers of Desire: The Politics of Sexuality* (New York, 1983), 350–367.

5. For the most influential reformulation of colonial American regionalism, see Jack P. Greene, *Pursuits of Happiness: The Social Development of Early Modern British Colonies and the Formation of American Culture* (Chapel Hill, N.C., 1988).

6. On shifts in colonial criminal justice, see Douglas Greenberg, "Crime, Law Enforcement, and Social Control in Colonial America," and Kathryn Preyer, "Penal Measures in the American Colonies: An Overview," both in the *American Journal of Legal History*, XXVI (1982), 293–325, 326–353. On seventeenth-century community sexual morality, see Cornelia Hughes Dayton, *Women before the Bar: Gender, Law, and Society in Connecticut, 1639–1789* (Chapel Hill, N.C., 1995), 158–160, 232; Else L. Hambleton, "'Playing the Rogue': Rape and Issues of Consent in Seventeenth-Century Massachusetts," in Smith, ed., *Sex without Consent*, 27–45; Ann M. Little, "'Shee Would Bump His Mouldy Britch': Authority, Masculinity, and the Harried Husbands of New Haven Colony, 1638–1670," in Michael A. Bellesiles, ed., *Lethal Imagination: Violence and Brutality in American History* (New York, 1999), 50; Kathleen M. Brown, "'Changed . . . into the Fashion of a Man': The

Rather than reinscribe the notion that the colonial period was a detachable prehistory of the United States, I continue my study to 1820, which reveals concurrent changes in the uses of rape and surprising stability in the practices of sexual coercion. Despite quantum shifts in print culture, urbanization, race, gender, and politics, the *enactment* of sexual coercion remained fundamentally intact throughout this period.[7] However, the image of rape took on new meaning in a post-Revolutionary America where slavery-based regional divisions as well as class and racial ties to sexual propriety increased. With the rising emphasis on white men's social crimes of seduction, consistently high prosecution rates for black rapists took on new meaning in the early Republic.[8]

Politics of Sexual Difference in a Seventeenth-Century British Settlement," *Jour. of Hist. of Sex.*, VI (1995), 171–193. Terri Snyder suggests that seventeenth-century Virginians might have been less concerned with moral offenses than were their northern neighbors. See Terri L. Snyder, "Sexual Consent and Sexual Coercion in Seventeenth-Century Virginia," in Smith, ed., *Sex without Consent*, 46–60.

On early American racial codifications, see Brown, *Good Wives, Nasty Wenches, and Anxious Patriarchs: Gender, Race, and Power in Colonial Virginia* (Chapel Hill, N.C., 1996), 107–136; Jennifer L. Morgan, "'Some Could Suckle over Their Shoulder': Male Travelers, Female Bodies, and the Gendering of Racial Ideology, 1500–1770," *William and Mary Quarterly*, 3d Ser., LIV (1997), 167–192; Alden T. Vaughan, "The Origins Debate: Slavery and Racism in Seventeenth-Century Virginia," in Vaughan, *Roots of American Racism: Essays on the Colonial Experience* (New York, 1995), 136–174; Joanne Pope Melish, *Disowning Slavery: Gradual Emancipation and "Race" in New England, 1780–1860* (Ithaca, N.Y., 1998), 34–35.

7. On rape's being, as one scholar of nineteenth-century crime found, "the one area of violence least impacted by the broader social changes," see Sean T. Moore, "'Justifiable Provocation': Violence against Women in Essex County, New York, 1799–1860," *Journal of Social History*, XXXV (2002), 896. For a later period, Karen Dubinsky has likewise found that the basic practices of sexual coercion remained surprisingly consistent; see Dubinsky, *Improper Advances: Rape and Heterosexual Conflict in Ontario, 1880–1929* (Chicago, 1993). On the consistency of the eighteenth-century "formal rules governing sexual practices," see Ruth Bloch, "Changing Conceptions of Sexuality and Romance in Eighteenth-Century America," *WMQ*, 3d Ser., LX (2003), 13. Although scholars (including Bloch) have pointed to evolutions and revolutions in middle-class consensual sexual ideals in the post-Revolutionary period, I have found that their conclusions are largely inapplicable to the process of sexual coercion. See, for instance, Richard Godbeer, *Sexual Revolution in Early America* (Baltimore, 2002); Clare Anna Lyons, "'Sex among the 'Rabble': Gender Transitions in the Age of Revolution, Philadelphia, 1750–1830" (Ph.D. diss., Yale University, 1996).

8. On the "compounding crisis of racial definitions and race relations" by the 1820s, see

While I have woven discussions of shifting ideologies, practices, and institutional possibilities into each chapter (and will return to summarize some of these shifts in the conclusion), chronological developments do not drive the narrative. I have attempted to balance a multitextured collage of individuals' experiences of sexual coercion with attention to the institutional shifts in the handling of rape. Scholars have repeatedly questioned how to historicize rape and sexuality. My approach begins from the assumption that sexual practices, desires, and ideologies are cultural constructs. But this does not necessarily mean that general societal or institutional transformations always brought about corresponding shifts in the ideologies or practices of sexual coercion.[9]

Indeed, to ask, Does rape have *a* history? may be posing the wrong question. Rape's history is a complicated one that yields neither singular nor linear answers. Rape is demanding to historicize precisely because it functioned at a variety of temporal levels that were not always equally affected by structural and large-scale ideological transformations. As a quintessential inversion of patriarchal control over women's sexual activities, rape seems widely transhistoric and transcultural. But the forms of that inversion (that is, who was seen as a believable rapist) in early America may be a specific product of a New World society built on particular social and racial relationships. Throughout this project, I struggled to mesh the importance of individual women's stories of sexual coercion — stories that bear depressing likeness to the processes of sexual coercion across time and place — with careful attention to the historical moment in which those acts occurred. Ultimately, I am not opposed to readers' seeing various parts of this book as transhistorical, but I also hope that they will see how sexual coercion was intricately tied to early America's specific social and cultural realities. Rape's imbrication in multiple strands of history, discourse, and popular culture makes rape both transhistoric and culturally specific.[10]

———

James Brewer Stewart, "The Emergence of Racial Modernity and the Rise of the White North, 1790–1840," *Journal of the Early Republic*, XVIII (1998), esp. 181–182; Melish, *Disowning Slavery*, 2–3.

9. For a useful overview of degrees of socially constructed sexuality, see Carol S. Vance, "Social Construction Theory: Problems in the History of Sexuality," in Dennis Altman et al., eds., *Homosexuality, Which Homosexuality? International Conference on Gay and Lesbian Studies* (London, 1989), 13–34.

10. See Roy Porter, "Rape — Does It Have a Historical Meaning?" in Sylvana Tomaselli and Roy Porter, eds., *Rape* (New York, 1986), 216–236; Catharine A. MacKinnon, "Does Sexuality Have a History?" in Domna C. Stanton, ed., *Discourses of Sexuality from Aristotle to AIDS* (Ann Arbor, Mich., 1992), 117–136.

The sheer breadth of sources I consulted allows me to make informed conclusions about early American rape from multiple perspectives. Sources for this project were gathered from more than twenty-five archives and historical societies. The 912 incidents of possible sexual coercion I have collected span 120 years and twenty colonies, states, and territories. Roughly 40 percent of these incidents occurred between 1700 and 1776 and 60 percent between 1777 and 1820. Of those 912 incidents, 761 were documented in criminal court records. I found the remaining unprosecuted incidents mostly in personal letters, diaries, civil court records, and through chance comments made in records of other crimes.[11]

Searching for criminal rape cases automatically biases the body of accusations toward those incidents that were most seriously prosecuted. Capital punishments were far more likely to lead to sermons, newspaper notices, and other surviving print records than were cases that ended in acquittal or lesser sentences. The acquittal of Benjamin Gilbert for raping a woman in Pennsylvania in 1781 was recorded, to my knowledge, only in manuscript court papers. Yet the conviction of a man named York for rape at the same court not only generated surviving court papers, but his death sentence was also confirmed in Pennsylvania's Supreme Council minutes, recorded in clemency papers, and published in a local newspaper. If original court records had not survived, we would still know about York's conviction but not Benjamin's acquittal. Given that extant records vary greatly by time period and region, I have been exceptionally cautious in drawing statistical conclusions from aggregated court records, making sure that qualitative evidence supports my identification of any general trends and that the statistics are not the by-product of source availability.[12]

11. I amassed evidence of rape prosecutions by searching known and available superior court and slave trial records from 1700 to 1820. I arrived at archives armed with a list of citations, either provided by generous colleagues or culled from published scholarship. After exhausting my citations, I examined superior court and slave court records, followed by, as time permitted, lower court records that had particularly rich supporting documents. For each colony, I also looked for newspaper reports of rape prosecutions and examined published and manuscript records where convicted rapists might have applied for a pardon. For a tabulation of my overall findings of sexual coercion incidents, see Appendix A.

12. For Gilbert, see Pennsylvania Court of Oyer and Terminer Dockets, 1778–1827, Bucks, Dec. 19, 1781, 120 (microfilm), PSA; Pennsylvania Court of Oyer and Terminer Court Papers, RG–33, box 1, PSA. For York, see *Minutes of the Supreme Executive Council of Pennsylvania* . . . , XIII (Harrisburg, Pa., 1853), 137; Clemency Papers, RG–27, reel 37, 688, PSA; *Freeman's Journal* (Philadelphia), Dec. 12, 1781; Pennsylvania Court of Oyer

To fully understand how early Americans thought about rape outside a legal setting, I have traced literary discussions of rape in fictional stories, propaganda, and humor. I systematically searched the *Pennsylvania Gazette* and the published index to the *Virginia Gazette* for any mention of rape, ravishment, or related keywords. I next examined scores of almanacs and fictional works at the Henry E. Huntington Library for stories of rape. Finally, I used a searchable version of Early American Imprints, Evans Digital, to find any relevant published documents. I collected a total of approximately five hundred manuscript and published documents that commented on some aspect of sexual coercion not pertaining to legal cases. Rape was the main topic of discussion in some of these documents and mentioned only in passing in others. This wide-ranging approach suggests a new way to study rape: instead of looking at one aspect of rape in law, literature, or print culture, I have recreated the complexities of early American rape in social, cultural, and legal history.

This expansive approach builds on more than one-quarter century of scholarship on sexual assaults in diverse fields of study. Although each group of scholars has approached the topic differently, the role of power has been central in all of their analyses. Feminist scholarship made rape a legitimate topic for scholarly study in the 1970s by arguing that it was the quintessential expression of patriarchal power. In the 1980s, women's historians began to use historical rape trials to explore the workings of particular patriarchal systems, scholars in sexuality studies deconstructed how modern-day rape prosecutions privileged male voices and perspectives, and literary critics began to analyze the rhetorical power of rape in fictional texts. By the 1990s, Michel Foucault's foundational work spurred research that problematized the operations of institutional power structures and asked how rape operated beyond the bounds

---

and Terminer Dockets, 1778–1827, Lancaster, Nov. 20, 1781, 121 (microfilm), PSA; Pennsylvania Court of Oyer and Terminer Court Papers, RG–33, box 4, PSA. On the problems of incomplete criminal records, see Preyer, "Penal Measures in the American Colonies," *Am. Jour. of Legal Hist.,* XXVI (1982), 347; Patrick J. Connor, "'The Law Should Be Her Protector': The Criminal Prosecution of Rape in Upper Canada, 1791–1850," in Smith, ed., *Sex without Consent,* 104–105.

Unfortunately, most colonies and states do not have a complete run of superior court records from 1700 through 1820. Surviving records of slaves' capital crimes are especially uneven: Virginia has some of the best records of slave trials, yet one expert still estimates that only 60 percent of the original documents have survived. See Merle Gerald Brouwer, "The Negro as a Slave and as a Free Black in Colonial Pennsylvania" (Ph.D. diss., Wayne State University, 1973), 180; Philip J. Schwarz, *Slave Laws in Virginia* (Athens, Ga., 1996), 65. For a full listing of court records consulted, see Appendix B.

of institutional ideology and punishment. Building on these insights, interdisciplinary scholars of colonialism linked the impact of ideologies of race, rape, and imperialism.[13]

Rape has appeared in similarly varied studies of American history. Sophisticated feminist scholars tackling the various intersections of gender, statehood, race, and sex have analyzed rape as a means through which gendered and racial ideologies were constructed in specific colonies. Such work has moved discussions of race beyond its meaning to nonwhite populations to show how colonial powers' developing racial ideologies could be enacted through sexual regulation. Scholars interested in American slavery and race relations have identified sexual violence as crucial to white mastery. Some have argued that the rape of enslaved women was both endemic to and representative of a race-based slave-labor system. Others have focused on the degree to which the punishing myth of black rapists—that African American men sought to rape white women—enacted slave owners' fears of their human chattel.[14]

13. See Michel Foucault, *History of Sexuality,* trans. Robert Hurley, I, *An Introduction* (New York, 1978). For a critique of Foucault, see Ann J. Cahill, "Foucault, Rape, and the Construction of the Feminine Body," *Hypatia,* XV, no. 1 (Winter 2000), 43–63.

Feminist scholarship on rape includes Susan Brownmiller, *Against Our Will: Men, Women, and Rape* (New York, 1975); Catharine A. MacKinnon, *Toward a Feminist Theory of the State* (Cambridge, Mass., 1989), esp. chap. 7. Women's histories include Anna Clark, *Women's Silence, Men's Violence: Sexual Assault in England, 1770–1845* (London, 1987); Barbara S. Lindemann, "'To Ravish and Carnally Know': Rape in Eighteenth-Century Massachusetts," *Signs,* X (1984), 63–82; Marybeth Hamilton Arnold, "'The Life of a Citizen in the Hands of a Woman': Sexual Assault in New York City, 1790–1820," in Kathy Peiss and Christina Simmons, eds., *Passion and Power: Sexuality in History* (Philadelphia, 1989), 35–56.

On present-day rape, see Susan Estrich, *Real Rape* (Cambridge, Mass., 1987); Kristin Bumiller, "Fallen Angels: The Representation of Violence against Women in Legal Culture," in Fineman and Thomadsen, eds., *At the Boundaries of Law,* 95–111; *Law and Philosophy: Philosophical Issues in Rape Law,* XI (1992).

On literary readings of rape, see Anthony B. Dawson, "*Women Beware Women* and the Economy of Rape," *SEL: Studies in English Literature, 1500–1900,* XXVII (1987), 303–320; Frances Ferguson, "Rape and the Rise of the Novel," *Representations,* XX (1987), 88–112.

For interdisciplinary imperial studies, see Ann Laura Stoler, *Carnal Knowledge and Imperial Power: Race and the Intimate in Colonial Rule* (Berkeley, Calif., 2002); Anne McClintock, *Imperial Leather: Race, Gender, and Sexuality in the Colonial Conquest* (New York, 1995).

14. Dayton, *Women before the Bar;* Brown, *Good Wives, Nasty Wenches, and Anxious*

Rape has attracted so much study, in part, because it can represent the ultimate perversion of the foundational act of heterosexual relationships: rape is the acceptable sexual act of heterosexual intercourse made transgressive solely by its circumstances. More than either illicit extramarital sex in which both parties were potentially complicit or sodomitic acts forbidden regardless of participants' consent, rape marked the distortion of a fundamental feature of patriarchal Western society — a man's sexual access to his wife and control over other men's sexual access to his female dependents. Yet rape was more than a violation of men's property rights. Unlike property, women could purposefully betray their husbands, fathers, or masters, making rape a tense testing ground for patriarchal hierarchies. As such, rape provides an exemplary moment to analyze what Foucault has called sexuality's "especially dense transfer point for relations of power." Early Americans adjudicated the gender confrontation in sexual coercion by using racial ideologies and social hierarchies to divide normative heterosexual relations from rape.[15]

This study begins with an exploration of the cultural definitions of rape. Chapter 1 explains the fundamental suspicion of women's claims of rape. Rather than resort to endpoint explanations of patriarchy or misogyny, I clar-

---

Patriarchs; Mary Beth Norton, *Founding Mothers and Fathers: Gendered Power and the Forming of American Society* (New York, 1996); Kirsten Fischer, *Suspect Relations: Sex, Race, and Resistance in Colonial North Carolina* (Ithaca, N.Y., 2002).

On the rape of enslaved women, see Nell Irvin Painter, "Soul Murder and Slavery: Toward a Fully Loaded Cost Accounting," in Linda K. Kerber, Alice Kessler-Harris, and Kathryn Kish Sklar, eds., *U.S. History as Women's History: New Feminist Essays* (Chapel Hill, N.C., 1995), 125–146; Thelma Jennings, "'Us Colord Women Had to Go though a Plenty': Sexual Exploitation of African-American Slave Women," *Journal of Women's History,* I, no. 3 (Winter 1990), 45–74.

On black-on-white rapes, see Jacquelyn Dowd Hall, "'The Mind That Burns in Each Body': Women, Rape, and Racial Violence," in Snitow, Stansell, and Thompson, eds., *Powers of Desire,* 328–349; Martha Hodes, *White Women, Black Men: Illicit Sex in the Nineteenth-Century South* (New Haven, Conn., 1997); Laura F. Edwards. "Sexual Violence, Gender, Reconstruction, and the Extension of Patriarchy in Granville County, North Carolina," *North Carolina Historical Review,* LXVIII (1991), 237–260; Daniel A. Cohen, "Social Injustice, Sexual Violence, Spiritual Transcendence: Constructions of Interracial Rape in Early American Crime Literature, 1767–1817," *WMQ,* 3d Ser., LVI (1999), 481–526; Lisa Lindquist Dorr, *White Women, Rape, and the Power of Race in Virginia, 1900–1960* (Chapel Hill, N.C., 2004); Diane Miller Sommerville, *Rape and Race in the Nineteenth-Century South* (Chapel Hill, N.C., 2004).

15. Foucault, *History of Sexuality,* trans. Hurley, I, 103.

ify how early American understandings of rape in relation to other sexual acts minimized the space for women's believable claims of rape. Because men were supposed to be sexually aggressive, consensual sex could contain violence without being classified as rape. And, because early Americans theoretically expected respectable women to resist all illicit sex, men could substitute their own judgment for women's consent. This made women, as a group, unreliable witnesses to their own resistance and left them very little room to show the true opposition necessary to prove a rape. These flexible ideologies could be adapted to changing historical epochs. As religiously oriented concern about sin shifted to social concern about morality and as belief in women's innate sexual depravity shifted toward an endorsement of respectable women's ability to control their sexual desires, early Americans found new ways to blur the lines between men's sexual force and women's sexual consent.

Chapters 2 and 3 set these ideologies alongside a detailed anatomy of sexual coercion. Early Americans prescribed social and sexual relations for abstract categories of men and women, but practices of sexual coercion were inseparable from the racial and status distinctions that organized their society. In these chapters, I reconstruct individual women's experiences and show that sexual coercion was a gendered act of power but was never divorced from other hierarchies. From the means of its commission through the likelihood of its definition as rape, men committed and women suffered acts of sexual coercion according to their social positions. Because these chapters decenter the criminal justice system as the principal arbiter of sexual coercion, I do not regularly reveal the criminal outcome of the incidents discussed. This allows the extralegal action to take center stage and avoids forwarding an anachronistic evaluation of the sexual coercion based on legal conclusions.

Chapter 2 illustrates how status was integral to the ways that men could force sex. The complexity of the process of sexual coercion belied the early American image of rape as a small sliver at one end of the continuum of sexual relations. White and elite men could use the power of their position to redefine coercion into consent while poor and enslaved men had no choice but to opt for the brute force that early Americans were most likely to recognize as rape. Economically dependent and racially marginalized women were exceptionally vulnerable to a wide range of coercive tactics that might not appear to include the force necessary for rape, whereas elite wives and daughters might have the protection of a patriarch to help avoid such manipulations. Thus, status and racial ties to rape were created in the very act of sexual coercion.

Chapter 3 explores the aftermath of coerced sex. Rather than immediately turn to judicial redress, some victims had to first overcome the cultural beliefs that held them responsible for all sexual relations. To make their claims public, assaulted women would often tell their story through female social and family networks; the women whom they told would then recruit patriarchal figures to bring the case to legal authorities. The path to legal remedy was structured through a victim's social position. Transferring the victim's story to her family and neighbors also meant that community beliefs about who was or was not capable of rape shaped the ultimate categorization of a sexual act. Most notably, widely held beliefs in the self-evident guilt of black men accused of raping white women decreased the need for women's mediation and elevated the importance of male authority figures in redressing sexual attacks. Long after the physical act ended, social relations continued to create the meaning of the sexual encounter.

The next two chapters juxtapose this cultural and social environment to the legalities of rape. The institutional treatment of rape combined a belief that rape should be harshly punished with the fear that women might regularly make false claims of rape. Chapter 4 traces the British legal influences on American legal handling of rape and explores the scores of colonial and state statutes that codified rape's criminal consequences. British law made rape of women or girls a capital crime, and British standards for proving rape rigorously interrogated women's claims. American courts largely embraced the British approach with two major changes: eighteenth-century Americans legalized a heightened attention to black-on-white rape, and, by the post-Revolutionary period, capital punishment reform meant that white men convicted of rape would rarely receive a death penalty. These legal shifts set the stage for the increasing racialization of American sexual coercion.

Chapter 5 examines how each step in the criminal process led inexorably to disparate outcomes for blacks and whites. From the likelihood of a trial to the chances of conviction, to the severity of punishment, courts gave tangible meaning to race and created a widespread image of black-on-white rapes. Here I engage with scholarship that sets the mid-to-late nineteenth century as a pivotal moment in the development of fears of black men as rapists. While many scholars focus on the persecution of blacks in the nineteenth-century South, I show that black men were consistently condemned as likely rapists throughout eighteenth-century America. Furthermore, early Americans' racial ties to rape depended as much on the positive meanings afforded to whiteness as on the negative imagery associated with blackness. The continuing prosecutorial attention to black men's rapes provided the backdrop for the nineteenth-century transformation to an image of a hypersexual black rapist, and shifts in the treatment of and publicity about white men were equally crucial to the post-Revolutionary hardening of racial ties to rape.

Chapter 6 returns us full circle to the world of public discourse. Instead of focusing on rape's place on a continuum of sexual relations or on the criminalization of sex acts, I examine the discourse surrounding the acts that early Americans clearly labeled as rape outside of a legal context. Rape's repeated appearance in American-read fiction, myth, and political propaganda reveals that, despite the comparatively low level of prosecutions, it held a prominent place in the early American psyche. Rape could condemn villains, mark racial differences, or demean political enemies. Using three sets of myths about Indians, slaves, and British soldiers, I show that the cultural work done by rape depended on early Americans' particular intertwinings of race, sexuality, and gender. The practice and image of rape converged in a public culture that used an assumed relationship between social identity and sexual behavior to mark the boundaries of the new American nation.

Throughout these chapters, I have gone against the conventional use of surnames when referring to individuals introduced previously. Instead I use given names to identify early Americans in sexual assault cases after their first full-name introduction. Slaves, who usually do not have identifiable surnames, were vastly overrepresented as rapists and vastly underrepresented as victims of rape. Given this pattern, the conventional use of surnames frequently sets African American men, identified only by first names, as rapists of white women who are identified with surnames. My use of given names attempts to avoid sentence constructions that reinscribe racial power imbalances and implicitly privilege free and white people through the use of their surnames. Although I do not want readers to lose sight of the profound racial inequities in early American society, I do want to avoid reifying subtle racism in my analysis. Furthermore, I am discussing intimate sexual interactions where the use of given names encourages readers to acknowledge the very personal element of these stories despite any initial discomfort over this unconventional usage. On a purely practical level, first names will also help readers keep track of the male and female participants and avoid confusion about multiple family members involved in a single incident.

We may not be able to chart accurately the amount of sexual coercion that early American women experienced, and we may not be able to fully recreate the mindsets either of individual men who raped or of individual women who were subjected to sexual force. But early Americans' widespread attention to rape highlights its significant role in their worldview. The scribes of personal diaries, travel narratives, biographies, histories, jokes, morality tales, and courtroom trials all expected rape to convey messages about how men and women should interact and how gender, social, and racial hierarchies should be maintained. History may remember George Washington better than Dolly Walden, but both played a crucial, if unknowing, role in connecting rape to early American social and sexual power.

CHAPTER ONE

CONSENT AND COERCION: THE CONTINUUM OF SEXUAL RELATIONS

In 1789, Rebecca McCarter told a Pennsylvania court about repeated sexual overtures made by her master, David Robb. To twenty-first-century ears, her testimony sounds like a clear case of sexual coercion. Rebecca recalled of several incidents, "He struggled with me . . . and left me so that I could scarcely lift my Arm to my head. . . . He threw me on the Bed . . . he caught hold of me and threw me down." Her account might have sounded like rape to eighteenth-century listeners as well: even though David was charged only with adultery, the grand jury had apparently inquired of Rebecca whether these sexual relations were "against my will or with my will." Ultimately, when cross-examined, Rebecca held, *"I consented to the Connection with Def[endan]t. . . .* I struggled each time — but consented at last."[1]

How can we reconcile these two sets of statements? On the one hand, Rebecca admitted being repeatedly thrown down and struggling to the point of exhaustion; on the other, she believed that she consented to sexual relations with her master. Rebecca's seemingly contradictory recollection of coercive acts alongside a choice of consent reflects the murky boundaries between coerced and consensual sex in eighteenth- and early-nineteenth-century America. While violence and physical force were necessary constituents of rape, their deployment did not necessarily turn a consensual sexual encounter into a coerced one.

What, then, made sexual intercourse a rape? The ubiquitous legal definition of rape as "carnal knowledge of a woman forcibly and against her will" did not provide details about how to distinguish between a man's seductive pressure

---

1. *Respublica v David Robb,* Yeates Legal Papers, March–April 1789, fol. 2, HSP, emphasis in original. I have regularized multiple spellings of individuals' names to a single spelling.

and a woman's inability to refuse. Instead, we need to look for the meanings of rape in wider cultural practices. We need to combine the descriptions of sexual interactions that might have been seen as rape with public depictions of men and women's sexual relations more generally. In this chapter, I look at the broad underlying understandings of proper heterosexual social and sexual relations in early America. Placing rape in this larger context reveals the difficulty in marking absolute boundaries between force and consent in early American sexual relations.[2]

Although Americans wrote surprisingly frequently about rape, it remained a difficult crime to charge and to successfully prove. Early Americans often saw the violence of forced sex as an unfortunate result of sexual desire rather than the original intent of a sexual act. Passions — understood as strong feelings or emotions — remained an explanation for sexual desires into the nineteenth century, as their meaning moved from a primarily religious focus to one that combined religious and secular concerns. As a result of passions, sexual coercion was less an aberrant act of violent sexual force than an extension of normative sexual practices. A rape might begin with voluntary social or sexual offers and end with the aggressor attempting to continue normal social relations after the rape. Contrary to modern expectations, physical force did not provide a clear dividing line between coercion and consent. Consensual sex could be physically forceful, and rape could originate in consensual sexual relations.

Early Americans did not divide sexual activity into sexual/consensual versus violent/coercive acts; instead, sexual and violent acts could bleed into each other. Rape fitted religiously, socially, and intellectually alongside an array of other sexual immoralities. Early Americans, like their early modern European counterparts, officially sanctioned sexual relations only within marriage. Thus, inappropriate sexuality included (among other acts) all heterosexual intercourse outside marriage. When ministers mused on the causes of rape, when soon-to-be-executed rapists were encouraged to explain their actions, and when the general populace talked about rape, they categorized sexual assaults with other forms of sexual misbehavior. Throughout the eighteenth century, concern about sexually sinful men and lustful women turned into anxiety about deceitful rakes and seduced innocents, adding a new narrative option to the interpretation of sexual coercion. Much of this shift can be traced to the increasing popularity in the early Republic of novels and sentimental stories that made seduction (and, less often, outright rape) integral to a story's

2. William Blackstone, *Commentaries on the Laws of England*, 4 vols. (1765–1769; rpt. Chicago, 1979), IV, 210.

plot and morals. These stories emphasized ruined chastity as the worst horror that could befall a virtuous woman, regardless of the force used in the sexual encounter.

The blurred divisions between consensual and coercive sexual relations provided the humor in almanacs, pushed the plot in fictional tales, and confounded juries' determination of the nature of a sexual interaction. Such ambiguous boundaries also shaped early American views of women's ability to provide believable evidence of resistance to a sexual overture. In light of rape's resemblance to other forms of sexual relations, women's claims of nonconsent often appeared to be self-serving deflections of responsibility for sexual misbehavior. By finding a woman's presumed physical (or, increasingly toward the nineteenth century, emotional) desires more trustworthy than her claims of resistance, early Americans severely circumscribed a woman's ability to consent · to or refuse a sexual interaction. Print descriptions further minimized the believability of rape and presented it as an exceedingly extraordinary occurrence, while seduction narratives that made women at least partially responsible for their own ruin contributed to the belief that women could and should control all sexual uses of their bodies.

Throughout the eighteenth and early nineteenth centuries, these understandings of rape adapted to changing social and political circumstances. Indeed, the sexual double standard that foisted the responsibility for and consequences of sexual acts onto women has been one of the most intractable features of Western society. While ideas about sexual desires and sexual morality would shift in colonial America, the inherited conceptualization of rape as an exceptional act that grew out of unexceptional sexual passion would endure.[3]

NORMATIVE SEXUAL RELATIONS:
BLURRED LINES OF FORCE AND CONSENT

Despite varying levels of premarital pregnancy throughout the American colonies, heterosexual sexual relations were legally and religiously acceptable only within marriage. Titles of sexual manuals, such as *Conjugal Love; or, The Pleasures of the Marriage Bed Considered,* assumed that heterosexual sexual relations would only occur within matrimony. Marital sex combined the twin goals of procreation and pleasure. As the popular eighteenth-century sex manual

3. Keith Thomas, "The Double Standard," *Journal of the History of Ideas,* XX (1959), 195–216.

Aristotle's Master-Piece proclaimed, "Mutual Enjoyment for Generation sake . . . is the chief end for which Wedlock was ordained." Marriage was the appropriate social arrangement for sexual relations.[4]

Authors might have written of mutual sexual enjoyment, but they did not envision sexual interactions as an equal partnership. At its most basic level, men's social superiority included an expected controlling role in sexual relations. For instance, *Conjugal Love* was addressed to only a male readership, who might conceivably choose to distill information for their brides. Biblical stories of Eve's creation from Adam's rib provided a foundational premise that women had been created to serve men. This belief would be echoed in multiple print genres throughout the eighteenth century. At the beginning of the century, British medical manuals had embraced a view of women's bodies primarily as useful receptacles for male-centered sexual practices. In the mid-eighteenth century, Benjamin Franklin proclaimed that women were "designed . . . to gratify our Passions." At the end of the century, William Boyd's poetry reading at Harvard University opined, "When time was young, and nature first began / To form this odd fantastic being, Man, / She rack'd her fancy to invent a joy / Unknown before, to please the smiling boy." Whether dictated by God, nature, or biological design, women were created to respond to — and to serve — men.[5]

4. Nicholas Venette, *Conjugal Love; or, The Pleasures of the Marriage Bed Considered*, 20th ed. (1750; rpt. New York, 1984); *Aristotle's Master-Piece; or, The Secrets of Generation* (1694; rpt. New York, 1986), 6. On early Americans' view of the place of pleasure versus reproduction in sexual relations, see Edmund S. Morgan, "The Puritans and Sex," *New England Quarterly*, XV (1942), 591–607; Kathleen Verduin, "'Our Cursed Natures': Sexuality and the Puritan Conscience," *NEQ*, LVI (1983), 220–237. On English advice manuals' emphasis on procreation, see Roy Porter, "The Literature of Sexual Advice before 1800," in Roy Porter and Mikuláš Teich, eds., *Sexual Knowledge, Sexual Science: The History of Attitudes to Sexuality* (Cambridge, 1994), 146–149.

On premarital pregnancy rates, see Daniel Scott Smith and Michael S. Hindus, "Premarital Pregnancy in America, 1640–1971: An Overview and Interpretation," *Journal of Interdisciplinary History*, V (1975), 537–570; Susan E. Klepp, "Revolutionary Bodies: Women and the Fertility Transition in the Mid-Atlantic Region, 1760–1820," *Journal of American History*, LXXXV (1998), 910–945; Cornelia Hughes Dayton, *Women before the Bar: Gender, Law, and Society in Connecticut, 1639–1789* (Chapel Hill, N.C., 1995), 174–175, 189–190, 208–209.

5. Venette, *Conjugal Love*, iii–iv; Mary Fissell, "Gender and Generation: Representing Reproduction in Early Modern England," *Gender and History*, VII (1995), 433–456; Benjamin Franklin, *Father Abraham's Speech to a Great Number of People, at a Vendue of*

An awareness of men's assumed leadership in sexual relations is crucial to understanding how early Americans viewed sex and rape. Because men's sexual dominance over women seemed naturally ordained, early Americans commonly spoke of sex as male action and female reception. In everyday parlance, men had carnal knowledge of women's bodies; sex was always formulated with man-as-subject and woman-as-object of the act. Men also encoded sex in military terms ("thrusting," "giving a flourish"), with the accompanying connotations of doing battle and subduing the female enemy. One midcentury British poet compared women to a fortress: "Women are so particularly form'd / Capitulate they will, but not be storm'd." A 1780 almanac used military metaphors for the punch line to a story about a "vigorrous young officer, who made love to a widow." The officer took the woman by surprise when he grabbed her, and she asked him whether he fought "after the French way, tak[ing] towns before you declare war?" He responded in the negative, but qualified, "I should be glad to imitate them so far as to be in the middle of the country, before you could resist me." Both the widow's and the soldier's words played on the parallels between military strategy and sexual pursuit. Later in the century, a New York lawyer explicitly referred to a woman's alleged promiscuity as her "surrendering the citadel." Sex was a battle, and women were expected to accept (if not enjoy) their defeat at men's hands gracefully.[6]

Such understandings of aggressive sexual relations blurred the distinction between voluntary and coercive sex. One scholar refers to the "overarching eighteenth-century discourse of male sexual drive, invariably portrayed as ag-

---

Merchant-Goods . . . to Which Are Added Seven Curious Pieces of Writing (Boston, [1758]), 19; William Boyd, *Woman: A Poem* (Boston, 1796), 5. See also *The Good Old Virginia Almanack, 1799* (Richmond, Va., [1798]), 19. Ellen Rooney summarizes this ideology: "The feminine part is to consent or refuse (to be taken) rather than to desire or will (to take)" (Rooney, "'A Little More Than Persuading': Tess and the Subject of Sexual Violence," in Lynn A. Higgins and Brenda R. Silver, eds., *Rape and Representation* [New York, 1991], 93).

6. *The Rape: A Poem Humbly Inscribed to the Ladies,* 2d ed. (London, 1768), 17; [Benjamin West], *Bickerstaff's New-England Almanack, for . . . 1780* (Norwich, Conn., [1779]), 15; *Report of the Trial of Henry Bedlow, for Committing a Rape on Lanah Sawyer* (New York, 1793), 41. See also Eliza Fowler Haywood, *Adventures of Eovaai, Princess of Ijaveo: A Pre-Adamite History* (London, 1736), 62; Isaac Bickerstaff, *The Rhode-Island Almanack . . . 1815 . . .* (Providence, [1814]), n.p.; Joy Wiltenburg, *Disorderly Women and Female Power in the Street Literature of Early Modern England and Germany* (Charlottesville, Va., 1992), 199–200; *The Commissioners of the Alms-House, vs. Alexander Whistelo, a Black Man; Being a Remarkable Case of Bastardy . . .* (New York, 1808), 52.

gressive," and another similarly notes that, in eighteenth-century literature, "men . . . solicit female chastity infinitely." By seeing men and women as desiring opposite ends (he sexual relations, she chastity), men could claim that forceful persuasion was justified. Thus, the line between forceful persuasion that led to consent, and rape — an act against a woman's will — was unclear in both representation and practice. Men's sexual pursuit of women through a variety of less than virtuous means of manipulation and coercion raised the specter that women's resistance to men's sexual overtures was not an honest representation of women's true sexual desires.[7]

Throughout the eighteenth century, individual men also seemed to assume that they might sexually overpower women as a matter of course. Such attitudes appear in court documents, diaries, and private recollections from the first decades of the century. Southern planter William Byrd's diaries are a well-mined source of information on his sexual beliefs and practices. In one entry, William confessed that he "kissed . . . [a visiting neighbor] on the bed till she was angry" and should have asked God's pardon "for the lust I had for another man's wife." Rather than regret that he forced himself on an unwilling woman, William instead lamented his sinful desire for another man's wife. He made her consent, or lack thereof, irrelevant to the sin that he believed he committed. Commenting more directly on the potential for force in everyday sexual relations, William recorded somewhat ironically other sexual encounters that he witnessed — one where the woman had "struggled just enough to make her Admirer more eager," one where a woman "wou'd certainly have been ravish't, if her timely consent had not prevented the Violence," and another where a man had "employ'd force, when he cou'd not succeed by fair means" to have sex with a woman. William interpreted women's struggles as, at best, performative, and, at worst, irrelevant. A woman's ultimate consent — even under duress — still did not appear as nonconsensual rape.[8]

7. James A. Steintrager, "'Are You There Yet?': Libertinage and the Semantics of the Orgasm," *differences: A Journal of Feminist Cultural Studies*, XI (1999), 33; Susan Staves, "Fielding and the Comedy of Attempted Rape," in Beth Fowkes Tobin, ed., *History, Gender, and Eighteenth-Century Literature* (Athens, Ga., 1994), 90.

8. Louis B. Wright and Marion Tinling, eds., *The Secret Diary of William Byrd of Westover, 1709–1712* (Richmond, Va., 1941), 91, 101; William Byrd, *Histories of the Dividing Line betwixt Virginia and North Carolina*, ed. William K. Boyd (New York, 1967), 57, 147–149. For just some of the voluminous writings on the sexual content of Byrd's diaries, see Kenneth A. Lockridge, *On the Sources of Patriarchal Rage: The Commonplace Books of William Byrd and Thomas Jefferson and the Gendering of Power in the Eighteenth Century* (New York, 1992), 24–27; Kathleen M. Brown, *Good Wives, Nasty Wenches, and Anxious Patriarchs:*

Such attitudes do not appear to be limited to southern planter gentry. Significant trickery, coercion, and even physical force might have been an acceptable means to achieve sexual goals. Dr. Alexander Hamilton recalled an incident during his travels to Long Island in the 1740s. His companion, a trader named Parker, was a man "who was apt to take flame upon all occasions." At one tavern, Alexander recorded, Parker saw a "pritty girl" with whom he was "mightily taken and would fain have staid that night." The girl was ill, so Parker "pretended to be a doctor and swore he could cure her if she would submitt to his directions." Only "with difficulty" did Alexander persuade Parker to leave the girl alone. Men such as Parker would resort to a variety of underhanded, if not explicitly violent, means to fulfill their sexual goals, because they assumed that women needed to be persuaded to have sexual relations.[9]

Two mid-eighteenth-century New England cases provide examples of men who thought that some degree of force might be acceptable in their sexual encounters. In a Rhode Island case in 1730, Mary Reynolds testified that Humphrey Sullivan had laid violent hands on her "in a very uncivil and Rapeous manner," while Humphrey claimed, "I offered to play with her." Humphrey's idea of an offer had apparently appeared as force to Mary, possibly suggesting a wider possible range of physical force in Humphrey's notion of consensual sexual relations than in Mary's. In 1756, Mary Seller testified that John Murphy stopped her mouth, threw her down, and tore off her petticoats, pleading to lie with her. She thought that "he wod have actually forced me" had others not heard her cries. John testified that he "did throw her down but had no design to force her . . . when she Cryed for help I took off of her." Perhaps John let Mary go when he thought that they might be discovered. But perhaps her cries convinced him that she was seriously resisting his advances — not just following courting rituals where some refusal might be expected. John thought his explanation exculpatory and believed that others might also. In both of these incidents, individual men had fairly expansive views of the degree of acceptable coercion, even when others objected to their activities.[10]

Gender, Race, and Power in Colonial Virginia (Chapel Hill, N.C., 1996), 328–334; Richard Godbeer, *Sexual Revolution in Early America* (Baltimore, 2002), 170–180, 194–200, 269–273.

9. Alexander Hamilton, *Gentleman's Progress: The Itinerarium of Dr. Alexander Hamilton, 1744* (Chapel Hill, N.C., 1948), 90, 96.

10. *Rex v Humphrey Sullivan,* March 1730, Rhode Island Superior Court of Judicature, Newport County File Papers, RIJRC; Murphy indicted, July 20, 1756, Massachusetts Superior Court of Judicature Records, Suffolk Files, no. 75839, MA. On courtship, see

At the end of the century, another diarist, this time in Philadelphia, reiterated more graphically how violence and resistance could become an acceptable part of his sexual encounters. He wrote that he lay all night with a woman he had just met. She told him that she had "never before enjoyed a man: she shrieked [illegible] and shrieked more but I made entry in due form and time." His written placement of "but" between the account of her shrieks and his completion of intercourse shows his recognition that the two were opposed: she resisted him. But such resistance did not mean, to him at least, that he had raped her. He still categorized the encounter as her "enjoying" a man. Further, the diarist did not regret such encounters because he had wronged the women; he repeatedly asked "god forgive me" and "god help me in my wickedness" for his sexual promiscuity. And, in the instance of the screaming woman, the diarist regretted that the woman might track him down if she became pregnant—he lied and told her that he lived in the Carolinas. Was he truly regretting his sexual sins or engaging in sexual boasting? Either way, his rationales did not encourage him to see a woman's resistance as signifying her nonconsent. Obviously, women's views of such sexual interactions are more difficult to reconstruct from men's stories or diary entries. Women who brought criminal charges certainly felt wronged by men's aggressive sexual behavior, and, in this case, the woman's request for information about the defendant's residence may indicate that she considered bringing some criminal charges (if not rape, then perhaps a bastardy claim) against him.[11]

Women might ultimately condemn physical force in sexual relations, but they also accepted a wide range of forceful sexual relations without charging a man with rape. As in Rebecca McCarter's case, this was especially true when the man was already in a position of mastery over a woman. In such situations, women seemed to accept a wide range of verbal and physical persuasion before categorizing the man's actions as attempted rape. In 1724, Margaret Connor told a Virginia court that her master was abusing her: he beat her when she refused to have sex with him. Margaret objected to her master's physical assaults but did not claim that his efforts to force her into sex were attempts at

---

Ruth H. Bloch, *Gender and Morality in Anglo-American Culture, 1650–1800* (Berkeley, Calif., 2003), 78–101; Cornelia Hughes Dayton, "Taking the Trade: Abortion and Gender Relations in an Eighteenth-Century New England Village," *William and Mary Quarterly,* 3d Ser., XLVIII (1991), 19–49; Karen Lystra, *Searching the Heart: Women, Men, and Romantic Love in Nineteenth-Century America* (New York, 1989).

11. [James Wilson?], Account Book and Diary, Feb. 15, 1773, MS, APS. Thanks to Susan Klepp for pointing me to this diary and for dating and authenticating the writing.

rape. A century later, the well-known fictionalized autobiography of Harriet Jacobs's enslavement clearly showed her master's repeated attempts to force her into sexual relationships. Yet, like Margaret, Harriet never characterized his actions as attempts at rape.[12]

Other court cases show how force and consensual sex might coexist. In Pennsylvania in 1734, Mindwell Fulfourd described how Thomas Beckett had followed her on horseback, eventually grabbing her horse's bridle and trying to lift her off her horse to make her have sex with him. Yet Mindwell characterized his efforts as having "offered to ly with her," as if he had simply made a verbal request that she could politely refuse. A decade later, a Connecticut court charged Isaac Willow with endeavoring "to tempt" Margaret Pearls into sexual relations, "all which was done with force and violence against [her] Consent." Isaac's actions were concurrently described as using temptation and violence to get Margaret to have sex. In 1800, Rachel Davis also characterized her master's overtures to her, which would later be charged as rape, as having "frequently tempted her" to sexual relations. The language used to describe these potentially coercive sexual interactions matched the language that could be used to describe consensual sexual liaisons.[13]

Consensual sexual relations and violent attacks could likewise be allied. In 1756, John Adams recorded an incident where a "fine Gentleman" persuaded a young woman to have sex with him for a three-farthing bribe. John disparaged this kind of behavior, complaining of men who claimed "exalted happiness" from "assaulting innocent People, breaking Windows or debauching young Girls." Although he wrote of a nominally consensual sexual interaction (a seduction, or, at worst, informal prostitution), John paired this voluntary sexual encounter with assault and property destruction — two violent acts that might more obviously parallel rape than seduction. Because coercion and con-

12. Case of Christopher Pridham, September 1724, Richmond Criminal Trials, 1710–1754, 85–87, 95–96, 119, LOV. For a sustained comparison of the role of class and race in the coercion of Harriet Jacobs and Rachel Davis, see Sharon Block, "Lines of Color, Sex, and Service: Comparative Sexual Coercion in Early America," in Martha Hodes, ed., *Sex, Love, Race: Crossing Boundaries in North American History* (New York, 1999), 141–163.

13. *D. v Thomas Beckett,* July 10, 13, August 1734, Chester County Quarter Sessions File Papers, CCA; *Rex v Isaac Willow,* Feb. 26, 1742/3, Windham County Court Files, February 1743–February 1744, box H–383, CSL; *Commonwealth v William Cress,* February 1808, Pennsylvania Court Papers, HSP. On the overlapping practices of seduction and rape in eighteenth-century working-class London, see Randolph Trumbach, *Sex and the Gender Revolution* (Chicago, 1998), 302.

sent overlapped, violence and sex could coexist in acts beyond the boundaries of rape.[14]

Women frequently presented rape as something done to them only when they refused to comply with sexual offers, highlighting the progression from consensual to coercive tactics in sexual assaults. In 1701, Elizabeth Pears testified that Seth Hills had used "all the allurements" to try to enter into a sexual relationship with her and turned to force only when she refused him. In 1737, Catherine Parry testified that Robert Mills had tried to persuade her to "commit adutry with him" for at least a year before he threw her down and raped her. In Massachusetts in 1784, Joseph Bedford repeatedly climbed into Mary Noble's bed, leaving each time after she told him to do so. But after doing this a half-dozen times, he told her that "if I stirred or got up he wd beat my brains out." In post-Revolutionary Pennsylvania, Christiana Waggoner testified that Abraham Moses "asked me if I would not do it" while she sat at her spinning wheel. When Christiana refused, he "would let me have no Peace . . . [he] caught me by the Petticoat and pulled me back" when she tried to run away, and then, she testified, Abraham raped her. In Virginia in 1810, Tom, an enslaved man, walked into freedwoman Dolly Boasman's house, told her he had "a favor to ask, she asked him what, he told her a stroke." When Dolly demanded that he go away, Tom threw her down and choked and raped her. For a man and woman of similar status — black or white — daily nonviolent social interactions could be a precursor to rape. These rapes did not appear to begin as violent physical attacks; physical force was a secondary recourse should a woman refuse a man's sexual overtures.[15]

Post-Revolutionary print descriptions of prosecuted rapes reinforced the idea that sexual relations could evolve into rape by portraying attackers who

14. L. H. Butterfield, ed., *The Diary and Autobiography of John Adams,* 4 vols. (Cambridge, Mass., 1961), I, 14. The young John Adams piously proclaimed about such behavior, "I had rather sit in school."

15. H. Clay Reed and George J. Miller, eds., *The Burlington Court Book of West New Jersey, 1680–1709,* American Legal Records, V (Washington, D.C., 1944), 254; examination of Catherine Parry, July 25, 1737, Chester County Quarter Sessions File Papers, CCA; indictment of Joseph Bedford, September 1784, Dockets of Cases and Notes of Evidence Taken by Hon. Increase Sumner, 1782–1786, II, 329–330, MHS; notes of evidence in *Respublica v Abraham Moses,* May 21, 1783, Yeates Legal Papers, April–May 1783, fol. 7, HSP. See also *Commonwealth v Long and Wilson,* May 1781, Pennsylvania Court of Oyer and Terminer Court Papers, RG–33, box 4, PSA; case of Tom, Jan. 22, 1810, Virginia Executive Papers, box 164, LOV.

first asked to have sexual relations. Only after that offer was refused would a man proceed to more forceful tactics. In the 1790s, Henry Bedlow "asked [a woman's] consent three or four times, which she refused," so he then forced himself on her. Joseph Mountain recounted that he had "attempted by persuasion" to have sexual relations with the woman he would eventually rape. In the early decades of the nineteenth century, convicted rapist Ezra Hutchinson testified that he would "obtain my will by compulsion, where free consent should be refused." Cato, an African American man who would be condemned for an unrelated crime, recounted that he was so "rash and inconsiderate" as to repeatedly "endeavour to obtain by violence what I could not effect by solicitation." These men presented sex as an offer that preceded any use of force, thereby making consensual relations slide into rape.[16]

Even in some of the clearly more physically violent rapes, the rapist claimed that he had made an initial attempt at replicating consensual social and sexual relationships. In 1771, Patrick Kennedy testified that he asked Jane Walker "if he should Shag her," and, when she refused, he "struck her and said he would have it." As several other men watched, Patrick tied her to a tree and raped her. In 1795, Edmund Fortis recounted that he had met his victim in the woods by saying, "How do you do, let me lie with you," and raped and murdered her only after she refused to comply with his wishes. In 1810, Elizabeth Vickers testified that, before her attacker's knife-wielding assault, he had previously "accosted her in a very familiar language, inquiring after the number of sweet hearts" she had. In framing their stories in these ways, the tellers assumed that forced and consensual sex were not clear and separate acts. The actions that might have led to a consensual sexual encounter could also be a prelude to forced sex. If only the women had consented, the men would not have had to commit rape.[17]

Beyond setting rape alongside normal, though illicit, sexual relations, men also tried to set rape within normal social relations. In 1796, Pompey, an

16. *Report of the Trial of Henry Bedlow*, 5; [David Daggett], *The Life and Adventures of Joseph Mountain, a Negro Highwayman* (Bennington, Vt., 1791), 13; *The Solemn Address, and Dying Advice, of Ezra Hutchinson* . . . (Stockbridge, Mass., [1813]), 9; *The Life and Confession of Cato, a Slave of Elijah Mount* (Johnstown, N.Y., 1803), 6.

17. *D. v Patrick Kennedy et al.*, 1771, Pennsylvania Court of Oyer and Terminer Court Papers, RG–33, box 2, PSA; *The Last Words and Dying Speech of Edmund Fortis, a Negro Man* (Exeter, N.H., 1795); case of Ben, Aug. 7, 1810, Virginia Executive Papers, box 168, 2 docs., LOV. For a story of a particularly violent rape and murder that began with attempts at seduction, see *Connecticut Courant* (Hartford), Nov. 16, 1767.

enslaved man, tried to rape Jane, a woman of African American descent, after offering to walk her home from church. Men might also continue normal social interactions with women after an incident as if no improper activity had taken place. In 1728, George Clinton walked Elizabeth Painter home after sexually assaulting her. After Abraham Moses forced Christiana Waggoner to have sex with him in 1783, he went to meet Christiana's husband, and all three spent several hours together. Abraham chose to have sexual relations (rape, according to Christiana) with a young woman he had known for several years, and, had she kept quiet, he seemed ready to continue his neighborly relations with her whole family. Perhaps these men did not see their actions as criminal and did not understand that women's cries and pleas were more than normal feminine modesty. Whether men did not believe or would not admit that their actions constituted a rape, they tried to maintain amiable relations with these women. Placing forced sexual acts into a setting of voluntary social relations could recreate rape as consensual sex.[18]

For lower-status women, men might assume that money could buy their consent and would use force only after the women refused to prostitute themselves. At a midcentury Connecticut court, Margaret Pearls testified that Isaac Willow had "ofered me if I would [have carnal relations with him] Eight pounds in money I told him I would not Consent to any such thin[g]," and Isaac then forced himself on her. In a 1787 New Jersey rape case, the victim recounted that her attacker had made "promises of money, a gown and ribbons" if she would have sexual relations with him and, when she refused, told her "he would now have his satisfaction of her without them." In 1817, Rebecca Day, Jr., testified that the man who raped her first offered her a dollar to have sexual relations with him and threw her down only when she refused. These offers of goods and money could have been intended as simple bribes or tokens of affection, or they might have been an offer to pay for sexual services. Regardless, the women's testimonies identified monetary exchange for sexual relations as a precursor to sexual force. If the women had been as bereft of virtue as the men apparently assumed, they might have sold the sexual favors that were instead forcibly taken from them. These women portrayed men who originally did not intend to commit rape; women offered their refusal of a

18. Case of Pompey, November 1796, indictments, no. 3376 and unnumbered doc., HHR; *Rex v George Clinton*, September 1728, New Haven County Court Files, 1720–1729, R–Y, no. 6, CSL; notes of evidence in *Respublica v Abraham Moses*, May 21, 1783, Yeates Legal Papers, April–May 1783, fol. 7, HSP. See also *State v James Rook*, 1788, New Jersey Supreme Court Actions-at-Law, no. 37902, NJSL; *Report of the Trial of Henry Bedlow*, 6.

variety of sexual propositions as evidence that the men forced them into sexual relations. These tactics might have been intended to prove women's nonconsent (why would she refuse money and then consent for nothing?) or men's immorality (he willingly offered money for sex), but they also further blurred the line between rape and illicit, nonforced sex.[19]

Rape and consensual sex fitted together in rhetoric and in practice because the processes of sexual coercion and consensual sex intersected: rape was an outgrowth of general illicit sexual relations. In a variety of settings, men and women pointed to the many ways that rape and illicit sex could be described with similar terms, begun with similar overtures, and completed under similar guises. These intersections of sex and rape in physical acts paralleled other early Americans' discussions of rape. The continuing acceptance of men's insatiable and potentially aggressive desire for sexual relations took multiple forms in early American law, religion, and print culture.

LEGAL, RELIGIOUS, AND PRINT DEFINITIONS OF RAPE

Public commentaries also set rape alongside general sexual misbehavior. Early Americans linked various forms of sexual misdeeds, in part, by a belief in a shared causality for all illicit sexual acts: unregulated sexual passions. Yet, even while providing an enduring explanation for sexual misbehavior, the passions took on different social meanings over time. Puritan emphasis on religious morality was joined by an emphasis on civic morality in the new nation; colonial concern about sinners transformed into concern about rakes in the early Republic; and images of respectable women ruined through love and bad marital choices eventually complemented seventeenth-century images of lustful women. As part of the general growth of sentimentalism, such changes required a corresponding resituating of rape's place in these new social dynamics.

Inherited legal language provided the basic definition of rape and exemplified the blurred boundaries between rape and consensual sexual relations.

19. *Rex v Isaac Willow*, Feb. 26, 1742/3, Windham County Court Files; exam of Polly, in *State v James Rook*, 1788, N.J. Supreme Court Actions-at-Law, no. 37902, NJSL. See also petitions for Andrew, 1793, Governor and Council, Pardon Papers, box 6, folder 54, MdSA; *Report of the Trials of Stephen Murphy and John Doyle before the Supreme Judicial Court at Dedham, Oct. 23, 1817* (Boston, 1817), 4–5. For a story of a European incident that progressed from seduction to prostitution to rape and murder, see *The Annual Register; or, A View of the History, Politics, and Literature for the Year*, X (London, 1767), 113.

Rape law grew out of more general laws against nonmarital sex. English jurist William Eden Auckland explained that "the English law hath made force necessary to the crime" of rape, whereas in Roman times, the "law made no distinction between seduction and force." Following British common law, early American law defined rape as *"unlawful and carnal Knowledge of a Woman by Force and against her Will."* The two concepts (by force and against her will), though perhaps indistinguishable now, were distinct in early America. Force alone did not mean rape; force could be an acceptable part of a sexual encounter, and a woman's will had to stand up to some force. In 1769, Joseph Latham, Jr., recognized the difference when he appealed his conviction for assault with intent to rape Rhoda Howel on the grounds that he was found guilty only of an assault with an attempt to have carnal knowledge of her, with no specification that it had been against her will. In other words, he (or his lawyer) thought it a defensible point that he could have assaulted a woman to have sex with her without violating her consent. Similarly, in a Virginia case at the end of the century, lawyers appealed a guilty verdict in part because the indictment omitted the words "with force."[20]

The overlapping language of forceful and consensual sexual relations appeared in legal formulations of charges other than rape. In one incident, a New York court charged a man with an "assault with an intent to seduce" a woman, despite the fact that assault might logically imply force beyond the limits of seduction. The legal language used to charge adultery frequently contained language of force, regardless of the degree of physical coercion involved. As William Blackstone wrote, if another man took a wife from her husband either by force or choice, "the law in both cases supposed force and constraint, the wife having no power to consent." The legal fiction of marital coverture that denied a woman's ability to act outside of her husband's will set a wife's adul-

20. William Eden Auckland, *Principles of Penal Law,* 2d ed. (London, 1771), 263, 264; Richard Starke, *The Office and Authority of a Justice of Peace, Explained and Digested, under Proper Titles* (Williamsburg, Va., 1774); case of Joseph Latham, Jr., April, May 1769, in David Thomas Konig, ed., *Plymouth Court Records, 1686–1859,* 16 vols. (Wilmington, Del., 1978–1981), III, *1748–1751,* 278, 279; case of Roz Norman, Apr. 15, 1797, Virginia Executive Papers, box 99, LOV. See also James Parker, comp., *Conductor Generalis; or, The Office, Duty, and Authority of Justices of the Peace . . .* (New York, 1788), 358; Jacob Giles, *The Modern Justice . . . ,* 3d ed. (London, 1720), 350. For a contemporary lawyer's notes on these terms, see C. J. Tilghman, "Definition of Crimes in 1806 or After," Pennsylvania Court Papers, box 6 (Tyson-Yard and Misc. Papers), 8, HSP. A defense attorney referred to the same idea in *Report of the Trial of Ephraim Wheeler for a Rape Committed on the Body of Betsy Wheeler, His Daughter, a Girl Thirteen Years of Age . . .* (Stockbridge, Mass., 1805), 8.

terous sex — whether consensual or forced — as a harm done to her husband. Multiple uses of this legal language surface in early American courts. In 1759, a North Carolina court ordered that Dr. Robert Lenox pay John Campbell five thousand pounds for assaulting and ravishing John's wife, by which John was "deprived of the Comfort and Society of his Wife." In 1803, Samuel Phillips had to answer Lewis Harding's charge of making "an Assault upon Ann Harding the wife of the said Lewis Harding . . . whereby the said Lewis Harding lost and was deprived of the comfort fello[w]ship and society of his said wife . . . to the great damage of the said Lewis Harding." The legal categorization of forceful and consensual sex as equivalent forms of adultery mimicked the blurring that occurred in the process of sexual coercion. Whether these incidents might have involved physical rapes or consensual adultery was irrelevant to the legal determination of adultery as an assault against a husband. Marriage set up a fiction of the invisibility of a woman's consent to individual sexual acts, which allowed a husband to define her consent for her.[21]

The treatment of rape as a form of sexual misbehavior was also prominent in religious publications, albeit for different purposes than legal documents. In keeping with the heightened religiosity inherited from their seventeenth-century forbears, early-eighteenth-century writers discussed the sinfulness of rape. As early as 1699, Cotton Mather expressed a New England minister's typical view of a man executed for a rape — he set the rape among the sinner's other sexual misdeeds. Mather wrote that the man had fornicated with women throughout his life and fathered nineteen or twenty children. In Mather's reckoning, the man was a menace because he could not control his sexual urges, not because he was physically violent. Another minister's 1736 sermon criticized the sinfulness evident in the British colonies, including "Sodomy,

21. *The Trial of Captain James Dunn, for an Assault, with Intent to Seduce Sylvia Patterson, a Black Woman* (New York, 1809), NYHS; Bernard Campbell Gavit, ed., *Blackstone's Commentaries on the Law from the Abridged Edition of Wm. Hardcastle Browne* . . . (Washington, D.C., 1941), book 3, chap. 8, 565; Robert J. Cain, ed., *Records of the Executive Council, 1755–1775,* Colonial Records of North Carolina, 2d Ser., IX (Raleigh, N.C., 1994), 400–401; petitions for Samuel Phillips, 1803, Governor and Council, Pardon Papers, box 10, folder 54, MdSA. On the history of coverture in American law, see Hendrik Hartog, *Man and Wife in America: A History* (Cambridge, Mass., 2000); Nancy F. Cott, *Public Vows: A History of Marriage and the Nation* (Cambridge, Mass., 2000), 11–12. For a discussion of a seventeenth-century "ravishment" of a man's wife that left the degree of force used unclear, see Kirsten Fischer, *Suspect Relations: Sex, Race, and Resistance in Colonial North Carolina* (Ithaca, N.Y., 2002), 14. For a fictional story of forced sex that is characterized as adultery, see Timothy Trueman, *The New Jersey Almanack for . . . 1779* (Trenton, N.J., [1778]), n.p.

Beastiality, Adultery, Incest, Rapes." A 1738 sermon bemoaned "the abominable Sin of *Buggery,* with Mankind or Beast, and the Sin of *Rape or Ravishment;* as also *Polygamy.*" These writers saw rape as an offense to God alongside
other sexual sins. The dual meanings of "ravish" likewise exemplified the religious emphasis on the sexual sin of rape rather than the force of violence.
Beyond being a synonym for rape, ravishment could also mean a rapturously
joyous experience, as in one author's discussion in 1700 of being "ravished
with the love of Christ."[22]

In the mid-eighteenth century, conflation of sexual desires with forced sexual acts also began to appear in publications with fewer religious overtones. In
1749, William Douglass described the sexual habits of the American Indians,
writing that they "are not so LASCIVIOUS as *Europeans* . . . they never offer
Violence to our Women Captives." For Douglass, sexual desires led (or lack of
desires, in this case, did not lead) directly to rape. Other midcentury publications set rape as a moral and social rather than an expressly sinful offense.
A 1753 New York publication that complained about men's bad behavior in
"this degenerate age" cited as proof the frequent lewdness, blasphemy, uncleanness, and brothel visiting, as well as the presence of men who "engaged in
Brawls, Rapes, or Duels." This author simultaneously associated rape with
immorality and overtly violent acts, though he still did not compare rape to
violent acts *against* an individual; brawls and duels were acts of primarily
consensual violence.[23]

By the Revolutionary era, commentaries on rape appeared in the many
publications about the executions of rapists. Such executions led to sermons,

22. [Cotton Mather], *Pillars of Salt* . . . (Boston, 1699), 69–71; *The Sad Estate of the
Unconverted, Discussed and Laid Open, with Many Inferences Thereon, Offered to the Inhabi-
tants of Sundry of His Majesty's Governments in North America* (Boston, 1736), 31; William
Williams, *The Serious Consideration, That God Will Visit and Judge Men for Sin, Would Be a
Happy Means to Keep Them from It* . . . (Boston, 1738), 10; James Janeway, *A Token for
Children* . . . (Boston, 1700), 10. For a similar comment in a non-Puritan publication, see
George Fox, *A Journal or Historical Account of the Life, Travels, Sufferings, Christian Experi-
ences, and Labour of Love . . . of . . . George Fox,* 4th ed., II (New York, 1800), 126. On the
Puritans' eroticization of spirituality, see Michael P. Winship, "Behold the Bridegroom
Cometh!: Marital Imagery in Massachusetts Preaching, 1630–1730," *Early American Liter-
ature,* XXVII (1992), 170–184; Godbeer, *Sexual Revolution in Early America,* 71–75.

23. William Douglass, *A Summary, Historical and Political, of the First Planting, Progressive Improvements, and Present State of the British Settlements in North-America* (Boston,
1749), I, 175; Francis Squire, *An Answer to Some Late Papers, Entitled the Independent Whig*
(New York, 1753), 124.

last words, and newspaper reports with both explicitly and implicitly religious content. New England execution sermons, intended as much for the listeners as for the condemned, told cautionary tales about the consequences of sinful living. As such, the tellers enlarged the sin in question beyond a capital crime, explaining how little sins led to bigger ones of the same kind, thereby tying the crime of rape to other kinds of sinful sexual behavior.[24]

Sermonizers focused on how the condemned had become a sinner, not on the specific rape for which the man would be executed. Aaron Hutchinson's sermon on a rapist's execution in 1768 repeatedly told listeners that the prisoner's lifelong "uncleanness" had led him to this unhappy end. The Reverend Thaddeus MacCarty told listeners about the same rapist's sins of *"stealing, lying, uncleanness, prophaneness,* and *drunkenness."* In a 1790 sermon, the Reverend James Dana concentrated on the many sins that the man had committed rather than discussed the specific crime of rape: "You have proceeded to *gaming, riot* and *debauch,* and from these to robbery. How many have you seduced?" Dana characterized the rapist as a seducer, implicitly ignoring the force against a woman's consent that was necessary for a rape.[25]

Because the ministers focused on criminals' progression to the scaffold, their sermons emphasized neither rape specifically nor the violence that modern readers would consider inherent to a sexual assault. As the Reverend Timothy Langdon explicitly stated of a condemned rapist in 1798, "His crimes are ruinous to society, whether he be an adulterer, a fornicator, or one who commits a rape." In 1817, the Reverend William Andrews reflected in a sermon at another rapist's execution, "How easy is the transition from fornication to adultery, and from adultery to the crime for which life must be taken." This "easy transition" lined up three sexual immoralities along a continuum of sexual misbehavior. Like adultery or fornication, rape was another version of

24. For scholarship on New England crime literature, see Daniel A. Cohen, *Pillars of Salt, Monuments of Grace: New England Crime Literature and the Origins of American Popular Culture, 1674–1860* (New York, 1993); Daniel Williams, "The Gratification of That Corrupt and Lawless Passion: Character Types and Themes in Early New England Rape Narratives," in Frank Shuffelton, ed., *A Mixed Race: Ethnicity in Early America* (New York, 1993), 194–221; Karen Halttunen, "Early American Murder Narratives: The Birth of Horror," in Richard Wightman Fox and T. J. Jackson Lears, eds., *The Power of Culture: Critical Essays in American History* (Chicago, 1993), 67–101.

25. Aaron Hutchinson, *Iniquity Purged by Mercy and Truth* (Boston, 1769), 19, 26; Thaddeus MacCarty, *The Power and Grace of Christ Display'd to a Dying Malefactor . . .* (Boston, 1768), 28; James Dana, *The Intent of Capital Punishment . . .* (New Haven, Conn., 1790), 23.

sexual misconduct. By considering the three as a group of progressive actions, Andrews overlooked the coercion that was necessary for a rape but theoretically absent from fornication or adultery. A close kinship among all sexual misbehavior allowed ministers to show their own concern about the powerful sins of the flesh. After all, sexual lust, and not physical assault, was one of Saint Augustine's three principal sins of fallen man. Through the early nineteenth century, New England ministers saw rape as one of the many sins of the "uncleanness" of sexual immorality.[26]

Like ministers, about-to-be-executed rapists filled published narratives of their lives with the illicit sexual activities that had preceded the rape. The relatively uniform structure of these narratives suggests that the men were creating lives to explain their misguided ways. Like execution sermons, these public dying words were meant to convey a message that would save souls. One condemned man's last words recounted "whoring with" women before committing the rape for which he was to be killed. Another cautioned listeners to avoid "paths of lewdness" and told tales of his "seducing the young women." Still another told how he had "devoted myself to acts of lewdness." One man, just before his execution for rape and murder was to take place, regretted his "whole life filled with sin, stealing, lying, whoring and drinking, and now murder." The rape went unmentioned, presumably categorized as whoring. These broadsides and pamphlets created a public stereotype of a sexually promiscuous rapist. Thus the force that had been involved in the sexual assault became secondary to the sexual immorality—the lewdness, the lustful, uncontrolled desire was what might make men rape or commit other immoral sexual acts.[27]

Commentaries in both printed and courtroom testimony also focused on whether convicted rapists had been sexually promiscuous. In a 1772 poem on an executed rapist, a printer proclaimed, "Your wicked Life, how lustful, how

26. Timothy Langdon, *A Sermon, Preached at Danbury, November 8th, A.D. 1798* . . . (Danbury, Conn., 1798), 11; William Andrews, *A Sermon Delivered at Danbury, Nov. 13, 1817, Being the Day Appointed for the Execution of Amos Adams for the Crime of Rape* (New Haven, Conn., 1817), 16, NYHS; Albert O. Hirschman, *The Passions and the Interests: Political Arguments for Capitalism before Its Triumph* (Princeton, N.J., 1977), 9.

27. *The Life, and Dying Speech of Arthur, a Negro Man* . . . (Boston, 1768); *The Last Words and Dying Speech of Robert Young, Who Was Executed at Worcester* . . . (New London, Conn., [1779]); *The Solemn Address, and Dying Advice, of Ezra Hutchinson*, 9, 14; *The Last Words and Dying Speech of Edmund Fortis, a Negro Man* (Exeter, N.H., 1795). For an insight into writing such tracts, see the editor's criticism of convicted rapist Ephraim Wheeler in *A Narrative of the Life of Ephraim Wheeler* . . . (Stockbridge, Mass., 1806), 10.

obscene! . . . To whore and drink has been your mighty Aim." A defense witness in a 1783 rape trial testified that the accused was of decent character and "not addicted to Women." In another rape trial that same year, a defense witness likewise testified that the accused "has not the Character of being a Lover of women." If these rapists had been accused of adultery or fornication instead of rape, the same poem and comments would have been appropriate.[28]

Popular early national sentimental novels condemned seducers and rakes in the same harsh terms as rapists. One seducer was described as "the disgrace of humanity and virtue, the assassin of honor," and another novel repeatedly opined that "With thee, SEDUCTION! are ally'd / HORROUR, DESPAIR and SUICIDE." Male seducers frequently received uniformly harsh condemnations in seduction stories of the early Republic. They were monsters, robbers, betrayers, or fiends. Men who sexually "ruined" good women were socially dangerous regardless of the force used in that destruction.[29]

Like their European counterparts, early Americans connected rape to these other forms of immoral sexual behavior through the passions, believing that passions were at the root of all unrestrained behavior. French painter Charles Le Brun's *Method to Learn to Design the Passions,* a treatise that analyzed the visual expression of emotions, was posthumously republished in at least sixty-three different editions throughout eighteenth-century Europe. In one British edition, Le Brun described the passions as "the main spring of every emotion of the heart, and which influence all our Actions." Passions were not, however, neutral influences. Without proper control, passions turned men into beasts and civilization into savagery. Le Brun emphasized that civilized societies must determine "how we may subject them to our Reason."[30]

American publications expressed similar concerns about the need to control

28. *On Bryan Sheehen, a Criminal This Day Executed in Salem* . . . ([Boston], 1772), AAS; notes of evidence in *Republic v James Paxton,* May 27, 1783, Yeates Legal Papers, April–May 1783, fol. 7, HSP; notes of evidence in *Respublica v Abraham Moses,* May 21, 1783, ibid.

29. Hannah Webster Foster, *The Coquette; or, The History of Eliza Wharton* (Boston, 1797), 91; [William Hill Brown], *The Power of Sympathy; or, The Triumph of Nature* (Boston, 1789), 118 (see also 105); Rodney Hessinger, "'Insidious Murderers of Female Innocence': Representations of Masculinity in the Seduction Tales of the Late Eighteenth Century," in Merril D. Smith, ed., *Sex and Sexuality in Early America* (New York, 1998), 272.

30. Charles Le Brun, *A Method to Learn to Design the Passions* . . . (London, 1734), preface. On the influence of Le Brun, see Jennifer Montagu, *The Expression of the Passions: The Origin and Influence of Charles Le Brun's Conférence sur l'Expression Générale et Particulière* (New Haven, Conn., 1994).

one's passions. An American midcentury writer discussed the dangers of uncontrolled passions with a more colorful metaphor. In the "Sea of Life," he
quoted Alexander Pope: "Reason [is] her Chart; but Passion is the Gale."
Passions could be a useful attribute only when channeled and controlled. A
Revolutionary-era writer recalled a woman's dinner party toast: "When passions rise may reason be the guide," and in 1774, *The Royal American Magazine*
advised "young gentleman" to "rule your passions with a sov'reign hand."
Uncontrolled passions were unquestionably dangerous; an early-nineteenth-
century commentator called passion "the threshold of madness and insanity"
that "deprives . . . [a man] of his reason." Even in an era that put increasing
value on expressions of feelings, passions still required tight control. As overpowering emotions that battled with the mind's reason, passions retained
explanatory power from the early modern period through the early nineteenth
century.[31]

Yet the interpretation of the exact dangers of uncontrolled passions shifted.
In the early colonial period, especially in Puritan New England, control over
one's passions was crucial to maintaining a godly society—sinners were those
who failed to employ reason over their passions. By the Revolutionary era, the
control of the passions became increasingly necessary to a well-ordered civil
society.[32] Rather than the concerns about religious disorder that character-

---

31. *Pennsylvania Gazette* (Philadelphia), May 27, 1762; *Journal of Josiah Quincy, Jun.* . . . ,
Massachusetts Historical Society, *Proceedings,* XL (Boston, 1916), 448; *Royal American
Magazine,* I (1774), 152; W[illiam] Dodd, *The Beauties of History; or, Pictures of Virtue and
Vice* . . . (Philadelphia, 1807), 175. For other midcentury examples of reason set in opposi-
tion to the passions, see *Penn. Gaz.,* Nov. 20, 1735, Dec. 27, 1739, Feb. 7, 1740, Jan. 17, Feb.
28, 1749. On the belief that unrestrained lust led to madness, see Lawrence Stone, *The
Family, Sex, and Marriage in England, 1500–1800* (New York, 1977), 188–189. On the
Puritan association of lust and general sinfulness, see Godbeer, *Sexual Revolution in Early
America,* 64–66.

32. On the shift toward the value of sympathy, see G. J. Barker-Benfield, *The Culture of
Sensibility: Sex and Society in Eighteenth-Century Britain* (Chicago, 1992); Markman Ellis,
The Politics of Sensibility: Race, Gender, and Commerce in the Sentimental Novel (Cambridge,
1996); Carla Mulford, introduction, in Mulford, ed., *The Power of Sympathy by William Hill
Brown and The Coquette by Hannah Webster Foster* (New York, 1996), xxii–xxiii. On the
larger historical meanings of the passions, see the *Oxford English Dictionary,* 2d ed., s.v.
"passion," definition no. 6. On a seventeenth-century New Englander enslaved to his
passions, see Alan Bray, "To Be a Man in Early Modern Society: The Curious Case
of Michael Wigglesworth," *History Workshop Journal,* XLI (1996), 155–165. On the social importance of the passions, see Jacquelyn C. Miller, "Governing the Passions: The

ized early colonial America, later commentaries focused on the political and social impact of uncontrolled passions. Thus, sentimental novels of the late eighteenth century frequently commented on the dangers of unrestricted passions; Hannah Webster Foster's *Coquette* mentioned "passion" at least thirty times, and Susanna Rowson's *Charlotte Temple* referred to it more than twenty. The title page of the first edition of William Hill Brown's *Power of Sympathy* exhorted readers to "Catch the warm Passions of the tender Youth, / And win the Mind to Sentiment and Truth" (Plate 1).[33]

As a cause of uncontrolled, potentially uncivilized behavior, the passions explained all forms of illicit sex, including rape. The publications and writings on rapists in the Revolutionary era repeatedly linked uncontrolled passions to rape. The execution of a rapist in 1773 was "a warning to others whose Passions are stronger than their Reason," and a 1768 poem contrasted a rapist with a real "man — not passion's slave." A preface to the report of a rape trial in 1805 explained that rape occurred "when the passions of man are let loose." In a request for a commuted sentence in 1816, one petition told the Maryland governor that an "unwarrantable ebullition of his passions" had caused the man to rape because he had "good principles but stronger passions." These petitioners all used the passions to illustrate the naturalness of rape. Just as all men could be sinners, all men might let go of the leash of their passions with unfortunately disastrous results.[34]

Eighteenth-Century Quest for Domestic Harmony in Philadelphia's Middle-Class Households," in Christine Daniels and Michael V. Kennedy, eds., *Over the Threshold: Intimate Violence in Early America* (New York, 1999), 45–62.

For examples of the politicization of passions, see *Federalist* No. X; *Penn. Gaz.*, Dec. 10, 1767, May 25, 1769, Aug. 22, 1781; Nathaniel Low, *An Astronomical Diary, 1783* (Boston, [1782]), December; John Adams to John Langdon, Feb. 27, 1812, in Alfred L. Elwyn, comp., *Letters by Washington, Adams, Jefferson, and Others . . . to John Langdon, New Hampshire* (Philadelphia, 1880), 17, cited in "Trivia," *WMQ*, 3d Ser., XXX (1973), 490.

33. Mulford, ed., *The Power of Sympathy and The Coquette*, 4. On passion's relation to dangerous sexuality in eighteenth-century literature, see Patricia Meyer Spacks, " 'Ev'ry Woman is at Heart a Rake,' " *Eighteenth-Century Studies*, VIII (1974), 27–46.

34. Purdie and Dixon's *Virginia Gazette* (Williamsburg), Jan. 7, 1773; *The Rape: A Poem Humbly Inscribed to the Ladies*, 20; *Report of the Trial of Ephraim Wheeler*; petitions for John Gibson, 1816, Governor and Council, Pardon Papers, box 17, folders 87, 91, MdSA. See also *The Life and Confession of Cato*, 6, 7. On the belief that passions caused rape in a European context, see Guido Ruggiero, *The Boundaries of Eros: Sex Crime and Sexuality in Renaissance Venice* (New York, 1985), 97.

In a post-Revolutionary era increasingly concerned with the social consequences of seduction, passion was also faulted for causing illicit, though presumably consensual, sexual encounters. Language virtually identical to that used in discussions of rape described the rake — a man who seduced women immorally but not forcibly (by early American standards, at least). He, too, was "Passion's Slave." The Philadelphia diarist who recorded both his consensual and coercive sexual exploits in the 1790s complained that he had "great passion and no self restraint" when it came to his sexual relations with women. When writing his autobiography shortly before his death in 1790, Benjamin Franklin criticized himself for his fornication, ascribing it to "that hard-to-be-govern'd Passion of Youth." Concerns in the Revolutionary era and early Republic about the impact of social morality on the newly formed nation set new secular consequences for age-old concerns about sexual misbehavior, but uncontrolled passions were still the impetus for multiple forms of illicit sexuality.[35]

The persistent rule of the passions bridged illicit sex and rape; both resulted from improperly controlled desires. Passions might lead to multiple forms of what early Americans deemed sexual misbehavior, whether consensual or coercive. Alongside religious attitudes toward sinful sexual behavior and legal language that blurred the boundaries of force, the popular discourse of rape related it to other sexual misdeeds rather than set rape off as an aberrant act of sexual violence.

⚥ WOMEN'S ROLE IN RAPE: RESPONSIBILITY AND SEDUCTION

Linking rape to other sexual misdeeds raised the issue of women's potential responsibility for rape. An early modern belief in women as sexual temptresses could make women's claims of rape look like consensual sex postcoitally regretted. Yet a declining eighteenth-century belief in all women's necessarily lustful nature did not translate into an automatic negation of women's respon-

35. Purdie and Dixon's *Vir. Gaz.*, July 16, 1772; [Wilson?], Account Book and Diary, May 12, 1773; Paul M. Zall and J. A. Leo Lemay, eds., *Benjamin Franklin's Autobiography: An Authoritative Text, Backgrounds, Criticism* (New York, 1986), 56. For historians' connecting early American men's libido to rates of sexual assaults, see Roger Thompson, *Sex in Middlesex: Popular Mores in a Massachusetts County, 1649–1699* (Amherst, Mass., 1986), 80; Lyle Koehler, *A Search for Power: The "Weaker Sex" in Seventeenth-Century New England* (Urbana, Ill., 1980), 93–94.

sibility for illicit sexual relations. An enduring sexual double standard still held women culpable for sexual immorality, and a growing emphasis on women's ability to make independent choices in love and marriage newly raised the issue of women's responsibility for their sexual predicaments. The multiple sites of overlap between consensual sex and rape allowed early Americans to reread women's resistance into tacit consent and minimized women's ability to believably label coercive sexual acts as rape.[36]

Early-eighteenth-century courts might find women legally culpable when they brought charges of rape or incest to a court's attention. In Maine in 1703, Sarah Tinny complained that John Amee "threw mee Down and pulled up my Close . . . got a Top or Mee . . . and Swore he would Nock mee." Witnesses corroborated that Sarah clearly seemed to be resisting John's violent attack; they recalled that John threatened to "Kick her" and that Sarah "Took a gon and Swore She would Shoot him." While the court found John guilty of "much rudeness," it also gave Sarah a "Publick Admonition" for her rudeness. In 1710, Maine courts dealt with an incident that Mary Jinkins claimed was an attempted rape, but the court punished both Mary and her attacker with fifteen stripes for lewdness. Such lingering enforcements of seventeenth-century morality codes would fade as the American population diversified beyond New England Puritan homogeneity. Eighteenth-century courts were more likely simply to dismiss rape cases than to punish women for charging an unproven rape, but a dismissal could have repercussions on a woman's reputation in the community. If a woman could prove sexual intercourse but a judge or jury did not conclude that she had been forced, they implicitly concluded that the woman must have consented to the illicit sexual relationship and therefore was sexually immoral.[37]

36. On early modern attitudes toward women's sexuality, see Katherine Usher Henderson and Barbara F. McManus, *Half Humankind: Contexts and Texts of the Controversy about Women in England, 1540–1640* (Urbana, Ill., 1985), 55–56. On eighteenth- and nineteenth-century modifications, see Ruth Bloch, "Changing Conceptions of Sexuality and Romance in Eighteenth-Century America," *WMQ*, 3d Ser., LX (2003), 13–42; Christine Stansell, *City of Women: Sex and Class in New York, 1789–1860* (Urbana, Ill., 1987), 76–101. On the double standard's persistence even in novels in the early Republic, see Cathy N. Davidson, *Revolution and the Word: The Rise of the Novel in America* (New York, 1986), 130–131.

37. Case of John Amee, January 1703, in Neal W. Allen, Jr., ed., *Province and Court Records of Maine*, IV (Portland, Maine, 1958), 288–289; case of John White and Mary, the wife of Rowland Jinkins, July 1710, ibid., 378–381. On similar treatment of women who claimed rape in seventeenth-century colonies, see Dayton, *Women before the Bar*, 240–242; Brown, *Good Wives, Nasty Wenches, and Anxious Patriarchs*, 193–194. On early New En-

Indeed, images of sexually eager and uncontrolled women persisted through the early nineteenth century, even as other images of less sexually driven women began to take hold. A woman's dual role as temptress and regulator meant that her stated "no" might still mean "yes" to sexual overtures. "The Sot-Weed Factor," first published in Maryland in 1731, told of the "maid upon the downy Field, [who] Pretends a Force, and Fights to yield." Women seemed to willingly engage in sexual relations, even when they regularly hid their desires behind a performance of resistance. British musical miscellanies reprinted songs with similar themes from the mid-eighteenth through the nineteenth centuries, and Marylander Alexander Hamilton included one in his comic novel manuscript, "The History of the Ancient and Honorable Tuesday Club" (1750s). In this song, "coy" maidens "swear if you're rude they will bawl, / But they whisper so low, / By which you may know / 'Tis artifice, artifice all, all, all." A Revolutionary-era poem reiterated that "a Gentle no, said with a smile, / Is worth a hundred *yesses,* / . . . Then, when I seize the rapturous joy, / Pray seemingly resist, / And, whilst you willingly comply, / Cry out, I won't be *kiss'd.*" These ditties created a world where sexual relations conformed to the format of male-female antagonism: men pursued, and women resisted. Within this world, women felt the simultaneous pressures toward chastity and sexual activity. As "The Maiden's Complaint," a poem printed repeatedly in southern and northern newspapers as early as 1736, surmised: "Poor girls are left if they deny, / And if they yield undone." Women were believed both to desire sex and to be responsible for upholding the social and religious disapprobation of premarital intercourse.[38]

The almanacs that became increasingly popular in the second half of the eighteenth century frequently told bawdy stories of women who were willingly promiscuous. In 1775, a Virginia almanac told the story of Dr. Bentley, who showed a "young lady" his bound books and asked her "how *she liked the binding:* The Lady answered they were extremely handsome, but she chose

---

gland women's sense of complicity, even in forced sexual relations, see Laurel Thatcher Ulrich, *Good Wives: Image and Reality in the Lives of Women in Northern New England, 1650–1750* (New York, 1980), 101.

38. Ebenezer Cook, "The Sot-Weed Factor; or, A Voyage to Maryland, Etc.," in Paul Lauter, ed., *Heath Anthology of American Literature,* 2d ed. (Lexington, Mass., 1994), I, 648; Alexander Hamilton, *The History of the Ancient and Honorable Tuesday Club,* ed. Robert Micklus, 3 vols. (Chapel Hill, N.C., 1990), I, 232 n. 1, 233, 269–270; Purdie and Dixon's *Vir. Gaz.,* Nov. 29, 1770; *Newport Mercury,* Nov. 28, 1771; *Vir. Gaz.,* Oct. 15–22, 1736; John Barry Talley, *Secular Music in Colonial Annapolis: The Tuesday Club, 1745–1756* (Urbana, Ill., 1988), 80–81.

rather to have his *works in sheets*." A 1798 anecdote told of a man who forced a young woman to drink until she was thoroughly intoxicated, at which point she consented to sexual relations with him. When she returned home and told her parents what had happened, they exclaimed that she was ruined, and she replied, "I wish I was to be ruined so every night of my life, and live to the age of *Methusalam*." Women wanted sex. Women enjoyed sex. These are the stories that early Americans told to each other, and, in the telling, much of rape was explained away.[39]

This dual construction of women's sexual role — always resisting, therefore never *really* resisting — had a powerful result: women could not be trusted to judge or represent their own consent. Accordingly, the discourse surrounding rape repeatedly implied that men had to determine a woman's consent for her. A defense attorney in a 1793 rape trial proclaimed, "Any woman [who] is not an abandoned Prostitute, will appear to be averse to what she inwardly desires; a virtuous girl upon the point of yielding, will not appear to give a willing consent, though her manner sufficiently evinces her wishes." Although this defense lawyer spoke with the express purpose of gaining an acquittal for his client, he was drawing on widespread cultural images. He tapped into the often repeated idea that a woman would at least *pretend* to resist sexual over-tures to show her supposed virtue. With such a standard, knowing when resistance meant that a woman was rejecting sexual relations rather than ex-pressing pro forma courting rituals could be difficult for the men involved (not to mention the men on a jury). Because women could not admit their true desires — they said one thing but meant another — they could not be trusted. Thus, the libertine who seduced a previously innocent woman in one late-eighteenth-century novel concluded that, while he loved the young woman, "it would hurt even my delicacy, little as you may think me to possess, to have a wife whom I know to be seducible." Men might forever pursue sexual relations with women but would not trust any woman who had engaged in extramarital sexual relations. Because women could not be trusted either to be honest or to be faithful, women's consent had to be surrendered to men's judgment, whether through marriage or through limitations on their claims to rape.[40]

39. *Virginia Almanack, 1775* (Williamsburg, Va., [1774]), illegible, HL; *The Farmer's Almanack, for . . . 1799* (Norwich, Conn., 1798).

40. *Report of the Trial of Henry Bedlow*, 45; Mulford, ed., *The Power of Sympathy and The Coquette*, 232. For a similar statement, see Benjamin Franklin, *The Complete Poor Richard Almanacks . . .* , 2 vols. (Barre, Mass., 1970), I, [July 1734], 36. On the ways that the

Such images of women shaped the stories of rape circulating in early America. In his narrative of travels to America in the 1750s, Gottlieb Mittelberger told of a rape trial where the defendant refused to speak or answer questions at his trial. Upon conviction, the man finally spoke, claiming that his victim had "cried out so horribly [at the rape] that he had lost his hearing." The "victim" then accused the defendant of lying: "You remember, I didn't say a word then," and the conviction was overturned to the spectators' "great laughter." Similarly, while stationed with the British army at Staten Island in 1776, Francis, Lord Rawdon, wrote a tongue-in-cheek letter stating that his troops were "as rioutous as satyrs. A girl cannot step into the bushes to pluck a rose without running the most imminent risk of being ravished, and they are so little accustomed to these vigorous methods that they don't bear them with the proper resignation." Rawdon's crude expectation that women would consent to rape again blurred the lines between consent and coercion. The post-Revolutionary explosion of cheap almanacs and jokebooks immortalized such personal stories.[41]

Published stories told of women who, once forced into sexual relations, admitted that they enjoyed (and had really desired) sex. One Revolutionary-era story recounted the tale of a woman who successfully sued a man for raping her. But the judge, convinced of the innocence of the "pretended Ravisher," ordered him to grab the bag of awarded money back from the supposed victim. When the woman held on to the money, the judge reversed the verdict, ordering that "she who had Strength enough to retain the Money, might have employed the same effectually, had she pleased, in the Defence of her Honour."

---

language of sexual discourse supported this view of rape, see Garthine Walker, "Rereading Rape and Sexual Violence in Early Modern England," *Gender and History*, X (1998), 5–6. On the relation between Enlightenment theories of political consent and women's sexual consent, see Carole Pateman, *The Sexual Contract* (Stanford, Calif., 1988), and chap. 4 in Pateman, *The Disorder of Women: Democracy, Feminism, and Political Theory* (Stanford, Calif., 1989).

41. Gottlieb Mittelberger, *Journey to Pennsylvania in the Year 1750 and Return to Germany in the Year 1754*, ed. and trans. Oscar Handlin and John Clive (Cambridge, Mass., 1960), 38–39; Francis, Lord Rawdon, to Francis, tenth earl of Huntingdon, Aug. 5, 1776, in Henry Steele Commager and Richard B. Morris, eds., *The Spirit of Seventy-Six: The Story of the American Revolution as Told by Participants*, I (New York, 1953), 424. Like others, Mittelberger's story simultaneously claims that the woman only claimed rape after realizing she was pregnant. See, for example, *Bickerstaff's Genuine Massachusetts, Rhodeisland and Connecticut Almanack, for the Year of Our Lord 1791* (Boston, [1790]), 24.

Another story focused on a man who defended himself against a woman's rape charge by explaining that he had caught the woman stealing beans from his garden and told her that "if she came again she might expect such consequences as those she swore to on the trial." When the woman returned to his garden, he "kept his word" and raped her. The defendant was acquitted, and the story's punch line warned the man, "You have made a most excellent defence to save your *bacon,* but a very bad one to save your *beans,*" because women would forever after be stealing beans (that is, asking for rape) in his garden.[42]

These stories' bawdy humor all hinged on the denial of women's claims of rape. The message of these stories was that despite having strong sexual desires, these women were unwilling to initiate a sexual encounter, so men had to read and fulfill their desires for them. Men focused on their own perception of women's sexual wishes, thereby creating consent for women who had not done so themselves. In the bean story, the accused rapist decided for the woman that her actions meant that she consented, rather than that she was poor and hungry; in the other stories, witnesses and judges dismissed the women's claims. By the end of each story, the speaking woman was no longer a victim of rape. She had been transformed into the sexually duplicitous wench who was a regular character in Anglo-American print. Such women might trick men into marrying, enjoy being ravished, or wrongfully claim paternity. And they falsely cried rape.[43]

While these images gained popularity in the expanding Revolutionary-era press, they did not create entirely new ideologies. They had parallels in actual early American rapes. Throughout the eighteenth century, when accused rapists portrayed their actions, they, too, might contend that the victim had con-

42. *Wilmington Almanack, or Ephemeris, for the Year of Our Lord 1779* (Wilmington, Del., [1778]), September–October; *Newport Mercury,* Dec. 16, 1789. For similar stories, see *The New Entertaining Philadelphia Jest-Book, and Chearful Witty Companion . . .* (Philadelphia, [1790]), 80–81; *The Kentucky Almanac, for the Year of Our Lord 1794 . . .* (Lexington, Ky., [1793]), 9. For a satire on the capriciousness of rape charges and the American legal system, see *The Trial of Atticus, before Justice Beau, for a Rape* (Boston, 1771).

43. For examples of eighteenth-century misogynistic bawdy humor, see Franklin, *The Complete Poor Richard Almanacks,* I, 36, 80; *Father Abraham's Almanac . . . for . . . 1761* (Philadelphia, [1760]); and *The Farmer's Almanack, for 1799.* See also Cornelia Hughes Dayton, "Satire and Sensationalism: The Emergence of Misogyny in Mid-Eighteenth-Century New England Newspapers and Almanacs," paper delivered at the New England Seminar in American History, Worcester, Mass., Nov. 15, 1991 (in Cornelia Hughes Dayton's possession).

sented and that, at worst, they were guilty of fornication but not rape. Often, this appeared to be a believable interpretation: if a woman were capable of consenting, courts might assume that she had indeed consented unless proved otherwise. Emmanuel Lewis, however, tried to stretch this ideology beyond its logical limits in 1734. Emmanuel admitted that he laid his mistress's five-year-old grandchild on his lap but denied that he forced himself on her sexually. He said that the "child did not Cry when he lay with it, but asked him to do it more — that the child pulled up its coats — put his yard to its body." Perhaps Emmanuel truly believed that the child was interested in him sexually, or perhaps he was trying to create a believable excuse for his behavior. Either way, he focused on her perceived sexual willingness to justify his own actions. At his trial in 1806, Ephraim Wheeler admitted that he led a loose and irregular life replete with drinking, bad company, and laziness, but he denied raping his daughter and admitted only to incest with her. The editor of his final words reconciled this stance with Ephraim's conviction for rape: "From the awe and respect, which a child naturally feels towards a parent, [perhaps she] did not make so violent and persevering resistance to the outrage, which he thought she must have done, had she been totally opposed to the perpetration of the deed." According to this statement, a girl could be opposed to sex without being "totally opposed"; she could indicate a lack of desire, but that did not mean that the sex was necessarily against her will. Emmanuel's and Ephraim's cases show that, even when the sexual relationship was totally inappropriate by any legal or moral standards (man-child or father-daughter), men might graft a narrative of female desire onto their explanations of the events. Because a woman's desire was seen as ubiquitous, neither it nor her consent was hers to own. By publicly negating a woman's resistance, men gave her consent for her in the discourse of rape, even when she had not done so during the original sexual encounter.[44]

Women's resistance might also be reread as a desire to control the *effects* of a sexual liaison rather than as a complete refusal of sex. When Sarah Hinton made "some resistance" to William Briscoe's sexual overtures toward her in 1779, he responded by telling her "that he would not get her with child." Rebecca McCarter reported of her attacker in 1789, "I would have nothing to do [with] him — he sd he could work long enough and not get me with Child."

44. Case of Emmanuel Lewis, Aug. 13, 1734, Massachusetts Superior Court of Judicature Records, Suffolk Files, no. 37793, MA; *A Narrative of the Life of Ephraim Wheeler*, 11–12. See also *Report of the Trial of Ephraim Wheeler*.

In these cases, men reinterpreted women's verbalized resistance to their sexual overtures as a concern only for the unwelcome outcome of pregnancy.[45]

One of the few ways that women could prove their resistance to rape was through a willingness to embrace death instead of the dishonor of a rape. Fictionalized women regularly claimed that they would rather die than be raped. In one adventure story reprinted throughout the eighteenth century, the heroine repeatedly claimed, "I had sooner resolved to die, than submit to his cursed proposals" of rape and forced marriage. In a 1790s publication, a German farmer's wife reputedly told French attackers that "she had rather meet death than dishonour." The 1807 Boston publication of an Algerian captivity narrative featured a heroine who told her Turkish captor, "I will sooner suffer death!" than consent to sexual coercion. Preferring death signified the reality of the rape — a woman's willingness to lose her life instead of her chastity proved that the incident was an attempted rape rather than a consensual encounter.[46]

Victims shared this belief that choosing death over dishonor could prove a woman's true resistance to rape. In 1728 Connecticut, Elizabeth Painter told her attacker that "she had rather he Should dash out her brains and Stamp her into the ground" than for him to rape her. In Pennsylvania in 1729, Anne Eastworthy was quoted as saying, "For Christ's sake, Man, don't abuse me thus, but rather kill me." Nearly a century later, Jane West would tell her attacker "I wd rather dye" than be raped. These women claimed rape by presenting their sexual virtue as equivalent to their physical life. In a 1798 trial, a judge endorsed this view, characterizing rape as an attack that robbed the victim "of what to a female is as dear as life." Women who could not prevent a rape might be expected to choose (like the historic Lucretia) a self-inflicted death as the only way to redeem their honor. In perhaps the most famous fictional eighteenth-century rape, Clarissa Harlowe willed herself to death

45. *William Briscoe v Henry Fleet,* Sept. 27, October 1779, April, June 1780, Lancaster Papers, frame 265, reel 192, LOV; *Respublica v David Robb,* Yeates Legal Papers, March–April 1789, fol. 2, HSP.

46. [W. R. Chetwood], *The Remarkable History of Miss Villars* (Keene, N.H., 1795), 9; Anthony Aufrer, *The Cannibals' Progress; or, The Dreadful Horrors of French Invasion* (Albany, N.Y., [1798]), 9; Maria Martin, *History of the Captivity and Sufferings of Mrs. Maria Martin, Who Was Six Years a Slave in Algiers* . . . (Boston, 1807), 65. See also Rinallo D'Elville, *The Rescue; or, The Villain Unmasked* (New York, 1813), 39; Rooney, "'A Little More Than Persuading,'" in Higgins and Silver, eds., *Rape and Representation,* 87–114; and Patricia Meyer Spacks, *Desire and Truth: Functions of Plot in Eighteenth-Century English Novels* (Chicago, 1990), 55–84.

after her libertine suitor drugged and raped her in Samuel Richardson's novel *Clarissa; or, The History of a Young Lady*.[47]

Like *Clarissa* (which was itself quite popular in pre- and post-Revolutionary America), American sentimental novels foregrounded sexually ruined women who chose to end their lives as penance for their sexual misdeeds, even though they were usually victims of seduction rather than rape. These novels of sexual and social danger gained tremendous popularity in America after the Revolution. Scholars have written extensively on the degree to which such novels presented a more sympathetic view of women's sexual misdeeds and the extent of women's agency (both as characters and readers) in these works. As did *Clarissa,* such novels often highlighted eighteenth-century tensions between personal love and parental control; the dangers of women's freedom and the need for their education; and, especially in the American context, tensions about the formation of a new body politic. A comparison of two popular sentimental American stories of seduction and rape reveals the overlap between these two kinds of sexual relations and the ways that blurry boundaries implicitly forwarded an image of women's responsibility for all illicit sexual acts.[48]

47. *Rex v George Clinton,* September 1728, New Haven County Court Files; *Penn. Gaz.,* Nov. 10–13, 1729; *Commonwealth v John Walker,* January 1815, Pennsylvania Court Papers, HSP; *Connecticut Journal,* Aug. 18, 1790, cited in Daniel E. Williams, comp., *Pillars of Salt: An Anthology of Early American Criminal Narratives* (Madison, Wis., 1993), 304–306. See also *State v John Morris,* December 1792, Kent County Oyer and Terminer File Papers, DPA; *The People v George Bowman,* July 24, 1798, New York County Court of General Sessions Indictment Papers, NYMA; trial of Gabriel Nolan, Mar. 17, 1761, WO 71/68, 136–140, TNA:PRO; case of Edmund Fortis, 1795, Robert Treat Paine Papers, Charges to Grand Juries, reel 17 (near the end of the reel), MHS. For this connection in a political commentary, see *Penn. Gaz.,* Aug. 2, 1780.

For some of the most influential scholarship on *Clarissa,* see Terry Eagleton, *The Rape of Clarissa: Writing, Sexuality, and Class Struggle in Samuel Richardson* (Minneapolis, Minn., 1982); Jay Fliegelman, *Prodigals and Pilgrims: The American Revolution against Patriarchal Authority* (Cambridge, 1982), 83–89; R. F. Brissenden, *Virtue in Distress: Studies in the Novel of Sentiment from Richardson to Sade* (London, 1974), 159–186; Frances Ferguson, "Rape and the Rise of the Novel," *Representations,* XX (1987), 88–112; Terry Castle, *Clarissa's Ciphers: Meaning and Disruption in Richardson's "Clarissa"* (Ithaca, N.Y., 1982).

48. For just some of the voluminous scholarship on seduction in American novels, see Marion Rust, "What's Wrong with *Charlotte Temple?"* *WMQ,* 3d Ser., LX (2003), 99–118; Elizabeth Barnes, *States of Sympathy: Seduction and Democracy in the American Novel* (New York, 1997); Davidson, *Revolution and the Word,* 110–150; Donna R. Bontatibus, *The Seduction Novel of the Early Nation: A Call for Socio-Political Reform* (East Lansing, Mich.,

Hannah Webster Foster's best-selling novel, *The Coquette,* was an archetypal sentimental tale of seduction. It told the tale of Eliza Wharton, a respectable and educated young woman who "made herself the victim, by her own indiscretion" "to the amusement of a seducer," rather than give herself wholeheartedly to the respectable though dispassionate minister who wanted to marry her. After learning of Eliza's continuing flirtation with the rake Peter Sanford, the minister avoided being "the dupe of coquetting artifice" by leaving Eliza. Subsequently, the rake with whom Eliza flirted married another woman solely to secure his financial future, yet still entered into an adulterous affair with Eliza that left her pregnant. The "ruined, lost Eliza" ran away from her friends and family and shortly thereafter died of consumption and heartbreak, leaving her friends to opine to the reader that "virtue alone" could "secure lasting felicity."[49]

The Coquette presented a largely sympathetic view of a respectable young woman whose errors in judgment were meant to warn readers of the dangers of libertine men and of the need to choose virtue and reason instead of the immediate gratification of passions. In keeping with general shifts toward sympathy, literary victims of seduction such as Eliza Wharton might be seen as "sweetly pathetic" rather than as the sexually voracious "loathsome temptresses" that populated seventeenth-century literature.[50]

A Very Surprising Narrative of a Young Woman, Who Was Discovered in the Gloomy Mansion of a Rocky Cave! combined features of seduction tales and captivity narratives. *A Very Surprising Narrative* was, perhaps, the most popular short fiction publication in the period, going through eighteen editions at fifteen presses in the twenty-one years after its pseudonymous first publication in the 1780s. It told the story of a New York woman who met a respectable man with whom she "vow[ed] mutual love" and planned "future happiness," until

---

1999); Hana Louise Layson, "Injured Innocence: Sexual Injury, Sentimentality, and Citizenship in the Early Republic" (Ph.D. diss., University of Chicago, 2003); Hessinger, "'Insidious Murderers of Female Innocence,'" in Smith, ed., *Sex and Sexuality in Early America,* 262–282. On the popularity of such novels, see Davidson, 112–114, 123, 136; Fliegelman, *Prodigals and Pilgrims,* 83, 87; Hessinger, 265–266; Jan Lewis, "The Republican Wife: Virtue and Seduction in the Early Republic," *WMQ,* 3d Ser., XLIV (1987), 692.

49. Mulford, ed., *The Power of Sympathy and The Coquette,* 134, 179, 219, 241.

50. Susan Staves, "British Seduced Maidens," *Eighteenth-Century Studies,* XIV (1980–1981), 109. On the image of bawdy women in early modern England, see Anthony Fletcher, *Gender, Sex, and Subordination in England, 1500–1800* (New Haven, Conn., 1995), chaps. 1–5.

her father found out about their plans and barred them from seeing each other. The young woman then ran away with her lover, hoping to change her father's mind. When her father "threatened vengeance to us both," the two moved farther into the country, where Indians captured the couple, imprisoned the beautiful woman, and "barberously murdered my lover." Luckily, the woman escaped and ran through the forest for weeks, until, unluckily, "a man of a gigantic figure. . . . accosted me in a language I did not understand" and took her with him to live in his cave. The giant then tried to force the woman to "accept of his bed, or expect death for my obstinacy." He gave her until sunrise to choose her fate, and the young woman used the time to chew through her bindings and "took up the hatchet" to "effectually put an end to his existence" with three blows. She then chopped off his head, cut him into quarters, and hid his body in the woods. She continued to live alone in the cave for nine years until some Anglo-American travelers discovered her. The travelers persuaded her to return to civilization, where she found her father on his deathbed, eager to welcome her into his arms and "acknowledg[e] he had been unjustly cruel to her." He then quickly expired, and proved his forgiveness by leaving his daughter "a handsome fortune."[51]

In many ways, this story conformed to forms of popular genres of the period. The melodramatic tale of repeated danger and near disaster was reminiscent of eighteenth-century adventure and captivity narratives. The story of the contest over love and patriarchal orders would have been equally familiar to eighteenth-century novel readers in Britain and America. And the image of the heroine, resisting foreigners and captors through her fantastic ability to protect her chastity, confirmed her as a trustworthy heroine for the nation.

How, then, should we compare this image of the heroic woman who escaped rape against overwhelming odds to the image of the fallible female victim of seduction? The image of Eliza's seduction directly contrasted with that of the cave-dwelling giant's near-rape of the beautiful heroine. The unnamed woman managed to miraculously resist rape, while Eliza was responsible for her own sexual downfall. But there is an important commonality in both stories: in keeping with debates about women's increased social power in the early Republic, both women were ultimately responsible for men's sexual use of their bodies. Eliza made choices that led to her downfall (as her seducer

51. Abraham Panther, pseud., *A Very Surprising Narrative of a Young Woman, Who Was Discovered in the Gloomy Mansion of a Rocky Cave! . . .* 3d ed. (Windsor, Vt., 1796), 5–11. For details on its publication history, see Fliegelman, *Prodigals and Pilgrims*, 140.

plainly warned early on, "If she will play with a lion, let her beware of his paw"), and the unnamed woman used her intellect to avoid rapacious Indians and giants. While the stories have diametrically opposed endings (Eliza's ruin led to her solitary death, removed from all those she loved, while the other woman's sexual integrity allowed her to have an eventual rebirth into Anglo-American society), they shared an underlying belief that all women were at least partially responsible for their participation in any form of sexual relations.

If the line between the responsibility of a seduced woman and a raped woman were potentially fine, then all women might likely have been suspected of contributing to their ruin via illicit sexual interactions. Indeed, Eliza Wharton's guardian traversed this slippery ground when she warned Eliza not to become "an object of seduction," like the fictional Clarissa, a woman who "made herself the victim, by her own indiscretion." Clarissa, like Eliza, trusted an untrustworthy man. However, unlike Eliza, Clarissa was tricked, drugged, and ultimately raped — physically forced to give up her chastity, rather than voluntarily surrendering it at a moment when passions overwhelmed reason. In trying to impress upon Eliza the need for social and sexual chastity, her adviser emphasized how women contributed to their own downfall — regardless of the degree of coercion or force men might use to lead women to sexual ruin.[52]

At the turn of the eighteenth century, women were not expected to possess the intellectual ability to control their passions. This early modern image of the sexually uncontrollable woman had undergone a transformation by the nineteenth century, when respectable women were believed to provide the balm to men's baser interests and to protect themselves through prudent behavior and choices. But these changes were neither linear nor complete. Two quotations from the turn of the nineteenth century show the conflicting ideologies circulating about women's sexual natures. In 1801, Alice DeLancey Izard, a South Carolina gentlewoman, anticipated notions of true womanhood in expecting a woman to control both her own and her man's passions. Alice held that a "good woman. . . . acts like a guardian angel by preventing the effects of evil desires and strong passions." Conversely, in a 1796 Pennsylvania book, William

52. Mulford, ed., *The Power of Sympathy and The Coquette,* 149. For examples of the scholarly classification of Clarissa as a seduction, see Lewis, "The Republican Wife," *WMQ,* 3d Ser., XLIV (1987), 693; Mulford, introduction, in Mulford, ed., *The Power of Sympathy and The Coquette,* 134n, 260. For a discussion of critics who have made Clarissa at least partly responsible for (or desirous of) the rape, see Eagleton, *The Rape of Clarissa,* 64–72; Brissenden, *Virtue in Distress,* 184.

PLATE I. *Frontispiece to William Hill Brown,* The Power of Sympathy *(Boston, 1789). This image shows, as the dedication page states, the "fatal consequences of* SEDUCTION," *underscoring women's responsibility for illicit sexual relations. As in stories of rape, virtuous women might regularly choose death over dishonor. Courtesy, American Antiquarian Society, Worcester, Mass.*

Alexander explicitly recognized the difficulty of vesting in women, "a sex so much guided by the impulses of passion," the power to claim rape.[53]

Despite their antithetical outlooks, both Alice's and William's constructions of women's sexual role made women largely responsible for rape. Women might be increasingly expected to regulate men's passions, even as their own passions provided a rationale for disbelief of their claims of rape. Such beliefs created circular arguments from which women could not easily escape. If women should regulate men's passions, then women were responsible for men whose passions caused them to rape. And if women were believed ruled by the impulses of their own passions, then any sexual encounter might be consensual. A woman gave the name of rape to a sexual act because her (non)consent was crucial to its very definition. But popular stories, firsthand testimonies, and cultural standards limited the belief in a woman's ability to refuse to consent. Hence much of rape was defined out of existence.

In 1768, Bennet Allen published a poem defending Lord Baltimore from a rape accusation. He titled his work *Modern Chastity; or, The Agreeable Rape*. This title contained some of the cultural assumptions that made Rebecca McCarter, the servant in the chapter's opening anecdote, hesitant to identify her master's ongoing sexual force as rape. Allen proposed that, because women secretly desired sex, their version of chastity allowed and even encouraged men to force women into agreeable rapes. This intractable construction of women's sexual desires left little room for women to carve out a rape from a continuum of illicit sexual interactions.[54]

53. Alice DeLancey Izard to Margaret Izard Manigault, May 29, 1801, Manigault Family Papers, South Carolina Library, University of South Carolina, quoted in Wylma Wates, "Precursor to the Victorian Age: The Concept of Marriage and Family as Revealed in the Correspondence of the Izard Family of South Carolina," in Carol Bleser, ed., *In Joy and in Sorrow: Women, Family, and Marriage in the Victorian South, 1830–1900* (New York, 1991), 6; William Alexander, *The History of Women: From the Earliest Antiquity, to the Present Time* (Philadelphia, 1796), II, 322. See also Jack P. Greene, ed., *The Diary of Colonel Landon Carter of Sabine Hall, 1752–1778,* 2 vols. (Charlottesville, Va., 1965), II, 1107. The best introduction to shifting notions of early Republic white womanhood remains Nancy F. Cott, *The Bonds of Womanhood: "Woman's Sphere" in New England, 1780–1835* (New Haven, Conn., 1977). On nineteenth-century passionlessness, see Nancy F. Cott, "Passionlessness: An Interpretation of Victorian Sexual Ideology, 1790–1850," *Signs,* IV (1978), 219–236; Steven Seidman, "The Power of Desire and the Danger of Pleasure: Victorian Sexuality Reconsidered," *Journal of Social History,* XXIV (1990), 47–67.

54. Bennet Allen, *Modern Chastity; or, The Agreeable Rape* (London, 1768). For the

Decades of feminism have schooled Americans to view rape as a crime of violence, not a sexual act run amok. Yet, from a historical perspective, the insistence that rape is an act of patriarchal violence obscures much about early American conceptions of sexual assaults. The permeable boundaries between force and consent in heterosexual relations encouraged early Americans to see rape as another form of illicit sex. From the early colonial period, ministers bemoaned the passions that caused all sins of uncleanness — whether adultery, fornication, or rape. In later print narratives, rapists themselves ascribed their actions to their early experiences of fornication. The Anglo-American legal language of force and assault might refer to either physically coercive or consensual sexual relations. Women who testified about rapes explained that they had originally refused sexual offers before the offer changed to a threat and ultimately an unrefusable demand. In countless stories of seduction in the early Republic where women willingly chose to have sexual relations with men (albeit against their better judgment), the morals of such stories paralleled the lessons of rape: in both cases, men were theoretically condemned; women were ruined victims who could redeem themselves only through death; and both sets of narratives presented the sexual misdeeds as an outgrowth of uncontrolled passions. This multiplicity of overlapping meanings could eclipse the issue of whether a woman had consented.[55]

Rape's slippage into consensual sex bolstered an image of women whose physical — or increasingly, in the early Republic, emotional — passions might overrule their verbal resistance. In keeping with the enduring double standard, women might *need* to be forced into sex. Men saw what women might intend as resistance as part of women's ruse as sexual temptresses. Although a disin-

---

complete trial, see *The Trial of Frederick Calvert . . . for a Rape on the Body of Sarah Woodcock; and of E. Griffinburg, and A. Harvey, otherwise Darby . . .* (London, 1768). Like Rebecca McCarter, Lord Baltimore's accuser was a servant in his household.

55. On the reconceptualization of rape and other heterosexual relations, see Susan Brownmiller, *Against Our Will: Men, Women, and Rape* (New York, 1975); Susan Rae Peterson, "Coercion and Rape: The State as a Male Protection Racket," in Mary Vetterling-Braggin et al., eds., *Feminism and Philosophy* (Tottowa, N.J., 1977), 360–371. More recent influential works include Patricia Searles and Ronald J. Berger, eds., *Rape and Society: Readings on the Problem of Sexual Assault* (Boulder, Colo., 1995); Emilie Buchwald, Pamela R. Fletcher, and Martha Roth, eds., *Transforming a Rape Culture* (Minneapolis, Minn., 1993). Ironically, as late as 2001, my own university's safety tips included the statement that "rape is a violent crime — a hostile attack — an attempt to hurt and humiliate. It is not the result of 'uncontrolled passions'" (http://www.abs.uci.edu/depts/police/safetytips/sexualassault.html [accessed Aug. 10, 2001]).

clination to believe women's claims of rape remained a fundamental hindrance to successful rape prosecutions, early Americans were more willing to believe some rape scenarios than others. When a community believed that the woman would *never* have consented to sexual relations with her attacker under any circumstances, a woman's claims of resistance carried more weight. In contrast, the increasing interest in seduction narratives promoted an image of white men as seducers rather than rapists. To make a fictional woman's temptation into illicit sexual relations believable, the seducer needed to be a white man that the readers might identify as attractive to a young white woman. This growing emphasis on white men as seducers would critically affect the hardening of racial lines in the early Republic, making ideologies of rape a fertile ground for the enactment of racial boundaries.

CHAPTER TWO

THE MEANS OF SEXUAL COERCION: IDENTITY, POWER, AND SOCIAL CONSENT

Sexual coercion took many forms in early America. In 1725, Sarah Perkins told a Connecticut court that her father had often pressured her to have sex with him. Sarah confessed to having repeated sexual relations with her father but maintained that "she always opposed him by argmts and was never willing to comply with him." In 1766, two Pennsylvania men raped and murdered two local Indian women, leaving their hatcheted bodies to decay by the roadside. In 1796, a woman named Jane was walking home from church when she ran into a neighbor who walked with her, helped her through a fence, and then tried to rape her in a New Jersey field. In 1808, Celia Evans testified to Virginia justices that a slave broke into her house and raped her at knifepoint, threatening to kill her if she made any noise or resistance.[1]

All of these women experienced a sexual attack that ultimately came to the attention of an early American court. The incidents spanned nearly a century, but nothing tied each incident to a limited historical epoch—an array of like incidents could be mixed and matched across any decade or region. Instead of regional or chronological specificities, these sexual assaults differed in the means of the sexual coercion. While any woman might theoretically fall victim to a knife-wielding stranger, different sets of identities, social standings, and societal expectations allowed for other particular forms of sexual coercion. Because sexual attacks were committed with social power as well as with physical force, a woman's standing in early American society left her differently

1. Indictment of John Perkins, Jr., and Sarah Perkins, March 1725, New Haven Superior Court Files, 1720–1727, drawer 324, CSL; *Pennsylvania Gazette* (Philadelphia), Aug. 7, 1766; case of Pompey, November 1796, indictments, no. 3376 and unnumbered doc., HHR; case of David, Apr. 18, 1808, Virginia Executive Papers, box 153, LOV.

vulnerable to sexually coercive tactics, and a man's standing allowed him to differently exploit these vulnerabilities.

We often talk about rape as if all forceful sex springs from the same cause and is implemented in identical ways. In reality, early Americans' limited definition of rape as an utterly irresistible act of overt physical force ignored the many forms of sexual coercion beyond physical battery. A stranger's surprise attack bore little resemblance to a father's continual sexual manipulation or a friendly neighbor's coercion, let alone to rapes committed in the course of murder. Yet, in all of these sexual attacks, social and economic power relations underwrote sexual power, not only in the ability to evade legal punishment but also through the very commission of sexual coercion. The porous boundaries between consensual and coercive sexual relations allowed some men to infuse sexual force with the appearance of consent. In other words, men could commit rape not just as an act of power—they could use their power to define the act.

The type of sexual assault that early Americans would most readily identify as an archetypal rape might have been one of the less common kinds of sexual assault. These unforeseeable rapes by strangers or community outsiders often involved excessive physical battery and occurred in isolated locations—the equivalent to the modern rape in a dark alley by an armed stranger. In these rapes, women's consent would least likely be an issue. Despite this common image of rape, far more sexual attacks might have occurred among neighbors and family members. Such incidents could combine a threat of brute force with more subtle forms of coercion that sought to make the victim a seemingly willing participant in the sexual encounter. While outsider rapes included only the most nominal effort at replicating consensual relationships, sexual assaults between people who knew one another could more effectively use social relationships to create an image of a consensual sexual interaction.

After a brief discussion of incidents enacted by pure physical force or threat, I focus on sexual coercion enacted through means other than sudden and brute force. In particular, I focus on rapes within households. As the primary economic, social, and familial configuration in early America, household hierarchies structured a variety of patterns of sexual coercion. Many sexual assaults depended on the relationship between the household members involved: masters and fathers could use their position as household patriarchs to coerce servants, slaves, or daughters. Most patriarchs did not need to resort to excessive physical force or weapons. Instead, masters could order their laborers into sexually vulnerable situations, and fathers could use their authority to order sexual obedience from their daughters. For enslaved women, virtually

nonexistent legal or community support meant that masters' sexual prerogatives would be a significant feature of a race-based slave labor system. Yet
household labor organization also blurred the lines between a patriarch's sexual and economic control over all of his dependent women's bodies. Case
studies of two exceptionally detailed incidents of master-on-dependent sexual
coercion suggest that we need to complicate any notion that racial or slave
status alone determined sexual vulnerability. White mastery as much as a servant's or slave's race shaped the form of sexual coercion.

Beyond outlining the common categories of sexual assaults enacted through
social relationships, I explore a group of sexual assaults that explicitly enforced
colonial boundaries. Throughout history, rape has been used in wartime as a
punishment of the vanquished and a reward for the victors. In the early American context, we also see sadistic sexual acts that displayed Anglo-American
men's direct punishment of subservient racial and ethnic groups through rape.
Such rapes were a tool of colonization against Native American and African
American women that marked a woman's gendered and racial inferiority. Thus,
contrary to early American definitions of rape as an attack by *a* man on *a*
woman, the act of sexual coercion gave rape social, racial, and specifically
colonial meanings.

RAPE BY STRANGERS, RAPE BY NEIGHBORS

The archetypal rape in early America — the type that newspaper editors
bemoaned, courts successfully prosecuted, and community members easily
condemned — was a onetime surprise attack by a virtual stranger. Such attackers might be expected to have surprised a woman in an isolated location
and threatened her with death or grave bodily harm if she did not comply with
his sexual force. Because such random attacks left little suspicion that the
woman might have consented, they were the most easily identified and likely
most prosecuted kind of rape. By providing a stark contrast to sexual relations
between people whose existing social relations with one another might imply
consensual sexual relations, such sudden-attack stranger rapes avoided an array
of concerns about a victim's chastity and sexual desires.

Violent rapes by men with whom the victims appear to have had no social
relations can be identified only sporadically in court records throughout the
eighteenth and early nineteenth centuries. In the most obvious of these cases,
attackers used weapons to force women's submission. In Massachusetts in
1731, a black laborer named London carried a young woman, whom he had
been ordered to transport to a nearby town, into the woods, threatened her

with a knife, and raped her. In Montreal in 1761, Catherine McCarter was walking when Gabriel Nolan, claiming he knew a shortcut, led her into the woods "where there was no path." In this remote area, Gabriel threw Catherine down at knifepoint, threatening that he would "cut her throat, or Rip up her Belly if she did not comply" with his sexual wishes. In 1787, Mary Murphy told a Maryland court that she was accosted by an enslaved man "she did not Remember ever to have seen" before, who held "a *Jackleg Knife* a cross her throat as if he intended to cut it." Such sudden attacks by an unfamiliar assailant with the threat or fulfillment of severe physical violence most easily fitted the quintessential image of rape.[2]

Although such stranger assaults might have been few, men of African descent were prosecuted for a disproportionate number of both weapon-wielding and stranger sexual assaults (about 40 percent of identifiable incidents). As social outsiders in most Anglo-American communities, African American men had few means other than physical threats and brute force for rape against white women. Unlike many white men, black men would have had little opportunity to build recognized social relationships with white women that might allow for less physically violent methods of sexual coercion. Black men who had little condoned opportunity to socialize with white women *seemed* more like rapists because they had little ability to reformulate social relations with white women

2. Examination of London, October 1734, Massachusetts Superior Court of Judicature Records, Suffolk Files, nos. 38267, 37890 (order for Special Assize), MA; trial of Gabriel Nolan, Mar. 17, 1761, WO 71/68, 136–140, TNA:PRO; petitions for Adam, November 1787, Governor and Council, Pardon Papers, box 3, folder 96, MdSA. Pistols were very rarely mentioned in connection with rape outside of wartime. For one such case, see *Carlisle Gazette, and the Western Repository of Knowledge* (Carlisle, Pa.), Nov. 19, 1788. Adopting a limited image of rape as acts committed randomly by violent strangers has allowed scholars critical of feminist interpretations of rape's relation to patriarchy to categorize rape as "flourish[ing] mainly on the margins" and rapists as "the waste of patriarchy" (Roy Porter, "Rape — Does It Have a Historical Meaning?" in Sylvana Tomaselli and Roy Porter, eds., *Rape* [New York, 1986], 235).

Of 321 incidents in which the relationship between the defendant and victim can be determined, fewer than twenty cases involved strangers. Although this number is undoubtedly an understatement (it is easier to identify a relationship than a lack of relationship), qualitative evidence does suggest that the "typical" rape popularized in published crime literature might have been far less typical than we may think. For a modern rape study that reached similar conclusions, see Diana E. H. Russell, *Rape in Marriage* (New York, 1982), 64–67.

into quasi-consensual sexual relations. Black and enslaved men might have had opportunities to coerce their own black neighbors into sexual relations, but the historical record is virtually silent about such acts. Consequently, their sexual assaults seemed to be more often committed as the kind of sudden, unavoidable attacks that early Americans associated with rape.[3]

This image of a rape committed through a stranger's use of extreme force was so much a part of communal consciousness that early Americans mimicked such violent attacks in their fabricated claims of rapes. In 1756, when Hannah Beebe made a rape accusation that she later recanted, she claimed that a black stranger had accosted her "in a bye and secret place," threatened to kill her, and made his threat real by pulling out a knife before he raped her. In the Revolutionary era, when Mary Bremer claimed that her pregnancy had resulted from a rape, she manufactured a story about an unknown assailant who accosted her in a wooded park (her uncle and guardian was eventually discovered to be the baby's father). Jacob Kester apparently concocted a story of rape to justify asking a neighbor to "use his medical knowledge in obtaining an abortion" for the servant he had impregnated in 1789. Jacob claimed that she had been accosted on a road by two unknown men "who menaced that they would murder her unless she consented to let them have the carnal enjoyment of her person." In all of these false rape stories, tellers claimed an image of rape that situated unknown, violent offenders as attackers of lone women in isolated locations, resorting to the archetypal image of rape for their fictional scenarios.[4]

But a world of sexual coercion existed outside the violent-outsider-as-attacker scenario—a world probably more common than the typical image of rape suggests. A man who sexually coerced a woman with whom he socialized did not have to rely exclusively on the physical violence and bodily threats of the stranger rapist. Neighbors, relatives, or family friends committed sexual assaults in ways that deviated sharply from the seemingly sudden brutality and

3. On the eighteenth-century image of rapists as community outsiders, see Cornelia Hughes Dayton, *Women before the Bar: Gender, Law, and Society in Connecticut, 1639–1789* (Chapel Hill, N.C., 1995), 233, 243, 249. I am in no way implying that black men raped any more than any other group of men might have. Rather, I am emphasizing the ways that social identities might have limited black men's means for sexual coercion in comparison to white men.

4. Philip M. Hamer et al., *The Papers of Henry Laurens,* 15 vols. (Columbia, S.C., 1968–[2000]), VIII, 558; *Andreas v Andreas,* 1789, Pennsylvania Supreme Court Eastern District Divorce Papers, RG–33, PSA.

absolute physical force of unambiguous rapes. In many of these incidents, daily forms of socializing went awry, as affable interactions led to what women experienced as acts of sexual coercion.[5]

When men and women shared an ongoing social relationship, men could blur the lines between persuasion and forceful attempts at sexual relations. We may most expect such blurring in courting relationships, when unmarried men and women worked toward adulthood through heterosocial and heterosexual pairings. Some rape accusations certainly seemed to originate out of young men's pursuit of young women, but men could also use the position of neighbor rather than suitor to shade social relationships into sexual ones. In Maine in 1710, Mary Jinkins told a court that John White came to her house when her husband was away "to Talke with her," and they chatted about Mary's "mother and other things" while John helped her put her children to bed. Afterward, John bolted the door and told Mary "hee cam to have his will of her." Mary used "all the meains Shee posebly Could to hender him" but "fell into a fitte" while he forced her into sexual relations. John then spent the night, not leaving until Mary's mother arrived in the morning. John's actions in front of others — helping with the children and greeting Mary's mother — suggested that he was being a friendly neighbor, perhaps protecting Mary from the hostile Indians she feared. But Mary's initial willingness to entertain him in her husband's absence might have simultaneously created his expectation that she would consent to sexual relations.[6]

In 1764, a married woman named Mary Burnside testified that she was working at a neighbor's house when David Clark sat beside her and repeatedly tried to pull her onto his lap. When she, "finding she did not Care to keep him Company," left the room, David followed her and "asked if he might not Kiss her." Mary refused, and David "pinched and Tickoled her" until she slapped

5. Of 321 incidents where the relationship between the defendant and victim can be identified, 126 (39 percent) involved people who were acquainted with one another but did not live in the same household. One hundred eighty-two (57 percent) involved people from the same town or region of the city (not living in the same house). Two studies of eighteenth-century London rapes found that similarly high percentages of prosecuted sexual assaults involved people who knew each other. See Antony E. Simpson, "Popular Perceptions of Rape as a Capital Crime in Eighteenth-Century England: The Press and the Trial of Francis Charteris in the Old Bailey, February 1730," *Law and History Review*, XXII (2004), par. 51; Randolph Trumbach, *Sex and the Gender Revolution* (Chicago, 1998), 307–308.

6. Case of John White and Mary, the wife of Rowland Jinkins, July 1710, in Neal W. Allen, Jr., ed., *Province and Court Records of Maine*, IV (Portland, Maine, 1958), 378–381.

him. According to Mary, David then carried her into a back room and threw her on the bed, attempting to rape her. John Baxter claimed that he had seen Mary sitting on David's knee and "some Toying between them," so when he heard Mary call for help from the back room, he told Mary that he would help her "when he thought She was in Need." When a servant woman and the homeowner's daughter tried to help Mary, other neighborhood men prevented their intervention. Although several men were aware of Mary's resistance to their neighbor, they chose not to intervene or to allow other young women to do so. Perhaps the men had determined that Mary was not truly resisting David, or that her admittance of some degree of familiarity meant that she likely wanted sexual relations. Yet, if these men had witnessed similar physical interactions where strangers or enslaved men were on top of neighbor women, they probably would have been more likely to consider that the woman was in real danger and the sexual interactions were forced.[7]

Women sometimes recalled that the neighbors they eventually charged with a crime had repeatedly pestered them for sex. In 1701, Sarah Aldridge accused William Hudson of attempting to rape her by "Divers times Attempting to lye with her." In 1798, Margaret Heyser complained that George Bowman "has several times attempted to take the advantage of this Deponent." In the early nineteenth century, Mary Ellis complained to a Mississippi court that Francis Surget made a dozen sexual overtures across several months before he came to her house, ostensibly to ask about her husband's farm business. During their conversation, Francis shut the window and door, ignored Mary's requests for him to "begone out of her presence," dragged her onto a bed and, according to Mary, raped her. The nuisance of a sexually forward neighbor might not seem like an actionable offense in communities that tacitly expected men to want illicit sex despite legal and religious condemnation of such acts. A community member might repeatedly attempt to have consensual sexual relations with a neighbor before escalating toward more overpowering tactics that led her to publicly complain about his behavior. Ironically, the hesitancy to turn on a neighbor might also distance a woman's accusation from the most believable image of rape as a sudden and physically irresistible attack.[8]

7. *D. v David Clark,* August 1764, Chester County Quarter Sessions File Papers, CCA.

8. Case of William Hudson, September 1701, in David Thomas Konig, ed., *Plymouth Court Records, 1686–1859,* 16 vols. (Wilmington, Del., 1978–1981), I, *1686–1721,* 253 (it is unclear from the court record whether Sarah was married); *The People v George Bowman,* July 24, 1798, New York County Court of General Sessions Indictment Papers, NYMA; *Territory of Mississippi v Francis Surget,* October 1808, in William Bakersville Hamilton, ed.,

In courting relationships, members of the community might be even more likely to see close social relationships that developed into sexual ones — even apparently coercive sexual relations — as private interactions that did not demand intercession. Unlike the seventeenth-century New Englanders who emphasized community policing, eighteenth-century community members who saw sexual tousling between their unmarried neighbors might avoid interfering. Perhaps they thought that the established social relationship between the parties meant that their sexual relationship was a consensual one or was a natural outgrowth of increasingly relaxed parental control over courting.[9]

In 1731 in Pennsylvania, Alice Yarnal complained that Lawrence MacGinnis had thrown her down and tried to rape her by the side of the road. Two men who accompanied Lawrence appeared to know that he planned to have sexual relations — forced if necessary — with Alice but did not seem to think intervention appropriate. John Howard testified that after Lawrence had seen Alice, Lawrence had claimed that if the road had been more isolated, he "would have taken the above alice yarnal into the woods and stopped her mouth." John apparently saw nothing wrong with Lawrence's plan; he later left Lawrence and Alice to go visit at a nearby house. Lawrence's second travel companion, Jacob Graves, likewise remarked that he had "no doubt but we shall find them in the bushes," and he was right. John and Jacob next saw Lawrence on top of Alice, who was hitting him and crying, "You shall not," but still did not intervene. Perhaps they thought that Alice's resistance was pro forma courting behavior or that interference in a neighbor's personal relations was not their right. Or perhaps, since they knew that Alice, though unmarried, had a small child, they took this evidence of her past sexual relations to mean that she had no virtue for them to protect and therefore would likely ultimately have con-

---

Anglo-American Law on the Frontier: Thomas Rodney and His Territorial Cases (Durham, N.C., 1953), 419–422. See also notes of evidence in Respublica v Abraham Moses, May 21, 1783, Yeates Legal Papers, April–May 1783, fol. 7, HSP.

9. On early colonial morals prosecutions, see Eli Faber, "The Evil That Men Do: Crime and Transgression in Colonial Massachusetts" (Ph.D. diss., Columbia University, 1974), 72, 110; Douglas Greenberg, "Crime, Law Enforcement, and Social Control in Colonial America," American Journal of Legal History, XXVI (1982), esp. 297–299, 305–307; Peter Charles Hoffer, Criminal Proceedings in Colonial Virginia . . . , American Legal Records, X (Athens, Ga., 1984), xxviii; Dayton, Women before the Bar, 173–187; Kathleen M. Brown, Good Wives, Nasty Wenches, and Anxious Patriarchs: Gender, Race, and Power in Colonial Virginia (Chapel Hill, N.C., 1996), 187–201. On changing courting practices, see Anne S. Lombard, Making Manhood: Growing up Male in Colonial New England (Cambridge, Mass., 2003), 57–97.

sented to Lawrence's overtures. Images of sexual courting as men's pursuit and women's resistance encouraged men to impose a consensual interpretation onto a female neighbor's or friend's sexual resistance.[10]

A sexual attacker could even purposefully use courting behavior to mask the appearance of coercion. In Pennsylvania in 1783, Jane Mathers described how James Paxton had approached her as she was walking through the woods, offered to walk her home, and asked what she would think "of his playing with me." Although Jane "begged him for God's sake not to touch" her, James "swore he would." When a man who had heard Jane's screams discovered them, James began brushing her hair, suggested that she wipe the dirt from her neck, and told the newly arrived witness that the scuffle was about Jane's refusal to give him any of her peaches. From beginning to end, even by Jane's own testimony, James had cast his actions into the normalcy of consensual sexual relations. He did not immediately force himself on Jane but asked to have sex with her. Brushing Jane's hair was a social interaction suggestive of intimacy and consent: after all, if she let him stroke her hair, was it not then reasonable to think that they had an amiable, even amorous relationship? Yet only accepted community members could replicate consensual amorous relations. An unfamiliar enslaved man could not have calmly stroked a white woman's hair, claiming that they had just had a tiff about some fruit.[11]

Indeed, even when white victims knew the identity of the black men they accused of rape, their courtroom testimony often reiterated that the women shared no social relationship with black attackers. Being literal neighbors rarely implied neighborliness between white victims and black attackers. In her testimony against a black man who broke into her house and raped her in Connecticut in 1817, Lelea Thorp specified that she knew him "but was, never, personally acquainted with him." A year later, Elizabeth Wright told a Virginia court that she had seen the slave she had accused of raping her only briefly on two previous occasions as he was passing through the plantation where she lived. One of the only known instances of a black man's sexual assault that stemmed from consensual social relations involved an attack on an African American

10. *D. v Lawrence MacGinnis,* June 1, 1731, Chester County Quarter Sessions File Papers, CCA.

11. Notes of evidence in *Respublic v James Paxton,* May 27, 1783, Yeates Legal Papers, April–May 1783, fol. 7, HSP. For other cases growing out of courting interactions, see case of John Amee, January 1703, in Allen, ed., *Province and Court Records of Maine,* IV, 288–289; indictment of Lenass Brawn, April 1792, Dockets of Cases and Notes of Evidence Taken by Hon. Increase Sumner, 1782–1797, 159–161, MHS.

woman. As previously mentioned, in New Jersey in 1796, Pompey tried to force Jane, a neighborhood woman whom he knew, into sexual relations when he accompanied her home from church services. Just as white male community members placed forced sexual acts into a setting of voluntary social relations to claim that sexual coercion of white women was consensual sex rather than rape, black men and women probably engaged in similar struggles in their own communities. Unfortunately, early American records are almost unanimously silent on the inner workings of African American sexual practices that were unrelated to Anglo-American culture.[12]

An increased concern about the dangers of unregulated courting and teenage socializing accompanied the rise of cities in the early Republic. Young women, often living outside the bounds of their fathers' protection and supervision, socialized more freely than ever with young men who might interpret that socializing as a license for sexual interactions. In one of the most infamous cases, a New York City court accused Henry Bedlow of raping Lanah Sawyer in 1793. Before Henry took Lanah to a brothel and, according to Lanah, raped her, they had gone on several dates, including walks in the Battery and on Broadway, out for some ice cream, and to a friend's house. Such socializing allowed witnesses to say that Lanah must have consented because they heard her laughing as she and Henry entered the house. Henry's lawyer proclaimed that her repeated acquaintance with Henry showed Lanah's "desire of gratifying her passions." Henry turned Lanah's unregulated heterosexual socializing into consent to future sexual relations.[13]

Other incidents likewise suggest that young men might have taken young

12. *Trial of Amos Adams, for a Rape, Committed on the Body of Lelea Thorp* (New Haven, Conn., 1817), 12–13, AAS; case of Jack, Aug. 25, 1818, Virginia Executive Papers, LOV; case of Pompey, November 1796, indictments, no. 3376 and unnumbered doc., HHR. For exceptional cases where white women's socializing with black men eventually undermined a rape accusation, see petitions for Jack, 1793, Governor and Council, Pardon Papers, box 6, folder 50, MdSA; case of George, Oct. 24, 1812, Virginia Executive Papers, LOV.

13. *Report of the Trial of Henry Bedlow, for Committing a Rape on Lanah Sawyer* (New York, 1793), 3–14, 40. On the community response to this case, see Christine Stansell, *City of Women: Sex and Class in New York, 1789–1860* (Urbana, Ill., 1982), 23–26. On socializing and sexual interactions, see ibid., 89–100; and, more generally, Clare A. Lyons, *Sex among the Rabble: An Intimate History of Gender and Power in the Age of Revolution, Philadelphia, 1730–1830* (Chapel Hill, N.C., 2006); Patricia Cline Cohen, *The Murder of Helen Jewett: The Life and Death of a Prostitute in Nineteenth-Century New York* (New York, 1998), 205–229. On the integration of sexual assault within working-class courtships in the British context, see Trumbach, *Sex and the Gender Revolution*, 301–305.

women's social interactions with them as presumed consent to sexual inter-actions. In 1812 in Philadelphia, fourteen-year-old Deborah Williams walked to a local tavern with Jacob Taylor before he threw her down, raped her, then walked her home. In 1817, Rebecca Day, Jr., was coming home from a night at a Boston tavern when she ran into two men with whom she had chatted earlier. The men offered her money for sex, and, when she refused, Rebecca told the court, they held her down and raped her. With the increase in heterosexual freedoms in cities in the early Republic, the single and often working-class women who either drank or socialized in public places with men were espe-cially vulnerable to unwelcome sexual interactions.[14]

Thus, some men used an array of social interactions as a springboard for sexual relations. These forms of sexual coercion differed greatly from the arche-typal stranger rape committed through brute force and grave bodily threat. Neighbors in small communities might use their everyday social relations to create opportunities for sexual force or read inappropriate socializing as evi-dence of a woman's consent to subsequent sexual relations. Did men pur-posefully plan such scenarios, or were they women's reconstructions of what retrospectively appeared to lead to their sexual predicaments? Either way, so-cial relations between men and women not only blurred the nature of the force in a given sexual interaction, but also coded race and status into the very process of sexual coercion — only white men could hope to blend coercive sex with white women into a seemingly consensual interaction. Still, the image of consent that white men could try to enact through neighborly familiarity paled in comparison to the sexual power of a patriarch over the women in his care.

COERCION IN THE HOUSEHOLD: MASTERS

A man's position as the head of a household might allow him ready access to dependent women within that household. Servants and slaves were prime targets for sexual coercion by their masters. A household head's power over a dependent woman's labor could be translated into opportunities for sexual coercion without the taboo of incest or child rape. A master's available tech-

---

14. *Commonwealth v Taylor*, Jan. 8, 1812, Pennsylvania Court Papers, HSP; *Report of the Trials of Stephen Murphy and John Doyle before the Supreme Judicial Court at Dedham, Oct. 23, 1817* (Boston, 1817), 2–6. For another incident of sexual coercion that grew out of imbib-ing with men, see *Commonwealth v John Walker*, January 1815, Pennsylvania Court Papers, HSP.

niques for sexual coercion also allowed forceful acts of coercion to appear more consensual than a stranger's onetime attack.[15]

Servants repeatedly told of unending pressure, if not coercion, to engage in sexual relations with their masters. Colonial court records are filled with fornication cases involving masters and servants. As early as 1662, Virginia law mandated the punishment of "dissolute masters" who impregnated their female servants. In a 1724 Virginia court, a servant complained that her master "continually Importuned" her "by all ways and means to prostitute her body to him which he Dayly practices to the other servant woman belonging to him." A decade later, Pennsylvania servant Hannah Gother testified that her master had "pretended to Court her and through great promises of marrying her he over came her and had Karnall knowledge of her body many times." Hannah did not mention overt physical coercion—perhaps trying to protect herself, she claimed only that she had sexual relations under false pretenses. Like Hannah, many women defended themselves against fornication charges with formulaic language of false promises of marriage. The incident might have straddled the margins of forced sex—if Hannah had refused her master, she might have lost her livelihood. Either way, women's testimony that they had been tricked into having sex made consensual sex seem at least slightly coerced, and, reciprocally, such master-servant cases as Hannah's might seem consensual. Occasional incidents were more clear-cut: in the 1750s, a Lutheran minister complained about a man who had repeatedly attempted "to rape the servant girl." But pinpointing the degree of coercion in many cases is impossible precisely because the power of mastery could blur the degree of coercion in master-servant sexual relations.[16]

15. Unfortunately, the very nature of the relationships between masters and their dependent laborers means that such cases are notoriously absent from historical records. Still, of 321 incidents where the defendant and victim's relationship is known, 51 (16 percent) took place between household members.

16. Quoted in Brown, *Good Wives, Nasty Wenches, and Anxious Patriarchs,* 134; case of Christopher Pridham, September 1724, Richmond Criminal Trials, 1710–1754, 85–87, 95–96, 119, LOV; *D. v Israell Taylor,* February 1734, Chester County Quarter Sessions File Papers, CCA; Theodore G. Tappert and John W. Doberstein, trans., *The Journals of Henry Melchior Muhlenberg,* 3 vols. (Philadelphia, 1942–1958), I, 265. For a case involving persuasion, if not coercion, see Lydia Morgan's deposition regarding David Howell, 1802, Shepley Collection, VII, 45, RIHS.

I have found few accusations of rape between servants. These cases could be dealt with out of court by masters or as fornication prosecutions. For a fornication case where a master physically punished one servant for impregnating another, see *D. v Terence Collins,*

Enslaved women faced similar pressures and were even more vulnerable to their masters' sexual coercion. By the eighteenth century, slavery followed the status of the mother, meaning that masters needed not fear paternity liability if a pregnancy resulted from the rape. Nor would masters have had to fear the legal repercussions of a rape charge, which was practically unheard of though legally possible. No rape conviction against a white man, let alone a victim's owner, for raping an enslaved woman has been found between at least 1700 and the Civil War. As with white servant women, scattered records suggest that enslaved black women also engaged in sexual relations — perhaps forced, perhaps nominally consensual — with their masters. In 1756, John Briggs complained to a Rhode Island court that he had been defamed by the charge that he had "offered to be naught[y] with his Negrow woman." In 1775, a Virginia Baptist church heard accusations that a member had offered "the Act of uncleaness to a Mulatto Girl of his own." In 1783, a Delaware court brought a bastardy charge against Michael Hart for impregnating his slave. The few such documented incidents most probably represent many more unrecorded ones. As early abolitionist David Rice rhetorically asked in 1792, "How often have [white] men children by their own slaves, by their fathers' slaves, or the slaves of their neighbours?" Even if only a small percentage of the forced interracial master-slave sexual relationships resulted in master-fathered enslaved children, the number of American mixed-race children born into slavery suggest that such relations were far more common than surviving documents reveal.[17]

November 1738, Chester County Quarter Sessions File Papers, CCA. For exceptional accusations against servants (two of which involved child victims), see case of Emmanuel Lewis, Aug. 13, 1734, Massachusetts Superior Court of Judicature Records, Suffolk Files, no. 37793, MA; *Penn. Gaz.*, Oct. 7–14, 1736; *Connecticut Journal* (New Haven), Sept. 14, 1770.

On servant-master sexual relations, see Sharon V. Salinger, *"To Serve Well and Faithfully": Labor and Indentured Servants in Pennsylvania, 1682–1800* (Cambridge, 1987), 111–112; Sharon Block, "Lines of Color, Sex, and Service: Comparative Sexual Coercion in Early America," in Martha Hodes, ed., *Sex, Love, Race: Crossing Boundaries in North American History* (New York, 1999), 141–163.

17. *John Briggs v Elizabeth Palmer,* November 1758, record of settlement in indictment of Job Almy, Newport General Sessions File Papers, RIJRC; Meharrin Baptist Church Record, September 1775, 35–36, LOV; examination of Phillis, Nov. 6, 1783, Northampton County Miscellaneous MSS, 1778–1797, 53, HSP; David Rice, "Slavery Inconsistent with Justice and Good Policy" (1792), in Charles S. Hyneman and Donald S. Lutz, eds., *American Political Writing during the Founding Era, 1760–1805,* 2 vols. (Indianapolis, Ind., 1983), II, 874. Harriet C. Frazier has found one presumably white man charged with raping a

Discussions of the duties of servants and slaves also implied that dependent women would naturally desire to sexually serve their masters. In a 1733 case of attempted rape in North Carolina, Robert Kingham first "talkt very rudely to [Elizabeth Montgomery] and then Sayed She should be his housekeeper." When Elizabeth refused that ostensible job offer, Robert tried to rape her. A midcentury Rhode Island divorce petition displayed a similar idea: David Thayer was reputed to have boasted that "he would hier no maid except they would have to do with him." For David, the explicit mastery over a servant in his household also extended to sexual mastery. A fictitious anecdote forwarded a like view of the overlap of master-servant sexual and social relations. A 1750s travel writer recalled the story of a Pennsylvania wife who, on her deathbed, requested that her husband marry their maid "who has all this time been such a faithful and hardworking servant in our house." When told of this arrangement, the servant happily "said she would do the master's will in everything." A Revolutionary-era *Virginia Gazette* poem described an ideal servant who cooked, cleaned, and made her master's bed, which the master was "certain [she] would think herself bless'd / If she could but partake it with me." These anecdotes conflated the labor a servant provided with the sexual services such wifely work implied. A woman who did a wife's work of caring for a man's household slipped easily into the role of sexual servant, which gave patriarchs opportunities for sexual access to the women in their households.[18]

---

slave in Missouri in 1834, but the case's outcome is unknown (Frazier, *Slavery and Crime in Missouri, 1773–1865* [Jefferson, N.C., 2001], 240–241).

On the relation of sexual prerogatives to the construction of white mastery, see Kirsten Fischer, *Suspect Relations: Sex, Race, and Resistance in Colonial North Carolina* (Ithaca, N.Y., 2002), 164–167. On America's mixed-race history, see Gary B. Nash, "The Hidden History of Mestizo America," *Journal of American History*, LXXXII (1995), 941–964. As with servant-servant rapes, there is a small handful of known slave-slave sexual assault allegations, but most appear to have led to dropped prosecutions or extralegal handling. For example, trial of Kitt, July 29, 1783, Westmoreland County, Va., Order Book, 148, LOV; petitions for Jerry, 1814, Governor and Council, Pardon Papers, box 16, folder 36, MdSA; Tate's Creek Baptist Church Record Book, May 1816, Southern Baptist Theological Seminary, Louisville, Ky. (thanks to Monica Najar for a transcription).

18. *Crown v Robert Kingham*, May 7, 1733, Criminal Papers, General Court Records, NCSA; Rebecca Thayer, petition for divorce, March 1766, Providence County Superior Court File Papers, RIJRC; Gottlieb Mittelberger, *Journey to Pennsylvania in the Year 1750 and Return to Germany in the Year 1754*, ed. and trans. Oscar Handlin and John Clive (Cambridge, Mass., 1960), 70–71; Purdie and Dixon's *Virginia Gazette* (Williamsburg), Dec. 9, 1773.

Women of African descent fell victim to such expectations from men who saw enslaved women as purchasable sexual and economic commodities. In the early national period, documents from the transatlantic slave trade show how economic ownership allowed for sexual mastery. One slave trader commented that the officers of a slave ship had "all provided themselves with three or four wives each . . . alleging that they would . . . bring a good price when we arrived in America." The trader's sentence related the officers' sexual possession to the economic ability to sell those same women. In 1787, an African's narrative of enslavement concurred, albeit from a vastly different perspective, that on slave ships "it was common for the dirty filthy sailors to take the African women and lie upon their bodies." The domestic slave trade continued the transatlantic overlap of economic and sexual possession. In the nineteenth century, William Wells Brown told of his journey with a New Orleans slave trader who forced one of his new possessions to spend the night in his stateroom. William recalled, "I had seen too much of the workings of slavery, not to know what this meant." In this case, the slave trader presented the woman with a choice: she could either establish a sexual relationship with him and be allowed to become a house servant or refuse him and get sold as a field hand to the "worst plantation on the river." The trader used his economic power over the African American woman to grant himself unrestricted sexual access to her. The power of absolute ownership included the largely unchecked power to extort sexual relations from one's chattel.[19]

While documented instances of sexual coercion of slaves or servants by their

19. Joseph Hawkins, "A Slave Trader's Description of a Voyage to Africa" (1797), in Gilbert Osofsky, *The Burden of Race: A Documentary History of Negro-White Relations in America* (New York, 1967), 12; Ottobah Cugoano, *Narrative of the Enslavement of Ottobah Cugoano, a Native of Africa; Published by Himself, in the Year 1787* (http://metalab.unc.edu/docsouth/neh/cugoano/cugoano.html [orig. publ. London, 1825]), 124; William Wells Brown, "Narrative of *William Wells Brown*, a Fugitive Slave" (Boston, 1847), in Osofsky, ed., *Puttin' on Ole Massa* (New York, 1969), 173–223.

As Nell Irvin Painter has written, "Extorted sex was part of a larger pattern of oppression embedded in the institution of slavery" (Painter, "Three Southern Women and Freud: A Non-Exceptionalist Approach to Race, Class, and Gender in the Slave South," in Ann-Louise Shapiro, ed., *Feminists Revision History* [New Brunswick, N.J., 1994], 207). See also Saidiya V. Hartman, *Scenes of Subjection: Terror, Slavery, and Self-Making in Nineteenth-Century America* (New York, 1997), 52, 81, 85–86; Joshua D. Rothman, *Notorious in the Neighborhood: Sex and Families across the Color Line in Virginia, 1787–1861* (Chapel Hill, N.C., 2003), 19; Peter Bardaglio, "Rape and the Law in the Old South: 'Calculated to Excite Indignation in Every Heart,'" *Journal of Southern History*, LX (1994), 757–758.

owners or masters exist, the brief notations that comprise most of these records make it difficult to see how a position of mastery allowed for specific practices of sexual coercion. However, an analysis of two particularly well-documented cases shows the similarities between a master's practices of sexual coercion with a white servant and with a black slave. The story of Harriet Jacobs, an enslaved woman in North Carolina who wrote a fictionalized autobiography detailing her struggles with a sexually forceful master in the early nineteenth century, is well known. Rachel Davis's story is less familiar; surviving in manuscript court records, it is the tale of a white servant in Pennsylvania who struggled with her own master's sexual attacks at the end of the eighteenth century.[20]

Slaves and servants faced vastly different legal options for redress of white masters' sexual assaults. Enslaved women had virtually no legal recourse for rape, but white servant women could have asked the courts, difficult though it might have been, for protection from a sexually abusive master. Despite these institutional differences, slaves and servants appeared to engage in largely similar struggles with masters' unwanted sexual overtures. Rachel Davis and Harriet Jacobs told nearly parallel narratives of sexual coercion. In both women's stories, the prerogatives of mastery went beyond their masters' abilities to force them physically into sexual intercourse: their masters attempted to control the parameters and definitions of these sexual acts. Rather than directly order his dependent to have sexual relations with him, each master took advantage of the woman's status to create a situation in which her ability to consent or refuse was whittled away. By translating authority over a woman's labor into opportunities for sexual coercion, economic mastery created sexual mastery, allowing masters to manipulate forced sexual encounters into a mimicry of consensual ones. Servants and slaves could not only be forced *to* consent, but this force was also refigured *as* consent.

Yet neither Harriet nor Rachel presented herself as an abject victim of her master's will. Each woman engaged in continual negotiations and struggles with her master; as much as he attempted to control the terms of any sexual

20. There are innumerable studies of Harriet Jacobs, as often from literary as historical perspectives. See Deborah M. Garfield and Rafia Zafar, eds., *Harriet Jacobs and Incidents in the Life of a Slave Girl: New Critical Essays* (New York, 1996); Painter, "Three Southern Women and Freud," in Shapiro, ed., *Feminists Revision History,* 195–216; Joanne M. Braxton, "Outraged Mother and Articulate Heroine: Linda Brent and the Slave Narrative Genre," in Braxton, *Black Women Writing Autobiography: A Tradition within a Tradition* (Philadelphia, 1989), 18–38. For a perceptive analysis specifically on the meaning of seduction and rape in Harriet Jacobs, see Hartman, *Scenes of Subjection,* 103–112.

interactions, she tried to change his definitions. Harriet's and Rachel's resistance to and strategic manipulation of their masters formed a vital part of their stories, but, by negotiating with a master, sexual coercion could be reformulated into a seemingly consensual relationship. Negotiation implied willingness, which contrasted with the early American image that rape consisted of irresistible force. Ironically, women's attempts to bargain their way out of sexual assaults made these encounters seem consensual.

Both Harriet and Rachel drew direct links between their status and their masters' sexual assaults. Each woman explained how her master had forced her into situations where he could sexually coerce her without being discovered. Rachel described several such incidents in her courtroom testimony. First, William Cress ordered her to hold the lantern for him one night in the stable, where he "tried to persuade me to something." While the two were alone measuring grain in the barn, "he caught hold of me and pulled me on the hay." In the most blatantly contrived incident, when they were reaping hay in the meadow, William "handed me his sickle and bad[e] me to lay it down. He saw where I put it." Later that night, William asked Rachel "where I put them sickles." Rachel offered to go with her sister to retrieve them, but William "said that was not as he bad[e] me." William and Rachel went out to find the sickles, but, before they reached them, William "threw me down. . . . I hallowed — he put his hand over my mouth . . . he pulled up my cloathes, and got upon me . . . [and] he did penetrate my body." According to Rachel's statement, William forced her to accompany him into a dark field on a contrived search for a purposefully lost farm implement so that he could rape her. William's authority to control where she went and what she did enabled him to force Rachel to have sex with him.[21]

Harriet Jacobs was even more explicit about the connections between James Norcum's mastery and his ability to force her into sexually vulnerable positions. It seemed to Harriet that James followed her everywhere; in her words, "My master met me at every turn" trying to force her to have sex with him. As William did with Rachel, James structured Harriet's work so that she was often alone with him. He ordered her to bring his meals to him so that while she watched him eat, he could verbally torture her with the possible consequences of refusing his sexual overtures. Harriet further recalled, "When I succeeded in avoiding opportunities for him to talk to me at home, I was ordered to come to his office, to do some errand." Tiring of Harriet's continued resistance, James

21. *Commonwealth v William Cress,* February 1808, Pennsylvania Court Papers, HSP, punctuation added. All future discussions of this case are based on this document.

ordered his four-year-old daughter to sleep near him, thus requiring that Harriet also sleep in his room in case the child needed attention during the night. After his wife objected to that arrangement, he tried to make Harriet accompany him on his solo trip to Louisiana.[22]

Other laborers likewise connected their masters' economic power over them to their own vulnerability to sexual coercion. In 1787, a Pennsylvania servant told a court that, after her master had "called me up to help to fill a bag of Grain," he threw her down in the loft and sexually assaulted her. Servant Unice Williamson told a New York City court in 1797 that her master "ordered her to go up stairs and make up the bed," and, once they were alone in the room, "he put her on the floor and Ravished her." In 1818, also in New York, thirteen-year-old Maria Forshee told a court that her master "sent her down Cellar to get some kindling wood to make a fire," followed her down there, seized her, and tried to rape her. Whether in rural or urban settings, servants recounted their experiences of a master's sexual assault in the context of their role as his servant.[23]

Masters or overseers might use similar techniques to manipulate enslaved women into sexual acts. In Josiah Henson's recollection of the overseer who raped his mother in the 1790s, he explained that the overseer "sent my mother away from the other field hands to a retired place" so that he could force himself on her. Ex-slave Lewis Clarke recalled that his sister's master "sent for her" repeatedly so that he could sexually assault her. Phillis, a Delaware slave, told detailed stories of how Michael Hart had sexual relations with her, stories that were strikingly similar to Harriet Jacobs's and Rachel Davis's recollections. Phillis told the court that Michael used to call her out to the stable to hold a light for him where he would "pull up her clothes and put into her his [scratched out]." When his wife was out of the house, Michael would order Phillis into the bedroom "and then follow her and sometimes threw her on the Bed and sometimes on the floor." He would get up in the night and call her into the kitchen to get him some water. Michael would then lay Phillis "down on the kitchen floor, and have carnal knowledge of her body." These physical

<hr>

22. Harriet A. Jacobs, *Incidents in the Life of a Slave Girl, Written by Herself,* ed. Jean Fagan Yellin (Cambridge, Mass., 1987), 27, 28, 31–32, 41.

23. *The Trial of Nathaniel Price: For Committing a Rape on the Body of Unice Williamson, a Child between 10 and 11 Years of Age, at Brooklyn in King's County, in May 1797* . . . (New York, [1797]), 2–3; *The People v Thomas Conlen,* Mar. 4, 1818, New York County Court of General Sessions Indictment Papers, NYMA; *Republica v David Robb,* Yeates Legal Papers, March–April 1789, fol. 2, HSP.

attacks were not random. They were enacted through social and economic labor relations. Controlling a woman's daily routine, her work requirements, and her physical presence — in other words, control over her labor and her body — gave men in positions of mastery access to a particular means of sexual coercion.[24]

A woman's servant or slave status also allowed for limited manipulation of a master's sexual overtures, something omitted from the standard image of rape. Any relationship, even the unquestionably inequitable one of slavery, depended on both participants' negotiations over its terms. If avoiding their masters did not work, then dependent laborers like Harriet and Rachel had to try to balance their actions on the fine line between covert resistance and outright disobedience. In commenting on the calculating techniques that their masters used to isolate them, each woman recalled how she had challenged her master's right to force her into a sexual relationship. Rachel recounted how she had "resisted" and "cried" when William tried to pull her into a darkened bedroom after sending the rest of the servants to bed and how she threatened to tell his wife about what he was doing. When these forms of resistance did not end his overtures, Rachel tried to carry out her master's orders in ways that might prevent her own sexual vulnerability. In her description of being raped in the dark field, Rachel recollected that she had first suggested that William could find the sickle himself and then offered to find it on her own or with her sister. Ultimately, William resorted to his position as a master — "He said that was not as he bad[e] me" — and issued a direct order for Rachel to accompany him. Rachel portrayed an evolving relationship with William: she might not have been able to override her master's orders, but she forced him to change their content. Rather than have sex in the bedroom while his children slept and his wife was away, Rachel forced William to order her into the dark field, thereby disrupting his original attempts at a seamless consensual interaction.

Harriet Jacobs told of similar efforts to avoid her master's sexual overtures that forced him to refigure his behavior. When Mary Norcum's suspicions made her husband revert to physical gestures instead of words to convey his sexual desires to Harriet, Harriet responded by letting "them pass, as if I did not understand what he meant." When James realized that Harriet could read,

24. Josiah Henson, *Truth Stranger Than Fiction: Father Henson's Story of His Own Life* (Boston, 1858), 3; Lewis Clarke, "Leaves from a Slave's Journal of Life," in John W. Blassingame, ed., *Slave Testimony: Two Centuries of Letters, Speeches, Interviews, and Autobiographies* (Baton Rouge, La., 1977), 156; examination of Phillis, Nov. 6, 1783, Northampton County Misc. MSS.

he wrote her notes that expressed his sexual intentions, but Harriet repeatedly claimed, "I can't read them, sir." Overall, "by managing to keep within sight of people, as much as possible, during the day time, I had hitherto succeeded in eluding my master. . . . At night I slept by the side of my great aunt, where I felt safe." Harriet forced James into baldly claiming his right for sexual access as a privilege of mastery. According to Harriet, James began constantly "reminding me that I belonged to him, and swearing by heaven and earth that he would compel me to submit to him" because "I was his property; that I must be subject to his will in all things." Like Rachel, Harriet engaged in an exchange of maneuvers with her master where each tried to foil the other's plans and counterplans. Despite her master's legal ownership of her body, Harriet did not portray herself as utterly powerless. By playing into an image of slaves as too stupid to understand signs and too illiterate to read notes, Harriet used her labor status to avoid her master's sexual overtures, forcing him to raise the stakes of his desires toward her. Harriet did not stop with games of cunning and indirect noncompliance. She recalled, "Sometimes I so openly expressed my contempt for him that he would become violently enraged." She recounted telling her master in a moment of anger, "You have no right to do as you like with me." Even to the extent of occasional outright disobedience, Harriet employed an array of tactics to shape the terms of her relationship with her master.[25]

If a master did not receive unquestioned acquiescence from a servant or slave, he had to create situations in which his laborers had little choice but to have sexual relations with him. Rachel's attempted refusal to go alone into a dark field with her master and Harriet's feigned ignorance of her master's intentions forced each man to modify his route to sexual interactions. By not consenting to a master's subtler attempts at sexual relations, a servant or slave might force her master into more overtly coercive sexual acts. Ironically, her resistance compelled a master to perform his laborer's interpretation of his overtures as nonconsensual. Rather than the sexual offers that the masters first proposed, the men were forced to use coercion to carry out their sexual plans. Theoretically, a master could use physical force to commit rape, but most did not have to depend exclusively on fists or whips. Instead, they could rely on the strength of their mastery.

While masters' manipulations of servant or slave labor could force women into sexually vulnerable positions, further pressure compelled them into sexual acts. As might be expected, William and James sometimes used the threat of

25. Jacobs, *Incidents in the Life of a Slave Girl*, ed. Yellin, 27, 28, 31, 32, 39.

physical violence to coerce Rachel and Harriet, respectively, into sexual relations. Although Harriet repeatedly stated that James never beat or whipped her, she also mentioned that "a razor was often held to my throat to force me to" consent to sexual overtures. Similarly, in the midst of one sexual struggle, Rachel recounted that William "said, if I did not go to bed he'd pull that topnot of mine to the damndest." If pushed, both of these men could rely on threats of physical assault in pursuit of their sexual goals.[26]

Because sexual coercion was often a running series of propositions, masters might purposefully alternate between persuasion and force, encouraging dependent laborers to consent to the best of two unpleasant paths to sexual relations. Harriet characterized her master as "a crafty man, . . . [who] resorted to many means to accomplish his purposes. Sometimes he had stormy, terrific ways, that made his victims tremble; sometimes he assumed a gentleness that he thought must surely subdue." James promised Harriet, if she would give in to him sexually: "I would cherish you. I would make a lady of you." The possibility of a better life that transcended her racial and labor status was more than a bribe to induce Harriet's consent. Such a promise created a fiction that she could voluntarily choose to have sexual relations with her master. James switched between the threats of physical harm and the gifts of courtship, thereby undercutting the appearance of a forced sexual interaction. By supposedly allowing space for Harriet's consent to his sexual overtures, James tried to redefine coercion into consensual sex.[27]

Similarly, William's verbal narration of consensual relations overlaid his forceful attempts at sex. While he had Rachel trapped underneath his body, William told her that "he wd have the good will of me." William's modification of the classic legal description of rape as a man's having carnal knowledge of a woman "*against* her will" verbally created a consensual act even as he used force. Even while making Rachel have sex with him, William used terms of endearment and called Rachel by her family nickname, saying, "Nate you dear creature." This masquerade substituted William's will for Rachel's consent as

26. Ibid., 32.

27. Ibid., 27, 35. On the ways that slaves were made responsible for their own violation, see Hartman, *Scenes of Subjection*, 226–227 n. 6. Historians have also fallen into the trap of contrasting forced sex with long-term, and therefore presumably consensual, sexual relations. See, for instance, Allan Kulikoff, *Tobacco and Slaves: The Development of Southern Cultures in the Chesapeake, 1680–1800* (Chapel Hill, N.C., 1986), 386; Francis S. Fox, *Sweet Land of Liberty: The Ordeal of the American Revolution in Northampton County, Pennsylvania* (University Park, Pa., 2000), 128.

his verbal intercourse of consensuality masked his actions of coercion. William's presentation of an affectionate and therefore consensual sexual relationship with Rachel differentiated his actions from the brutality that early Americans would most easily recognize as rape.[28]

Unlike in an assailant's surprise attack, a master did not have to rely on explicit physical force to coerce his dependents into a sexual act. Instead, he might use the power of his position to create opportunities for sexual coercion, backing a woman into a corner where capitulation seemed her best option. A servant or enslaved woman often recognized this manipulation and tried to negotiate her way around her master's overtures rather than confront him with direct resistance. This attempt at negotiation further contributed to an image of master-laborer sex as a consensual encounter rather than a forced rape, simultaneously bolstering the overlap of consensual and coercive sex. Similar factors would encourage the redefinition of other forms of household sexual coercion as well.

COERCION IN THE HOUSEHOLD: FATHERS AND HUSBANDS

Along with their position as masters of servants or slaves, many male household heads were husbands and/or fathers. Under a patriarchal system, these identities carried with them particular privileges of sexual control and access. By definition, a husband had automatic and indisputable sexual access to his wife, making marital rape a legal and conceptual impossibility in early America. As with servants and slaves, patriarchs also had extensive social and economic control over their children. While incestuous sexual relations were unquestionably prohibited, some fathers nevertheless ordered their daughters into forced sexual liaisons that depended on the powers of fatherhood instead of the brute force of a believable rape. Making their actions appear unlike early American images of sudden and physically (rather than socially or psychologically) irresistible rape was crucial to their ability to force their daughters into ongoing sexual relations.

Despite the biblical, social, and ethical proscriptions against incest, some fathers sexually assaulted their daughters for years without discovery. Polly and Betsy Johnson were sexually assaulted by their father for several years before a Connecticut court formally charged him with attempted rape at the end of the

28. Emphasis added. For the British standard of this classic legal formulation of rape, see William Hawkins, *A Treatise of the Pleas of the Crown* . . . (1724–1726; rpt. New York, 1972), I, 108.

eighteenth century. In Virginia a few years later, Ursula Fogg's incestuous relations with her father came to light only when her new husband realized that Ursula was pregnant with his father-in-law's child. A South Carolina man repeatedly tried to have sexual relations with his teenage stepdaughter in 1808. Some men recurrently abused the dependent girls in their households as well. In Revolutionary New England, Silas Gates allegedly attempted to have sex with both his four-year-old daughter and a nine-year-old apprentice girl who lived with him, and Asa Bailey was accused of having sex with two servants and his daughter.[29]

Just as masters might order their servants into sexually compromising situations, fathers did not have to resort to brute force to have sexual relations with their daughters: they could use their patriarchal authority. In the 1720s, Sarah Perkins's father, John Perkins, repeatedly tried to coerce her into sexual relations. Sarah's testimony outlines several common features of father-daughter sexual coercion. Sarah recalled that at first her father "only tempted and sollisted her," but that "when he found that would not prevail, he proceeded to threatening" to accomplish his purpose. John kicked Sarah out of his house "because she would not comply with him" and continued to pressure Sarah to have sex with him while she lived with neighbors. He commanded her "to go forth abroad with him" and threatened to "have her hand cut off for being a dissobedient child and to disinherit her" and to have her "[pounded]-to death for her not falling in with his motions and being a disobedient child," because, as her father, he "had Right to Require my obedience." As with dependent laborers, Sarah's noncompliance compelled John to resort to threats and disownment to force her consent. But John could set his threats of physical violence within the purview of fatherhood, repeatedly couching his threatened punishment in terms of his right to correct his daughter's misbehavior. Fathers could use the expectations of a child's obedience to her parents as leverage to force sexual consent. Ultimately, despite Sarah's continuing resistance (neigh-

29. *State v Moses Johnson*, August 1794, Fairfield County Superior Court Files, 1790–1799, A–K, box 625, CSL; petitions of John Fogg, Sr., and William Fogg, Dec. 11, 1800, Legislative Petitions, Essex County, LOV; *State v Nathan Darby*, April, May 1808, Union County General Sessions Court, Sessions Rolls, nos. 103, 117, SCDAH; petitions of Mary Gates, Salisbury, Mar. 3, 1777, Windham County Superior Court Records, Subject: Divorce 1752–1922, microfilm no. 418, CSL; Ann Taves, ed., *Religion and Domestic Violence in Early New England: The Memoirs of Abigail Abbot Bailey* (Bloomington, Ind., 1989), 59–60, 70–80. See also *State v John Ely*, November 1804, Hartford County Superior Court Files, November 1804–September 1805, box 36, CSL.

bors noted that she acted "as if she was going among rattlesnakes" when forced to be with her father), Sarah "acknowledged herself guilty of the crime" of incest with her father.[30]

Other fathers made similar claims of necessary enforcement of hierarchical familial order while coercing their daughters into sexual relations. In early-eighteenth-century Connecticut, Hannah Rood's stepfather told her that "if I did not obey him I would resist . . . the holy ghost," and her mother, too, said that "it was no sin it was my fathers command" to have sexual relations with him. In Massachusetts a few decades later, Peter Harding took the logic of a father's authority one step further. He told his daughter that having sex with him "was no Sin. That the Dutch always lay with their daughter that it was no sin til they were married." Peter mixed the two patriarchal roles of father and husband into one—a patriarch had the right to have sexual relations with any woman under his care. Similarly, when confronted about his sexual relations with his stepdaughter in the 1780s, James Weller reportedly replied, "Who has a better right—and laughed." And, at the end of the eighteenth century, Abigail Bailey recounted that when her husband began sexually abusing their daughter, he tried to take the girl away with him so he could have unencumbered sexual access to her. Abigail recalled his claim that "as a father, he had a right to command her to go."[31]

When manipulation and recourse to patriarchal privileges failed, a father could proceed to threats and physical force. Maria Cottle told a New York court in 1800 that "her father frequently told her if ever she told [of his continual sexual abuse], he would kill her." When Maria did run away from home, her father's threats escalated into physical violence. He "whipped her severely and chained her . . . and kept her chained for about a week." These kinds of punishments might be possible only within the patriarchally con-

30. Indictment of John Perkins, Jr., and Sarah Perkins, March 1725, New Haven Superior Court Files, 1720–1727, drawer 324, CSL. It was common for seventeenth- and early-eighteenth-century courts to punish both fathers and daughters guilty of incest. See Dayton, *Women before the Bar*, 275.

31. Case against Thomas Hall, May 1703, Connecticut Archives, Crimes and Misdemeanors, 1st Ser., I, 322–331, CSL; case of Peter Harding, October 1729, Massachusetts Superior Court of Judicature Records, Suffolk Files, no. 26074, MA; indictment against James Weller and Monicha Strick, October 1783, Dockets of Cases and Notes of Evidence Taken by Hon. Increase Sumner, 1782–1786, II, 231–233, MHS; Taves, ed., *Religion and Domestic Violence in Early New England*, 65, 77–78. James Weller also used scriptures to justify sexual relations with his stepdaughter. See indictment against James Weller and Monicha Strick, 231–233.

trolled household: a stranger or neighbor would most likely be unable to enact such punishments, but a father could discipline a daughter's "misbehavior" with relative impunity.[32]

Even when a father ultimately resorted to brute force, his daughter's general obedience to him could later be used as evidence of the girl's willing consent. In the early nineteenth century, Betsy Wheeler's father, Ephraim Wheeler, first "tried to persuade . . . [me] to let him have *to do* with me." When Betsy refused, he offered her a gown and petticoat if she would consent to him. When she again refused, he took Betsy into the secluded woods and told her that "he would kill her if she did not" lie down on the ground, and "he then took hold of her and threw her on the ground." Despite this testimony, Ephraim's lawyer claimed that if they had sexual relations, it was with his daughter's consent. After all, "Why did she go [into the woods with him, where she was raped], without being dragged by violence?. . . Would you not strongly suspect that these transactions were not much against her will?" Lawyers could play on the fact that a father did not look like the early American image of a rapist — a man who forced a woman to have sex with him under sudden threat of death. The social obedience to a father that was expected of early American daughters could be alternatively read as consent to sexual relations.[33]

Although incestuous relationships were theoretically taboo, some of them could never be recognized as such in a race-based labor system. Across centuries, enslaved women bore their masters' children. Sometimes, these children would in turn be impregnated by their master-fathers, but, because children of slave mothers could not claim their patrilineal lineage, a father could not legally be prevented from having sex with his daughter on the basis of this biological relationship. As one ex-slave recounted, "My grandmother was her master's daughter; and my mother was her master's daughter; and I was my master's son." An early abolitionist complained that the "innocent offspring of the master" would become "the slave of her unnatural brother," and therefore be "forced to submit to his horrid and incestuous passion." Generations of incest would go unrecognized and unprohibited for enslaved women.[34]

---

32. *The People v Grant Cottle,* Aug. 15, 1800, New York County Court of General Sessions Indictment Papers, reel 4 (in Oct. 9, 1800, folder), NYMA.

33. *Report of the Trial of Ephraim Wheeler for a Rape Committed on the Body of Betsy Wheeler, His Daughter, a Girl Thirteen Years of Age* . . . (Stockbridge, Mass., 1805), 12; *Liberty Hall and Cincinnati Mercury* (Ohio), Oct. 29, 1805.

34. Clarke, "Leaves from a Slave's Journal of Life," in Blassingame, ed., *Slave Testimony,* 156; Theodore Dwight, "An Oration, Spoken before the Connecticut Society, for the

Virtually no evidence of sexual coercion in African American families exists. White masters or community members did not note sexual assaults by enslaved men on their own daughters. Without Anglo-American concern for a slave's sexual chastity or future marital prospects, rape, incest, or extramarital sex were generally not worthy of prosecution. Furthermore, enslaved men could not be convicted of incest, because they were not legally recognized as fathers of their biological children. Free black men could have been convicted of incest, but there do not appear to be any records of such incidents. Certainly, this should not be read as an absence of such acts of sexual coercion; there is no reason to believe that African American fathers could not use their power as adult men to force their daughters into sexual relations. Regardless, black men's ability to commit such acts undetected and undeterred by the larger community did not translate into widely recognized identities of mastery as for white men; rather, the very lack of documentation of black-on-black sexual coercion reminds us that there was little institutional interest in the protection of some women and girls' sexual integrity.[35]

Men's almost unlimited sexual access to their wives created another unrecognized form of household sexual assault — marital rape. Tracing coerced sex within marriage in early America is nearly impossible because such acts were neither a legal nor a conceptual possibility. An early-nineteenth-century American publication of the influential British legal manual, *A Treatise of the Pleas of the Crown,* explained that "a husband cannot by law be guilty of ravishing his wife, on account of the matrimonial consent which she cannot retract." Legally, marriage provided a woman's perpetual sexual consent to her husband, making the notion of rape within marriage an impossibility and all sexual relations within marriage automatically consensual.[36]

Nevertheless, wives might feel forced to participate in sexual encounters with their husbands. One series of William Byrd's diary entries indirectly hints

---

Promotion of Freedom and the Relief of Persons Unlawfully Holden in Bondage" (1794), in Hyneman and Lutz, eds., *American Political Writing during the Founding Era,* II, 892.

35. We know comparatively little about African Americans' perspectives on their familial relationships, let alone sexual relations, in early America. For discussion of African American families, see John Wood Sweet, *Bodies Politic: Negotiating Race in the American North, 1730–1830* (Baltimore, 2003), 151–161; Jennifer L. Morgan, *Laboring Women: Reproduction and Gender in New World Slavery* (Philadelphia, 2004), 128–143; Philip D. Morgan, *Slave Counterpoint: Black Culture in the Eighteenth-Century Chesapeake and Lowcountry* (Chapel Hill, N.C., 1998), 541–548.

36. Sir Edward Hyde East, *A Treatise of the Pleas of the Crown* (Philadelphia, 1806), I, 446.

at the irrelevance of his wife's desires for sexual intercourse. On May 15 and 16, 1711, he wrote that his wife was "much indisposed" and "sick" due to her pregnancy, yet, also on May 16, he marked down, "I rogered my wife, in which she took but little pleasure in her condition." Mrs. Byrd's lack of pleasure in sexual intercourse was a far cry from rape, but William's entries clearly show that his wife's desires for sexual relations were irrelevant to his sexual fulfillment. This is not necessarily evidence of William's lack of love or care for his wife. When she grew even more ill in June of that year, her sickness made him "weep for her." Even loving relationships included a woman's acquiescence to her husband's sexual demands as a matter of course. With an ideology of a husband's unreserved sexual access to his wife, her sexual choices might be synonymous with his sexual demands.[37]

One of the exceptionally rare records of what might have been a form of marital rape appears in a 1793 Pennsylvania county court record. Eleanor Pettit accused her husband, Samuel, of committing that "sodomitical detestable and abominable sin called buggery" in her "fundament." Sodomy or buggery did not require the force necessary to a rape charge—all such acts were criminalized regardless of consent, yet Eleanor's complaint still suggests the limits of marital sexual prerogatives. Husbands could not be prosecuted for forcing their wives into appropriate (penis-vagina) sexual relations but could be prosecuted for committing other transgressive sexual acts. Still, the appearance of this case in a lower court, rather than in the superior courts where sodomy was usually prosecuted, as well as the grand jury's decision not to indict Samuel may suggest that early Americans did not quite know how to deal with a wife's accusation of sexual misconduct against her husband.[38]

It was no accident that the most intimate relation in the household, the marital bond, could not by definition include rape. The criminalization of a

---

37. Louis B. Wright and Marion Tinling, eds., *The Secret Diary of William Byrd of Westover, 1709–1712* (Richmond, Va., 1941), 345. On the ways that eighteenth-century European literature inscribed male sexual pleasure on women's bodies, see James A. Steintrager, "'Are You There Yet?': Libertinage and the Semantics of the Orgasm," *differences: A Journal of Feminist Cultural Studies,* XI (1999), 22–52.

38. *D. v Samuel Pettit,* February 1793, Chester County Quarter Sessions File Papers, CCA. The charge was dismissed as *ignoramus.* Scholarship on early American sodomy focuses almost exclusively on prosecutions of sex between men. See Richard Godbeer, "'The Cry of Sodom': Discourse, Intercourse, and Desire in Colonial New England," *William and Mary Quarterly,* 3d Ser., LII (1995), 259–286; Colin L. Talley, "Gender and Male Same-Sex Erotic Behavior in British North America in the Seventeenth Century," *Journal of the History of Sexuality,* VI (1996), 385–408.

broader category of sexual coercion was a direct challenge to the patriarchal system that ordered and legitimated men's access to women. The household was meant to be a place where the patriarchal figure, as a husband, father, or master, necessarily ruled over and protected dependents; as such, it implicitly allowed for various forms of sexual coercion that did not fit with the early American image of rape. A household head had an array of indirect means to force a dependent to have sex with him that simultaneously denied both her resistance to him and his coercive behavior. Because early Americans imagined rape as an act committed through sudden and utterly irresistible physical force, men's use of social power to compel women's submission fell less easily under the rubric of actionable rape. Women's social status was thus crucial to their sexual vulnerability, not only because lower-status women often had less powerful patriarchal protectors but also because more powerful men could enact a wider range of coercive tactics against them.

COLONIALISM'S PURPOSEFUL PUNISHMENT

Feminists may argue that rape always stems from a man's desire to punish, prove his superiority over his victim, and replace her will with his own. But some sexual attacks show direct evidence of motives beyond the pursuit of individual sexual superiority. Some attackers seemed to use sexual attacks expressly to punish individual women. In wartime, soldiers historically displayed their military success by raping the vanquished enemy's women, marking their victory with sexual release. In the colonial context, nonwhite women repeatedly fell victim to sexual attacks that extended far beyond desires for sexual satisfaction into a purposeful lesson about their cultural groups' degraded status. Both African American and Native American women were far more likely than white women to be the victims of sadistic and horrific sexual violence that went beyond the gratification of men's sexual desires and starkly expressed relations of subordination through intentional sexual cruelty.[39]

39. For modern cases of rape and sexual humiliation as a tool for racial subordination and punishment, see James Risen, "G.I.'s Are Accused of Abusing Iraqi Captives," *New York Times,* Apr. 29, 2004, http://www.nytimes.com/2004/04/29/politics/29ABUS.html?ex=1084344022&ei=1&en= 87a8b0b3999c9d79 (accessed Apr. 29, 2004); Peter Landesman, "A Woman's Work [on mass-militarized rape of Tutsi women in Rwanda]," *New York Times Magazine,* Sept. 15, 2002; Beverly Allen, *Rape Warfare: The Hidden Genocide in Bosnia-Herzegovina and Croatia* (Minneapolis, Minn., 1996). On early modern fears of rape by soldiers, see Lois G. Schwoerer, *"No Standing Armies!": The Antiarmy Ideology in*

A few known cases involving sexual attacks on white women that might have been punishment for a perceived sexual or other misdeed exist. Most of them occurred in New England, perhaps suggesting New Englanders' stronger belief (even into the nineteenth century) in community enforcement of gendered morality. In 1756 in Rhode Island, several community members stripped Mary Tefft and pulled "the Hair out from off her Private parts," and one man attempted to rape her. In 1769, three Massachusetts men were charged with lewdness against Pegge Keen when they "exposed her secret parts to open view" and "violently plucked out much of the hair of her secret parts." Perhaps a dispute in Connecticut between neighbors led five members of the Stoddard family to chase Anna Stoles and Mary Clark, strip the two women, and leave them cut and nearly naked in an open field in 1812. But these occasional group attacks, aimed at public humiliation through sexual disfigurement or exposure, were the exception rather than the rule in attacks on white women.[40]

In contrast to these occasional incidents, wartime rapes have occurred throughout history as victors claimed their success in a sexual right to their defeated enemy. Wartime rapes often involved multiple assailants and usually did not attempt to replicate consensual social or sexual relations. Instead, they were an explicit exercise of sexual power over a defeated enemy. During the American Revolution, Elizabeth Cain testified that two British soldiers had raped her and several other young women at gunpoint, then took them to their camp to sexually service other soldiers. A Pennsylvania newspaper reported that a thirteen-year-old girl was "carried to a barn" by some British soldiers and "there ravished, and afterwards made use of by five more of these brutes." A

Seventeenth-Century England (Baltimore, 1974), 62. My emphasis on the purposeful cruelty of these rapes in no way means to minimize the harm done to women in the other kinds of rapes discussed — I would not presume to debate the degree of personal harm done by years of inescapable sexual manipulation v. the harm done by a short-term sadistic sexual event. Rather, I am pointing to the differences in men's seeming intent. In many of the cases discussed earlier, men tried to make sexual coercion resemble sexual consent; in these cases, men made no such attempts. Indeed, they seemed to be purposefully avoiding any image of sex as consensual and normative.

40. *Rex v Amos Lewis*, August 1757, Washington County Court of General Sessions of the Peace, Minute Book, RIJRC (docket page says August 1756, possible clerk's mistake); case of Joshua Ransom et al., in David Thomas Konig, ed., *Plymouth Court Records, 1686–1859*, 16 vols. (Wilmington, Del., 1978–1981), III, *1748–1751*, 285, 293; *State v Robert Stoddard et al.*, September 1814, New London Superior Court Files, January 1813–January 1815, box 41, CSL. On tarring white women for sexual misdeeds in the eighteenth-century South, see Fischer, *Suspect Relations*, 172–174.

publication on the War of 1812 detailed the rape of a Mrs. Turnbull, who was chased into a river, then "dragged on shore by ten or twelve of these [British] ruffians, who satiated their brutal desires upon her after pulling off her clothes, stockings, shoes, etc." These rapes were intended as marks of one's military prowess and not just attainment of a soldier's individual sexual gratification. When asked about their rape of a New York woman during the American Revolution, two British soldiers reportedly claimed "that she was a Yankee whore or a Yankee bitch, and it was no great matter." White women could be momentarily reduced to available sexual property in a military conflict. Women of color, however, were far more likely to have their social inferiority consistently marked by white men's sexual attacks.[41]

Officially, British Americans were not constantly at war with Native Americans, but the two did engage in frequent hostilities. Some scholars have seen the rape of Indian women as a form of sexual imperialism that was part of colonization, and one argues that the rape of indigenous women could be ideologically justified as the symbolic castration of Indian men. We may be reluctant to "call the conqueror a rapist," but incidents of sexual abuse of Native American women by European traders, soldiers, and settlers were far more common than accounts of sexual abuse of European women by Native American men. Anglo-Indian conflicts could be "as much sexual as they were economic, diplomatic, and military." Additionally, Native Americans were increasingly part of early American society and did not just live as separate entities on the outer edge of the proverbial frontier.[42]

41. "Papers and Affidavits relating to the Plunderings, Burnings, and Ravages Committed by the British, 1775–1784," Papers of the Continental Congress, reel 66, item 53, 29, U.S. National Archives and Records Administration, College Park, Md.; *Pennsylvania Evening Post* (Philadelphia), Dec. 28, 1776, in *Archives of the State of New Jersey,* 2d Ser. (Trenton, N.J., 1901), I, 245–246; *Documents Demonstrating . . . the Brutal Violence and Cruelty Practised by the British, on Private and Unarmed Citizens, and on Helpless American Females . . .* (n.p., 1813?), 11; trial of John Dunn and John Lusty, Sept. 7, 1776, WO 71/82, 419–420, TNA:PRO. See also trial of Sergeant Boswell, June 7, 1779, WO 71/88, 524–528, TNA:PRO; J. F. D. Smyth, *A Tour in the United States of America* (London, 1784), II, 302.

42. Antonia I. Castañeda, "Sexual Violence in the Politics and Policies of Conquest: Amerindian Women and the Spanish Conquest of Alta California," in Adela De La Torre and Beatríz Pesquera, eds., *Building with Our Hands: New Directions in Chicana Studies* (Berkeley, Calif., 1993), 15–33; Stephanie Wood, "Rape as a Tool of Conquest in Early Latin America," *University of Oregon Center for the Study of Women in Society Review* (1992), 18; Richard Godbeer, "Eroticizing the Middle Ground: Anglo-Indian Relations along the Eighteenth-Century Frontier," in Hodes, ed., *Sex, Love, Race,* 92. See also Carl A. Bras-

The few nonfrontier court cases involving women identified as Native Americans stand out from other rape cases. These cases were exceptionally rare (less than a half-dozen out of more than seven hundred sexual assault prosecutions) despite the constant presence of Native Americans in British colonies. Of this small number, two of the recorded sexual attacks on Indian women in early American society suggest that white men's prosecutable attacks on Indians were far different from most sexual assaults on white women. In these incidents, rape appears to have been a purposeful attempt to mark the distance between white and Indian through forced sex and sexual torture.[43]

In Pennsylvania in 1722, James Browne followed a "Squaw" known as Betty or "Great Hills" into a field. Several Indian girls then saw James having sexual relations with her. After James finished with Betty, he told Thomas Pryor that he could "show him a sight." James took Thomas to the field where Betty still lay, apparently unconscious, with her clothes up around her waist. James turned Betty onto her back, "took both his thumbs[,] and ground her privot parts and Looked In." James then had Thomas cut a stick of wood, "and James browne Hold open Her privot parts while he put in the Stick." Besides having had possibly forced sex with Betty, James appropriated control of her body and made her an object of purposefully public humiliation. Beyond James's sexual pleasure, this sexualized violence reflects a sadistic brutality that depended on Betty's inferior status as a "squaw." Rather than committing a secretive assault in an isolated location or mimicking typical consensual sexual relations, James showed no apparent fear of discovery. He had sexual relations with Betty in front of several Indian girls, and then invited a friend to join him in his sexual mutilation of her limp body, as if he had the right to lay claim to her body as he saw fit.[44]

Nearly fifty years later, a second incident in Pennsylvania suggests an exceptional use of rape to punish Indian women. In June 1766, James Annin and James McKinzy apparently had a disagreement with two Indian women known as Hannah and Catherine. After "the youngest of the Men gave them

---

seaux, "The Moral Climate of French Colonial Louisiana, 1699–1763," *Louisiana History,* XXVII (1986), 27–42, esp. 18; David J. Weber, *The Spanish Frontier in North America* (New Haven, Conn., 1992), 16, 48, 247.

43. On the persistent underrepresentation of Indian presence in Anglo-American colonies, see James H. Merrell, "Some Thoughts on Colonial Historians and American Indians," *WMQ,* 3d Ser., XLVI (1989), 94–119.

44. *D. v James Browne,* August 1722, Chester County Quarter Sessions Indictments, CCA.

abusive Language," Hannah and Catherine went to rest in some nearby woods. The next day, residents noticed a stench coming from where the women had lain and realized that they had been hatcheted to death. Witnesses were outraged that the youngest of the women, who was pregnant and "near the Time of Delivery," had particularly savage "Marks of shocking Treatment." Local officials arrested the two Jameses after witnesses noticed that they were carrying goods that had belonged to the women. The men eventually admitted that "they went to the Indians with Intent to ravish them," and one claimed that he had attacked the women because "he thought it a Duty to extirpate the Heathen."[45]

This was one of the most gruesome and violent attacks connected to a sexual assault and was unlike typical attacks on white women. White women might also occasionally be murdered in conjunction with a sexual attack, but none of these rape-murders involved multiple attackers and victims. As "Heathen," Indian women were vulnerable to particularly sadistic assaults that were expressions of more than men's overt sexual gratification. Sexual interactions with nonwhite women were characterized by a degree of hostility and brutality that moved beyond simple sexual pleasure into torture as a purposeful expression of racial superiority. Sexual attacks on socially vulnerable nonwhite women became an opportunity for white men to bond through rape.[46]

These kinds of sexually vicious attacks also occurred against African American victims. In her study of sexual violence in colonial North Carolina, Kirsten Fischer argues that the ability "to enforce the use of another person's body in a sexual act, or to obliterate another person's sexual agency, had long been privileges of power," and, in the context of a racial slave labor system, "sexualized violence also served to mark a body as 'raced.'" Enslaved women were especially vulnerable to attacks by their masters, who might think themselves able to rightfully claim sexual access to the women they owned. Trevor Burnard's analysis of slave owner Thomas Thistlewood's Jamaican diary brings to light the actions of a particularly sadistic slave owner who used sex as a weapon, systematically punishing enslaved women by having sexual relations with them. When one free African American woman was kidnapped into slavery by several

---

45. *Penn. Gaz.,* Aug. 7, 1766. For a gang rape of a Native American woman in 1821, see Sean T. Moore, "'Justifiable Provocation': Violence against Women in Essex County, New York, 1799–1860," *Journal of Social History,* XXXV (2002), 897.

46. For one exceptional case of murder, robbery, and rape that involved several men but only one woman, see *Penn. Gaz.,* Sept. 12, 1787.

men in Delaware in 1816, her return to slavery meant that she was sexually vulnerable to her new owners; they raped her while transporting her south.[47]

In one of the most disturbing recorded incidents, a white man named William Holland petitioned the governor in post-Revolutionary Maryland for a pardon after his conviction for assault and battery on Elizabeth Amwood, a free black woman. There was no sexual content to the assault on Elizabeth: William was convicted of cutting off her hair, a potentially erotic but not explicitly sexual assault. Yet a memorandum included in the pardon request suggests an additional story of sexual assault. Elizabeth told the magistrate that, after shearing her head, William forced her to "Pull up her Close and Lie Down he then Called a Negrow Man Slave . . . and ordered him to pull Down his Britches and gitt upon the said Amwood and to bee grate with her." During all of this, another man named John Pettigrew held a pistol on Elizabeth and the enslaved man, and William repeatedly asked her if it "was in" and "if it was sweet." Then, William "went up into the Company and Called for Water to wash his hand, saying he had bin putting a Mare to a horse."[48]

In physically disfiguring Elizabeth and forcing an enslaved man to rape her, William's primary goal did not seem to be his own immediate sexual release. His explicit comparison of black people to mating animals emphasized William's use of forced sexual relations as a means to mark racial and gender status as two interrelated forms of vulnerability; yet, even here, William attempted to impose a narrative of consensuality by pressuring Elizabeth to say that she enjoyed the sexual act. If free African American women were vulnerable to these kinds of sadistic and vile sexual attacks, one can only imagine the degree to which enslaved women, for whom far fewer records survive, suffered sexual punishments at the hands of cruel and violent masters.

For nonwhite women generally, their social status made them vulnerable to punitive sexual attacks that went beyond physically forceful attempts at sexual

47. Fischer, *Suspect Relations,* 161; Trevor Burnard, "The Sexual Life of an Eighteenth-Century Jamaican Slave Overseer," in Merril D. Smith, ed., *Sex and Sexuality in Early America* (New York, 1998), 176–177; Morgan, *Slave Counterpoint,* 411; *State v William Gossage et al.,* February 1817, New Castle Oyer and Terminer Docket, RG–2825, microfilm p. 0133b, DPA. On the ideology underlying the degradation of black women's bodies, see Jennifer Morgan, "'Some Could Suckle over Their Shoulder': Male Travelers, Female Bodies, and the Gendering of Racial Ideology, 1500–1770," *WMQ,* 3d Ser., LIV (1997), 167–192.

48. Petitions for William Holland, March 1787, Governor and Council, Pardon Papers, box 4, folder 47, MdSA.

relations. This distinction in the processes of sexual coercion for white and nonwhite victims allowed rape to directly express racial divisions. Rather than sex that was meant to appear consensual, negotiated, or manipulated, these purposefully cruel acts were performed through relations of subordination.

The African American man's rape of Celia Evans at knifepoint would better fit early American understandings of rape than would Sarah Perkins's ultimate consent to her father's sexual coercion, but none of the multiple forms of rape introduced at the beginning of this chapter was random. Daughters, wives, servants, slaves, neighbor women, and subordinated racial groups were all differently vulnerable to particular kinds of sexual force. Men in positions of power could extort sex from their dependents and their workers without causing them grave bodily harm. Masters might force their servants into vulnerable situations, fathers might invoke their patriarchal right to gain sexual access to a daughter, and neighbors might create opportunities for sexual coercion through socializing. In contrast, an African American man would most likely resort to blatant force in his attempt to sexually coerce a white woman into sexual relations. In all of these situations, the relationship between the parties determined the nature and course of a possible sexual attack. These multiple forms of sexual coercion contributed to the porous boundaries between consensual and coerced sex. With the power to shape the form of sexual coercion without the use of physically irresistible brute force, privileged men could coerce sex in ways that might undercut the appearance of their coercion. The power to reshape force into consent inextricably intertwined coerced and consensual sex.

Rape was explicitly racialized through the early American legal system, but institutional racial biases do not adequately explain the patterns of early American sexual assaults. Sexual attacks were race-based in their commission: white men were generally less likely to negotiate with nonwhite women for sexual relations. Instead, white men might expressly use sexual assaults on nonwhite women as a marker of their degraded racial status. Black men, without the privileges of mastery or community-insider status, did not share their white counterparts' range of options for sexual coercion of white women. A patriarch's social and economic power translated into an ability to coerce or extort sex, making sexual access and control a sign of mastery, prosperity, and, ultimately, whiteness.

I have emphasized the means of sexual coercion here, but the legal system provided a backdrop to these incidents. It functioned as a possible realm for redress and as a shaper of the stories that circulated about a forced sexual encounter. Some of the many aforementioned incidents were charged as rape or attempted rape, some were brought to trial for lesser charges, and some appear never to have entered the criminal justice system. Community and judicial responses to acts of sexual coercion were built both on a system of law and on images of believable rapes. The social dynamics that influenced the process of coercion continued to shape women's and girls' reactions to sexual assaults.

CHAPTER THREE

AFTER COERCED SEX: THE PROGRESSION OF KNOWLEDGE

In 1803, Cato, an African American New Yorker convicted of rape and murder, explained why another young woman he had previously tried to rape had not complained to the authorities. He supposed that she "from motives of modesty declined complaining, or pursuing measures to bring me to justice." Perhaps Cato or, more likely, the editors of his published life story felt the need to explain why a presumably innocent young woman would not complain to authorities about an attempted rape—especially one committed by an African American man who later murdered another young woman. Modesty, the hallmark of proper womanhood, seemed as likely an explanation as any. But the decision to involve legal authorities was far more complex than a victim's concern about propriety. Women's view of their relation to the legal system, of the actual harm done by a sexual assault, and of their right to complain led many to agonize over the proper course of action following a sexual attack. An assaulted woman had to arrive at two basic conclusions before she shared her story: she had to realize that an actionable wrong had been done to her, and she had to believe that telling someone else might physically or emotionally improve her situation.[1]

Still, bringing a sexual assault to the attention of court officials was not just an individual woman's choice. A woman made her attack known to others through social networks of custom, ritual, and responsibility. A woman's family and community proved as crucial to the reporting of an attack as a jury was to the conviction of a rapist. Other women evaluated the likelihood of her claim, and a household patriarch often physically brought the victim to a justice of the peace to file her complaint, providing the final link to the all-male judicial system. Thus, a victim's position in a household, the labor

1. *The Life and Confession of Cato, a Slave of Elijah Mount* (Johnstown, N.Y., 1803), 7.

system, and the community greatly influenced her actions. Social and economic power relations continued to underwrite sexual power even after the sex act itself.

Interactions with family or close community members provided a victim's first introduction to the community's standards for rape. Because a woman made her assault a matter of public concern by progressively giving her story away to others, family, friends, and neighbors played a crucial role in improving or worsening her outlook. Those who learned of the assault formed their own judgments about what had happened. Long before an alleged attacker faced a court's judgment on a rape charge, his accuser faced the verdict of her community, and before anyone might face the institutionalized prejudices of the courtroom, beliefs about who would and would not rape influenced the categorization of a sexual act. Hierarchies of race, age, gender, and kinship limited and guided the reception and redress of the attack.

Legal sources, which comprise the lion's share of surviving records on sexual assaults, methodologically predispose us toward seeing legal redress as a victim's sole legitimate response. If we consider legal intervention the only valid reaction to an assault, we neglect much of the story. A court's intervention would be a virtual impossibility for some women and an unwelcome option for others. An entire world of interactions, decisions, and compromises preceded or supplanted legal intervention. Rather than ask the unanswerable question of how many women never reported a sexual attack, I explore *how* women decided on a course of action after a sexual attack. The transition from the act of sexual assault to a criminal prosecution was neither automatic nor linear. Cultural ideology, social status, and community reactions to a woman's claim of a sexual assault circumscribed the path from her reaction to her ability to speak her case before a courtroom full of men. Thus, the process of extralegal reaction to a sexual assault was as complex as any case adjudicated within a courtroom.[2]

2. Scholars who have compared the prosecution and occurrence of sexual attacks have largely debated the degree to which rape was an unreported crime. See Edward Shorter, "On Writing the History of Rape," *Signs,* III (1978), 471–482; Heidi I. Hartman and Ellen Ross, "Comment on 'On Writing the History of Rape,'" *Signs,* III (1978), 931–935; Nazife Bashar, "Rape in England between 1550 and 1700," in London Feminist History Group, ed., *The Sexual Dynamics of History: Men's Power, Women's Resistance* (London, 1983), 28–42. For unintentional equation of prosecution and actual rapes, see Else Hambleton, "'Playing the Rogue': Rape and Issues of Consent in Seventeenth-Century Massachusetts," in Merril D. Smith, ed., *Sex without Consent: Rape and Sexual Coercion in America* (New York, 2001), 27.

Many women did not even seem to consider turning to the legal system after a sexual assault, especially if that attack stopped short of a rape. Victims' explanations of their own hesitancy revolved around fears of both their own culpability and the physical consequences of making a complaint. Some women feared the wrath of the judicial system or the reaction of the community; some were afraid of the fury of parents, masters, or their attackers. The hurdles for women who ultimately brought legal complaints suggest that many other women chose to be silent about sexual attacks. In all cases, the decision to make a sexual attack public knowledge depended greatly on a woman's place in society and her relation to her attacker. Before community members could react to the claim and legal officials could debate the strength of the case, a victim often had to choose whether to make an intimate assault a matter of public concern.

Early Americans imagined an idealized rape victim whose extreme modesty removed any doubt of her true resistance to the sexual attack. Perhaps the most famous rape victim was Lucretia, the Roman wife who killed herself rather than live with her chastity ruined. In a 1747 publication, William Penn called Lucretia "most Chaste" and praised her *"Vertue."* A 1760s mid-Atlantic bookseller's advertisement for five volumes of historical biographies listed Lucretia's story shortly after Thomas Hobbes's and right before Martin Luther's. In 1774, a popular sentimental novel identified Lucretia as the "most celebrated" example of female chastity. Even if early Americans did not expect their own raped women to kill themselves, the fascination with Lucretia's devotion to her own chastity implicitly emphasized a raped woman's perceived disgrace. Violated women might be thought to shame their husbands and families, diminish their own marital prospects, and be ostracized by their communities. Thus, their families and society might be better served if victims kept their misfortunes to themselves. And indeed, many sexual assault victims hesitated to share their stories.[3]

---

3. William Penn, *No Cross, No Crown: A Discourse Shewing the Nature and Discipline of the Holy Cross of Christ*, 7th ed. (Boston, 1747), 83–84; *A Catalogue of Books, Sold by Rivington and Brown, Booksellers and Stationers from London, at Their Stores* . . . ([Philadelphia?], 1762), 22 (the book was *Bayle's Historical and Critical Dictionary*); [Henry] Brooke, *Juliet Grenville; or, The History of the Human Heart*, 2 vols. (Philadelphia, 1774), II, 49. For a criticism of Lucretia's suicide as un-Christian, see Mary Wortley Montagu, *Letters of the Right Honourable Lady M——y W——y M——e*, 4th ed. (New York, 1766), 161. Similarly, in Richardson's immensely popular novel, *Clarissa*, the heroine wills herself into death after

The modesty that contemporary writers believed held back a victim's natural urge for justice might be better understood as the historically persistent double standard. Women's perceived responsibility for all extramarital sexual affairs weighed heavily on them as they considered reporting a sexual assault. A woman might ask herself: Had she somehow encouraged the man's overtures? Would she be punished? Was his behavior wrong enough to trouble with legal involvement? Concerns about her own perceived complicity might dissuade a woman from telling anyone about a sexual assault. Because women's sexual reputations were directly tied to their social standing, women risked a great deal by bringing forward a charge of sexual attack that ultimately might be doubted.[4]

Women also sometimes hesitated to complain because they were unsure of the kind of reception they might get from legal officials. Even though British common law (the centuries-old law of court precedents) had long made quick complaint essential to a believable rape accusation, most victims did not immediately turn to the judicial system. Beyond the generic and quite possibly real assertion that fear of retribution kept them quiet, women described halting attempts to get advice about their legal recourse, their social responsibilities, and their best options. These explanations underscore the distance between women's personal reactions to a rape and a court's institutional expectations of a rape victim. Common law might have expected that a truly raped woman would file complaint against her attacker without delay, but many early American victims hesitated to complain about an attacker. A woman was far more likely to first involve others in her decision to seek out criminal justice.

In deciding whether to share the story of a sexual assault, women had to consider the possibility that they would be held responsible for any extramarital sexual activity, regardless of a claim of force. In the early eighteenth century,

---

being drugged and forced into sexual relations by her suitor. See Samuel Richardson, *Clarissa; or, The History of a Young Lady,* ed. Angus Ross (1747–1748; rpt. New York, 1985).

4. See Keith Thomas, "The Double Standard," *Journal of the History of Ideas,* XX (1959), 195–216. On the relation of slander to women's sexual reputations, see Kirsten Fischer, *Suspect Relations: Sex, Race, and Resistance in Colonial North Carolina* (Ithaca, N.Y., 2002), 141; Clara Ann Bowler, "Carted Whores and White Shrouded Apologies: Slander in the County Courts of Seventeenth-Century Virginia," *Virginia Magazine of History and Biography,* LXXXV (1977), 411–426. On the concern that reporting a rape could be seen to make a woman appear unchaste, see Susan Staves, "Fielding and the Comedy of Attempted Rape," in Beth Fowkes Tobin, ed., *History, Gender, and Eighteenth-Century Literature* (Athens, Ga., 1994), 105–106.

women in Puritan New England had experienced decades of strict accountability for all forms of sexual sin. In Connecticut in 1706, Sarah Beach displayed her knowledge of stern Puritan treatment of sexual misbehavior: she reminded the married man who tried to have sex with her that he would answer to God and man for his actions. However, court proceedings also might hold the complaining women responsible for encouraging extramarital sexual relations. In 1703, Sarah Tinny complained that John Amee had thrown her down, put his hands under her clothes, and "swore he would Nock mee." When several witnesses supported Sarah's story, a northern New England court convicted John of un-Christian behavior and rudeness, but the court also sentenced Sarah to public admonition for her rudeness. In the same year, a Connecticut court charged Hannah Rood with being pregnant with her stepfather's child when she complained to the court that he had forced her to have sex with him. In 1710, another New England court whipped Mary Jinkins for lewdness after she complained that John White had forced himself on her. Less is known about early southern colonies' treatment of sexual misdeeds, but here, too, sexual misbehavior made up a significant portion of courtroom prosecutions. Women might rightly consider whether complaints to early-eighteenth-century legal authorities would be as likely to implicate them in criminal proceedings as to punish their attackers.[5]

5. Case of Joseph Mallery, 1706, Connecticut Archives, Crimes and Misdemeanors, 1st Ser., I, 405b, CSL; case of John Amee, January 1703, in Neal W. Allen, Jr., ed., *Province and Court Records of Maine* (Portland, Maine, 1958), IV, 288–289; case of Thomas Hall and Hannah Rood, 1702–1703, Connecticut Archives, Crimes and Misdemeanors, 1st Ser., I, 322–331. See also case of John and Sarah Perkins, 1725, ibid., III, 42–43; case of John White and Mary, the wife of Rowland Jinkins, July 1710, in Allen, ed., *Province and Court Records of Maine,* IV, 378–381. On prosecution of and attitudes toward illicit sex in early southern colonies, see Fischer, *Suspect Relations,* 53, 112–113; Kathleen M. Brown, *Good Wives, Nasty Wenches, and Anxious Patriarchs: Gender, Race, and Power in Colonial Virginia* (Chapel Hill, N.C., 1996), 188–201; Mary Beth Norton, *Founding Mothers and Fathers: Gendered Power and the Forming of American Society* (New York, 1996), 335–347. On seventeenth-century Puritan prosecution of sex crimes, see Cornelia Hughes Dayton, *Women before the Bar: Gender, Law, and Society in Connecticut, 1639–1789* (Chapel Hill, N.C., 1995), 173–181, 235–243; Norton, *Founding Mothers and Fathers,* 262–264; Lyle Koehler, *A Search for Power: The "Weaker Sex" in Seventeenth-Century New England* (Urbana, Ill., 1980), 351–353; Roger Thompson, *Sex in Middlesex: Popular Mores in a Massachusetts County, 1649–1699* (Amherst, Mass., 1986), 10–11, 53–82; Else Knudsen Hambleton, "'The World Fill'd with a Generation of Bastards': Pregnant Brides and Unwed Mothers in Seventeenth-Century Massachusetts" (Ph.D. diss., University of Massachusetts at Amherst, 2000).

By the later eighteenth century, women, especially unmarried ones, seemed to fear extralegal punishment from parents or masters more than a court's retribution. In 1778, Maria Nichols told her mother "that if she would not beat her, she would tell her" about the man who had sexually assaulted her. In 1793, Lanah Sawyer told a New York court that she had not told her father that she had been raped, for fear he would beat her before hearing her full story. In 1799 South Carolina, Eleander Hill waited nearly a month to tell her mother that Samuel Casey had sexually assaulted her, believing his threat that "if she did that her mother would beat her up and whip her well." In Philadelphia in 1812, Deborah Williams would not explain to anyone what had happened to her until her mistress promised that she would not beat her. Although such fears might have been at work a century earlier, victims in the early 1700s seemed less likely to openly attribute a delayed complaint to their fear of a parent's or master's punishment. Perhaps the religious emphasis on admission of one's sins made a claim of silence because of fear seem less exculpatory. Regardless, wavering prosecutorial interest in women's sexual misdeeds did not automatically translate to a declining belief in women's responsibility for sexual misbehavior. The threat of a negative reception by either institutionalized religious morality or concerned authority figures could deter individual victims from telling others about a sexual assault.[6]

This initial hesitancy to make a sexual attack public meant that men might repeatedly coerce women before facing the possibility of prosecution. Mary Fryley testified that Seth Hills had tried to get her to have sexual relations with him several times before she finally complained to the Burlington, New Jersey, court in 1701, and another witness likewise testified that Seth had also tried to force her into a sexual relationship. Catherine Parry recounted that her attacker had attempted to force her to have sex with him for almost a year before she complained publicly to a Pennsylvania court in 1737. In 1761, Elizabeth Swindle told a North Carolina court that Robert Jones had "importuned . . . [her] to lie with him" before the day he brutally raped her. Despite legal holdings that quick complaint supported a rape claim, the indistinct line between escap-

6. Trial of John Fisher, Feb. 24, 1778, WO 71 / 149, no. 8, 7–19, TNA:PRO; *Report of the Trial of Henry Bedlow, for Committing a Rape on Lanah Sawyer* (New York, 1793); *State v Samuel Casey,* August 1799, Pinckney District General Sessions Court, Sessions Rolls, no. 25, SCDAH; *Commonwealth v Taylor,* Jan. 8, 1812, Pennsylvania Court Papers, HSP. See also trial of William McDermott, Sept. 23, 1773, WO 71/79, 5, TNA:PRO; trial of John Barron, Jan. 27, 1763, WO 71/73, 101–108, ibid.; testimony in *King v John Domaine,* Oct. 30, 1766, John Tabor Kempe Papers, Lawsuits C–F (in back of unlabeled folder), NYHS.

able sexual pressure and actionable sexual assault led many women to choose to avoid the legal system until a man's sexual pressure became unbearable or unavoidable.[7]

A woman would easily report only those attacks heinous enough to immediately overcome her fears of negative reception and possible damage to her reputation. The many acts of sexual coercion that were less than outright rapes (either incomplete intercourse or sex with a disputable level of force) were difficult for women to act on precisely because they fell into the expansive gray area between forceful sex and sexual force. Forceful sex was acceptable; sexual force was not, but the distinction between the two was in the eye of the beholder.

A rare personal recollection gives us insight into how women might interpret sexual force that still fell short of the degree necessary for prosecution. While traveling in Ohio in 1810, Margaret Van Horn Dwight wrote about an incident "as bad as can befal us." After she undressed and went to bed at a tavern, a wagoner "came into the room and lay down by me . . . I was frighten'd almost to death . . . trembling, begging of him to leave me." Eventually, the man left, telling Margaret "not to take it amiss, as he intended no harm and only wish'd to become acquainted with me." Two other women in her party were likewise tremendously frightened by "one of the creatures [who] had been into their room, and they could scarcely get him out." When one man came back to their room, Margaret and another woman ran "out into the mud in our stocking feet." The women then lay awake together all night, fearing that the men would return.[8]

Even though Margaret and her traveling companions felt menaced by these

7. H. Clay Reed and George J. Miller, eds., *The Burlington Court Book of West New Jersey, 1680–1709,* American Legal Records, V (Washington, D.C., 1944), 254; examination of Catherine Parry, July 25, 1737, Chester County Quarter Sessions File Papers, CCA; complaint against Robert Jones, February 1764, in Robert J. Cain, ed., *Records of the Executive Council, 1755–1775,* Colonial Records of North Carolina, 2d Ser., IX (Raleigh, N.C., 1994), 453. See also *Rex v George Clinton,* September 1728, New Haven County Court Files, 1720–1729, R–Y, no. 6, CSL; Leo Hershkowitz, ed., "Tom's Case: An Incident, 1741," *New York History,* LII (1971), 63–71; *The People v George Bowman,* July 24, 1798, New York County Court of General Sessions Indictment Papers, NYMA; *Territory of Mississippi v Francis Surget,* October 1808, in William Bakersville Hamilton, ed., *Anglo-American Law on the Frontier: Thomas Rodney and His Territorial Cases* (Durham, N.C., 1953), 419–422.

8. Margaret Van Horn Dwight, *A Journey to Ohio in 1810,* ed. Max Farrand (New Haven, Conn., 1912), 40–41.

men, they also felt that they had little recourse from the men's behavior. She certainly knew that legal action was a possibility: "Mr W," a traveling companion, "threaten'd them [the wagoners] with a prosecution" the next morning. But Margaret instead first criticized the tavernkeeper who would not stand up to the wagoners and blamed one of her female traveling companions "who is much too familiar with them, and I believe it was owing entirely to that" that the wagoners harassed the women in her party. After all, Margaret could not imagine that she had done anything "that could give him reason to suppose I would authorise such abominable insolence." The lessons once taught by Puritan institutions remained a part of nineteenth-century notions of proper womanhood. Women still held themselves responsible for encouraging—and, more importantly in sexual assaults, *discouraging*—male sexual attention. The ideological transformation toward a belief in less naturally passionate womanhood over the course of the eighteenth century did not change women's perceived responsibility for sexual virtue. Instead, the overlapping of coerced and consensual sexual relations prompted Margaret to wonder how she or her companions had encouraged that sort of male behavior. Was this truly an attempt at rape or simply an incident of disreputable men pushing women for all the sexual favors they might be willing to bestow? Margaret believed that a clearer display of female chastity would have protected them from such sexually hyperforceful men; perhaps this was one reason why Mr. W. did not follow through on his threat of legal action. If Margaret, an elite, literate woman, would not prosecute this kind of unwelcome sexual pressure, legal recourse for a servant or slave must have seemed very distant indeed.[9]

To report an attack, a sexual assault victim had to move beyond her internal trepidation that she might be partly to blame for her own suffering. The degree to which women held themselves responsible or feared others would hold them accountable for a sexual attack varied, often according to the circumstances of the attack, the social position of the victim and attacker, and the

---

9. Ibid., 40, 42, 43. On women's sexual responsibility for rape in early modern rape cases, see Garthine Walker, "Rereading Rape and Sexual Violence in Early Modern England," *Gender and History*, X (1998), 5–6. On the transformation in courtship norms, see Ruth H. Bloch, *Gender and Morality in Anglo-American Culture, 1650–1800* (Berkeley, Calif., 2003), 78–101. On early modern women's reactions to physical and sexual abuse, see Lawrence Stone, *Road to Divorce: England, 1530–1987* (Oxford, 1990), 199–201; Margaret Hunt, "Wife Beating, Domesticity, and Women's Independence in Eighteenth-Century London," *Gender and Hist.*, IV (1992), 10–33.

degree to which the attack looked like an archetypal, excessively violent rape. Victims who did not have confidence in community and family support for their accusations often chose to keep silent for extended periods.

Young girls seemed especially likely to suffer repeated sexual assaults before telling others what had happened. Perhaps the most vulnerable to long-term abuse were daughters whose fathers sexually abused them. In 1703, Hannah Rood told a Connecticut court that she did not see how to complain about her stepfather's persistent sexual assaults. She recounted, "I knew not what to do. I went to one house and to another and to a third thinking to declare my grife to them, but when I came thear, thear being strangers to me, I had not the power to speake, but sat downe and cry." Nearly a century later, Phoebe Bailey reacted similarly to her father's abuse. Her mother "often saw her cheeks bedewed with tears, on account of his new and astonishing behaviour" but recounted that "such were . . . [Phoebe's] fears of him, that she did not dare to talk with me, or any other person upon her situation." In early-nineteenth-century Massachusetts, Betsy Wheeler's father threatened to "kill me in the most cruel way he could think of" if she told of his abuse. So Betsy did not complain of his attempts on her until after her mother had ordered him out of their house. Betsy's mother, as the new household head, directly challenged the father's authority in the family and, in so doing, created a space for her daughter to speak. A daughter had difficulty complaining about a sexual attack because she could not see how to complain against the man who was meant to be her protector. He was the one who should have helped her out of an abusive situation by prosecuting her attacker. Fear of retribution and confusion about the limits of a father's authority made outside assistance a particularly thorny issue for abused daughters. Fathers not only had access to their daughters' bodies but also control over their daughters' ability to seek redress for their actions.[10]

10. Case of Thomas Hall, Sarah Hall, and Hannah Rood, 1703, Connecticut Archives, Crimes and Misdemeanors, 1st Ser., I, 325a, CSL; Ann Taves, ed., *Religion and Domestic Violence in Early New England: The Memoirs of Abigail Abbot Bailey* (Bloomington, Ind., 1989), 71; *Report of the Trial of Ephraim Wheeler for a Rape Committed on the Body of Betsy Wheeler, His Daughter, a Girl Thirteen Years of Age* . . . (Stockbridge, Mass., 1805), 12–13. See also *Rex v John Perkins, Jr.,* March 1725, New Haven Superior Court Files, 1720–1727, drawer 324, CSL; *State v Moses Johnson,* August 1794, Fairfield County Superior Court Files, 1790–1799, A–K, box 625, CSL; *State v John Ely,* November 1804, Hartford County Superior Court Files, November 1804–September 1805, box 36, CSL; *State v Nathan Darby,* March 1808, Union County General Sessions Court Journal, WPA transcript, 148, 150, 167, and Union County General Sessions Court, Sessions Rolls, nos. 103, 117, SCDAH.

Like daughters, female servants also had to rely on the household patriarch for guidance and assistance. This level of control could make it exceptionally difficult for servants to accuse a master of sexual abuse. Margaret Connor withstood continual sexual pressure and abuse from her master before she complained to a Virginia court in 1724. In 1789, Rebecca McCarter told a Pennsylvania court that her master had been forcing her to have sexual relations with him since shortly after she had become his servant two years earlier. Even if she did not live in her abuser's house, an authority figure might seem difficult to accuse. Unice Williamson continued to be a servant to Nathaniel Price for more than a week after he bound, gagged, and raped her, and she did not tell anyone about his attack for two months. The prerogatives of mastery went beyond a master's ability to force a servant into sexual intercourse because servants found it very difficult to complain against repeated abuse by their supervisor and guardian. But, if a servant did not complain right away, others might view her as complicit in the sexual relationship. Master-servant sexual relations, though certainly illicit and possibly adulterous, did not fall under the kind of incest taboos that automatically condemned all father-daughter sexual relations; therefore, a young servant's claims of resistance to ongoing sexual relations were automatically suspect.[11]

Other young girls had difficulty complaining about continuing abuse by men who were outside of their households. Though we see multiple cases of father-daughter molestation in the early eighteenth century, comparatively few girls reported repeated sexual assaults by unrelated men in the first quarter of the century. Some of this absence may be due to the variable content of surviving testimonies or to differing prosecution strategies across time periods. Also, significant patriarchal control and community policing likely made it more difficult for men to coerce neighbor girls in tight-knit communities. Young girls, too, might have been hesitant to report sexual abusers early in the century for fear that they would be held accountable for engaging in any sexual acts. Regardless of the exact reasons, the number of reports of nonincestuous, repeated sexual abuse of children increased as time progressed. In one of the earliest cases, in Massachusetts in 1739, six-year-old Sarah Blewitt admitted

11. Trial of Christopher Pridham, September 1724, Richmond Criminal Trials, 1710–1754, 85–87, 95–96, 119, LOV; *Respublica v David Robb*, Yeates Legal Papers, March–April 1789, fol. 2, HSP; *The Trial of Nathaniel Price: For Committing a Rape on the Body of Unice Williamson, a Child between 10 and 11 Years of Age, at Brooklyn in King's County, in May 1797* . . . (New York, [1797]), 2–3. See also Norton, *Founding Mothers and Fathers,* 265–268.

that James Gatton "often had hurt her" sexually. In 1777, Mary Gates complained to a Connecticut court that her husband had sexually assaulted their young apprentice for years. In 1804, thirteen-year-old Polly Waldo told a Hartford, Connecticut, court that John Ely had sexually assaulted her a "great number" of times.[12]

With the increased availability of women's education in the Revolutionary era came multiple cases involving schoolteachers who repeatedly assaulted their pupils. A New Jersey court charged schoolmaster Peter Galvin with raping or trying to rape four girls who were less than ten years old in 1774; a Massachusetts court accused Stephen Burroughs, a quondam schoolmaster, of sexually assaulting two young women in 1791; and, in 1817, a New York court charged William Genner with sexually assaulting at least three of his students. Men's positions of direct authority over young girls gave them an opportunity to commit multiple sexual assaults without discovery — if they could legitimately command their victims' behavior, then they might be able to command their silence. In addition to fears of their own culpability, young victims might not know their legal rights or how to challenge an adult male abuser.[13]

Young victims were especially fearful of their attackers' threats. For a child victim, any adult white man was an authority figure and could therefore level horrifyingly believable threats. In a 1797 case, ten-year-old Unice Williamson did not tell anyone for weeks about her master's assaults, because he threatened to kill her. The man who raped six-year-old Sally Carver persuaded her to keep silent after an assault in 1810 New York City with a particularly vivid warning. Sally recalled that her attacker had "told her not to tell and if she did tell he

12. Case of James Gatton, June 5, 1739, Massachusetts Superior Court of Judicature Docket, reel 6, 106, MA; petition of Mary Gates, Salisbury, Mar. 3, 1777, Windham County Superior Court Records, Subject: Divorce 1752–1922, microfilm no. 418, CSL; *State v John Ely,* November 1804, Hartford County Superior Court Files, November 1804–September 1805, box 36, CSL. Many early-eighteenth-century court documents consist of indictments or depositions that focus solely on the crime charged, whereas later sources include trial transcripts and lawyers' notes that might record fuller questioning and cross-examination about incidents of ongoing sexual abuse other than the specific incident being prosecuted.

13. *King v Peter Galvin,* November 1774, New Jersey Supreme Court Minutes, September 1772–April 1775, no. 59, 400, 402, 411, 414, 422, NJSL; *King v Peter Galvin,* 1774, New Jersey Supreme Court Actions-at-Law, no. 20684, NJSL; *Commonwealth v Stephen Burroughs,* 1791, Massachusetts Superior Court of Judicature Records, Suffolk Files, nos. 155602, 155603, 155604, 155605, MA; *The People v William Genner,* Aug. 13, 1817, New York County Court of General Sessions Indictment Papers, NYMA.

would buy two cow skins and two horse whips and would Twist them up together and would whip her — also that he would borrow a knife . . . and would cut her ears off and her head." In nineteenth-century Philadelphia, John Kinless made a more succinct but probably no less scary threat to four-year-old Mary McElroy: John said he would "give her to the sweep" if she told anyone that he had raped her, and, as a result, Mary said nothing for nearly a month. Older women might recognize that community involvement and legal prosecution could possibly protect them from retribution, but young girls were especially susceptible to believing that the men who had already hurt them so much could make good on their horrific threats.[14]

Black men's threats to white victims appeared to be less effective than white men's threats. Once a rapist who had little socially recognized power released his victim, she did not have to sleep in his house, follow his orders, or worry whether he could turn the community against her. When a black man attacked fourteen-year-old Susannah Sylvester in 1734 in New York City, she shouted "that she knew him and who was his Master." In 1748, a Connecticut woman picked up a stone and threatened to kill her African American attacker as soon as she got away from him, telling him "she would have him hanged." Records from early-nineteenth-century Virginia courts, where black men were regularly convicted of rape, show that white victims reported little hesitation in threatening retribution. In 1804, Phebe Pool told Jesse, a mulatto man, that, despite his threats, she would certainly inform her parents that he had raped her. When a Virginia slave named Reuben raped Sarah Fox in 1819, she promised him that she would never mention the attack, but, as soon as she was away from him, Sarah ran to the first house she saw and told the residents of her ordeal. These women reported the attacks immediately without fear of being blamed themselves; they were able to confront their attackers with the knowledge that when they did tell, few white community members would believe that a white victim had encouraged a black attacker.[15]

14. *Trial of Nathaniel Price,* 2–3; *Commonwealth v Kinless,* Jan. 18, 1815, Pennsylvania Court Papers, HSP. See also *State v Samuel Casey,* August 1799, Pinckney District General Sessions Court, Sessions Rolls, no. 25, SCDAH. For an adult victim citing fear of a rapist's threats, see *The People v George Bowman,* July 24, 1798, New York County Court of General Sessions Indictment Papers, NYMA.

15. *King v Cato,* Jan. 21, 1733/4, Rough Minutes of the General Quarter Sessions of the Peace for the City and County of New York, 329–334, NYHR; *Rex v Cuff,* September 1748, New Haven Superior Court Files, drawer 327 (record book missing), CSL; case of Mulatto Jesse, Aug. 6, 1804, Virginia Executive Papers, box 131, LOV; case of Reuben, July 12, 1819, ibid., box 255. See also *D. v Joe,* n.d., Kent County Oyer and Terminer File Papers,

Although crucial to white women's interpretation of their right to redress, color lines were not indelible. When black men assaulted young girls, the victims might be hesitant to make the attack known, even in a state where rape convictions of slaves were common. In 1808, five-year-old Virginian Sally Briggs would not tell her mother how an enslaved man had sexually assaulted her until her mother could assure her that "there was no danger of his killing her." In 1804, Lucy Ann Steel, who was about a decade older than Sally, seemed equally afraid of the enslaved man who had attacked her, and she did not complain of the attack until a month later. Perhaps Lucy did not immediately complain because they both worked on the same plantation — class similarities might have disturbed any simple racial hierarchies. While racial relationships are most easily identified, a variety of social relations influenced how sex could be coerced and how victims interpreted and sought assistance after a sexual attack.[16]

For enslaved African American women, continuing sexual abuse was often a fact of life; these women had little hope of legal or other redress, and this lack of recourse greatly affected their reaction to sexual attacks. In 1774, Philip Vickers Fithian noted repeated sexual attempts toward Sukey, a "likely Negro Girl about sixteen" who was a slave on Robert Carter III's Virginia plantation. Despite repeated rumors that a Carter son tried to force himself on Sukey, Philip dismissed the claim as "calumny" and showed little interest in finding or condemning Sukey's attacker. Because others' knowledge of a sexual assault would net them little protection or chance at legal redress, the question of whether to tell someone about sexual assaults did not have the same significance for enslaved victims as it might for white victims.[17]

Slaves whose masters assaulted them had virtually no chance at outside intervention. In the nineteenth century, Lewis Clarke recalled that his sixteen-year-old enslaved sister could do nothing in response to her master's sexual abuse but "hold her head up over such things, if she could." Slaves had good reason to believe their masters' threats of violence — a master could brutally assault his slave with virtual impunity. Harriet Jacobs recalled that her master

DPA; case of Archy, Apr. 10, 1805, Virginia Executive Papers, box 134, LOV. For a victim's similar reaction to a servant's order, see Francis G. Walett, ed., *The Diary of Ebenezer Parkman, 1703–1782* (Worcester, Mass., 1974), I, 64.

16. Case of Dick, Nov. 19, 1808, Virginia Executive Papers, box 157, LOV; case of Luke, Mar. 7, 1804, ibid., box 129.

17. Hunter Dickinson Farish, ed., *Journal and Letters of Philip Vickers Fithian, 1773–1774: A Plantation Tutor of the Old Dominion* (Williamsburg, Va., 1957), 86, 184–185.

"threatened me with death, and worse than death, if I made any complaint" of his treatment, so she rhetorically asked, "Where could I turn for protection?" Enslaved women lived with the constant threat of sale if they sufficiently displeased a master. Unfortunately, sexual involvement, even if not of an enslaved woman's own choosing, with a member of the master's family could cause just such displeasure. James Pennington recalled a fellow slave who had been "degraded" by her master's son in the early nineteenth century. Upon learning of this, the master restored his family's honor by selling her to the Deep South, and James reported that her family never heard from the woman again.[18]

Telling others about sexual assaults led to a very different outcome for enslaved victims than the one hoped for by white victims. Even if a white woman's complaint would not ultimately be believed, she at least stood a chance of assistance from family or friends. In contrast, slaves might escape sexual assault only by being sold away from their families and communities — an option that might be worse than the recurrent sexual assaults. Enslaved victims might have told their family members of their suffering in the hopes of getting personal support or informal community assistance in avoiding their attackers, but sharing their stories could cost those who took action on their behalf. Ex-slave Josiah Henson recounted that his father had intervened in an overseer's attempted rape of his mother in Maryland in the 1790s, springing "upon him [the overseer] like a tiger." The overseer punished Josiah's father with one hundred lashings and severed his ear. The father, now marked as a recalcitrant slave, was eventually sent to Alabama. The punishment endured by Josiah's father physically marked the exclusion of enslaved black men from free white men's right to protect a wife from rape. Enslaved women might have ultimately decided that there was little benefit in telling others about the sexual assaults that were one more abuse in the horrific daily reality of slavery.[19]

Some victims, however, did not have the option of deciding for themselves whether to make an assault known to others. Witnesses to the attack or to its effects could force a victim to tell her story. Assaults on children seemed most likely to come to light through others' actions. Sometimes witnesses inter-

18. Lewis Clarke, "Leaves from a Slave's Journal of Life," in John W. Blassingame, ed., *Slave Testimony: Two Centuries of Letters, Speeches, Interviews, and Autobiographies* (Baton Rouge, La., 1977), 156; Harriet A. Jacobs, *Incidents in the Life of a Slave Girl, Written by Herself,* ed. Jean Fagan Yellin (Cambridge, Mass., 1987), 27, 32; James W. C. Pennington, *The Fugitive Blacksmith* . . . (1850; Westport, Conn., 1971), vi–vii.

19. Josiah Henson, *An Autobiography of the Rev. Josiah Henson* . . . , in Robin W. Winks, ed., *Four Fugitive Slave Narratives* (1881; rpt. Reading, Mass., 1969), 13–14.

rupted the assault in progress. In 1745, a father found his daughter's teacher "in the very Posture of Perpetuating his abominable Intention" and, within an hour, brought his daughter to complain to the Georgia authorities. Mary Clarkson saw John Domaine lying across eight-year-old Catharine Larkings in their New York home in 1766 and, "not in the Least mistrusting what he had been about," helped to get him quickly convicted. In 1819, when Sarah Duffy found a visitor assaulting her nine-year-old servant in her Philadelphia home, she immediately yelled for her husband to "stop that villan, he has ruined the child." Such cases suggest that men who sexually assaulted children might more likely be stopped when witnesses caught them, not because the girls reported the attacks.[20]

Continuing incestuous sexual abuse might also eventually be discovered by witnesses, most often women, who noticed something amiss in a father-daughter relationship. Early in the eighteenth century, women actively looked for breaches in sexual morality. In 1725, Elizabeth Chatterson told a Connecticut court that she thought that John Perkins showed a "a lasivious air" toward his daughter, so she peeked through a crack in the door and found him having sex with her. A few years later, Mary Brown, a Massachusetts resident, listened at a bedroom door to sounds that convinced her that a father and daughter were having sexual intercourse. Rather than report her concern right away, Mary continued her investigation a few months later, this time looking through a crack to see the father lying on top of his daughter. Women also discovered incestuous sexual relations later in the century but seemingly more by chance than through purposeful investigation. For instance, in 1781, a Mrs. Ocane nudged her husband awake to look at their overnight visitors, a father who had insisted on sleeping in bed with his stepdaughter and who appeared to be having sexual relations with her. Whether as part of community policing efforts or through happenstance, these witnesses gave molested daughters the possibility of legal redress without the daughters' having to make the extraordinarily difficult decision to oppose their fathers in a public legal setting.[21]

20. Letter from John Terry to the Trustees of Georgia regarding the rape of Christina Pennikar, in Allen D. Candler, ed., *Colonial Records of the State of Georgia, 1742–1745*, 25 vols., XXIV (New York, 1970), 406–407; testimony in *King v John Domaine*, Oct. 30, 1766, Kempe Papers; *Commonwealth v Boyle*, Jan. 7, 1819, Pennsylvania Court Papers, box for 1807–1809, HSP.

21. *Rex v John Perkins, Jr.*, March 1725, New Haven Superior Court Files, 1720–1727, drawer 324, CSL; *Rex v Peter Harding*, October 1729, Massachusetts Superior Court of Judicature Records, Suffolk Files, no. 26074, MA; indictment against James Weller and

More common than witnesses to the actual attack were witnesses to its effects. Family and household members might question a victim about how she had received visible injuries. In 1736, Elizabeth Bissell told her sister that she had been assaulted only after the sister had noticed that Elizabeth had difficulty walking. In nineteenth-century Philadelphia, Deborah Williams testified, "I don't know that I shd have said any thing [about being raped] if Mr. S. [her master] had not spoken to me," questioning why she looked so muddy and disheveled. Attacks on children, who were perhaps least able to dissemble and most likely to show signs of abuse, often came to light through bodily injuries. Jane Briggs realized that her five-year-old daughter had been sexually assaulted when she found her "feet and legs in a gore of blood." Nine-year-old Alice Workenson's injuries from a sexual assault were equally obvious: she stood in a "stream of blood running down on [the] floor."[22]

Sometimes others learned about a sexual attack when victims eventually became sick from the injuries they sustained. Four days after a sexual assault in 1763, Mary Tolany's mother demanded to know what was making the seven-year-old girl so ill, and Mary eventually told her that John Barron had raped her. In 1797, Unice Williamson, who was too afraid of her attacker to tell anyone, eventually related her story after she became ill with what doctors diagnosed as a sexually transmitted disease. Injuries did not necessarily lead to immediate action. Despite the bloody handprint on her daughter, Mary, and the blood on a neighborhood man who would prove to be her attacker, Ann McElroy told a Philadelphia court in 1815 that she "had no suspicion of any crime" committed on her daughter until a month after the attack, when she appeared "wasted away" and "ready to drop." Barring catastrophic visible wounds, family members had to purposefully examine and pursue possible physical evidence of sexual assaults.[23]

Monicha Strick, October 1783, Dockets of Cases and Notes of Evidence Taken by Hon. Increase Sumner, 1782–1786, II, 231–233, MHS.

22. *Rex v John Green,* September 1736, Hartford County Superior Court Files, box 83, CSL. Elizabeth was still reluctant to divulge the full extent of the assault—she waited another day to admit that she had been raped. See *Commonwealth v Taylor,* Jan. 8, 1812, Pennsylvania Court Papers, HSP; case of Dick, Nov. 19, 1808, Virginia Executive Papers, box 157, LOV; *Commonwealth v Boyle,* Jan. 7, 1819, Pennsylvania Court Papers, box for 1807–1809, HSP.

23. Trial of John Barron, Jan. 27, 1763, WO 71/73, TNA:PRO; *Trial of Nathaniel Price,* 2–3; *Commonwealth v Kinless,* Jan. 18, 1815, Pennsylvania Court Papers, box for 1807–1809, HSP. For other rape victims' contracting venereal diseases, see case of Samuel Corey, April 1784, Massachusetts Superior Court of Judicature Records, Suffolk Files, nos. 15366,

If some family members did not appear to see obvious signs of a sexual attack, others would tenaciously look for indications of sexual misconduct, if not sexual assault. Several mothers learned of attacks on their daughters from doing laundry. In Revolutionary-era Philadelphia, Hannah Downs noticed stains on her daughter's linen, so she asked her daughter "if any body had done any thing to her." A seven-year-old girl in nineteenth-century South Carolina did not tell her mother about a sexual attack until her mother found blood on her underclothes. Direct questioning by an observant family or household member could lead a victim to explain what had happened to her before she might have chosen to do so.[24]

Yet signs of possible abuse did not mean that victims immediately told their stories. Young girls might still fear that they would be punished for a sexual assault. Even after noticing her daughter's physical injuries, Mary Tolany's mother in 1763 had to "beat her till she told" that John Barron had raped her. In 1781, Ellenor Wilson refused to tell anyone how she contracted a "venereal disorder" until a doctor told her "she would certainly die of the disorder if she did not tell him who had used her thus." Perhaps the threat of corporal punishment or death counterbalanced the attackers' threats of physical harm and overcame the victims' reluctance to tell their stories. Future retribution from an assailant or fear of one's own culpability might have seemed less formidable when compared to a guarantee of immediate suffering.[25]

Sexually mature women's bodies might provide another impetus to reveal a sexual assault. Even if not evidence of *forced* sexual intercourse, telltale signs of pregnancy were tangible proof that sexual intercourse had indeed taken place. A woman who had chosen not to tell anyone about a sexual attack might eventually be obligated to explain the cause of her pregnancy. In 1754 in Massachusetts, Mary Packard waited until she realized that her attacker had impregnated her to complain about the assault. In Revolutionary-era Pennsylvania, Rebecca McCarter, pregnant and homeless, appeared before the Overseers of the Poor. After two years of abuse, her master had kicked her out of his house once she became pregnant, and the overseers demanded she swear the

---

154180, MA; *State v LeBlanc*, 1 Treadway's Constitutional Reports (SC), 354 (1813); trial of William McDermott, Sept. 23, 1773, WO 71/79, TNA:PRO.

24. Trial of John Fisher, Feb. 24, 1778, WO 71/149, no. 8, 7–19, TNA:PRO; *State v LeBlanc*, 1 Treadway's Constitutional Reports, 354. See also trial of William Sanders, Aug. 6, 1779, WO 71/149, 7, TNA:PRO.

25. Trial of John Barron, Jan. 27, 1763, WO 71/73; trial of John Wilson, July 18, 1781, WO 71/94, 253–260, TNA:PRO.

child to someone or leave the county. Only then did Rebecca tell her story. In 1797, Virginia authorities learned that Ursula Fogg's father had been abusing her for years after her new husband complained that she "was pregnant by her Father Taylor Noel in consequence of an incestuous intercourse between them . . . which originated from Violence."[26]

A woman making such a belated claim of rape was automatically suspect — had she only cried rape to diminish her culpability? One mid-eighteenth-century traveler recounted the story of a woman who falsely claimed rape after becoming pregnant. When asked why she did not cry out her resistance during the sexual encounter, "she answered that if she had thought that this time she would become pregnant, then she would certainly have cried for help." A 1791 almanac satirically told a similar story of a woman who charged a "gentleman" with rape and was asked by the court if she had resisted his advances. She replied that she had cried out, "Please your lordship." Another trial witness delivered the punch line, agreeing that she had cried out, but only *"nine months after."* Pregnancy might have forced a woman to admit that she had been raped but in no way forced others to believe her. And community reaction would prove a crucial determinant of the outcome of a victim's attempts at legal redress.[27]

A sexually assaulted woman based her decision to tell or not tell on a variety of factors. The attack had to be serious enough for a victim to involve others in her personal problems. A woman had to believe that the attack was more than a man's acceptable forceful attempt at sexual relations and went beyond her own ability to prevent such illicit acts. Notions of modesty did not necessarily encourage a woman's silence. Rather, the circular logic of the sexual double standard suggested that, if it were a woman's responsibility to prevent sexual

26. Case of James Lindsay, 1754–1755, in David Thomas Konig, ed., *Plymouth Court Records, 1686–1859,* 16 vols. (Wilmington, Del., 1978–1981), III, *1748–1751,* 55, 57–58; *Respublica v David Robb,* Yeates Legal Papers, March–April 1789, fol. 2, HSP; petitions of John Fogg, Sr., and William Fogg, Dec. 11, 1800, Legislative Petitions, Essex County, box 67, folder 47, LOV. See also divorce petition of Ann Teal, February 1770, New Haven County Superior Court Divorce Files, 1712–1773, box 461, A–Z, CSL; *Rex v George Clinton,* September 1728, New Haven County Court Files, 1720–1729, R–Y, no. 6, CSL; *Mercer v Walmsely,* 5 Harris and Johnson (Md.), 27 (1820). Laurel Thatcher Ulrich suggests a similar scenario in her discussion of the 1789 North-Foster rape case in *A Midwife's Tale: The Life of Martha Ballard, Based on Her Diary, 1785–1812* (New York, 1990), 115–127.

27. Gottlieb Mittelberger, *Journey to Pennsylvania in the Year 1750 and Return to Germany in the Year 1754,* ed. and trans. Oscar Handlin and John Clive (Cambridge, Mass., 1960), 38–39; *Bickerstaff's Genuine Massachusetts, Rhodeisland, and Connecticut Almanack, for . . . 1791* (Boston, [1790]), 24, emphasis in original.

assaults, then a woman who was sexually assaulted had failed in her feminine duties. If she had failed, then she, too, might be responsible for the sexual encounter. Thus, a victim needed to categorize an assault as an actionable wrong for which she would not be held responsible before sharing her story with others.

Even beyond the obstacle of this sexual double standard, not all victims had the same opportunities or desires to share their stories. Barring obvious physical injury or pregnancy, a woman had to weigh the pros and cons of telling others about a sexual assault, and, for the most vulnerable members of society, there were often more disadvantages than advantages in asking for help. Daughters abused by fathers as well as servants or slaves abused by masters were the most likely to suffer years of continuing sexual abuse before reaching out for assistance. Children and victims who were directly subordinate to their assailants were especially influenced by the threats of an attacker. If victims decided to publicly allege a sexual assault, they did so through a series of cultural scripts shaped by their social and economic status. For many women, the path to redressing a sexual assault began with a community of women.

TELLING THE TALE AND TELLING THE BODY

When thirteen-year-old Margaret Miller testified about being raped in early-nineteenth-century New York City, the prosecutor asked her whether she told her surrogate mother about the attack. Lawyers expected that unmarried victims would first tell the women around them that they had been assaulted. Although the official matrons' juries that traditionally testified about sexual crimes became less common throughout the eighteenth century, women still maintained an informal role in the encouragement or discouragement of sexual assault prosecutions. They provided the victim's first introduction to community standards for rape, and their opinions could be influential in court determinations of the severity and believability of the crime. More important, these women could provide care, nurturing, and assistance, giving the victim the support she needed to publicly confront her attacker. Their reactions could convince a victim to pursue legal redress or to keep her story to herself. Once that decision was made, communities of women acted as gatekeepers to legal redress for young victimized women by mediating believable claims to a wider, male audience.[28]

28. *Report of the Trial of Richard D. Croucher, on an Indictment for a Rape on Margaret Miller; on Tuesday, the 8th Day of July, 1800* (New York, 1800), 5–9. On seventeenth-century

Victims followed a basic pattern in their choices of confidantes. Women's stories of rape moved up social hierarchies, beginning with someone in a position of relatively more power than themselves. For single victims, this usually meant an older, married woman. The assistance of a married, and therefore presumably sexually experienced, woman could also address one of the stumbling blocks to an unmarried woman's charge of rape: if she were supposed to have never engaged in sexual relations, how could she testify to the intercourse required for a rape prosecution? By reading victims' bodies for signs of the sexual assault they claimed, female confidantes could establish the veracity (or falsehood) of the claims. This made women crucial determinants of both community and legal reactions to sexual assaults on unmarried women.

Most unmarried victims chose other women as their first confidantes about a sexual attack. After two men raped Anna Grubb in 1781, she "imidiatley informed her aunt and [an]other woman what had happened." In 1817, when Rebecca Day, Jr., was assaulted on the way to her boardinghouse, she told three women that night and her mother at five o'clock the next morning. Even victims who had waited years to share their stories eventually broke their silence with other women. Phoebe Bailey ended two years of her father's sexual abuse by confessing to her mother with "the help of her aunt." These choices emphasize that women lived in a social world filled with other women—a world where intimate tragedies (and joys) were shared among groups of women.[29]

The choice to turn to other women was more than a happenstance of social proximity; sexually assaulted young women deliberately sought out other women with whom to share their woes. Assaulted unmarried women who had

---

matron's juries, see Kathleen M. Brown, "'Changed . . . into the Fashion of a Man': The Politics of Sexual Difference in a Seventeenth-Century British Settlement," *Journal of the History of Sexuality*, VI (1995), 171–193; Dayton, *Women before the Bar*, 21, 246; Rebecca J. Tannenbaum, *The Healer's Calling: Woman and Medicine in Early New England* (Ithaca, N.Y., 2002), 93–113. On English women's roles in examining rape victims, see David Harley, "The Scope of Legal Medicine in Lancashire and Cheshire, 1660–1760," in Michael Clark and Catherine Crawford, eds., *Legal Medicine in History* (Cambridge, 1994), 53.

29. *Commonwealth v Long and Wilson*, May 1781, Pennsylvania Court of Oyer and Terminer Court Papers, RG–33, box 4, PSA; *Report of the Trials of Stephen Murphy and John Doyle* . . . (Boston, 1817), 4–6; Taves, ed., *Religion and Domestic Violence in Early New England*, 87. Even an older woman might first turn to her mother. See, for example, case of Joseph Mallery, 1706, Connecticut Archives, Crimes and Misdemeanors, 1st Ser., I, 405b, CSL. Similarly, Richardson's fictional heroine, Clarissa, chose to tell several women (two of whom were older widows) about her sexual assault (Richardson, *Clarissa*, letters 306, 307, 311–315).

an opportunity to first tell a man what had happened might keep quiet until they could instead tell a woman. In Pennsylvania in 1782, Andrew Blair found Jane Mathers just after she had been sexually assaulted. Jane begged him to keep her attacker away from her and ran home. Under cross-examination at the trial she testified, "I did not tell Blair what was done to me—but told my mother when I went home." Perhaps the defense lawyer wanted to cast doubt on Jane's story by emphasizing that she did not immediately tell someone about the attack, but Jane's answer illustrated the acceptable choice of turning first to a female confidante with news of a rape.[30]

Individual victims might turn to other women because they were too embarrassed to talk about sexual details with male neighbors or relatives or hoped that women might provide a more sympathetic ear. Beyond such individual rationales, unmarried victims first told other women about assaults primarily because sexual matters had long been women's purview. Communities of women helped one another with birth, provided health advice, and, before the nineteenth-century challenge of male midwives, were considered the experts on the female body. Courts regularly heard women's testimony in sex-related cases. A witness list for an attempted rape trial in 1734 included a midwife and the girl's mother, who both searched her for evidence of the crime. In 1750, Elizabeth Bethy testified that she, "a Stranger then in the house," had helped Ann Hunter examine her daughter's body for signs of a rape. On the day after Christmas in 1754, Mary Gordon called her neighbor, Elizabeth Scott, "as an Evidence" to "come and See" her crying, bloodied daughter. As in these cases, other women were more involved in court proceedings when the victim was young and likely sexually inexperienced.[31]

30. Notes of evidence in *Respublic v James Paxton,* May 27, 1783, Yeates Legal Papers, April–May 1783, fol. 7, HSP. See also case of James Gibson, March 1783, Connecticut Archives, Crimes and Misdemeanors, 1st Ser., VI, 220–222, CSL; *Report of the Trial of Ephraim Wheeler,* 13; *Report of the Trial of Henry Bedlow,* 6–7.

31. Case of Emmanuel Lewis, Aug. 13, 1734, Massachusetts Superior Court of Judicature Records, Suffolk Files, no. 37793, MA; Conrad Weiser Papers, call no. 700, I, 25, HSP (thanks to Birte Pfleger for this citation); *D. v John McVaugh (McVay),* May 1755, Chester County Quarter Sessions File Papers, CCA. See also Carl J. Ekberg, *Colonial Ste. Genevieve: An Adventure on the Mississippi Frontier* (Gerald, Mo., 1985), 374. On the traditional women's communities surrounding birth and sexual matters, see Laurel Thatcher Ulrich, *Good Wives: Image and Reality in the Lives of Women in Northern New England, 1650–1750* (New York, 1980), 126–145; Norton, *Founding Mothers and Fathers,* 222–239. On the shift to male physicians for obstetric care, see Judith Walzer Leavitt, *Brought to Bed: Childbearing in America, 1750 to 1950* (New York, 1986), 36–63. On early modern female sexual subculture,

Both women and men recognized this embodiment of sexual truth as women's exclusive domain. James Parker's 1788 guide for justices of the peace stated explicitly that only women could properly determine whether another woman had been raped. Accordingly, when Deborah Williams's master took her to file a rape complaint before his wife returned home, the judge in the 1812 case instructed the jury, "It was indiscretion [for her master] to take her to the Justice, until his wife came home and the Girl had been examined by respectable women." Even after matrons' juries were no longer common, communities and legal authorities recognized that women remained the proper readers of other women's bodies. The opinions of other women could provide crucial support both for the individual victim and for any future prosecution.[32]

Unlike single women, married victims did not regularly turn to other women when moving toward legal redress. While other women might have provided moral support, married women uniformly turned first to their husbands with their own claims of rape. Married women knew what sexual intercourse felt like and were assumed to know their bodies well enough to testify to the act. One married woman made this connection explicit, stating in 1783 that the rapist "did as my husband did." Even though Elizabeth Truax, a married woman, fell into an insensible state while being raped, a 1792 Delaware court accepted without supporting testimony from other women her statement that the effects she felt on her body gave her "the greatest reason to believe" that a man had sexual relations with her. A married woman's assumed knowledge about sexual intercourse rendered her a reasonable witness to her own body.[33]

But a chaste, sexually inexperienced woman would not be able to testify to

---

see Patricia Crawford, "Sexual Knowledge in England, 1500–1750," in Roy Porter and Mikuláš Teich, eds., *Sexual Knowledge, Sexual Science: The History of Attitudes to Sexuality* (Cambridge, 1994), 94–96.

32. James Parker, comp., *Conductor Generalis; or, The Office, Duty, and Authority of Justices of the Peace* . . . (New York, 1788), 359; *Commonwealth v Taylor,* Jan. 8., 1812, Pennsylvania Court Papers, HSP. See also *A Narrative of the Life of Ephraim Wheeler* . . . (Stockbridge, Mass., 1806). On the absence of matrons' juries in rape cases in the British context, see Antony E. Simpson, "Popular Perceptions of Rape as a Capital Crime in Eighteenth-Century England: The Press and the Trial of Francis Charteris in the Old Bailey, February 1730," *Law and History Review,* XXII (2004), 27–70. On matrons' juries more generally, see James C. Oldham, "On Pleading the Belly: A History of the Jury of Matrons," *Criminal Justice History,* VI (1985), 1–64.

33. Notes of evidence in *Respublica v Abraham Moses,* May 21, 1783, Yeates Legal Papers, April–May 1783, fol. 7, HSP; *State v John Morris,* December 1792, Kent County Oyer and Terminer File Papers, DPA.

the commission of an act of which she was supposed to have no firsthand knowledge. Barbara Witmer testified under cross-examination that she had not immediately said anything about being raped because "I was ignorant whether i was ravished." Eight-year-old Eleander Hill testified that she "felt something go into her body, but does not know what it was." In an 1819 case, Elizabeth Smith, a single woman, told a Virginia court that she was raped but then claimed that the attacker had not entered her body. When asked if she understood what "entering her body" meant, she said that she did not. A sexually inexperienced victim (or a victim who needed to appear sexually inexperienced) had to present the rape committed on her through the examination and opinions of others, so women's networks played a crucial role in the expanding knowledge of a sexual assault. Because an unmarried woman, meant to be sexually inactive, could not speak for her own body, other women made her body public for her, either in support or refutation of her claim of sexual coercion. Women could look for physical signs of resistance, such as cuts or bruises, and visually examine her genital area for evidence of recent sexual intercourse. Through this examination of possible sexual assault victims, women read the truth of the sexual encounter. Rather than having to trust a supposedly untrustworthy individual woman's claim of rape, other women had the power to (re)create and reveal a recent sexual encounter by the perceived signs on another woman's body.[34]

Reading bodies for evidence was the sole province of women — they were the examiners and the examined. Accused rapists' bodies neither condemned nor exonerated them. Nearby men or legal officials did not regularly examine a man's genitals to see whether he had recently ejaculated. Nor did they strip him

34. Notes of evidence in *Respublica v Timothy Cockly, Timothy Lane, Patrick O'Hara, Thomas Marony, Michael Snoddy,* May 10, 1786, Yeates Legal Papers, May–June 1786, fol. 4, HSP; *State v Samuel Casey,* August 1799, Pinckney District General Sessions Court, Sessions Rolls, no. 25, SCDAH; case of Dennis, June 1819, Virginia Executive Papers, box 254, June 24–30 folder, LOV.

On the naturalized sexed body, see Moira Gatens, "A Critique of the Sex/Gender Distinction," in Sneja Gunew, ed., *A Reader in Feminist Knowledge* (New York, 1991), 139–157; Judith Butler, *Gender Trouble: Feminism and the Subversion of Identity* (New York, 1990). On the social implications of this constructed body, see Catherine Bell, *Ritual Theory, Ritual Practice* (New York, 1992), chap. 5, 94–117. On raped women's reading themselves through others, see Mae G. Henderson's insightful analysis, "Toni Morrison's *Beloved*: Re-membering the Body as Historical Text," in Domna C. Stanton, ed., *Discourses of Sexuality from Aristotle to AIDS* (Ann Arbor, Mich., 1992), 321.

to see if he had any scratches, bruises, or bodily fluids on him. The few accused men's bodies that were described or analyzed were those of African American men. White community members brought Tom, a Virginia slave, before Dolly Boasman to see whether he was the man who had raped her a few hours earlier. Since Dolly's attacker had been barefoot, his captors made Tom remove his shoes and socks to see whether she could identify him. Court records do not mention whether anyone examined his body for any signs of recent sexual activity. I have found only one case where the body of a (black) man was purposely examined for signs of recent sexual intercourse, and he was convicted and hanged, regardless of the physical corroboration of his innocence.[35]

The rise of the field of medical jurisprudence further institutionalized the readability of women's bodies. Samuel Farr's 1785 foundational text, *Elements of Medical Jurisprudence,* listed seven physical criteria to show that a girl was still a virgin and nine to show that a woman was accustomed to venereal habits and thus "less to be believed upon a deposition for a rape." A woman could be categorized as virgin or whore, truth teller or liar, according to the perceived signs of her physical body.[36]

Reconstructing the corporal details that women looked for when they examined a possible rape victim is difficult. Published trial transcripts left out the details of a sexual assault, citing the desire not to offend the reader with immodest language. Even court file papers contain few particulars of the physical damage on which women based their assessments of rape. This nod to modesty might have been an empowering tool for women because it required that women's words stand as facts and that women analyze the evidence within their own heads and among their own social circles before reporting their findings. The two women who examined Diana Parish's body in 1748 testified that they had been "very Particular in their Examination" and "according to

35. Case of Tom, Jan. 22, 1810, Virginia Executive Papers, box 164, LOV; case of Roz Norman, Apr. 15, 1797, Virginia Executive Papers, box 99, LOV. For an exceptional case where witnesses found semen on the shirt of a community and cultural outsider, see case of Vanskelly Mully, 1760, Connecticut Archives, Crimes and Misdemeanors, 1st Ser., V, 144–146, CSL, and discussion in Dayton, *Women before the Bar,* 254–256. On reading enslaved bodies, see Walter Johnson, *Soul by Soul: Life inside the Antebellum Slave Market* (Cambridge, Mass., 1999), 138–161.

36. Samuel Farr, *Elements of Medical Jurisprudence* . . . (1788; rpt., London, 1815), 47–49.

their best Judgment the Body of the said Diana had been entered by some man." Mary Gordon told a Pennsylvania court in 1755 that, after examining her assaulted daughter, "it is the Oppinion of Sd Dep[onan]t that [the accused] was Guilty of a Rape." Jane Briggs examined her daughter and, without describing to the court what injuries she saw, assuredly testified that "I do fully believe" that she was raped. Only women could participate in the examination of possible rape victims, and only these women knew the details of their findings. The rest of the community would have to trust their conclusions if they were to believe the rape victim's story.[37]

The growing, though still infrequent, reliance on physicians in post-1750 rape cases shows that, despite their increasing status as respected professionals, doctors did not provide the same kind of definitive conclusions about their examinations of women's bodies that communities of women regularly forwarded. Women generally involved doctors when there were abnormalities beyond their experiences of the female body. A surgeon was called to testify in a 1766 trial involving an eight-year-old rape victim because she was thought to have contracted a sexually transmitted disease. In 1779, Ann Tobin's mother first called another married woman to examine her daughter's genital injuries, and the two women determined that her "private parts were found to be harmed So much, that I was obliged to make application to surgeons." In 1804, Margaret Sweeney testified that she had stripped and examined her daughter, "found her much hurt," and only then called for a doctor.[38]

When they were called in, doctors seemed less likely than women to pass unambiguous judgments about the events that led to the victim's injury. Doctors focused instead on a description of physical injuries and theoretical possibilities. In a 1792 case, a doctor testified that either sexual assault or jumping might have caused a ten-year-old's genital injuries. Although a doctor testified at one 1808 rape trial about the physiological possibility of a man's penetration

37. For examples of concern over immodest language, see *Report of the Trial of Ephraim Wheeler,* 12; *Report of the Trial of Henry Bedlow,* 6; *Pennsylvania Gazette* (Philadelphia), Nov. 11–13, 1729; *Rex v Cuff,* September 1748, New Haven Superior Court Files, drawer 327 (record book missing), CSL; *D. v John McVaugh (McVay),* May 1755, Chester County Quarter Sessions File Papers, CCA; case of Dick, Nov. 19, 1808, Virginia Executive Papers, box 157, LOV.

38. Testimony in *King v John Domaine,* Oct. 30, 1766, Kempe Papers; trial of William Sanders, Aug. 6, 1779, WO 71/149, TNA:PRO; *Commonwealth v Amos Penross,* Nov. 27, 1804, Pennsylvania Court Papers, box for 1799–1800, HSP. For another case where a doctor was called in to testify about a sexually transmitted disease, see *State v Le Blanc,* 1 Treadway's Constitutional Reports, 354.

of a five-year-old, the girl's mother was asked whether she thought the defendant had entered her daughter's body. Unlike women who focused on their conclusions, doctors gave clinical information about a victim's body—they discussed labia, discoloration, fluids, and lacerations. Dr. Henry Clapp examined an assaulted Philadelphia nine-year-old in 1819. At the trial, he testified to the specific damage done to her genitals: there was "some laceration and some hemorrage . . . the Hymen was ruptured." He concluded, "If she had been ravished, the appearance wd have been such as I saw." Dr. Clapp spoke in the subjunctive, stating probable conjecture rather than fact. Unlike the women who testified, doctors had to describe what they saw, supporting their conclusions with the visual evidence they had gathered. Women's intimate relationship to the female body stood in for medical description. Their opinions passed as a truth knowable only to women.[39]

Women's roles as helpers, confidantes, and supporting witnesses in a sexual assault trial gave them significant power over the possibility of legal redress for a young victim who claimed a sexual assault, but this power did not necessarily translate into a uniformly supportive community of women. They might question whether the victim had really been raped, or they might react negatively to protect their own interests. Even if they believed the victim, they might decide that the risks of prosecution outweighed its potential benefits. Some did not want to bring charges that might take the life of the rapist, some feared that the jury would not believe the victim's story, and some worried that a public trial would cause embarrassment or dishonor to the victim and her family. Even if neighbor women believed a victim, they had only as much power as the value a community placed on their words—male juries and judges might believe a male doctor's conjecture over the assured statements of female examiners.

Accordingly, family and neighbors sometimes betrayed a willingness *not* to know what had happened to an assaulted woman. Laurel Thatcher Ulrich summarized midwife Martha Ballard's reticent attitude toward a neighbor's 1789 confession that a prominent man in the community had raped her: "Mar-

---

39. *Trial of Nathaniel Price*, 3; case of Dick, Nov. 19, 1808, Virginia Executive Papers, box 157, LOV; *Commonwealth v Boyle*, Jan. 7, 1819, Pennsylvania Court Papers, box for 1807–1809, HSP. For an earlier case where women called a doctor to examine an injured girl, see *Rex v Sam*, 1737, Fairfield County Court Files, box 180, folder 17, CSL, cited in Dayton, *Women before the Bar*, 252 n. 29. On nineteenth-century shifts in medical testimony about rape, see Stephen Robertson, "Signs, Marks, and Private Parts: Doctors, Legal Discourses, and Evidence of Rape in the United States, 1823–1930," *Jour. of Hist. of Sex.*, VIII (1998), 345–388.

tha was unwilling to invite any more information than she was given unbidden." Other victims met with even more direct disinterest and lack of assistance. In 1800, Maria Cottle told a woman who lived in her house that she wanted her father's long-term abuse made known to the proper officials, but the woman declined to help Maria because "she was poor and knew but little of law" and instead suggested that Maria just run away if it happened again. Nearly two decades later, Maria Forshee told her mistress and some neighbors that her master had tried to rape her, but, rather than helping her bring charges, they apparently told her master what she had said, "and he then turned her away calling her a whore."[40]

Like the two Marias, daughters and servants were the victims most likely to meet with resistance from their confidantes. The detailed interactions of William Cress and his servant, Rachel Davis, allow for an exploration of multiple commentaries on this resistance. As discussed in the previous chapter, the 1808 case involved Rachel Davis's rape complaint against William Cress, her master. The testimony in this case exemplifies the difficulty abused servants could have when they tried to escape an abuser. William's wife, Becky, appeared to know about her husband's sexual behavior and repeatedly questioned him about why he had to be alone with Rachel. When Becky heard her husband trying to kiss Rachel in the cellar, she "said she had caught him and he wd deceive her no longer," but William denied any wrongdoing, and his wife left in tears. Finally, Rachel's mistress "saw something was the matter with me, and asked what it was. I told her." When Becky again confronted her husband, he denied the attack. She suggested that "if it was lies, he ought to whip" Rachel, and he did so.[41]

Instead of bringing charges against her husband or applying for a divorce on the grounds of adultery, Becky Cress told Rachel Davis that she must "leave the house." Rachel's mistress might have ultimately recognized that her husband was at best complicit in his sexual relations with Rachel, but she also recognized that, as his wife, she was in a poor position to mandate a reform in his behavior. She could, however, as mistress of the household, remove the more disposable partner in the sexual relationship, so she ordered Rachel to leave their home. Whether or not Becky believed Rachel's story of rape, she did not consider her entirely innocent of wrongdoing. At the very least, she spread

40. Ulrich, *A Midwife's Tale*, 116; *The People v Grant Cottle*, Aug. 15, 1800, New York County Court of General Sessions Indictment Papers, folder for Oct. 9, 1800, NYMA; *The People v Thomas Conlen*, Mar. 4, 1818, ibid.

41. *Commonwealth v William Cress*, February 1808, Pennsylvania Court Papers, HSP.

blame equally between her servant and her husband, with much of the resulting punishment falling on the more vulnerable of the two parties. As Rachel stated, "Before I was hired out, [my mistress] used me very bad and said she would knowck me down if I came to table to eat."[42]

Because William was a master of both Rachel and his household, his wife could enact only limited direct retribution against him. She could watch his behavior, confront him, and let him know her displeasure, but removing the object of his overtures was easier than publicly accusing him of wrongdoing. A husband's sexual overtures toward another woman placed his wife in opposition to his victim, whether the other woman welcomed his overtures or not. In addition to her personal resentment, a wife's economic well-being was greatly jeopardized if her husband were removed from the household through incarceration or marital separation. Given the chance, a wife might strike out at the victim rather then her husband.

Becky's reaction to growing evidence of her husband's sexual misbehavior, if not abuse, toward their servant was not uncommon. A 1795 joke book told a story of this exact scenario in which a mistress punished the servant for a husband's sexual misdeeds: "A certain lady, finding her husband somewhat too familiar with her chamber-maid, turned her away, saying *'Hussy, I have no occasion for such sluts as you, I hired you to do your own business, not mine.'*" The story set up a husband propositioning the chambermaid (the occurrence of physical coercion is indeterminate), but the wife clearly blamed the servant for encouraging the encounter. Abigail Bailey recounted a similar sentiment when she noticed "very improper conduct" between her husband and a servant. Abigail pleaded with her husband to "consider the evil of his ways" but blamed the "rude" and "disagreeable" servant and "prevailed to send the vile young woman from our family." Household mistresses felt that they were in sexual competition with the servant, even if the servant was not a willing competitor. The mistress might blame the servant, not her husband, for any sexual activities, with the bulk of the resulting punishment falling on the young woman.[43]

Becky Cress was not the only community member loath to challenge her husband's treatment of Rachel. Rachel eventually told several women close to her — one of her sisters who was a servant in another household, her aunt, and her new mistress — about William's sexual assaults. Her aunt purposefully avoided asking how badly Rachel had been abused. As she told the court, "I

42. Ibid.

43. *Feast of Merriment: A New American Jester* (Burlington, N.J., 1795), 33, emphasis in original; Taves, ed., *Religion and Domestic Violence in Early New England*, 58–59.

did not enquire whether he obtained his will in the meadow." When Rachel's sister told her own mistress that "Mr Cress wanted to be gret [great] with her sister Rachael," the mistress replied, "I wanted to hear no more." The community of adult women who could have assisted Rachel wanted neither to hear nor to tell the full extent of William's abuse.[44]

Enslaved women were even more disadvantaged than free servants in their attempts to seek assistance from mistresses and communities. Like Rachel, North Carolina enslaved woman Harriet Jacobs had a mistress who repeatedly confronted Harriet with suspicions of her husband's sexual improprieties and tried to get her husband to whip Harriet for her "lies" about their relationship. Harriet Jacobs's fellow slaves were also hesitant to volunteer their verbal or physical assistance. Harriet believed that her friends and relatives were unable to speak of the abuse they knew she suffered. She recalled: "The other slaves in my master's house noticed" her changed behavior as a result of her master's treatment of her, but "none dared to ask the cause. . . . They knew too well the guilty practices under that roof; and they were aware that to speak of them was an offence that never went unpunished." Harriet's fellow slaves' silence, necessary for their own self-preservation, limited their ability to help her resist their master's overtures.[45]

Women's examinations of young women and girls who had been raped could reassure the victim of her story's veracity, introduce her to the community's definitions of rape, and eventually bolster or destroy her claims of her body's experiences. Other women could provide support for a future prosecution or protect their own interests at the victim's expense. If women believed that a victim should pursue legal redress, they mediated between the assaulted woman and the rest of the community. But to widen the circle of knowledge about an assault, women's next step usually involved men.

FROM WOMAN TO WOMEN TO MEN: PUBLIC KNOWLEDGE

Mary Mathers's testimony about her family's reaction to her daughter Jane's rape in 1783 epitomizes the expansion of knowledge of a sexual assault:

> My daughter came home crying and dirty like — When I met her, she said Jam paxton had catched her and ravished her. . . . When my Husbd came home I told him — He went to Alex. Harvey's that Night [in search of her attacker] . . . next morning my sister Betty and I examined her.

44. *Commonwealth v William Cress*, February 1808, Pennsylvania Court Papers, HSP.
45. Jacobs, *Incidents in the Life of a Slave Girl*, ed. Yellin, 28, 34–35.

Like most other young victims, Jane Mathers first turned to an older female relative—in this case, her mother. Mary then took control of the situation. She heard her daughter's story, joined with a female relative to examine her body, and informed her husband of the attack. In contrast, Jane's father's version of the attack was: "My wife told me of the Affair—I got a Warrant for Pris." His testimony contained no reference to his daughter and no indication that he examined or directly interacted with her. He focused instead on the outward-directed activity of bringing the attacker to justice, leaving Jane's care to a circle of women.[46]

This division of labor repeatedly structured reactions to rape; women tended to the victim, and men went to a community of other men for restitution or retribution. In New York in 1766, Mary Clarkson found her daughter being sexually assaulted, and her husband got a warrant for the attacker. In Pennsylvania in 1799, two women examined a victim, and her father arrested her attacker. After a rape on their servant, Alice Workenson, in Philadelphia in 1817, Sarah Duffy "asked the child how [the attacker] came to meddle with her," while her husband, Francis, said that he "took my wife and the child to Squire Freyerson's—my wife brought alice back and washed her." Francis did not mention any direct interaction with the victim, instead focusing his efforts toward legal redress and leaving his wife to communicate with and care for the assaulted girl. Women's corroboration of a victim's story became a way to involve a patriarch in righting the wrong of a sexual assault. As mothers, mistresses of households, and wives, married women smoothed the path to justice for an assaulted girl or young woman by providing a link to a patriarchal figure.[47]

The reading of women's bodies would become more superfluous in the increasingly racialized post-Revolutionary period. A series of early-nineteenth-century Virginia incidents involving slaves accused of raping young white women—the prime candidates for examination by female community members—show that these victims regularly bypassed other women's mediation of their rape claim. When a man found Anne Miller on the side of the road after an enslaved man raped her in 1805, "she immediately communicated . . . what had been done to her." At the 1808 trial of Mooklar for raping Ann Jett, the

46. Notes of evidence in *Republic v James Paxton,* May 27, 1783, Yeates Legal Papers, April–May 1783, fol. 7, HSP.

47. Testimony in *King v John Domaine,* Oct. 30, 1766, Kempe Papers; *Commonwealth v Amos Penross,* Nov. 27, 1804, Pennsylvania Court Papers, box for 1799–1800, HSP; *Commonwealth v Boyle,* Jan. 7, 1819, Pennsylvania Court Papers, box for 1807–1809, HSP. See also trial of William McDermott, Sept. 23, 1773, WO 71/79, TNA:PRO.

only female witness talked about seeing Mooklar throw Ann down, not about any examination of Ann's body. When an enslaved man raped Polly Butler, she first told a male neighbor about the attack. Sixteen-year-old Juriah Young immediately told her father that she was raped by an enslaved man, and no women testified at the trial. In such cases, the significance attributed to the color of the attacker's body likely overshadowed the evidence a white victim's body might provide. Unless the victim was too young to testify in such cases, other women did not need to examine the victim's body for signs of a rape. In the slave system of the nineteenth-century South, women's ability to provide crucial information for rape prosecutions was trumped by assumptions (and frequent courtroom conclusions) of black guilt.[48]

While we see some evidence of women's involvement in black-on-white rape cases in mid-eighteenth-century New England, the records for the nineteenth-century North are largely silent on this issue, making it difficult to determine the extent to which this was a national or regional phenomenon. At least in the southern cases, a black man's identity appeared to be sufficient evidence that a decent white woman would never consent to him. Thus, a black man's rape of a white woman might have discounted much of the media-

48. Case of Billy Scott, 1805, Auditor of Public Accounts, no. 756, Condemned Slaves, box 1967, LOV; case of Mooklar, 1808, ibid.; case of Isaac, Sept. 1, 1812, Virginia Executive Papers, box 190, LOV; case of Anthony, Sept. 15, 1817, ibid., box 241. See also case of David, Apr. 18, 1808, ibid., box 153; *D. v Joe*, n.d., Kent County Oyer and Terminer File Papers, DPA. For an exceptional case where a woman's testimony about a white victim's lack of physical injury was used to try to exonerate the slave female witnesses accused of her rape, see case of Jerry, June 4, July 1807, Virginia Executive Papers, box 145–146, June 1–18, July 1–9 folders, LOV.

For mothers' testifying about the rape of their very young daughters by enslaved men, see case of Dick, Nov. 19, 1808, Virginia Executive Papers, box 157, LOV; *Rex v Sam*, 1737, Fairfield County Court Files, box 180, folder 17, cited in Dayton, *Women before the Bar*, 252 n. 29. For debate in such a case, see *The People v Harry*, Aug. 12, 1805, New York County Court of General Sessions Indictment Papers, NYMA. For examples of eighteenth-century New England women examining young white victims who accused black men of rape, see *Rex v Cuff*, September 1748, New Haven Superior Court Files, drawer 327 (record book missing), CSL; case of Bristo, January 1757, Connecticut Archives, Crimes and Misdemeanors, 1st Ser., V, 47–53, CSL.

Although community women filled crucial supporting roles for sexual assault victims, it is less clear how important these women's statements were to legal officials. At the very least, women's findings were a filter for prosecutable cases.

tion that was needed in those rapes with less stark racial and social differences. Women's words generally seemed to bear more importance in sexual assaults involving people of similar status, where women would question the victim, examine her body, and pass judgment on the likelihood of her claim.

Regardless of the race of the accused, once men learned of a sexual assault, they focused on seeking retribution, often first attempting to find the attacker. Some men went after him themselves, usually without assistance from the women who had told them about the crime. In 1766, a Sergeant Clarkson wanted to track down the runaway rapist who assaulted his stepdaughter. In late-eighteenth-century New York, once John Callahan's wife told him about his daughter's rape, John went to the place where she said the crime had occurred, questioned the people there, and wound up in a scuffle with her attacker. Virginian Samuel King tracked down his wife's attacker after an 1806 assault and brought him back for her to identify. In 1817, at least four men were involved in catching Parthena Rucks's rapist in Virginia, examining the tracks he left behind and waking him up in the middle of the night to imprison him. Whether the accused attacker was black or white, slave or free, once male relatives of the victim believed in the guilt of the rapist, they took it upon themselves to capture, question, and bring him to justice.[49]

Occasionally, a husband or father might go to even greater lengths to personally punish a sexual attacker. In 1771, the *Virginia Gazette* described an incident where a man had made repeated unwelcome sexual overtures to a married woman. Upon being told of these indiscretions, her husband dressed up in his wife's nightgown and waited for the man. When the prospective lover arrived, the husband and three waiting friends attacked the intruder, "who met with an irreparable [loss]" — they apparently castrated him. While this might have been an apocryphal case, one New York man did set up his own elaborate ruse to catch his wife's attacker in 1810. Rebecca Fay's husband originally wanted to shoot the attacker who had raped her on their dining room table, but she convinced him that it was a bad idea. He then tried to create a situation where he could catch the man in the midst of again assaulting his wife. When that failed, he claimed he began socializing with the attacker, hoping that "he

49. Testimony in *King v John Domaine*, Oct. 30, 1766, Kempe Papers; *Report of the Trial of Henry Bedlow*, 15–16; case of Peter Twine, Auditor of Public Accounts, no. 756, Condemned Slaves, box 1967, LOV; case of Lewis, Aug. 1, 1818, Virginia Executive Papers, box 248, LOV. For another case of men's examining the tracks where rape was supposed to have taken place, see case of Isaac, Sept. 1, 1812, Virginia Executive Papers, box 190, LOV.

was apt to boast to his companions . . . of his violence to other women." In a more direct example of retribution, an 1817 North Carolina court that charged Timothy Hilliard with trying to rape Ann Hall also charged a man named Almond Hall, presumably a relative of Ann's, with trying to murder Timothy. Most men would probably not resort to such extremes, but they took their responsibility and right to protect the women in their households seriously. As patriarchs, these men focused on protecting their dependent women from outsiders and left the comforting and examining of the victim to other women.[50]

However enraged husbands or fathers might have been by the rape of a loved one, most men shied from vigilante justice and turned instead to the legal system. Bringing raped girls and women to the legal authorities was men's role. John Waggoner took his wife to the justice of the peace to file a complaint the morning after she had been raped in 1783. Once Foster Evans found out that his wife had been raped in 1808, he immediately complained to the local magistrate. In 1811 Philadelphia, one of Moses Sell's first questions to his raped servant was whether she would make a complaint to the justice. If men were unsure of a victim's story, they were more likely to look elsewhere for circumstantial evidence than to examine women directly before complaining to a justice of the peace. In eighteenth-century Delaware, Mary Crippen's father examined the spot in the road where Mary said she had been raped. In 1817 in Virginia, George Saub inspected the field where his daughter said she had been raped, and, after finding trampled ground and signs of a struggle, went to the local magistrate. These men investigated the veracity of a sexual assault claim in a very different way from women who examined bodies and heard details of victims' stories. Men tried to reconstruct external circumstances rather than read the event from the victim's body. This separation between the victim and those who made the leap to the criminal justice system increased as men decided how to redress a sexual assault on a household member.[51]

50. Purdie and Dixon's *Virginia Gazette* (Williamsburg), Feb. 21, 1771; *Trial of Charles Wakely, for a Rape on Mrs. Rebecca Fay* (New York, 1810); *State v Timothy Hilliard* and *State v Almond Hall*, October 1817, both in Salisbury District State Appearance and Trial Docket, NCSA. See also notes of evidence in *Republic v James Paxton*, May 27, 1783, Yeates Legal Papers, April–May 1783, fol. 7, HSP; *The People v Terry Scandlin*, July 3, 1816, New York County Court of General Sessions Indictment Papers, NYMA.

51. Notes of evidence in *Respublica v Abraham Moses*, May 21, 1783, Yeates Legal Papers, April–May 1783, fol. 7, HSP; case of David, Apr. 18, 1808, Virginia Executive Papers, box 153, LOV; *Commonwealth v Taylor*, Jan. 8, 1812, Pennsylvania Court Papers, HSP; *D. v Joe*, n.d., Kent County Oyer and Terminer File Papers, DPA; case of Anthony, Sept. 15, 1817, Virginia Executive Papers, box 241, LOV.

Despite women's involvement, men were the ultimate arbiters of whether to file a complaint. Ebenezer Parkman's diary entries about a sexual attack on his daughter in 1739 show how he and not his daughter or anyone else in the family decided whether to take her complaint of a sexual assault to court. After a servant attempted to rape his fourteen-year-old daughter, Ebenezer debated more than two weeks what to do "at so important a Juncture." He asked advice from friends, ministers, and legal authorities. He prayed to God and read law books before deciding to go to the court clerk about the attack. Not once did Ebenezer mention talking to his daughter or wife about which action they preferred. As the household patriarch, he determined the proper course of public action. Similarly, Mary Ann Marsh recalled that, when she told her husband of a neighbor's near rape on her in 1815, he "thought that it might better be dropped than to go to court and expose herself," and she did not report the crime.[52]

Men's concerns that a court trial would be time-consuming or potentially embarrassing meant that cases might often be settled informally. Attackers understood that a victim's husband or father held the key to prosecutorial efforts, so they usually addressed their efforts to him. The servant who attacked Ebenezer Parkman's daughter repeatedly begged Ebenezer not to prosecute him, pleading on bended knee and making "promises of great Reformation." After John Morrow raped Celia Holloman in Kentucky in 1806, he went to her father and begged "not to be lawed." One victim explained that her husband had told her that "he would make Some arrangement with . . . [her attacker] — therefore She did not Lodge her Comp[lain]t" with a justice of the peace after an 1808 rape. When Sylvia Patterson's husband discovered James Dunn trying to have sex with her in New York City, James's attack turned into a negotiation between the men: James alternately begged the husband's forgiveness, tried to get him drunk, and offered him a pocket watch if he would not report the incident. Sometimes an attacker's efforts at persuading fathers or husbands to derail a prosecution were successful. After a Kentucky court accused Richard Tomlinson of raping his niece, Frances, or "Franky," in 1803, Richard came to speak with her father. Franky's father then ordered her to stay with her cousin in another town until the trial ended so that she could not be called to testify

52. Walett, ed., *Diary of Ebenezer Parkman*, I, 64–65; *The People v Patterson Jolly*, Oct. 6, 1815, New York County Court of General Sessions Indictment Papers, NYMA. For another father's supposedly turning to other men for advice after a daughter's rape, see John Terry to the Trustees of Georgia, in Candler, ed., *Colonial Records of the State of Georgia*, XXIV, 254–255.

against her uncle. Instead of trying to make restitution to the victim, an attacker focused his energies on the father or husband, who would likely determine the course of any criminal prosecution.[53]

Since male household heads typically drove prosecution efforts, fatherless families faced additional obstacles to judicial redress. Female household heads seemed particularly hesitant to usher their assaulted daughters through the judicial process. In 1754, Mary Anderson's widowed mother eventually took Mary to complain before a magistrate but told him that, if the men who had attacked her daughter would only give assurances not to bother Mary, she would prefer to drop all charges. In Boston in 1817, another mother baldly refused to go with her daughter to file a complaint about a sexual assault, explaining, "I am a poor woman, and did not wish the trouble." Especially for lower-class women without husbands, the legal system could be a site of intimidation rather than salvation.[54]

Cases where a patriarch was temporarily absent illustrate again his crucial role in approaching a magistrate about a sexual assault. In 1789 in Maine, Rebecca Foster told a female friend that "shee believed it was best for her to keep her trouble [of a sexual assault] to her Selfe as mutch as shee Could till her Husband returnd" from a prolonged trip. Servant Rachel Davis would not swear a complaint against her sexually abusive master until her father returned to town. No fewer than five women knew of the assaults, but none of them would begin any legal action without Rachel's father's involvement. When a neighbor asked Rachel "why she did not go to a Squire to complain — she said, she did not dare — she a bound girl and her father absent." Rachel and the other women who kept her secret recognized that a woman needed a male figure to stand with her when challenging another man in a court.[55]

Accordingly, victims abused by a master or father might be able to look for

53. Walett, ed., *Diary of Ebenezer Parkman,* I, 64–65; *Commonwealth v John Morrow,* October 1806, Warren County Circuit Court File Papers, KLA; *Territory of Mississippi v Francis Surget,* October 1808, in Hamilton, ed., *Anglo-American Law on the Frontier,* 420; *The Trial of Captain James Dunn, for an Assault, with Intent to Seduce Sylvia Patterson, a Black Woman* (New York, 1809), NYHS; *Commonwealth v Tomlinsons et al.,* March 1804, Fayette County Circuit Court Decided Cases, drawer 58, KLA. See also notes of evidence in *Respublica v Abraham Moses,* May 21, 1783, Yeates Legal Papers, April–May 1783, fol. 7, HSP.

54. *King v John Lawrence et al.,* Aug. 1, 1754, Supreme Court Pleadings, reels 48–49, K–501, K–650, NYHR; *Report of the Trials of Stephen Murphy and John Doyle,* 6–7.

55. Quoted in Ulrich, *A Midwife's Tale,* 116; *Commonwealth v William Cress,* February 1808, Pennsylvania Court Papers, HSP.

redress only when marriage gave them a new male protector. In early Connecticut, Hannah Rood did not complain about her stepfather's sexual attacks on her until her new husband brought her to court. Traveler and writer J. P. Brissot de Warville described such a case in post-Revolutionary Pittsburgh in which an indentured servant's new husband "purchased her freedom and rescued her from a barbaric and libidinous white master who had made every effort to seduce her." As mentioned previously, in the early nineteenth century, a Virginia man's ongoing abuse of his daughter did not come to light until her new husband realized she was pregnant with her father's baby. Because patriarchs provided the final link to the all-male legal system, woman could often not complain about a sexually abusive patriarch until he was replaced.[56]

Bringing a complaint to court began a whole new series of interactions that returned focus to the victim. A father or husband could notify a magistrate about the crime, but the victim would have to give a deposition with specifics of the attack. Here the victim's world of women fell away as she had to tell her story to what was sometimes a roomful of men. Victims who had already been questioned or examined by other women probably had some idea what a magistrate would expect in a rape accusation and might have been bolstered by the support of mothers, fathers, husbands, or masters. Regardless, victims had a difficult time telling male officials the details of their traumatic experiences. For instance, while one New York woman immediately complained to British officers that a soldier had raped her daughter during the American Revolution, she only later told the officers that she had been raped as well. When asked why she did not immediately complain about her own rape, she explained that she "thought it a shocking thing to tell of, [so] she only mentioned the Circumstances of her Daughter, for which alone she thought that he would suffer severely." Even women who could speak for other victims had difficulty talking to male authorities about their own violations.[57]

The 1786 case of a young Pennsylvania woman clearly shows women's fear and consequent hesitation before legal officials. After she was kidnapped and raped, Barbara Witmer's rescuers quickly brought her to local justices of the peace to press charges against the attackers. But Barbara, possibly still in shock,

56. Case of Thomas and Sarah Hall, 1703, Connecticut Archives, Crimes and Misdemeanors, 1st Ser., I, 328, CSL; J. P. Brissot de Warville, *New Travels in the United States of America,* ed. Durand Echeverria, trans. Mara Soceanu Vamos and Durand Echeverria (Cambridge, Mass., 1964), 232–233; petitions of John Fogg, Sr., and William Fogg, Dec. 11, 1800, Legislative Petitions, Essex County, LOV.

57. Trial of Bartholomew McDonough, Aug. 6, 1778, WO 71/86, 201–202, TNA:PRO.

had great difficulty telling the magistrates about her ordeal. One justice of the peace asked her "8 or 10 times to begin" her testimony. When she said nothing, the justice decided that Barbara was "confused" about what had happened, so he gave up and went to bed. Another magistrate, however, seemed to understand that she might be too traumatized to tell her story. Rather than immediately categorizing her as a confused witness, he saw her as "very bashful" about what had happened to her. This justice "spoke very mildly and told her no one could hurt her for telling the Truth." After waiting through ten or fifteen more minutes of Barbara's silence, the magistrate called in her mother and uncle to provide support, and Barbara hesitatingly began telling her story.[58]

Some victims had to face the even more daunting task of telling a justice of the peace about a rape while her attacker was in the same room. In front of both the magistrate and her attacker, John Waggoner tried to get his silent wife to answer questions about her rape by threatening *"to kick her with my Foot* if she did not answer." In Virginia in 1810, James Wilkinson noted that Dolly Boasman "appeared to be very much frightened . . . which I suppose was the Cause of her refusing to swear" that the man in front of her was the one who raped her. When Dolly "said she did not like to swear that day," her husband ordered her to. Once involved, husbands expected their wives to follow through on their accusations of rape. Women could provide support for a victim, read her body for evidence, and prepare her for the kinds of statements a legal complaint would entail, but, ultimately, a victim had to stand up before male family members and court officials to tell her story.[59]

Redress for sexual assault began long before a victim showed up at the courtroom doors, and the legal prosecution of rape involved more than what went on in front of male lawyers, judges, and jurors. Of crucial importance were the

58. Notes of evidence in *Respublica v Timothy Cockly, Timothy Lane, Patrick O'Hara, Thomas Marony, Michael Snoddy,* May 10, 1786, Yeates Legal Papers, May–June 1786, fol. 4, HSP. See also *Commonwealth v Boyle,* Jan. 7, 1819, Pennsylvania Court Papers, box for 1807–1809, HSP. On seventeenth-century raped women's interactions with magistrates, see Terri L. Snyder, "Sexual Consent and Sexual Coercion in Seventeenth-Century Virginia," in Smith, ed., *Sex without Consent,* 50–53.

59. Notes of evidence in *Respublica v Abraham Moses,* May 21, 1783, Yeates Legal Papers, April–May 1783, fol. 7, HSP, emphasis in original; case of Tom, Jan. 22, 1810, Virginia Executive Papers, box 164, LOV. As a free black woman, Dolly might have been more hesitant to put a black attacker at the mercy of the courts than a white victim would have been. See also *Rex v Michael Carel,* September 1724, Rhode Island General Court of Trials, Newport County File Papers, RIJRC.

extensive negotiations that preceded any direct involvement of the judicial system, negotiations governed by long-held social and cultural conventions. While many sexual assault victims hesitated before sharing details of the attack, this reluctance was more informed by the early American cultural context than by transhistoric notions of modesty or propriety. Rather than solitary decisions to endure Lucretia-like, stoic suffering, victims decided how to deal with a sexual assault within social networks. Women had a variety of options in response to a sexual attack that depended on the social positions of the victims and the attackers, the reaction of those around them, and their own perceptions of the assault.

Early American patriarchy required substantial action and influence by its female participants. By following the lines of household and social organization, sexually assaulted women gave meaning to that patriarchy. While women might comfort, corroborate, and mediate, it was men's involvement that turned the assault into a crime. Raped women, then, arrived at court in an odd position — they were the crucial players in a sexual assault prosecution, but they had already been separated from the public discourse of their victimization.

These cultural scripts also meant that race mattered in the reception of the story of a sexual assault. Beyond the hugely prejudicial treatment of African American men accused of rape, the importance of an alleged attacker's and victim's status challenged the weight of white women's words and communities. A defendant's racial status could stand in as a sign of guilt or innocence that need not be read by an experienced community of women but rather was visible to any who laid eyes on the attacker and victim. The racialization of rape would have gendered consequences for white women — both in the increased ease of some rape convictions at black men's expense and in a decreased need for women's specialized knowledge. Women might have been the unofficial gatekeepers to legal redress, but white men held the keys to the courthouse door.

CHAPTER FOUR

THE CRIME OF RAPE: TRANSATLANTIC STANDARDS, AMERICAN RACIALIZATION, AND LOCAL JUDGMENT

In 1776, Elizabeth Johnstone told a British military court about the two soldiers from the 28th Regiment who had raped her in her Long Island home. She testified that John Dunn and John Lusty entered her house, held her down, threatened to kill her, and took turns raping her in front of her four-year-old daughter. After her testimony, the court asked Elizabeth a series of questions: Was she certain that the men entered and emitted in her body? Was the attack done by force and against her consent? Did she resist with all of her power? How soon after the attack did she complain to officials? Did she have marks of violence on her body? Did she call for help as much as she could? How close was her nearest neighbor?[1]

Few observers could have doubted the guilt of the two Johns. Witnesses in the house corroborated Elizabeth's story, and two other soldiers immediately captured the attackers and brought them, still "very much in liquor," to military officials. Indeed, both soldiers were court-martialed and executed. Regardless of the strength of this case, though, the court's pointed questions were meant to test the veracity of Elizabeth's claim of rape. Such questions institutionalized cultural doubts about women's claims of rape and formed the cornerstone of transatlantic legal standards for rape.[2]

Major seventeenth- and eighteenth-century British legal scholars and the eighteenth- and early-nineteenth-century American legal guidebooks that built on their opinions emphasized the difficulty in proving the crime of rape and the consequent need for detailed circumstantial evidence independent of women's accusations. Local lawmakers learned of procedural opinions from these

1. Trial of John Dunn and John Lusty, Sept. 7, 1776, WO 71/82, 405–406, 413–415, TNA:PRO.

2. Ibid.

popular justice of the peace manuals. Meant to provide legal information to often uneducated local justices of the peace, such publications presented anywhere from a few sentences to a few pages on the treatment of each type of criminal and civil litigation. For rape, some simply specified its standards, and others provided detailed histories of its punishment alongside sample indictment forms.[3]

British law provided the skeleton on which early American society framed its punishment of rape. Rape had undergone a series of transformations in medieval and early modern Britain. At the beginning of British colonization in America, rape was firmly established as a capital crime for both England and its colonies. As a capital crime, rape was tried in each colony's superior (that is, highest) court or in specially called courts of oyer and terminer. Once capital punishment came under moral attack after the Revolutionary era, a rape conviction no longer necessarily led to a death sentence but still consistently received some of the stiffest punishments allowed. The expanded and revised penal codes in the early Republic even began treating attempted rape as a separate statutory crime with its own set of regulated punishments.[4]

Yet the most distinctive modification of the British treatment of rape was its racialization, which occurred in two main stages of institutional legal development. First, Americans' attention to rape and attempted rape as acts of slave rebellion put a decidedly colonialist spin on rape. In the early eighteenth

3. On the popularity of such legal manuals, see William Hamilton Bryson, *Census of Law Books in Colonial Virginia* (Charlottesville, Va., 1978), esp. xiv–xvii. I have traced these legal trends in more than thirty justice of the peace manuals printed in America before 1820.

4. Originally a capital crime, rape then became a high misdemeanor, with a rapist punished by the loss of his eyes and castration. In 1275, Edward I reduced the punishment for a rape to a trespass, subject to two years' imprisonment, but in 1285, rape was made a felony again. In 1576, Elizabeth I set the age of consent at ten years old and excluded rape from the benefit of clergy. For contemporary summaries of the history of the British law of rape, see Matthew Hale, *Pleas of the Crown: A Methodical Summary* (1678; rpt. London, 1972), 117; William Blackstone, *Blackstone's Commentaries on the Laws of England* (Philadelphia, 1803), IV, chap. 15, 212; Robert Chambers, *A Course of Lectures on the English Law Delivered at the University of Oxford, 1767–1773*, ed. Thomas M. Curley, 2 vols. (Madison, Wis., 1986), I, 404–407. For a modern discussion of British legal developments, see Antony E. Simpson, "Vulnerability and the Age of Female Consent: Legal Innovation and Its Effect on Prosecutions for Rape in Eighteenth-Century London," in G. S. Rousseau and Roy Porter, eds., *Sexual Underworlds of the Enlightenment* (Chapel Hill, N.C., 1988), 182–185. On the shift away from capital punishment, see Louis P. Masur, *Rites of Execution: Capital Punishment and the Transformation of American Culture* (New York, 1989).

century, black and enslaved men began to be singled out for separate punishments in sexual attacks on white women in most colonies outside of New England. Second, what had begun as New England legal exceptionalism in the colonial period would become statutory distinctions between northern and southern slave systems in the new United States. Statutory shifts in the early Republic's treatment of white criminals eliminated the threat of a death penalty for most white rapists and increased the racialization of rape.

This examination of law and legal opinions relates to formal charges of rapes and attempted rapes, yet much of the story of sexual coercion is missed if we focus only on those acts that fell under the criminal category of rape. Local community courts regularly addressed incidents of possible sexual coercion that did not qualify as the crime of rape. Thus, the final section of this chapter examines a decade of a lower court's prosecutions of sexual coercion. The very seriousness of rape law meant that community members might hesitate to prosecute a sexual attack as a life-and-death matter. Instead, they used an array of lesser charges that still allowed for some punishment of acts of sexual coercion.

Together, these approaches paint a picture of laws that made rape a serious crime alongside a court system that found multiple ways to minimize its prosecution against certain male subjects or citizens. The racialization of rape law created a two-tiered system that allowed flexibility in local prosecutions of free community members while mandating exceptionally harsh treatment of enslaved men. Rather than a simple listing of statutes or a quantitative study of formal charges of rape, this chapter explores both the law and the legalities of rape in early America. Beyond transatlantic inheritances and the linear history of statutory law, the multiple forms in which sexual attacks intersected with American criminal justice systems show how the cultural meanings of rape were institutionalized into law.[5]

TRANSATLANTIC INFLUENCES ON THE DETERMINATION
OF RAPE

The common-law definition of rape was seemingly straightforward. In the early eighteenth century, William Hawkins's *Treatise of the Pleas of the Crown*, a major authority on British law, defined rape as "unlawful and carnal Knowl-

5. For a theoretical construction of legalities v. law, see Christopher Tomlins, "The Many Legalities of Colonization: A Manifesto of Destiny for Early American Legal History," introduction in Tomlins and Bruce H. Mann, eds., *The Many Legalities of Early America* (Chapel Hill, N.C., 2001), esp. 2–3.

edge of a Woman, by Force and against her Will." American jurists, statutes, and justice of the peace manuals were still using this basic definition through the early nineteenth century. Early American lawmakers also agreed, virtually unanimously, with the British statute that set ten as the age of consent, meaning that for girls under ten years old, a successful rape prosecution did not depend on whether she had consented. Americans likewise adopted the British custom that men needed to be fourteen years of age to be found guilty of a rape because at an age less than fourteen "the law supposes an imbecility of body as well as mind."[6]

The most significant legal statement on the adjudication of rape cases was a cautionary note that Sir Matthew Hale, lord chief justice of England, proposed in his *Historia Placitorum Coronae* and writers, lawyers, and judges reiterated throughout Britain and America. Hale wrote that rape "is an accusation easily to be made and hard to be proved, and harder to be defended by the party

6. William Hawkins, *A Treatise of the Pleas of the Crown* . . . (1724–1726; rpt. New York, 1972), I, 108. For examples of this common formulation, see *[Massachusetts] Act and Laws* . . . (Boston, 1697), 235; Samuel Chew, *The Speech of Samuel Chew, Esq.* . . . (Philadelphia, 1741), 14; James Parker, comp., *Conductor Generalis* . . . (Woodbridge, N.J., 1764), 360; William Simpson, *The Practical Justice of the Peace of South-Carolina* (1761; rpt. New York, 1972), 207. On the persistence of statutory law, see Faith H. Biggs, "Rape Law in Massachusetts: Our Puritan Forbearers and Other Cultural Remnants," *New England Law Review*, XXII (1987), 93. For ten as the age of consent, see *Conductor Generalis; or, The Office, Duty, and Authority of Justices of the Peace* . . . (Philadelphia, 1722), 194; George Webb, *The Office and Authority of a Justice of Peace* . . . (Williamsburg, Va., 1736), 260; William Simpson, *The Practical Justice of the Peace of South-Carolina*, 207; James Parker, comp., *Conductor Generalis; or The Office, Duty and Authority of Justices of the Peace* . . . (New York, 1788), 358.

Although modern thinking views incest as a type of sexual assault, early American incest statutes more often appeared under acts to regulate marriage. On the incest statutes, see Cornelia Hughes Dayton, *Women before the Bar: Gender, Law, and Society in Connecticut, 1639–1789* (Chapel Hill, N.C., 1995), 274; Albert Stillman Batchellor, ed., *Laws of New Hampshire* . . . , 10 vols. (Manchester, N.H., 1904–1922), II, 124–125; John D. Cushing, ed., *The Earliest Printed Laws of Pennsylvania, 1681–1713* (Wilmington, Del., 1978), 41; *Acts and Laws of the State of Connecticut in America* (Hartford, Conn., 1805), 286–287.

On fourteen as the age of criminal responsibility, see John Haywood, comp., *The Duty and Authority of Justices of the Peace, in the State of Tennessee* (Nashville, 1810), 67; Nathaniel Pope, *Laws of the Territory of Illinois* . . . , 2 vols. (Kaskaskia, Ill., 1815), 106; William S. Pennington, comp., *Laws of the State of New-Jersey* (Trenton, N.J., 1821), 246. For this holding in a British context, see Matthew Hale, *Historia Placitorum Coronae*, 2 vols. (London, 1736), II, 730.

accused, tho never so innocent." In other words, Hale contended that women would easily charge a man with rape, and, although proving that a rape had occurred might be difficult, Hale's sympathies lay with the problems the accused would face in defending himself. Justice of the peace manuals regularly reprinted Hale's conclusion, often alongside stories of men who had been mistakenly convicted of rape.[7]

To protect men from these difficult-to-defend-against rape prosecutions, Hale proposed specific criteria to evaluate the credibility of a woman's rape claim. Hale maintained that "the credibility of [the victim's] testimony, and how far forth she is to be believed must be left to the jury, and is more or less credible according to the circumstances of fact that concur in that testimony." Hale's "circumstances of fact" to bolster or destroy the victim's credibility were a series of interpretations about the woman's actions during and after the incident:

> If she presently discovered the offence, and made pursuit after the offender; shewed circumstances and signs of the injury . . . if the place, wherein the fact was done, was remote from people, inhabitants or passengers; . . . these, and the like, are concurring evidences to give greater probability to her testimony, when proved by others as well as herself.
>
> But, on the other side, if she concealed the injury for any considerable time . . . and she made no outcry when the fact was supposed to be done, when and where it is probable she might be heard by others . . . these and the like circumstances carry a strong presumption, that her testimony is false or feigned.[8]

These paragraphs gave legal standing to the cultural doubt about women's claims of rape. As Americans began to publish more elaborate justice of the peace manuals in the second half of the eighteenth century, many reprinted

7. Hale, *Historia Placitorum Coronae,* II, 635. For manuals that included this statement by a "very learned judge and a good man," see John Haywood, *The Duty and Office of Justices of Peace . . . of North Carolina* (Halifax, N.C., 1800), 197; Lewis Kerr, *An Exposition of the Criminal Laws of the Territory of Orleans . . .* (New Orleans, 1806), 42; Parker, comp., *Conductor Generalis* (1764), 361; *A New Conductor Generalis . . .* (Albany, N.Y., 1803), 391; William Waller Hening, *The New Virginia Justice . . .* (Richmond, Va., 1795), 358. For stories of mistaken convictions, see Haywood, *Justices of Peace of North Carolina,* 197; *A New Conductor Generalis* (1803), 391.

8. Hale, *Historia Placitorum Coronae,* II, 633. These paragraphs additionally mentioned whether the complainant was "of good fame" and whether a defendant had acted guilty. Questions of women's reputations will be discussed in Chapter 5.

complete paragraphs from Hale's *Historia Placitorum Coronae*. Hale's standards of evidence and cautionary advice would be repeated in courtrooms well into the nineteenth century and beyond (a televised rape trial in 2003 featured a defense lawyer paraphrasing Hale's warning about the difficulty of defending an innocent man from rape in his closing argument). Hale gave jurists specific means to corroborate or dispute a woman's claim of sexual attack: Did she quickly report the offense? Did she try to call for help? Could others have heard her resistance? Was she physically injured? Rather than believe a woman's charge of rape unless it were proved false, Hale suggested that her accusation was suspect until she could prove otherwise. These questions allowed jurors to decrease their reliance on the complaining woman's word in favor of a set of seemingly objective social behaviors.[9]

First and foremost, a woman needed to scream for help to show that she had resisted a man's sexual overtures. When Patience Matthewson charged a man with rape in Rhode Island in 1769, she was asked, "Did you call aloud for Assistance?" She answered, "I did hallow for help, but he soon stopped my mouth and prevented my hallowing as much as he could." Patience's preemptive answer suggests that she knew that courts regularly expected women to have signified their nonconsent by screaming for assistance. The first question

9. For reprints of Hale, see William Graydon, *The Justices and Constables Assistant . . .* (Harrisburg, Pa., 1805), 335; Parker, comp., *Conductor Generalis* (1764), 361; Parker, comp., *Conductor Generalis* (1788), 359; [Richard Burn], *Burn's Abridgment; or, The American Justice . . .* , 2d ed. (Dover, N.H., 1792), 338; François X. Martin, *The Office and Authority of a Justice of the Peace . . . of North Carolina* (New Bern, N.C., 1804), 267–268; John E. Hall, *The Office and Authority of a Justice of the Peace in the State of Maryland* (Baltimore, 1815), 173.

For lawyers' discussions of Hale, see *Report of the Trial of Henry Bedlow, for Committing a Rape on Lanah Sawyer* (New York, 1793), 20, 30–33; *Report of the Trial of Ephraim Wheeler for a Rape Committed on the Body of Betsy Wheeler, His Daughter, a Girl Thirteen Years of Age . . .* (Stockbridge, Mass., 1805), 20; *Report of the Trial of Richard D. Croucher, on an Indictment for a Rape on Margaret Miller; on Tuesday, the 8th Day of July, 1800* (New York, 1800), 12–13; *Report of the Trials of Stephen Murphy and John Doyle before the Supreme Judicial Court at Dedham, Oct. 23, 1817* (Boston, 1817), 9, 13; *Commonwealth v Taylor,* Jan. 8, 1812, Pennsylvania Court Papers, HSP; petitions for Andrew, 1793, Governor and Council, Pardon Papers, box 6, folder 54, MdSA; file of Jacob Azzett Lewis, Mar. 12, 1802, Governor's Council, Pardon Papers, MA. On Hale's standards, see David Lanham, "Hale: Misogyny and Rape," *Criminal Law Journal,* VII (1983), 156–160. For the modern use of Hale, see *People v Hugo Alcazar,* San Diego, October 2002, on *Crime and Punishment,* NBC, July 6, 2003.

defense lawyers posed to Rebecca Fay at an 1810 trial was whether she had cried for help. Not crying out could provide justification for an acquittal, especially if the attack had occurred in a place where screams might have alerted others to a woman's need for help. Several witnesses testified for the defense at a rape trial in 1793 that they had been in the house where the supposed rape occurred and heard no screams. A witness in a South Carolina rape case in 1799 testified that he did not hear "any cries from [the victim] as if solliciting assistance." Judges, too, advised juries that a woman's screams could help prove her true resistance, and humorous stories of false rape charges repeatedly exposed the victim's duplicity by showing that she had not really cried for help during sexual relations. Rather than a sign of fear, shock, or physical restraint, courts interpreted a woman's not crying out for help as a sign of her consent to sexual relations.[10]

A woman's cries not only signified her lack of full-fledged consent to her attacker but also signaled to anyone within shouting distance her complete resistance. Accordingly, Hale made the location of the attack ("if the place, wherein the fact was done, was remote from people, inhabitants or passengers") another determinant of the likely truthfulness of a woman's claim. Thus, a witness at Joseph Dudley's Connecticut rape trial in 1767 reported measuring the distance from the field where the attack supposedly took place to the nearest house and shop; he even squatted down to determine whether there was a clear view to the house. In an 1805 case, the attorney general assured the jury that the wooded area where the rape was said to have occurred was indeed private enough to perpetrate such a crime. In 1812, a victim testified explicitly that "there were no homes near where he threw me down." Conversely, a

10. *Rex v Benjamin Smith,* Sept. 3, 1769, Providence County Superior Court File Papers, RIJRC; *Trial of Charles Wakely, for a Rape on Mrs. Rebecca Fay* (New York, 1810), 6 (for similar questioning, see *Report of the Trial of Richard D. Croucher,* 5–9); *Report of the Trial of Henry Bedlow,* 14–15; *State v Samuel Casey,* August 1799, Pinckney District General Sessions Court, Sessions Rolls, no. 25, SCDAH. See also *The People v George Bowman,* July 24, 1798, New York County Court of General Sessions Indictment Papers, NYMA; *The People v Grant Cottle,* Aug. 15, 1800, ibid., reel 4, folder for Oct. 9, 1800; *D. v Patrick Kennedy et al.,* 1771, Pennsylvania Court of Oyer and Terminer Court Papers, RG–33, box 2, PSA. For judges' comments to juries on the necessity of a victim's cries for help, see *Commonwealth v Taylor,* Jan. 8, 1812, Pennsylvania Court Papers, HSP; *Report of the Trial of Ephraim Wheeler,* 73. For false rape stories, see Gottlieb Mittelberger, *Journey to Pennsylvania in the Year 1750 and Return to Germany in the Year 1754,* ed. and trans. Oscar Handlin and John Clive (Cambridge, Mass., 1960), 38–39; *Bickerstaff's Genuine Massachusetts, Rhodeisland, and Connecticut Almanack, for . . . 1791* (Boston, [1790]), 24.

defense lawyer in a 1797 case tried to convince the jury that a man would not likely have raped a girl in a house where others might walk in and discover them. These testimonies tried to adjudge the coercive degree of a sexual act by determining whether the woman could have received assistance from others. Rapes were most believable if they occurred outside the physical bounds of protective intervention of family and communities.[11]

Complaining immediately after a rape (in Hale's words, "if she presently discovered the offence") could be another crucial determinant of a woman's credibility. Connecticut incorporated the requirement that "complaint be made forthwith" into its 1702 rape statute, and justice of the peace manuals throughout the colonies frequently concurred with that idea. From the court's perspective, a woman who complained immediately after an attack showed that she knew the wrong done to her and that malicious relatives or her own hurt feelings about a romance gone awry had not unduly influenced her. By the time they appeared in court (if not before), assaulted women seemed to know the importance of their immediate complaint. Witnesses who testified in a Connecticut case in 1706 clarified that the victim had gone to town to bring charges against her attacker the day after the attack, but illness and inclement weather had prevented her from actually filing her complaint. In 1781, Anna Grubb testified that, after telling her aunt she had been raped, "They then Imediately went and got the Constable." In 1810, Elizabeth Vickers testified that she went "in as Short a time [as] it could be effected and lodged information before a Magistrate of the attempt made by Ben to commit a rape on her." Even though many sexual assaults came to the attention of legal authorities after the mediation of other women, a victim's immediate recourse to law indicated a more believable accusation to judges and juries.[12]

11. Testimony of Thomas Willcox, Oct. 27, 1767, Connecticut Superior Court Record Book, XVIII, misc. leaves at the back, CSL; *Report of the Trial of Ephraim Wheeler,* 58; *Commonwealth v Taylor,* Jan. 8, 1812, Pennsylvania Court Papers, HSP; *The Trial of Nathaniel Price: For Committing a Rape on the Body of Unice Williamson, a Child between 10 and 11 Years of Age, at Brooklyn in King's County, in May 1797* . . . (New York, [1797]), 6–7. See also *D. v Joe,* n.d., Kent County Oyer and Terminer File Papers, DPA.

12. An Act for the Punishing of Capital Offenders, *Acts and Laws, of His Majesties Colony of Connecticut in New-England* (Boston, 1702), 12; case of Joseph Mallery, 1706, Connecticut Archives, Crimes and Misdemeanors, 1st Ser., I, 236, 405–433, CSL; *Commonwealth v Long and Wilson,* May 1781, Pennsylvania Court of Oyer and Terminer Court Papers, RG–33, box 4, PSA; case of Ben, Aug. 7, 1810, Virginia Executive Papers, box 168, 2 docs., LOV. For manuals discussing timely complaint, see James Davis, *The Office and Authority of a Justice of Peace* (New Bern, N.C., 1774), 286; *A New Conductor Generalis* (1803), 390;

Prosecutors, judges, and defendants repeatedly focused on the speed with which a woman had leveled her complaint. One prosecutor specified in his opening statement in a 1781 trial that the victim had immediately gone to the justice of the peace with her accusation while the blood and bruises on her body were still fresh. Conversely, defendants might convincingly use a victim's delayed complaint as justification for an acquittal or commutation of a sentence. In 1769, a Virginia court still convicted a slave of rape but gave him a much lighter sentence than usual, citing the woman's delay in lodging her complaint. When John Dolbe's mother-in-law accused him of raping her in 1774, the court dismissed him with a stiff warning because she "did not make hir complaint so soon as she aught." In an indictment filed two months after an 1809 rape, the attorney general added the note, "NB: This complaint was made immediately after the fact was committed but the Atty Genl has mislaid the affidavit," ostensibly to ensure that the delay in filing charges would not be held against the victim. Despite the mediation by communities of women that often preceded formal charges against an assailant, the law expected raped women to act immediately, and this discrepancy between customary practices and legal expectations further undermined many women's claims of rape.[13]

The law did recognize the need for women's communities in testifying to the physical damage done by a rape. Hale stated that many of the signs of sexual injury "are of that nature, that only women are the most proper examiners and inspectors." Women might also testify to the physical damage they saw on victims' bodies. Witnesses reported bruised throats from strangula-

---

Hening, *The New Virginia Justice*, 356; Martin, *The Office and Authority of a Justice of the Peace of North Carolina*, 267; Graydon, *The Justices and Constables Assistant*, 335; Hall, *The Office and Authority of a Justice of the Peace in Maryland*, 173.

13. John A. Graham, *Speeches Delivered at the City-Hall of the City of New-York, in the Courts of Oyer and Terminer, Common Pleas and General Sessions of the Peace* (New York, 1812), 87–91; trial of Will, Apr. 10, 1769, Bedford County Order Book, reel 39, 516, LOV, in printed page nos. (92 in originals); petition for divorce of Patience Dolbe, September 1774, Scituate Superior Court File Papers, RIJRC; *The People v Charles Wakely*, Feb. 12, 24, 1810, New York County Court of General Sessions Indictment Papers, 1790–1820, NYMA. See also *Report of the Trial of Henry Bedlow*, 61; Laurel Thatcher Ulrich, *A Midwife's Tale: The Life of Martha Ballard, Based on Her Diary, 1785–1812* (New York, 1991), 123. For defendants' arguing for pardons or commutation specifically on the basis of a delayed complaint, see case of John Ely, November 1804, Connecticut Archives, Crimes and Misdemeanors, 2d Ser., I, 146, CSL; *State v David Marvin*, January 1811, New Haven Superior Court Criminal Files, box 598, CSL; *The People v William Van Tassell*, Feb. 8, 1800, New York County Court of General Sessions Indictment Papers, NYMA.

tion attempts and other assorted injuries and cuts. One female neighbor testified that the day after Ruth Stufflemine's rape in 1800, Ruth had "upon her arms the marks of four fingers, . . . that her body was much bruised. her left Cheek . . . her shoulders were bruised, her breast scratched, her loins bruised, and her left thigh." Visible physical injuries minimized the possibility that a woman had willingly engaged in sexual relations that she now regretted and charged as a rape.[14]

Although legal scholars agreed that the physical body provided crucial evidence of rape, they did not agree on how to read the sexual and reproductive natures of forced sex. British scholars forwarded contradictory claims on the role of emission in rape prosecutions. William Hawkins stated, "No Assault upon a Woman in order to ravish her, howsoever shameless and outrageous it may be, if it proceed not to some Degree of Penetration, and also of Emission, can amount to a Rape." But Hale directly challenged Hawkins, contending that "the least penetration meaketh it rape or buggery, yea although there be not *emissio seminis*." These opposing opinions reflected some of the most fundamental questions about rape: Was rape a crime of ruined chastity, or of possible impregnation? Should it be determined by the immediate act done to the woman (penetration) or by a man's standards of sexual completion (emission)? Perhaps because there was no clear consensus in answering such questions, many justice of the peace manuals, both the relatively succinct early-eighteenth-century manuals and some of the more expansive nineteenth-century ones, bypassed a discussion of emission and penetration altogether. Only four of the more than thirty manuals I examined explicitly discussed emission, and all four adopted Hawkins's claim that "some Degree of Penetration, and also . . . [of] Emission" was necessary for a rape.[15]

14. Hale, *Historia Placitorum Coronae,* II, 633; deposition of Hannah Boyles, in Justice Powell's Report from Mt. Dorchester, Sept. 22, 1800, Civil Secretary, Correspondence, Upper Canada and West Upper Canadian Sundries, 508, NAC. For other examples of physical injuries caused by rape attempts, see *Rex v Cuff,* March 1743, Rhode Island Superior Court of Judicature, Newport County Records, C, 127–128, RIJRC; *Aurora: General Advertiser* (Philadelphia), Aug. 25, 1796; *Pennsylvania Gazette* (Philadelphia), Nov. 10–13, 1729; *Virginia Gazette* (Williamsburg), Oct. 27, 1738. On the "seemingly unshakeable association of rape with physically violent misconduct," see Stephen J. Schulhofer, "Taking Sexual Autonomy Seriously: Rape Law and Beyond," *Law and Philosophy: An International Journal for Jurisprudence and Legal Philosophy,* XI (1992), 35.

15. Hawkins, *A Treatise of the Pleas of the Crown,* I, 108; Hale, *Historia Placitorum Coronae,* I, 628; Richard Starke, *The Office and Authority of a Justice of Peace, Explained and Digested, under Proper Titles* (Williamsburg, Va., 1774), 292. See also Hening, *The New*

All legal commentators agreed with Hale that rape involved, at the very least, the crime of penetration of a vagina by a penis — the modern concept of sexual battery by an object other than a penis had no place in early American courts. Accordingly, courts could not charge rape or attempted rape for violent sexual assaults that did not include penile penetration. In 1769, a Massachusetts court charged three men only with lewdness for their assault on Pegge Keen when they "exposed her secret parts to open views" and "violently plucked out much of the hair." A Pennsylvania court charged Barney Boyle with raping nine-year-old Alice Workenson after she was found with streams of blood running down her legs in 1819, but when Alice testified at the trial that Barney had only "hurt me with his thumb," the prosecution reduced the charge to attempted rape. The judge in the case then told the jury that Barney could only be guilty of attempted rape if he had "inserted his finger with a view of enlarging the orefice, in order afterwards to have carnal knowledge of her." In other words, a sexual assault could not be an attempted rape unless sexual intercourse were the clear objective.[16]

By the nineteenth century, lawmakers and commentators seemed to be moving away from emission as a necessary proof of rape; penile penetration was sufficient. In 1805, *The Laws of the Indiana Territory* repealed the previous laws "regulating the evidence in case of a rape, as makes emission necessary." An Indiana legislative committee had found that "proof of penetration ought to [be] sufficient to convict" because proof of emission "can very rarely be obtained unless at the risque of perjury." A review of Kentucky criminal laws in the same year stated that the least degree of penetration was a rape, "although there be no seminal emission." In 1806, a Pennsylvania lawyer rhetorically asked, "If the *Emission* be in the body, and it be necessary to constitute these

---

Virginia Justice, 355; *A New Conductor Generalis* (1803), 389; *A New Conductor Generalis . . .* (Albany, N.Y., 1819), 394. For the absence of emission and penetration discussions, see *Conductor Generalis* (1722), 193–194; Davis, *The Office and Authority of a Justice of Peace*, n.p.; Hall, *The Office and Authority of a Justice of the Peace in Maryland*, 172–174; Martin, *The Office and Authority of a Justice of the Peace of North Carolina*, 266–268; Parker, comp., *Conductor Generalis* (1764), 360–361; Simpson, *The Practical Justice of the Peace of South-Carolina*, 207–208.

16. Case of Joshua Ransom et al., December 1769, in David Thomas Konig, ed., *Plymouth Court Records, 1686–1859*, 16 vols. (Wilmington, Del., 1978–1981), III, *1748–1751*, 285, 293; *Commonwealth v Boyle*, Jan. 7, 1819, Pennsylvania Court Papers, box for 1807–1809, HSP. On the late-twentieth-century shift to gradations of sexual battery, see Leigh Bienen, "Rape III — National Developments in Rape Reform Legislation," *Women's Rights Law Reporter*, VI (1979–1980), 170–213.

offenses, how can [rape] be proved?" In the 1820s, one of the early medical jurisprudence treatises published in America devoted five pages to a discussion of the necessity of emission as proof of rape, concluding that "it is objectionable to insist on this proof" because women "may not be sensible" of emission during a rape. Two editions of *Digest of the Laws of Virginia* show the developing acceptance of penetration as sufficient proof of rape. In the 1823 edition, an 1820 rape law made no mention of penetration or emission, but a footnote to that same law in the 1841 edition clarified that, "if *penetration* be proved, the offence is complete, without proof of *emissio seminis*." In commentaries and statutes, emission as a necessary criterion for rape seemed to be falling out of favor in the nineteenth century.[17]

Yet legal *practice* did not follow such a straightforward pattern. Only a few rape cases seemed to explicitly hinge on emission versus penetration. I found no debate on the necessity of emission in eighteenth-century rape cases. Colonial rape cases generally required women to provide the formulaic language that a man had carnal knowledge of her, complete with penetration but without specification of emission. In a 1724 rape prosecution in Rhode Island, Mary Phalet testified that Michael Carel had "penetrate[d] in a violent manner so as to have compleat and carnal knowledge" of her body. Other women testified that men had had carnal knowledge of them "by actuall Penetration" or, more commonly, that "he entered her Body."[18]

17. Francis S. Philbrick, ed., *The Laws of the Indiana Territory, 1801–1809*, Collections of the Illinois State Historical Library, XXI (Springfield, Ill., 1930), 118; Gayle Thornbrough and Dorothy Riker, eds., *Journals of the General Assembly of Indiana Territory, 1805–1815*, Indiana Historical Collection (Indianapolis, 1950), 52–53; Harry Toulmin and James Blair, *A Review of the Criminal Law of the Commonwealth of Kentucky*, 3 vols. (1804; Holmes Beach, Fla., 1983), I, 130. See also Kerr, *An Exposition of the Criminal Laws of the Territory of Orleans*, 38; C. J. Tilghman, "Definition of Crimes in 1806 or After," Pennsylvania Court Papers, box 6 (Tyson-Yard and Misc. Papers), 8, HSP, emphasis in original; Theodoric Romeyn Beck, *Elements of Medical Jurisprudence* (Albany, N.Y., 1823), 95–99; Act of Feb. 8, 1819–Jan. 1, 1820, in Joseph Tate, *Digest of the Laws of Virginia* . . . (Richmond, Va., 1823), 127; Tate, *Digest of the Laws of Virginia* (Richmond, Va., 1841), 212. See also Pope, *Laws of the Territory of Illinois*, 106. On the nineteenth-century shift away from emission requirements, see Stephen Robertson, "Signs, Marks, and Private Parts: Doctors, Legal Discourses, and Evidence of Rape in the United States, 1823–1930," *Journal of the History of Sexuality*, VIII (1998), 353–355.

18. *Rex v Michael Carel*, September 1724, Rhode Island General Court of Trials, Newport County File Papers, RIJRC; *Rex v John Green*, September 1736, Hartford County Superior Court Files, box 83, CSL; *Rex v Cuff*, September 1748, New Haven Superior

In the early Republic, court documents still emphasized penetration but more often began to include mention of emission. Occasional rape victims were probably encouraged to use the formulaic legal language that an attacker had, as Juriah Young testified in 1817, "raped her by penetration and emission." Sometimes lawyers asked victims if the man had ejaculated during the assault. During a cross-examination in an 1818 New York case, one woman answered that "he made her all wet." Not surprisingly, defense lawyers were more likely to claim the necessity of emission in the hopes of acquittals for their clients. In an 1812 case, one defense lawyer emphasized in his closing statement that "there s[houl]d be Emmission, as well as Penetration" to prove a rape. Penetration alone might have no longer been considered sufficient to convict a man of rape. In an 1801 case, the court charged a defendant with *attempted* rape even though the victim testified that he "had Entered her Body." Such language implicitly forwarded emission as a necessary proof of rape.[19]

Still, legal officials in the early Republic did not agree on the importance of emission to rape. Local jurists advanced multiple opinions on the matter. In

---

Court Files, drawer 327 (record book missing), CSL. For other statements that sexual attackers had "entered" a woman's body, see *Rex v Jack,* September 1743, Hartford County Superior Court Files, box 86, CSL; case of Vanskelly Mully, August 1760, Connecticut Archives, Crimes and Misdemeanors, 1st Ser., V, 144–146, CSL; exam of Polly, in *State v James Rook,* 1788, New Jersey Supreme Court Actions-at-Law, no. 37902, NJSL; *D. v Joe,* n.d., Kent County Oyer and Terminer File Papers, DPA.

19. For court discussions that show the necessity of penetration, see case of Dick, Nov. 19, 1808, Virginia Executive Papers, box 157, LOV; *Commonwealth v Boyle,* Jan. 7, 1819, Pennsylvania Court Papers, box for 1807–1809, HSP; case of Anthony, Sept. 15, 1817, Virginia Executive Papers, box 241, LOV; *The People v Charles Carpenter,* Nov. 13, 1818, New York County Court of General Sessions Indictment Papers, NYMA; *Commonwealth v Taylor,* Jan. 8, 1812, Pennsylvania Court Papers, HSP; *State v Mark Boston,* September 1801, Hartford County Superior Court Files, drawer 31, CSL. For courts-martial cases that discussed whether a defendant emitted, see trial of Thomas Higgins, July 17, 1760, WO 71/46, 306–308, TNA:PRO; trial of McClear, Hunter, and Lyons, September 1761, WO 71/71, 5–8, ibid.; trial of John Wilson, July 18, 1781, WO 71/94, 255–256, ibid. For statements on emission, see case of Mulatto Jesse, Aug. 6, 1804, Virginia Executive Papers, box 131, LOV. For a court's statement that specified emission and penetration in a rape charge, see *Crown v Harry,* July 1740, Secretary of State Court Records, Magistrates and Freeholders Courts, 1740–1886, Miscellaneous, SS311, NCSA. For a British-Canadian prosecution that dismissed the need for "technical evidence of the rape," see Justice Powell's Report from Mt. Dorchester, Sept. 22, 1800, Civil Secretary, Correspondence, Upper Canada and West Upper Canadian Sundries, 502–512, NAC.

1793, a Pennsylvania appellate court found only penetration necessary to prove a rape, concluding that the harm of rape is "the violence done to the person and feeling of the woman, which is completed by penetration without emission." This decision was unique in suggesting that the damage of rape was an attack on a woman, perhaps reflecting Pennsylvania's more egalitarian Quaker heritage, the Revolutionary rhetoric on individual rights, and the growing value given to emotions. Other courts concurred with the Pennsylvania opinion; an 1813 southern appellate court likewise found emission not necessary to prove a rape. Perhaps judges thought that emission relied too heavily on a woman's unsubstantiated testimony: female examiners might be able to detect the presence of seminal fluid, but it was likely that only the victim could know whether the attacker had emitted inside or outside her body. Nevertheless, in 1808, fifteen years after the Pennsylvania appellate decision, another Pennsylvania judge instructed the jury that it was the "opinion of Court, that Emission as well as penetration is necessary." Scholars' opposing stands on emission carried over to courtroom practice, where American jurists expressed opposed positions on the need for emission in rape cases.[20]

The confusion about emission might have also related to shifting understandings of reproductive physiology: could rape result in conception? Pregnancy proved penetration and most likely emission, but an early modern belief that conception required a woman's orgasm meant that a pregnancy could stand for a woman's consent to an alleged rape. Notions of parallel male and female reproductive physiology encouraged the idea that women, like men, had to reach orgasm to create new life. Accordingly, some British legal scholars claimed that pregnancy negated a rape, but Hawkins and Hale disagreed on both practical and philosophical levels. As Hawkins explained, "If it were necessary to shew that the Woman did not conceive, this Offender could not be tried till such Time as it might appear whether she did or not." Furthermore, Hawkins continued, "the Philosophy of this Notion [that pregnancy could not result from rape] may be very well doubted of." In the early Republic,

20. *Pennsylvania v Sullivan,* 1793, in Alexander Addison, *Reports of Cases in the County Courts of the Fifth Circuit . . . ,* 2d ed. (Philadelphia, 1883), 143; *State v LeBlanc,* 1 Treadway's Constitutional Reports (SC), 356 (1813); *Commonwealth v William Cress,* February 1808, Pennsylvania Court Papers, HSP. Cress's defense attorney, as one witness recorded, entered "minutely into question of Emission" during his nearly two-hour opening statement. See also trial of John Wilson, July 18, 1781, WO 71/94, TNA:PRO. On New York State's shift away from emission requirements, see Sean T. Moore, "'Justifiable Provocation': Violence against Women in Essex County, New York, 1799–1860," *Journal of Social History,* XXXV (2002), 898.

justice of the peace manuals seemed to agree that conception could occur during a rape. Still, folk beliefs persisted that a woman needed to enjoy sex (if not have an orgasm) in order for pregnancy to result. *The Experienced Midwife,* published in 1798 as a companion to the popular pseudonymous *Works of Aristotle,* claimed that "there never follows a conception on a rape" because conception required that "their hearts as well as their bodies" be united.[21]

In the post-Revolutionary period, medical experts entered the controversy about whether women could become pregnant without consenting to sex. In his 1788 publication, Samuel Farr claimed, "If an absolute rape were to be perpetrated, it is not likely that she would become pregnant," suggesting that at least some degree of sexual force could still lead to conception. In 1823, Theodoric Beck presented a different kind of argument gleaned from European medical discourse. He claimed that fright could cause an orgasm "sufficient to induce the required state, although the will itself is not consenting." Women's wombs might consent to rape and impregnation even if the women themselves did not.[22]

Few colonial rape charges involved women who were impregnated from the attack. Several cases involving the forced impregnation of mentally incompetent women were addressed with charges less serious than rape, perhaps because the women could not effectively testify on their own behalf. Pregnancy

---

21. Thomas Laqueur, *Making Sex: Body and Gender from the Greeks to Freud* (Cambridge, Mass., 1990), 161–162; Hawkins, *A Treatise of the Pleas of the Crown,* I, 108; Hale, *Historia Placitorum Coronae,* I, 731; [Burn], *Burn's Abridgment,* 337; [John Faucherand Grimké], *The South-Carolina Justice of Peace . . .* (Philadelphia, 1796), 496; Aristotle, pseud., *The Works of Aristotle, the Famous Philosopher, in Four Parts* (Philadelphia, 1798), pt. 2, 78. On the eighteenth-century transformation of this belief in England, see Patricia Crawford, "Sexual Knowledge in England, 1500–1750," in Roy Porter and Mikuláš Teich, eds., *Sexual Knowledge, Sexual Science: The History of Attitudes to Sexuality* (Cambridge, 1994), 87–88. On the ideological transformation of ideas of the necessity of women's pleasure for conception, see Angus McLaren, *Reproductive Rituals: The Perception of Fertility in England from the Sixteenth Century to the Nineteenth Century* (London, 1984), 20–21, 26–27. Early Americans seemed to accept stories about Rome's original descendants' resulting from rape. See, for example, *Fables of Aesop and Others* (Philadelphia, 1777), 145.

22. Samuel Farr, *The Elements of Medical Jurisprudence . . .* (1788; London, 1815), 46; Beck, *Elements of Medical Jurisprudence,* 101. For a discussion of this in an 1825 southern rape trial, see Martha Hodes, *White Women, Black Men: Illicit Sex in the Nineteenth-Century South* (New Haven, Conn., 1997), 47–48. On the transatlantic influence on the nineteenth-century medical jurisprudence of rape, see Robertson, "Signs, Marks, and Private Parts," *Jour. of Hist. of Sex.,* VIII (1998), 351–352.

probably more often encouraged courts to try a claim of sexual assault as fornication, adultery, or bastardy — all charges where pregnancy provided proof of a criminal act. A 1728 Connecticut court acquitted a woman of fornication charges after judges determined that her impregnation was a result of force and "not . . . by her consent." A Massachusetts court illogically charged a man with the lesser charge of an attempted rape in 1755, even though the defense tried to quash the indictment on the grounds that the woman did not complain of the assault until after she was "begotten with child by him." If the woman had become pregnant with the accused's child, the two had likely had sexual intercourse, thus negating a charge of *attempted* rape.[23]

By the nineteenth century, a few American appellate cases supported the notion that women could conceive from rape. An 1820 Arkansas appellate judge gave a definitive ruling: "The old notion that if the woman conceived, it could not be a rape, because she must in such case have consented, is quite exploded." Yet most Americans did not necessarily follow judicial decrees. One New York woman involved in a bastardy case in 1808 testified that she "had a connexion" with a particular man but "was sure they had made no one young, for they *fit* [fought] all the while." For this woman, at least, conception and sexual pleasure still went hand in hand. An 1817 petition for the commutation of one Virginia rapist's sentence similarly used a pregnancy to argue for the man's innocence: petitioners suggested that the child's birth strongly urged that "the connection called a rape was by *consent*." Despite some declining beliefs that pregnancy negated a rape, conception remained, at best, an uncertain means to disprove a rape.[24]

All jurists agreed that rape was a serious crime that could cost a man his life.

---

23. Petition for Christeen Pauper, August 1734, Chester County Quarter Sessions File Papers, CCA; *State v Caesar Parker,* October 1805, Hillsborough County Superior Court Judgments, April 1805–1807, box 606113, 190–191, NHA; *Rex v George Clinton,* September 1728, New Haven County Court Files, 1720–1729, R–Y, no. 6, CSL; case of James Lindsay, 1755, in Konig, ed., *Plymouth Court Records,* III, *1748–1751,* 44, 55, 57–58. For an adultery case that resulted in pregnancy and included questioning about the woman's consent, see *Respublica v David Robb,* Yeates Legal Papers, March–April 1789, fol. 2, HSP.

24. *United States v Dickinson,* 14 Federal Cases (U.S.) 957a (1820); *The Commissioners of the Alms-House, vs. Alexander Whistelo, a Black Man; Being a Remarkable Case of Bastardy . . .* (New York, 1808), 12; case of John Holloman, October 1817, Virginia Executive Papers, box 3, LOV, emphasis in original. For a case that addressed a pregnancy resulting from a forced assault, see *Wallace v Clark,* in John Overton et al., eds., *Tennessee Reports; or, Cases Ruled and Adjudged in the Superior Courts of Law and Equity, and Federal Court and Supreme Courts of Errors and Appeals for the State of Tennessee* ([Nashville], 1809–1815), II, 93–96.

They also agreed that, as such, courts and communities should be hesitant to prosecute rape. Hale's standards reflected the general view that a woman's claim of rape had to be proved well beyond reasonable doubt before she would be believed. Accordingly, Americans repeatedly sought, though they did not always agree on, supplemental proofs of rape beyond a woman's words: a victim's cries needed to have been heard by witnesses, she needed to show signs of physical violence, and she needed to immediately recognize that she had been legally wronged and complain to others. The need for such elaborated standards (unmatched in Hale's work save for witchcraft prosecutions) foreshadowed the prosecutorial difficulties in instances of possible sexual coercion. Women needed to meet legal standards of behavior far removed from their likely experiences of and reactions to a sexual attack. Disagreements about the possible physical outcomes of a rape left further room for dispute of women's claims and legal maneuvering. Overall, rape was indeed, as Hale had predicted, a difficult crime to prove. Once the crime was proved, however, the institutional process moved on to sentencing and punishment, where Americans' racially based rape law diverged from inherited British standards.[25]

AMERICAN INTERVENTIONS: STATUTORY PUNISHMENT OF RAPE

From the time of its founding through the early nineteenth century, each colony passed at least a few laws related to rape. Most early statutes simply reiterated that rape was a capital crime, punishable by death, and some colonies enforced British common law without passing specific local statutes. Plymouth was the first colony to include rape in its list of capital crimes in 1637, followed by Rhode Island in 1647, Massachusetts Bay in 1648, Connecticut in 1672, South Carolina in 1712, and Delaware in 1719. A few colonies briefly experimented with alternative, noncapital punishments. Close to the turn of the eighteenth century, Pennsylvania mandated imprisonment and forfeiture of one's estate for first offenses of rape, but this statute was quickly repealed. Such exceptions highlighted the rule: rape was overwhelmingly treated as a capital crime throughout the colonial period. Of the seventy-three guilty verdicts in eighteenth-century colonial rape cases (1700–1776) where the sentence is known, sixty-eight resulted in a death sentence. Colonial Americans, like their British counterparts, varied little in the sentencing of convicted rapists.[26]

25. Lanham, "Hale: Misogyny and Rape," *Crim. Law Jour.,* VII (1983), 157.
26. For example, William Brigham, ed., *The Compact with the Charter and Laws of the*

After the American Revolution, individual states and territories sought to define their judicial systems apart from British common law by passing more elaborate criminal codes. Post-Revolutionary capital punishment reform efforts made the statutes pertaining to rape sentences more varied. Several New England states and northern territories continued to rely on capital punishment. Other states and territories rewrote rape into a noncapital crime. Such a shift is visible in Vermont's criminal statutes. Vermont's 1779 Act for the Punishment of Rape still mandated death, but, in 1791, its Act for the Punishment of Rape legislated a penalty of fines, imprisonment, corporal punishment, and public marking instead. By 1800, more than a half-dozen states and territories substituted incarceration for capital punishment in rape convictions — at least for free men. Incarceration time differed from state to state, generally from ten years to life.[27]

Colony of New Plymouth (1836; Buffalo, N.Y., 1986), 42–43; John Russell Bartlett, ed., Records of the Colony of Rhode Island and Providence Plantations, in New England, 10 vols. (Providence, 1856–1865), I, 173; The Book of the General Lawes and Libertyes concerning the Inhabitants of the Massachusets (1648; rpt. San Marino, Calif., 1975), 6; John D. Cushing, ed., The Earliest Laws of the New Haven and Connecticut Colonies, 1639–1673 (Wilmington, Del., 1977), 83; George Staughton et al., comps. and eds., Charter to William Penn, and Laws of the Province of Pennsylvania, Passed between the Years 1682 and 1700 . . . (Harrisburg, Pa., 1879), 110. There was at least one case prosecuted under this law: Rex v Nicholas Guatan, 1712, Philadelphia Legal Papers, 1702–1744, HSP.

The remaining noncapital convictions resulted in heavy whippings, fines, or exile. A few defendants sentenced to death ultimately received a commuted sentence or pardon. For example, in 1760, a Connecticut court sentenced Vanskelly Mully to death for a rape, but the state commuted his sentence to a severe whipping when Vanskelly claimed that, as a foreigner, he had not known rape was a capital crime. See case of Vanskelly Mully, August 1760, Connecticut Archives, Crimes and Misdemeanors; Purdie and Dixon's Vir. Gaz., Nov. 8, 1770; Penn. Gaz., Dec. 15, 1763; case of Bristo, January 1757, Connecticut Archives, Crimes and Misdemeanors, 1st Ser., V, 47–53, CSL; case of Negro Harry, November 1752, in Archives of Maryland, 72 vols. (Baltimore, 1883–1972), XXVIII, 577.

27. On punishments for rape, see Rodolphus Dickinson, A Digest of the Common Law, the Statute Laws of Massachusetts, and of the United States . . . (Deerfield, Mass., 1818), n.p.; John D. Cushing, comp. and ed., The First Laws of the State of Connecticut (Wilmington, Del., 1982), 197 (laws in effect in 1784); The Public Statute Laws of the State of Connecticut . . . (Hartford, Conn., 1821), 152; Allen Soule, ed., Laws of Vermont [1777–1780], State Papers of Vermont, XII (Montpelier, Vt., 1964), 40; John A. Williams, ed., Laws of Vermont [1791–1795], State Papers of Vermont, XV (Montpelier, Vt., 1967), 20; The Public Statute Laws of the State of Connecticut (Hartford, Conn., 1808), I, 300; Pennington, comp., Laws of the State of New-Jersey, 246; The Statutes at Large of Pennsylvania from 1682 to 1801, XV,

The partial elimination of capital punishment for rape reflected large-scale shifts in attitudes toward state-sponsored executions, not toward the crime of rape. In fact, rape continued to be one of the most harshly punished crimes. In spite of changing statutes, death sentences were still the norm for the men (mostly enslaved) who were convicted of rape after the Revolution: of 139 rape prosecutions in the early Republic (1777–1820), more than 100 led to death sentences, 21 to incarceration, and the remaining sentences included exile or corporal punishment. Even laws that set noncapital sentences for rape continued to punish the crime harshly. The 1794 Pennsylvania law that abolished capital punishment for all crimes but first-degree murder set stiffer incarceration terms for rape than for any other crime mentioned: high treason and arson could result in up to twelve years in prison, forgery up to fifteen and second-degree murder up to eighteen years, but men convicted of rape might receive up to twenty-one years in Pennsylvania jails, and some convicted rapists did receive this maximum sentence. In practice, rape sentences varied widely in the early Republic. A Pennsylvania man was sentenced to ten years for a rape in 1795, a New York man to life in 1797, a Connecticut man to seven years in 1801, a Kentucky man to ten years in 1804, and a Georgia man to four years in 1817. Because of statutory differences and judges' discretion, men might be subject to a variable range of years in prison for the crime of rape.[28]

1794–1797 (Harrisburg, Pa., 1911), 174–176; Lucius Q. C. Lamar, comp., *A Compilation of the Laws of the State of Georgia . . . 1810–1819* (Augusta, Ga., 1821), 571; John Faucherand Grimké, comp., *The Public Laws of the State of South-Carolina* (Philadelphia, 1790), 30; Peter Bardaglio, "Rape and the Law in the Old South: 'Calculated to Excite Indignation in Every Heart,'" *Journal of Southern History,* LX (1994), 755; Beck, *Elements of Medical Jurisprudence,* 95; Pope, *Laws of the Territory of Illinois,* 106; Harry Toulmin, *The Magistrates Assistant . . .* (Natchez, Miss., 1807), 172; Haywood, *The Duty and Authority of Justices of the Peace in the State of Tennessee,* 67; *Laws of the Indiana Territory . . .* (Vincennes, Ind., 1807), 35; *The Statutes at Large of Pennsylvania,* XV, *1794–1797,* 175; Toulmin and Blair, *A Review of the Criminal Law of the Commonwealth of Kentucky,* I, 129–130; Oliver H. Prince, comp., *A Digest of the Laws of Georgia . . .* (Milledgeville, Ga., 1822), 349.

28. *The Statutes at Large of Pennsylvania,* XV, *1794–1797,* 174–175; *Commonwealth v John Bergenhof et al.,* 1795, Pennsylvania Court Papers, box for 1802–1803, HSP, and Pardon Book, Oct. 23, 1795, RG–26, reel 435, 246, PSA; *Trial of Nathaniel Price,* 8; *State v Mark Boston,* September 1801, Hartford County Superior Court Files, CSL; *Commonwealth v Tomlinsons et al.,* March 1804, Fayette County Circuit Court Decided Cases, drawer 58, KLA; Robert Scott Davis, *The Georgia Black Book: Morbid, Macabre, and Sometimes Disgusting Records of Genealogical Value,* 2 vols. (Easley, S.C., 1982–1987), I, 52. For examples of maximum sentences for rape, see Henry Graham Ashmead, *History of Delaware County,*

Judges had even more discretion in attempted rape cases. As a felony, rape was prosecuted in each colony or state's highest court, but attempted rape cases might appear before a county's quarter sessions (lower court) judges or before higher court judges. In Lancaster, Pennsylvania, in November 1802, Daniel McCloskey was brought before the county's special court of oyer and terminer on a charge of assault with intent to rape; yet, six months later, James Kyle was charged with attempted rape at the Lancaster court of quarter sessions. The severity of the specific attack as well as local custom might have led neighborhood justices to seek various prosecutorial venues.[29]

In contrast to the statutory consistency for rape sentencing, colonial statutory punishments for *attempted* rape were virtually nonexistent. Some colonies passed statutes against *"lascivious carriages,"* defined by one early Connecticut statute as a *"variety of Circumstances,* [to which] *particular and express Laws cannot suddenly be suited,"* but few specified an *attempt* at forced sexual relations. Without specific statutory directions, local justices determined punishments, which varied according to local customs and the perceived seriousness of the offense. For colonial free men, punishments could include a combination of fines, time in the pillory, and whippings. In the 1750s alone, fines for attempted rape convictions ranged from a Delaware court's one-shilling fine to a Rhode Island court's one hundred–pound penalty. Between these extremes was a New Jersey court's twenty-shilling fine and a Pennsylvania court's five-pound fine. Other courts in the same decade applied a combination of punishments: a Massachusetts court levied a five-pound fine along with twenty lashes for a 1755 attempted rape conviction and an eight-pound fine without lashes for a 1758 conviction. When colonial punishments included whippings, convicts were usually given up to thirty-nine lashes, although occasionally an offender might be forced to undergo multiple sessions of lashings. Because attempted rapes could cover a wide range of sexual harm, judges used their discretion to determine an appropriate punishment.[30]

Pennsylvania (Philadelphia, 1884), 176; *Commonwealth v Robert Henderson,* May 1808, Chester County Quarter Sessions Court Docket, 122, CCA.

29. *Commonwealth v Daniel McCloskey,* November 1802, Lancaster County Oyer and Terminer Docket, 1792–1820, 118, LCHS; *Commonwealth v James Kyle,* May 1803, Lancaster County Quarter Sessions Docket, 450–451, LCHS. For similar alternative venues, see *State v Pompey,* November 1796, Hunterdon County Common Pleas Minutes, 1794–1800, XV, 433, 444, HHR; *State v Christopher Rockefeller,* September 1796, New Jersey Supreme Court Actions-at-Law, no. 37865, NJSL.

30. *The Book of the General Laws for the People within the Jurisdiction of Connecticut . . .* (Cambridge, Mass., 1673), 37; *Rex v Amos Lewis,* August 1757, Washington County Court

Laws that specified the sentence for attempted rape began appearing in the elaborated penal codes passed at the end of the eighteenth century. Vermont passed a law on attempted rape in 1791, Connecticut in 1792, and New York in 1813, and each one specified a punishment that centered on incarceration. Most states designated a range of years of imprisonment, leaving judges to determine the severity of the individual assault. In the early nineteenth century, Georgia mandated a punishment of between one and five years' incarceration at hard labor for attempted rape, and Maryland mandated two to ten years.[31]

In practice, New England states tended to impose longer prison sentences for attempted rape, perhaps as a holdover from earlier concerns with moral policing. Massachusetts, one of the few states to retain capital punishment for rape, sentenced attempted rapists to imprisonment for anywhere from one to ten years, with an average sentence of more than five years. Vermont's and New Hampshire's sentences also hovered at five years. Connecticut repeatedly sentenced men to life imprisonment (as well as to lesser sentences) for attempted rape. Pennsylvania's average sentence was three years in prison. Keeping attempted rape charges out of a colony or state's higher court might have also allowed for significantly more leniency in the sentencing process. A Maryland

------

of General Sessions of the Peace, Minute Book, RIJRC (docket page says August 1756, possible clerk's mistake); *King v Richard Jones,* March 1752, Perth Amboy Supreme Court, 170, 174, 176, NJSL; *King v Richard Jones,* 1752, New Jersey Supreme Court Actions-at-Law, no. 20888, NJSL; *D. v Thomas Brown,* August, November 1751, Chester County Quarter Sessions Court Docket, 168, 172, CCA; *D. v Andrew Opperman,* May 1753, New Castle Oyer and Terminer Docket, RG–2825, 47, DPA; case of James Lindsay, May 1754, January 1755, in Konig, ed., *Plymouth Court Records,* III, *1748–1751,* 44, 55, 57–58; case of James Studley, April 1758, ibid., 97. For a 1680 New Hampshire statute forbidding the attempting or "offering any Insolence or Violence to any Woman . . . of Despoiling them, Damnifying, or Defacing any of their Attire," see John D. Cushing, ed., *Acts and Laws of New Hampshire, 1680–1726* (Wilmington, Del., 1978), 87–88. For a sentence of three rounds of thirty-nine lashes, see *The People v John Domaine,* Nov. 1, 1766, Rough Supreme Court Minutes, n.p., NYMA. For an exceptionally harsh punishment of two hundred lashes for an attempted rape, see *Rex v Moses Tuttle,* November 1727, New Haven County Court, III, CSL.

31. *Public Statute Laws of Connecticut,* 300; *Laws of the State of New-York, Passed at the Thirty-Sixth Session of the Legislature* (Albany, N.Y., 1813), 409; Prince, comp., *A Digest of the Laws of Georgia,* 350; *The Laws of Maryland . . . [1799–1810?]* (Annapolis, Md., [1811]), III, 460. See also Dickinson, *A Digest of the Common Law,* n.p. The city of Baltimore punished attempted rape by any "free male person, or any male servant or apprentice" with seven years at labor on the public roads. See *An Appendix, to A Digest of the Law of Maryland* (Baltimore, 1799), 196.

lower court sentenced John Welsh to a ten-shilling fine for an attempted rape in 1744. In that same year, William Lyndall was fined twenty pounds by Maryland's provincial (higher) court for an attempted rape. Connecticut consistently prosecuted attempted rape at its superior court in the early Republic, which may partly explain its particularly stiff sentences for attempted rape. In contrast, southern states seemed especially reluctant to sentence free white men to long prison terms: Maryland's punishment of free men for attempted rape was generally two years, and North Carolina courts repeatedly punished free men with months instead of years in prison. The southern reluctance to sentence white men for attempted rapes hints at the racial distinctions that increasingly underlay eighteenth- and nineteenth-century rape statutes.[32]

Although statutes expressly setting the punishment for attempted rape appeared only in the post-Revolutionary era, in the first half of the eighteenth century, many colonies had set punishments specifically for slaves and blacks who attempted to rape white women. These statutes were extensive in their geographic and chronologic reach; most colonies outside of New England passed some. As early as 1705, Pennsylvania specified a punishment of thirty-nine lashes, branding, and exile for any "Negro" who attempted to rape a white woman. New York passed a law specifically targeting slaves' attempted rape of

32. Entries of convicts in the state prison, Charlestown, Mass., 1805–1818, MA; *State v Johnson Loverin,* Rockingham County Superior Court Record Book, September 1817–September 1818, 397–398, NHA; John Russel, *An Authoritative History of the Vermont State Prison* . . . (Windsor, Vt., 1812), 25; *State v Moses Johnson,* August 1794, Fairfield County Superior Court Files, 1790–1799, A–K, box 625, CSL; case of John Ely, November 1804, Connecticut Archives, Crimes and Misdemeanors, 2d Ser., I, 99n, 109, 119, 990, IV, 135–136, CSL; C. Ashley Ellefson, *The County Courts and the Provincial Court in Maryland, 1733–63* (New York, 1990), 289; case of William Lyndall, April 1744, Maryland Provincial Court Judgments, microfilm no. 2507–2, Liber E.I., no. 7, 480–481, MdSA; petitions for Jonathan Abell, 1818, Governor and Council, Pardon Papers, box 18, folder 75, MdSA; petitions for John Lewis, 1818, Governor and Council, Pardon Papers, box 18, folder 74, MdSA; petitions for Richard Burket alias Dick, 1815, Governor and Council, Pardon Papers, box 17, folder 16, MdSA; *State v Daniel Swinney,* March 1809, Surry County Supreme Court State Docket, 1807–1814, NCSA; *State v James Long,* October 1801, Fayetteville District State Trial Docket, 1788–1816, NCSA. Connecticut also imposed shorter incarcerations for attempted rape, and several of these convicts received early release. Pennsylvania average based on eleven convictions for attempted rape in Lancaster County Oyer and Terminer Docket, 1792–1820, LCHS; Pennsylvania Court of Oyer and Terminer Dockets, 1778–1827, PSA. Enslaved men in North Carolina still received corporal punishment for attempted rape.

free women in 1712, as did New Jersey in 1714. An eighteenth-century Delaware statute specified a punishment of four hours with the convict's ears nailed to the pillory and then "cut off close to his Head" for any slave convicted of attempting to rape a white woman. In 1750, a Maryland statute condemned any slave who attempted to "commit a Rape upon any White Woman" to death. Rhode Island was the only New England colony with a statutory punishment for black-on-white attempted rape: in 1743, Rhode Island mandated whipping, branding, and expulsion from the colony. Other New England colonies, with their minimal African American populations, might not have felt the need for such statutes. The lack of racially based rape statutes made Massachusetts and Connecticut the exceptions: the racialization of rape was the primary Americanization of British common law regarding rape.[33]

Colonies simultaneously institutionalized the statutory emphasis, not just on black and enslaved rapists, but specifically on nonwhite attackers of white women. In 1714, New Jersey specified punishments for enslaved men of multiple racial backgrounds — any "Negro, Indian or other Slave" — who raped any of the "Majesties Leige People, not being Slaves." The lack of racial designation for victims of rape in this section of the law may reflect the still-developing shift from social to racial distinctions in early-eighteenth-century America. Similarly, an early draft of Maryland's 1737 Act for the More Effectual Punishment of Negroes and Other Slaves for the "Rape upon any White Woman" might

33. Cushing, ed., *The Earliest Printed Laws of Pennsylvania*, 69; *A Collection of All the Laws of the Province of Pennsylvania, Now in Force* (Philadelphia, 1742), 83–84. (A 1700 Pennsylvania law that was disallowed by the queen set castration as a punishment for black-on-white attempted rape. See http://www.palrb.us/statutesatlarge/17001799/1700/0/act/0158.pdf, from the Commonwealth of Pennsylvania Legislative Reference Bureau [accessed April 15, 2004].) See also Bernard Bush, comp. and ed., *Laws of the Royal Colony of New Jersey, 1703–1745*, New Jersey Archives, 3d Ser., II (Trenton, N.J., 1977), 28–30; *Acts of Assembly Passed in the Province of New-York from 1691 to 1725* (New York, 1726), 84; John D. Cushing, ed., *The Earliest Printed Laws of New Jersey, 1703–1722* (Wilmington, Del., 1978), 22; *Laws of the Government of New-Castle, Kent, and Sussex, upon Delaware* (Philadelphia, 1752), 70 (statute is undated); Thomas Bacon, comp., *Laws of Maryland at Large . . .* (Annapolis, Md., 1765), chap. 14; *Acts and Laws of the English Colony of Rhode-Island and Providence Plantations, in New England, in America* (Newport, R.I., 1767), 195–196. This statute might have been a reaction to a slave's rape attempt on a white woman in 1742 that produced a flurry of litigation in multiple courts. See *Rex v Cuff*, March 1743, Rhode Island Superior Court of Judicature, Newport County Records, C, 127–128, RIJRC; *Comfort Taylor v Cuff*, May 1743, Newport County Inferior Court of Common Pleas, 404B, RIJRC.

have initially referred only to the rape of non–racially specified women: the assembly instructed that "after the word Rape" the words "upon any White Woman" be inserted. Status implication had become distinct racial division by the mid-eighteenth century.[34]

Colonial statutes not only set harsher punishments for enslaved men's attempted rapes on white women than those to which white men would ever be subject; they also removed local justices' flexibility to minimize the seriousness of the attack. Statutes set black-on-white sexual assaults in a category with other rebellious and dangerous slave behavior. Statutes on sexual assaults that were not expressly racial often appeared alongside other sexual crimes such as sodomy, buggery, adultery, or fornication, but black-on-white rape and attempted rape statutes were uniformly part of colonies' attempts to regulate dangerous slaves. In 1636, Plymouth's list of capital crimes grouped rape alongside sodomy and buggery. Likewise, New Hampshire's 1718 Act against Murder Etc. listed the punishment for rape after the punishment for buggery. Nearly a century later, a review of the laws of Kentucky repeatedly mentioned buggery in the discussion of rape and grouped sample indictments for "Rape, Sodomy, Forcible Abduction and Adultery."[35]

In contrast, the first mention of rape in specific relation to slavery in the British colonies might have been in a Barbados statute of 1688 that set special trial courts to deal with slaves who "many Times" committed grievous crimes, including "Murder, Burglaries, Robbing in the Highways, Rapes, burning of Houses or Canes." A 1714 New Jersey law specified punishments against slaves who murdered, raped, burned, or dismembered. New York's 1730 Act for the More Effectual Preventing and Punishing the Conspiracy and Insurrection of Negro and Other Slaves included punishments for "Murders Rapes Mayhems Insurrections or Conspiracies." A 1751 Maryland statute condemned slaves who had committed insurrection, murder, arson, or rape of white women to death without benefit of clergy. An 1816 Georgia statute specified that slaves

---

34. Cushing, ed., *The Earliest Printed Laws of New Jersey*, 20–22; *Archives of Maryland*, LX, 92–93. On a similar conceptual shift in Virginia, see Kathleen M. Brown, *Good Wives, Nasty Wenches, and Anxious Patriarchs: Gender, Race, and Power in Colonial Virginia* (Chapel Hill, N.C., 1996), 107–136.

35. Brigham, ed., *Compact with the Charter and Laws of . . . New Plymouth*, 43; Cushing, ed., *Acts and Laws of New Hampshire*, 121; Toulmin and Blair, *A Review of the Criminal Law of the Commonwealth of Kentucky*, I, 136, III, 137. See also Kerr, *An Exposition of the Criminal Laws of the Territory of Orleans*, 42.

and free people of color would be tried for the capital offenses of insurrection, poisoning, murder, maiming, burglary, arson, and rape of whites. Early American laws labeled black-on-white rape as a crime of resistance to white authority rather than an act of sexual immorality.[36]

The distinctions drawn by statutory sentences for black and white rape defendants continued in the early Republic. The general shift away from corporal punishment seen in rape and attempted rape sentences did not carry over to statutes that mandated slaves' punishments. Southern states reiterated exceptional punishments for most black-on-white attempted rapes, even while they lessened punishments for white-on-white crimes. In 1770, Georgia prescribed death for slaves convicted of rape or attempted rape of a white woman and reiterated this punishment in 1816, at the same time that it instituted imprisonment for white men convicted of rape. Virginia legislators passed an 1820 statute that did likewise. In 1809, Maryland specified that a slave convicted of rape or attempted rape who was not hanged might be given one hundred lashes, exile, or both, rather than the two to twenty-one years in prison to which whites might be sentenced. These race-based differences were enacted in the prosecution of attempted rape as well: all but one of the known death sentences for attempted rape in the new Republic were handed down to slaves.[37]

Other sentencing changes also began to apply only to slaves. In the second half of the eighteenth century, castration began to be used against enslaved men convicted of attempted rape and as commuted sentences for rape convic-

36. Sheila Lambert, ed., *House of Commons Sessional Papers of the Eighteenth Century,* 147 vols., LVIX (Wilmington, Del., 1975), no. 329; Cushing, ed., *The Earliest Printed Laws of New Jersey,* 20; *The Colonial Laws of New York from the Year 1664 to the Revolution* . . . (Albany, N.Y., 1894), II, 679–685; Bacon, comp., *Laws of Maryland at Large,* n.p.; Lamar, comp., *A Compilation of the Laws of the State of Georgia,* 804. For a similar listing in an earlier Georgia law, see Horatio Marbury and William H. Crawford, eds., *The Laws of the State of Georgia* . . . (Savannah, Ga., 1802), 429–431.

37. Marbury and Crawford, eds., *Laws of the State of Georgia,* 430; Prince, comp., *A Digest of the Laws of Georgia,* 349, 461; see also John D. Cushing, ed., *The First Laws of the State of Delaware* (Wilmington, Del., 1981), II, pt. 2, 1324; Tate, *Digest of the Laws of Virginia,* 127; *The Laws of Maryland,* III, 458–461. For a side-by-side comparison of punishments for slaves and freemen convicted of rape, see *The Revised Code of Laws of Virginia* (Richmond, Va., 1819), chap. 158. The remaining execution sentence for an attempted rape was against a free man of unknown racial background, whose crimes also included burglary. See case of Jesse Martin, June 1797, Virginia Executive Papers, box 99, June 16–30 folder, LOV.

tions. Castration had appeared as a punishment for slaves in several southern and West Indian colonies, as often for nonsexual crimes as for rape. New Jersey had first attempted to punish enslaved men's sexual attacks with castration in 1704, but its law was repealed, and no evidence exists that the prescribed punishment was applied to any slaves. In fact, no castrations appear to have been carried out in the mainland colonies as a rape or attempted rape sentence until close to the time of the American Revolution. In 1769, Virginia expressly limited castration to a slave's attempted rape of a white woman and castrated more than a dozen black men for sexual attacks in the next fifty years. Also by the Revolutionary era, southern colonies began exiling slaves instead of executing them. In a time of diminishing support for capital punishment, exile or castration could be more publicly palatable and financially advantageous to the slave's owner. One rape victim in Maryland in 1770 joined with the slave's owner in asking that the man be exiled instead of executed: "I am not willing said Negro should be Executed for the Crime."[38]

Together, these shifts in sentencing practices increasingly marked the institutional differences between northern and southern societies. The early-eighteenth-century attention to black-on-white sexual assaults as crimes that deserved special mention and uniformly harsh punishment first increased attention to interracial rapes in the majority of colonies. After the Revolution, the exclusion of most white convicted rapists from capital punishment left

38. Bush, comp. and ed., *Laws of the Royal Colony of New Jersey*, 28–30; William Waller Hening, comp., *The Statutes at Large; Being a Collection of All the Laws of Virginia* . . . , 13 vols. (Richmond, Va., 1809–1823), VIII, 358; case of Abraham, June 1770, in *Archives of Maryland*, XXXII, 368–370. For other commutations, see petitions for Joseph Pherill, 1780, Governor and Council, Pardon Papers, box 1, MdSA; petitions for Adam, 1787, Governor and Council, Pardon Papers, box 3, folder 96, MdSA; *Raleigh Register, and North-Carolina Weekly Advertiser*, Oct. 22, 1804; case of Luke, Mar. 7, 1804, Virginia Executive Papers, box 129, Mar. 1–10 folder, LOV. On punishments of castration, see Philip J. Schwarz, *Twice Condemned: Slaves and the Criminal Laws of Virginia, 1705–1865* (Baton Rouge, La., 1988), 22, 206; John Pendleton Kennedy, ed., *Journals of the House of Burgesses of Virginia, 1773–1776* . . . (Richmond, Va., 1905), 208, 224; case of James Gibson, 1783, Connecticut Archives, Crimes and Misdemeanors, 1st Ser., VI, 220–222, CSL; Winthrop D. Jordan, *White over Black: American Attitudes toward the Negro, 1550–1812* (Chapel Hill, N.C., 1968), 154–155; attorney general to Council of Trade and Plantation, Oct. 13, 1704, in Karen Ordahl Kupperman, John C. Appleby, and Mandy Banton, eds., *Calendar of State Papers, Colonial: North America and West Indies, 1574–1739* (CD-ROM, 2000), XXII, 277, item 604. On the growth of transportation over execution, see Philip J. Schwarz, *Slave Laws in Virginia* (Athens, Ga., 1996), 97–119.

blacks as the overwhelming majority of executed rapists, as only southern slave states reinstituted their corporal punishments against black men. Thus, by the early Republic, what had been statutory New England exceptionalism in the punishment of rape had become an increasingly widening gap between North and South. The abolition of slavery in the North eliminated de jure differences, though not necessarily de facto ones, in the treatment of most black men and white men.

Overall, early Americans made few interventions in the British legal handling of rape. Rape began its American history as a capital crime, as in Britain, and was transformed by general shifts in attitudes toward capital punishment. The major Americanization of British law was the racialization of rape. Increasingly throughout the eighteenth and early nineteenth centuries, American lawmakers affirmed that black-on-white sexual assaults deserved special attention and punishments. At the end of the eighteenth century, many colonies substituted incarceration for execution at the same time that abolition began to take hold in northern states. Black-on-white rape executions became a predominantly southern spectacle. The racially institutionalized differences in rape statutes set the stage for race-based prosecutions of individual cases.

Yet legal standards and statutory punishments for rape and attempted rape prosecutions provide only a partial glimpse of the possible legal redress available for incidents of sexual coercion in early America. By turning to the punishment of those sexual assaults that courts identified as something less than rape or attempted rape, we get a more complete sense of the place of sexual coercion in the early American legal system. Beyond the many sexual assaults that never appeared before the criminal justice system, colonial courts also dealt with sexual attacks in a variety of ways that might provide less life-threatening judicial redress than rape charges required.

LOCAL FLEXIBILITY: LESS-THAN-RAPE AT
THE CHESTER COUNTY COURT OF QUARTER SESSIONS

Despite the statutes and legal directives on rape, many sexual assault cases came before local justices who hesitated to charge a community member with the capital crime of rape. An examination of prosecutions at the Chester County, Pennsylvania, court of quarter sessions from 1730 to 1739 reveals how such justices tried to address women's needs for sexual safety without charging free white men in the community with crimes that necessitated harsh corporal or capital punishments. Official documents can hide many sexual assault prosecutions from the historian's view; thus, the prosecution of acts of sexual coercion may be far more varied than official charges of rape or attempted rape suggest.[39]

Chester County, located just outside Philadelphia, was one of the first English settlements in Pennsylvania. It was originally colonized by the Dutch in the seventeenth century; by the 1730s, more than ten thousand people of European descent comprised a largely agrarian community of thriving towns and a less-populated hinterland. Scotch-Irish Protestants and English Quakers populated its towns, and German-speaking immigrants were beginning to arrive in significant numbers. European residents enslaved Africans, but slavery was less common than white servitude. Native Americans still lived within the area, although they no longer had their own towns within the county's boundaries. Rich in archival records, Chester County was socially diverse, and one decade of its court of quarter sessions records serves as a microcosm of a local court's handling of incidents of sexual coercion.[40]

More than one thousand people were involved in the roughly three hundred cases that made up the activities of the court of quarter sessions in the 1730s. While such cases did not have the notoriety of less frequent and often more sensational capital crimes, the local court was a place for social gatherings, dissemination of information, and regulation of community ideals. One historian has estimated that roughly 40 percent of a community's population might be involved with the court of quarter sessions in a single decade. This lower court addressed criminal incidents that ranged from formulaic prosecutions for selling liquor without a license to a variety of assault, theft, counterfeiting, and fornication charges. Between 1730 and 1739, at least ten prosecutions included some allegation of sexual coercion. Ten incidents out of three hundred cases (about 3 percent) seems to be a typically low occurrence of

39. Virtually all defendants at this local court appear to have been white; enslaved men would be tried in separate slave courts, as is discussed in Chapter 5.

40. On colonial Chester County, see James T. Lemon, *The Best Poor Man's Country: A Geographical Study of Early Southeastern Pennsylvania* (Baltimore, 1972); Lucy Simler, "Tenancy in Colonial Pennsylvania: The Case of Chester County," *William and Mary Quarterly,* 3d Ser., XLIII (1986), 542–569; Duane E. Ball, "Dynamics of Population and Wealth in Eighteenth-Century Chester County, Pennsylvania," *Journal of Interdisciplinary History,* VI (1976), 621–644; Jack D. Marietta, "The Distribution of Wealth in Eighteenth-Century America: Nine Chester County Tax Lists, 1693–1799," *Pennsylvania History,* LXII (1995), 532–545; Adrienne D. Hood, "The Material World of Cloth Production and Use in Eighteenth-Century Rural Pennsylvania," *WMQ,* 3d Ser., LIII (1996), 43–66.

sexual coercion, only somewhat higher than the rate of rape or attempted rape cases prosecuted in other regions.[41]

Yet these numbers take on a different significance if only those cases involving female victims are considered. Women were victims in only approximately one-quarter of all criminal cases, and most of these appearances were for fornication, where women were more likely to be conspirators than victims. Even so, cases involving accusations of sexual violence accounted for approximately 15 percent of all of the cases where women were ostensible victims. Further, nearly one-half of all the assaults against women included accusations of sexual violence. Several scholars have documented similar percentages in other locales. Thus, from the perspective of women's interactions with local justice, an institutional 3 percent of cases conceals a much higher proportion of sexual assaults.[42]

41. For a complete discussion of rates of rape prosecutions, see Introduction, n. 3. On local courts, see Rhys Isaac, *The Transformation of Virginia, 1740–1790* (Chapel Hill, N.C., 1982), 88–93. For contemporary commentary on the audience at rape trials, see Louis B. Wright and Marion Tinling, eds., *The Secret Diary of William Byrd of Westover, 1709–1712* (Richmond, Va., 1941), 95; Mittelberger, *Journey to Pennsylvania in the Year 1750,* eds. and trans. Handlin and Clive, 38; Laura L. Becker, "The People and the System: Legal Activities in a Colonial Pennsylvania Town," *Pennsylvania Magazine of History and Biography,* CV (1981), 139–140. See also G. S. Rowe, "The Role of Courthouses in the Lives of Eighteenth Century Pennsylvania Women," *Western Pennsylvania Historical Magazine,* LXVIII (1985), 5–23. For dated, though useful, general studies of Pennsylvania courts, see Herbert William Keith Fitzroy, "The Punishment of Crime in Provincial Pennsylvania," *PMHB,* LX (1936), 242–269; Lawrence H. Gipson, "Crime and Its Punishment in Provincial Pennsylvania: A Phase of the Social History of the Commonwealth," *Penn. Hist.,* II (1935), 3–16; William H. Loyd, Jr., "The Courts of Pennsylvania in the Eighteenth Century Prior to the Revolution," *University of Pennsylvania Law Review,* LVI (1908), 28–51. Even though enslaved defendants did not appear in the quarter sessions court (Pennsylvania law mandated that their transgressions be handled by the magistrates and freeholders court, whose records have not survived), they, too, likely would have been aware of the community gossip surrounding court proceedings.

42. James Rice's work suggests that, out of more than four thousand minor and serious crimes prosecuted in Maryland from 1749 to 1837, rapes accounted for 34 percent of violent crimes. James D. Rice, "Crime and Punishment in Frederick County and Maryland, 1748–1837: A Study in Culture, Society, and Law" (Ph.D. diss., University of Maryland at College Park, 1994), 251, 286, 339. In his study of an antebellum New York county court, Sean T. Moore found that nearly half of all reported violence against women involved sexual violence (Moore, "'Justifiable Provocation,'" *Jour. Soc. Hist.,* XXXV [2002], 902 and n. 65).

The ten cases involving possible sexual coercion in the 1730s Chester County quarter sessions records encompass an array of charges, circumstances, and court responses. Three involved charges of intent or attempt to rape, three of assault, two of fornication, one of theft, and one was labeled as rape and adultery. If just the court docket for this decade rather than the surviving loose file papers were read, only one case would have appeared as a sexual assault, because cases listed as assaults in the docket were described as *sexual* assaults only in supplemental papers (Table 1). In 1731, the court charged Thomas Culling with an assault on a servant named Martha Claypool in the docket, but in the loose indictment and recognizances Thomas was charged with an attempted rape. In 1736, the docket indicates that James White was charged with assaulting Hannah McCradle, but in the loose indictment he was charged with an assault with an intent to ravish; in other file papers in the case, his actions were categorized as attempted rape and adultery. Although the court convicted Daniel Patterson of assaulting Hannah Tanner in 1734, the supplemental papers clearly show that he was accused of trying to rape her. Whether resulting from a court clerk's shorthand or a deliberate minimization of sexual crimes, the characterization of sexual assault as assault in the court's official docket tends to hide incidents of sexual coercion.[43]

Other accusations of sexual coercion brought before a Chester County justice of the peace never appeared in the court's official record books. In 1731, Alice Yarnal accused Lawrence MacGinnis of trying to rape her. Alice told the court that, while she was "going along the Road" one evening, she met up with Lawrence, who "throwd her down and Indeavoured to have Carnal knowlege of her body." With the help of her daughter, Alice escaped. On another occasion, Alice testified, she was tricked into walking into a shop where Lawrence lay in wait and again tried to rape her. After this second incident, she went to a justice of the peace with her complaint, and the justice deposed Alice, Lawrence, and several witnesses. Despite the multiple examinations, the case was apparently never prosecuted and thus never listed in the quarter sessions

43. *D. v Thomas Culling,* February 1731, Chester County Quarter Sessions Court Docket, 213, 215, 223, and Chester County Quarter Sessions File Papers, CCA; *D. v James White,* February 1736, Chester County Quarter Sessions Court Docket, and Chester County Quarter Sessions File Papers, CCA; *D. v Daniel Patterson,* March 1734, Chester County Quarter Sessions Court Docket, 44, 49, and Chester County Quarter Sessions File Papers, CCA. "Attempted rape" and "assault with intent to rape" seem to have been used interchangeably throughout early American indictments, with no discernible chronologic, regional, or substantive meanings.

TABLE 1. Summary of Cases Involving Sexual Coercion in
Chester County Quarter Sessions Court, 1730–1739

Date	Defendant/ Victim	Charge on Indictment or in Testimony	Charge in Docket
1731	Lawrence MacGinnis/ Alice Yarnal	Assault with intent to rape	None
1731	Thomas Culling/ Martha Claypool	Assault with attempt of rape	Assault
1734	Abraham Richardson/ Mary Smith	Attempted rape	Assault
1734	Thomas Beckett/ Mindwell Fulfourd	Theft (testimony of attempted rape)	Theft
1734	Unknown/ Christeen Pauper	(Fornication charge against Christine)	None
1735	Daniel Patterson/ Hannah Tanner	Violent assault to ravish	Assault
1736	James White/ Hannah McCradle	Attempted rape/ adultery	Assault
1737	Robert Mills/ Catherine Parry	Rape	None
1738	John West/ Isabella Gibson	Attempt to ravish/ assault	Fornication
1739	Thomas Halladay/ Mary Mouks	Assault with intent to ravish	None

Source: Chester County Quarter Sessions Docket Books and File Papers,
1730–1739, CCA.

docket. Catherine Parry accused Robert Mills of repeatedly trying to rape her in July 1737, and a justice of the peace took her statement, but there is no record of this case in the court docket. The attempted rape case against Thomas Halladay was dropped even before the indictment form was completed in 1739, which presumably explains why the docket book never listed the prosecution against him. Such cases might have been settled out of court, justices might have been hesitant to pursue them, or participants might have been pressured to drop their complaints. Whatever the reasons, the official court docket indicates a much smaller number of sexual assault incidents than might have been brought to court officials' attention.[44]

Overall, cases involving direct charges of sexual violence were unlikely to be entered as such in the docket book. Of the four cases that could have been charged as attempted rape, only one assault with intent to rape appeared in the official court record. In contrast, five of the six incidents that involved possible sexual violence but were prosecuted without rape-related charges appear in the court docket. Although these numbers are too few for definitive conclusions, they may suggest a real hesitancy to fully, officially, and seriously prosecute attempts at sexual violence. At the very least, they definitively illustrate that court records bear little resemblance to the prevalence of coerced sex in society. As noted crime historian J. M. Beattie concludes, "Court cases can throw little light" on the existence of rape in a given community.[45]

The Chester County record also shows that sexual assaults could be redressed under other sex-related charges. The 1738 court docket contains a charge against John West for fornicating with Isabella Gibson, yet Isabella believed the sexual interaction was nonconsensual. She quoted John as saying, while she resisted him, that "he would force her," and John's loose indictment paper charged him with an attempted rape. Another incident raises decidedly modern questions about the ability to consent. In 1734, more than a dozen

44. *D. v Lawrence MacGinnis,* June 1, 1731, Chester County Quarter Sessions File Papers, CCA; examination of Catherine Parry, July 25, 1737, Chester County Quarter Sessions File Papers, CCA; *D. v Thomas Halladay,* July 1739, Chester County Quarter Sessions File Papers, CCA. Because Catherine Parry claimed that Robert eventually succeeded in raping her, this case might have been tried in a court of oyer and terminer, but no records have survived, and the indictment does not mention (as others do) a removal to an o. and t. court.

45. J. M. Beattie, *Crime and the Courts in England, 1660–1800* (Princeton, N.J., 1986), 132. For an early American scholar who makes conclusions about the frequency of rape directly from criminal prosecutions, see Barbara S. Lindemann, "'To Ravish and Carnally Know': Rape in Eighteenth-Century Massachusetts," *Signs,* X (1984), 82.

county residents petitioned on behalf of "Christeen Pauper" who had given birth to a bastard child. The petitioners asked the judge not to prosecute Christeen for fornication, because she was "a Nattural fool; and Divested of Reason to that degree, That wee Think She could not Count four; if it were to Save her Life." There is no evidence that any man was prosecuted for having sexual relations with Christeen, a woman who was not mentally capable of, as her neighbors put it, being "Sencible of her Crime." It is not hard to imagine Christeen's pregnancy as resulting from sexual coercion, at least by modern standards. Although early Americans might have condemned the act that resulted in a disabled woman's pregnancy, charging such an act as rape was inconceivable because an inability to consent did not equal resistance.[46]

Another Chester County case shows how charges with no explicit sexual content might still be used to redress an incident that involved sexual coercion. In 1734, the court charged Thomas Beckett with committing felonious theft on Abraham Fulfourd. In actuality, however, Thomas's crime involved only Mindwell Fulfourd, Abraham's wife. While Mindwell was riding her horse along the road, she testified, Thomas came up to her, told her, "I have amind to ly with you," and tried to force her off her horse. When "at last through perswation he let her go," she realized that he had stolen her goods out of her saddlebag. Ultimately, Thomas was convicted of theft of Abraham's goods, but there is no indication that the court gave any attention to his unwelcome sexual pressure on Mindwell. Perhaps theft was an easier crime to prove, or perhaps the court thought that, since she had repelled his sexual overtures, there was no reason to charge him with an attempted rape. Either way, the court clearly did not feel the need to charge a community member with sexual assault.[47]

Cases from other jurisdictions suggest that Chester County clerks' use of non-rape-related charges for incidents of sexual assaults might have been a common practice. Like Thomas Beckett, Jack York was officially convicted of burglary in British Canada in 1800, but his crime including breaking into a

46. *D. v John West,* August 1738, Chester County Quarter Sessions Court Docket, 142, 147, 153, 157, 161, CCA, and separate page of docket for August 1738; and Chester County Quarter Sessions File Papers, CCA. Note that this is an impossible combination of charges: it seems counterintuitive to accuse a man of both fornication (unmarried sexual intercourse) and an *attempted* rape (unconsummated sexual intercourse). See petition for Christeen Pauper, August 1734, Chester County Quarter Sessions File Papers.

47. *D. v Thomas Beckett,* August 1734, Chester County Quarter Sessions Court Docket, and July 10, 13, 1734, Chester County Quarter Sessions File Papers, CCA. For a military case where a court filed robbery charges in lieu of attempted rape charges, see trial of Gabriel Nolan, Mar. 17, 1761, WO 71/68, 136–140, TNA:PRO.

house and raping Ruth Stufflemine. As in the Chester case of Christeen Pauper, a New Hampshire court convicted a man of adultery for getting a "distracted" woman drunk and forcing himself on her. Other colonies' court dockets might also record official charges of assault for sexual attacks. When Richard Kearns was charged with an assault in a New Jersey docket book in 1766, only the supplemental papers showed that he had assaulted Anne Barson "in a very indecent and Unbecoming manner makeing Proposals to her for to admit him to Unlawful freedoms Indeavoring to throw her on a bed." In early-eighteenth-century Virginia, Christopher Pridham was convicted of abusing his servant—not because he repeatedly tried to force her "to prostitute her body to him," but because he beat her when she refused.[48]

Even higher court record books might list a sexual attack only as assault. In the Rhode Island Superior Court record book, Elisha Thomas was accused of assaulting Katherine Beck in New Hampshire in 1793, but the corresponding file papers show that Katherine accused him of attempting "to have Carnal knowledge" of her. On occasion, extralegal documents provide information completely absent from court records. In 1777, a Pennsylvania man named James McConnaughy was charged with an assault on Ann Patton. Neither the docket book nor the supplemental papers mention that this violent attack was a sexual one. But, when James escaped from jail, the *Pennsylvania Gazette* described him as a tall, curly-haired man who had been imprisoned for rape.[49]

48. Justice Powell's Report from Mt. Dorchester, Sept. 22, 1800, Civil Secretary, Correspondence, Upper Canada and West Upper Canadian Sundries, 502–512, NAC. See a discussion of the case in William Renwick Riddell, "Upper Canada—Early Period," *Journal of Negro History,* V (1920), 334. For a similar case, see trial of Jack, Jan. 7, 1741/2, Elizabeth City County Order Book, reel 17, 265, LOV; *State v Caesar Parker,* October 1805, Hillsborough County Superior Court Judgments, April 1805–April 1807, box 606113, 190–191, NHA; recognizance of Kearns et al., July 19, 1766, Miscellaneous Documents, no. 2351, HHR, and *King v Richard Kearns,* Hunterdon County Common Pleas Minutes, 1765–1767, X, 374, 378, 385, 408, HHR; case of Christopher Pridham, September 1724, Richmond Criminal Trials, 1710–1754, 85–86, LOV. For examples of other docket books listing charges of assault while supplemental indictment papers specified an assault with an attempt to rape, see *State v Richard Horsly,* August 1719/20, Chester County Quarter Sessions Court Docket, CCA, and Chester County Quarter Sessions File Papers, February 1719/20, CCA; *King v John Lawrence et al.,* Aug. 1, 1754, Supreme Court Pleadings, reels 48–49, K–501, K–650, NYHR. For a similar example in a military court, see trial of Timothy Spillman, Dec. 26, 1775, WO 71/82, 250–256, TNA:PRO.

49. *State v Elisha Thomas,* April 1793, Rockingham County Superior Court Record Book, 1789–1792, 536, NHA, and Rockingham County Superior Court Cases, no. 13253,

If we had looked at the prosecuted cases of sexual coercion from surviving court dockets and newspaper reports for all of Pennsylvania in the 1730s, we would know of a handful of cases of rape and attempted rape. These records reveal that rape was a capital crime, and a few men were executed for rape, but sexual attacks would seem to be a comparatively small part of the colony's criminal justice system. The Chester County court of quarter sessions dockets would show us several assaults on women, fornication cases, and a theft. But such records vastly underestimate the sexual attacks that women brought to this local court. Cases that were not charged as rape or attempted rape but involved some form of sexual assault are often extraordinarily difficult to identify. Even a small number of such cases remind us that, within the bounds of the criminal justice system, there could be a world of difference between the prosecution of rape and the practice of sexual coercion.[50]

Despite the fairly clear minimization of sexual assault cases in historical records, an important interpretive question remains. Does the appearance of less-than-rape cases in local courts suggest a community's attentiveness to sexual assaults, or does it suggest a downgrading of more serious crimes to a more informal realm of justice? Although to some degree this question is unanswerable, in the case of rape, I am persuaded that the difficulties women faced in reporting rape in addition to the law's general suspicion of rape accusations indicate a downgrading rather than a heightened concern for sexual crimes against women. Indeed, in the Chester County court of quarter sessions records, one of the cases charged as assault might even have qualified as a superior court prosecution for rape: six-year-old Mary Smith apparently told her mother that the man who attacked her "Laid her down on the bed and took up her Close and Lay upon her and was Like to Kill her and took a Long Red thing out of his trousers and hurt her belly with it." This defendant received only a £2 fine as punishment for this crime — just slightly more than the average overall fine of £1.78 in that decade's crimes. Such cases remind us not only that the historical record should be used with caution but also that local prose-

---

NHA; case against James McConnaughy, August 1777, Chester County Quarter Sessions Court Docket, and Chester County Quarter Sessions File Papers, CCA; *Penn. Gaz.,* Sept. 3, 1777.

50. Because oyer and terminer court records have not survived for this period, our knowledge of 1730s Pennsylvania rape prosecutions comes primarily from newspapers. See *Penn. Gaz.,* July 22–Aug. 2, 1736; *Penn. Gaz.,* Apr. 8–15, 1736; *New-York Gazette,* July 28–Aug. 4, 1735; *American Weekly Mercury* (Philadelphia), Oct. 29–Nov. 5, 1730.

cutorial decisions gave white community members an opportunity to receive a more flexible form of justice than increasingly rigid statutes allowed to non-white and unfree men.[51]

In 1771, a Boston printer published a fictional rape trial in which a Mrs. Chuckle accused her neighbor, Atticus, of sitting on a bed with her two years before. This accusation transformed into a full-fledged rape trial with the help of Atticus's enemies, a justice of the peace who was easily insulted by Atticus's lack of deference, the blustery and greedy Lawyer Rattle, and bad blood between Atticus and the Chuckle family. Along the way, Mrs. Chuckle was coached into saying that Atticus raped her with force and against her will, that she screamed when he attacked her, and that she told her husband what had happened right away. The satirical trial was a stark condemnation of, in the author's words, "Justices, Lawyers, Complainants, Evidences, Doctors, Conjurers, Innholders and Deacons" who purposefully manipulated the criminal justice system for their own ends. But its focus on a rape charge also reveals the degree to which Americans considered rape an easily falsifiable crime. Mrs. Chuckle was led by others into charging an innocent man with a sexual assault, and she quickly learned to provide the correct answers to the standard interrogative questions on rape.[52]

Whether in fiction, before a British military tribunal, or in a variety of colonial courts, Anglo-Americans paired the recognition of the seriousness of a rape with doubts about the veracity of a woman's accusation. Moreover, the statutes that consistently made rape a harshly punished crime were enervated by criminal courts unwilling to easily charge many men with such a serious felony. Accordingly, local justices regularly decided to prosecute sexual attacks under charges other than rape or even attempted rape. Such lesser charges gave communities more flexibility in prosecution and punishment but also minimized the apparent level of sexual coercion in historical records.

Yet these incongruities in the institutional handling of rape did not apply evenly to all the men accused of rape. At the beginning of the eighteenth

51. *D. v Abraham Richardson*, Aug. 5, 1734, Chester County Quarter Sessions File Papers, CCA. Other scholars have found evidence of "downgrading" and dropping of rape and attempted rape charges in other jurisdictions. See Beattie, *Crime and the Courts in England*, 127–132; Moore, "'Justifiable Provocation,'" *Jour. Soc. Hist.*, XXXV (2002), 897.

52. *The Trial of Atticus, before Justice Beau, for a Rape* (Boston, 1771). For a brief analysis of this pamphlet, see Ulrich, *A Midwife's Tale*, 120–121.

century, Americans first started to institutionalize an image of rape that was expressly tied to race-based slavery. American statutory law harshly punished all of enslaved men's sexual assaults on white women by viewing such attacks as akin to slave rebellion. Such statutes meant that local justices had far less leeway in charging and punishing enslaved men. Further, the image of rape as a kind of resistance to slavery meant that some of the doubts about (white) women's motives for rape accusations faded when compared to Anglo-American concerns about rebellions by enslaved African men. A second wave of hardening racial lines in the early Republic followed the shifts in punishment for white rapists, as abolition of death sentences left black men as the overwhelming majority of executed rapists. Just as Atticus was eventually prosecuted, not for his actions toward Mrs. Chuckle, but for his alleged bad character, the meanings ascribed to the race of both the defendant and the victim greatly influenced the criminal prosecution of rape.

CHAPTER FIVE

CONSTRUCTING RAPE AND
RACE AT EARLY AMERICAN
COURTS

Just a few weeks after the Chester County, Pennsylvania, court of quarter sessions dropped attempted rape charges against a white man named Lawrence MacGinnis in 1731, the *Pennsylvania Gazette* reported that a "Negro Man" convicted of raping "a young white Woman" in nearby New Castle was "condemned to die" by a court set up specifically to try slaves. Taken by themselves, these two cases seem like serendipitously timed charges against two individuals, but viewing them alongside hundreds of such cases reveals clear patterns in the racialized criminalization of sexual assault. First, white women were the ubiquitous victims in prosecuted sexual assaults. Second, white men accused of sexual assaults were far more likely to be charged with noncapital crimes at lower courts, while black men were frequently charged with capital crimes at courts with fewer procedural safeguards. Just as for Lawrence and the unnamed "Negro Man," these differences led to very different outcomes for individual defendants and for early American society.[1]

Of the 174 men known to have been executed for criminal charges related to a rape between 1700 and 1820, 142 — more than 80 percent — were identified as being of African descent. Given that whites outnumbered blacks in every region (New England, mid-Atlantic, South) throughout this period, this number is especially striking. The only more conspicuous racial disparity related to the victims of criminally prosecuted sexual assaults: approximately 95 percent

---

1. *D. v Lawrence MacGinnis,* June 1, 1731, Chester County Quarter Sessions File Papers, CCA; *Pennsylvania Gazette* (Philadelphia), June 24–July 1, 1731; *Penn. Gaz.*, July 15–22, 1731. For Delaware's slave trial court statute, see An Act for the Trial of Negroes, 1719, in *Laws of the State of Delaware . . .* (New Castle, Del., 1798), 103–104.

of them were white. Racial identities of both victims and defendants most strongly predicted the outcome of a sexual assault prosecution.[2]

Yet the leap from a (white) woman's accusation of sexual assault to a (black) man's death sentence was not a single racist step. Every stage of prosecution offered options, advantages, and safeguards to whites that were denied to blacks. Although rape could be a very difficult crime for a white woman to prove, black and enslaved women were usually de facto (if not de jure) prevented from even bringing criminal charges against almost any defendant. A defendant's race frequently correlated to the court in which he would be tried, the charges leveled against him, the proof needed to convict him, his sentence, and his punishment. Through this criminal process, early Americans gave tangible meaning to the social construction of race and turned multiplicities of racial identities into a binary of black and white. The archetypal criminally prosecuted rape was a black man's violent attack on a white woman.

The historiography on interracial rape is extensive. Foundational scholars, such as Winthrop Jordan, argued for early and consistent beliefs in black men's hypersexuality from the seventeenth century on. Others later detailed the transformation and intensification of whites' fear of black men's sexual threats. Literary scholars such as Richard Slotkin used New England's criminal narratives to argue for an increasing late-eighteenth-century emphasis on black rapists, and Daniel Williams connected these narratives to the eighteenth-century production of racist stereotypes of black sexuality. In contrast, Daniel Cohen used the narratives to argue that protoracist views of dangerous black rapists were largely absent until the early nineteenth century. Social and legal

2. For colonial population statistics, see U.S. Bureau of the Census, *Historical Statistics of the United States, Colonial Times to 1957* (Washington, D.C., 1960), 756. For census data from 1790 to 1820, see http://fisher.lib.virginia.edu/census/ (accessed July 1, 2003). On issues of nomenclature for early American people of color, see Joanne Pope Melish, *Disowning Slavery: Gradual Emancipation and "Race" in New England, 1780–1860* (Ithaca, N.Y., 1998), 9–10, 37–38; John Wood Sweet, *Bodies Politic: Negotiating Race in the American North, 1730–1830* (Baltimore, 2003), 9.

Of 557 prosecuted cases involving victims whose racial identity can be identified, 22 were of African descent and 4 of Native American. For a summary of historians' attempts to quantify the sexual exploitation of enslaved women, see Joshua D. Rothman, *Notorious in the Neighborhood: Sex and Families across the Color Line in Virginia, 1787–1861* (Chapel Hill, N.C., 2003), 249 n. 14. Statistics in this chapter were computed using SAS software. On the quantification of historical legal records, see Michael Stephen Hindus and Douglas Lamar Jones, "Quantitative Methods or *Quantum Meruit*? Tactics for Early American Legal History," *Historical Methods*, XIII, no. 1 (Winter 1980), 63–74.

historians of New England, such as Cornelia Hughes Dayton and John Wood Sweet, used manuscript legal records to argue for a century-earlier emphasis on black-on-white rape.[3]

Scholars of the Old South have primarily used legal and social history to analyze interracial rape. Those who have addressed the prosecution of rape in particular colonies have found an emphasis on black-on-white rape throughout the eighteenth century. Historians who focus on the nineteenth-century South have examined the legal treatment of enslaved men accused of rape or have debated the myth of the black rapist. Using statutes and appellate trial records, Peter Bardaglio concluded that white antebellum southerners "widely shared the belief that black men were obsessed with the desire to rape white women." Yet Martha Hodes suggested that black men and white women had more leeway for interracial sexual relations in the antebellum South than they had once post–Civil War emancipation led to both a significant decrease in tolerance for all forms of black men's sexual relationships with white women and a consequent rise in the image of the hypersexual black rapist. Calling specific attention to the ways that white women's negative reputations could undermine slave executions for rape, Diane Sommerville agreed with Hodes's later timetable for the myth of the black rapist and explicitly argued that there was no pre–Civil War anxiety over black men's sexuality.[4]

3. Winthrop D. Jordan, *White over Black: American Attitudes toward the Negro, 1550–1812* (Chapel Hill, N.C., 1968), 151–154, 158, 162; also Jordan, *Tumult and Silence at Second Creek: An Inquiry into a Civil War Slave Conspiracy* (Baton Rouge, La., 1993), 149; Richard Slotkin, "Narratives of Negro Crime in New England, 1675–1800," *American Quarterly,* XXV (1973), 18–28; Daniel Williams, "The Gratification of That Corrupt and Lawless Passion: Character Types and Themes in Early New England Rape Narratives," in Frank Shuffelton, ed., *A Mixed Race: Ethnicity in Early America* (New York, 1993), 194–221; Daniel A. Cohen, "Social Injustice, Sexual Violence, Spiritual Transcendence: Constructions of Interracial Rape in Early American Crime Literature, 1767–1817," *William and Mary Quarterly,* 3d Ser., LVI (1999), 481–526; Cornelia Hughes Dayton, *Women before the Bar: Gender, Law, and Society in Connecticut, 1639–1789* (Chapel Hill, N.C., 1995), 243; Sweet, *Bodies Politic,* 165, 167–169. For a more general foundational work on this topic, see Jacquelyn Dowd Hall, "'The Mind That Burns in Each Body': Women, Rape, and Racial Violence," in Ann Snitow, Christine Stansell, and Sharon Thompson, eds., *Powers of Desire: The Politics of Sexuality* (New York, 1983), 328–349.

4. Kirsten Fischer, *Suspect Relations: Sex, Race, and Resistance in Colonial North Carolina* (Ithaca, N.Y., 2002), 181–186; Kathleen M. Brown, *Good Wives, Nasty Wenches, and Anxious Patriarchs: Gender, Race, and Power in Colonial Virginia* (Chapel Hill, N.C., 1996), 209–210; Martha Hodes, *White Women, Black Men: Illicit Sex in the Nineteenth-Century South*

How do we reconcile studies that reach such varied and, in some cases, opposite conclusions to the question of when and how the image of the black rapist took hold in America? In some ways, comparing all of these pieces of scholarship is like comparing apples to oranges to beach balls: authors work with not only different sources, time periods, and geographic locales but also individual definitions of what constitutes racism, protoracism, or racial prejudice and varied definitions of black men's "hypersexuality" and white men's "anxiety." In early America, there were virtually no known lynchings and comparatively few polemical treatises on black hypersexuality of the kind that appeared by the end of the nineteenth century, when expressions of whites' extreme fear of black men's sexuality were used as justifications for horrific acts of oppression and torture. The early American belief in black men's proclivity to rape should not be taken as equivalent to a late-nineteenth-century widespread fear of black men's hypersexuality. Yet neither should the ultimate heights of outwardly racist persecution blind us to the more subtle — yet no less crucial — racial meanings of rape in early America.[5]

Accordingly, I make several interventions to the substantial histories of rape and race. First, I show that, despite the hardening of racial lines after the American Revolution, the prosecutorial treatment of black men accused of

---

(New Haven, Conn., 1997); Diane Miller Sommerville, "The Rape Myth in the Old South Reconsidered," *Journal of Southern History,* LXI (1995), 481–518; Peter Bardaglio, "Rape and the Law in the Old South: 'Calculated to Excite Indignation in Every Heart,'" *JSH,* LX (1994), 749–771, quotation on 752. For a recent work that challenges the relationship of the rhetoric and practice of the black rape myth in the twentieth century, see Lisa Lindquist Dorr, *White Women, Rape, and the Power of Race in Virginia, 1900–1960* (Chapel Hill, N.C., 2004).

5. On the ideological construction of race, see Barbara Jeanne Fields, "Slavery, Race, and Ideology in the United States of America," *New Left Review,* CLXXXI (1990), 95–118; Shelley Fisher Fishkin, "Interrogating 'Whiteness,' Complicating 'Blackness': Remapping American Culture," *AQ,* XLVII (1995), 428–466. On the shifting meanings of race, see Nicholas Hudson, "From 'Nation' to 'Race': The Origin of Racial Classification in Eighteenth-Century Thought," *Eighteenth-Century Studies,* XXIX (1996), 247–264. On the increased sexualization of black danger after the Civil War, see Martha Hodes, "The Sexualization of Reconstruction Politics: White Women and Black Men in the South after the Civil War," *Journal of the History of Sexuality,* III (1993), 402–417; Laura F. Edwards, "Sexual Violence, Gender, Reconstruction, and the Extension of Patriarchy in Granville County, North Carolina," *North Carolina Historical Review,* LXVIII (1991), 237–260. On lynching, see W. Fitzhugh Brundage, *Lynching in the New South: Georgia and Virginia, 1880–1930* (Urbana, Ill., 1993).

raping white women remained surprisingly consistent in the colonial period and in the early Republic. When occasional acquittals of colonial-era black men are read against the overwhelming exoneration of white rape defendants, we see that the image of black men as rapists developed not just because black men were frequently convicted of rape (they were more frequently convicted of most crimes) but because white men were only very irregularly convicted of rape. Furthermore, social and legal shifts in the post-Revolutionary era that were not necessarily related to rape were nevertheless crucial to an increasing public image of rape as a black-on-white crime. Although these shifts most directly affected white men's relationship to rape, they might have been as critical as the unchangingly harsh prosecutions of black-on-white rapes to the shifting notions of dangerous black rapists.

A fundamental societal distrust in women's ability to believably claim rape underlay the race-based criminal treatment of rape. Long before Americans expressly articulated a myth of black rapists, they used the privileges of whiteness and subjugations of blackness to circumvent this default disbelief in women's rape allegations. Because early Americans had a vested interest in concluding that white women (practically the only legitimate victims in prosecuted rapes) would not voluntarily have sexual relations with black men, black men were the most believable rapists of white women. The prosecution of rape was part of the ongoing production of racial ideologies. And the cost of a criminal prosecution that at every stage reinforced the image of black men as sexually dangerous and white men as sexually privileged can be counted in the numbers of lives lost.

COURTS AND CHARGES

America's British heritage guaranteed the right to a jury trial for its subjects. Early American criminal proceedings thus usually involved a grand jury's evaluation of an indictment (to determine whether there was sufficient information to warrant a trial), followed by a trial before a twelve-man petit jury to unanimously determine the defendant's guilt or innocence. For charges of rape, this process occurred at the colony's superior court, which had original jurisdiction over capital offenses. Colonists accused of lesser crimes (such as assault, fornication, lewdness, and sometimes attempted rape) were tried in a lower court. Colonists charged here also had to be indicted before a grand jury before they could be tried before a petit jury of their peers.[6]

6. On the Americanization of British jury practices, see John M. Murrin, "Magistrates, Sinners, and a Precarious Liberty: Trial by Jury in Seventeenth-Century New England," in

However, most colonies and states created special courts to try slaves (and occasionally free black men) for serious crimes. Originally meant to provide, as a Virginia statute specified, *"for the more speedy prosecution of slaves committing Capitall Crimes. . . .* without the sollemnitie of jury,"* these courts could condemn a slave without a grand or petit jury trial, relying instead on the majority decision of several county justices or slaveholders for a verdict. Barbados's 1688 statute created the first of these New World courts with a clear racial justification: "Being brutish Slaves, [they] deserve not, for the Baseness of their Condition, to be tried by the legal Trial of 12 Men of their Peers or Neighbourhood." Such courts both policed and marked the newly created racial class of slaves by separating them from the traditional legal rights afforded to British subjects, and most mainland colonies (with the exception of most of those in New England) came to depend on these courts. The singularity of this secondary court system set up specifically for slaves made manifest the permanent segregation of those of African descent in race-based slavery: no other dependents (women, indentured servants, or children) would be systematically deprived of the rights of English subjects.[7]

Almost all of the mid-Atlantic and southern colonies held special slave courts. In 1692, Virginia became the first mainland colony to create courts of oyer and terminer for slaves accused of felonies, and these courts continued through the antebellum period. North Carolina's magistrates and freeholders courts tried slaves for capital crimes before county magistrates and slave owners from 1715 through 1816, at which point superior courts took over jurisdiction for slaves' capital crimes. South Carolina created a magistrates and freeholders court to try both slaves and free blacks after 1690. By 1755, Georgia, too, began holding such freeholders courts for all blacks accused of serious crimes. All of these colonies' courts replaced the grand jury and petit jury trial guaranteed to whites accused of capital crimes with a single trial in front of

---

David D. Hall, John M. Murrin, and Thad W. Tate, eds., *Saints and Revolutionaries: Essays on Early American History* (New York, 1984), 152–206; Lawrence M. Friedman, *Crime and Punishment in American History* (New York, 1993), 20, 24–25.

7. William Waller Hening, comp., *The Statutes at Large; Being a Collection of All the Laws of Virginia . . .*, 13 vols. (Richmond, Va., 1809–1823), III, 102–103; Sheila Lambert, ed., *House of Commons Sessional Papers of the Eighteenth Century* (Wilmington, Del., 1975), pt. 2, 59, 70. On the creation and evolution of these courts, see Peter Charles Hoffer, *Criminal Proceedings in Colonial Virginia . . .*, American Legal Records, X (Athens, Ga., 1984), xlv–lii; Thomas D. Morris, *Southern Slavery and the Law, 1619–1860* (Chapel Hill, N.C., 1996), 228.

several justices and freeholders, and most did not require a unanimous verdict for conviction.[8]

Mid-Atlantic colonies also instituted separate court systems for African Americans accused of serious crimes. A Pennsylvania act passed in 1705 established a special court for the speedy trial of free and enslaved blacks before two judges and six freeholders and excluded them from a right to a jury trial until its repeal in 1780. In colonial New York, five freeholders and three justices of the peace could try a slave for a capital offense, though a master could, for a fee, request a jury trial. New Jersey created freeholders courts in 1713 to try slaves accused of rape, murder, or arson.[9]

8. See Hening, comp., *The Statutes at Large of Virginia*, III, 102–103; Thad W. Tate, *The Negro in Eighteenth-Century Williamsburg* (Charlottesville, Va., 1965), 164–181; Philip Schwarz, *Twice Condemned: Slaves and the Criminal Laws of Virginia, 1705–1865* (Baton Rouge, La., 1988), 17–27; John D. Cushing, ed., *The Earliest Printed Laws of North Carolina, 1669–1751*, 2 vols. (Wilmington, Del., 1977), 64; John Haywood, *The Duty and Office of Justices of Peace . . . of North Carolina* (Halifax, N.C., 1800), 238; George Stevenson and Ruby D. Arnold, "North Carolina Courts of Law and Equity Prior to 1868," *Archives Information Circular*, no. 9 (March 1977), 7–8, NCSA; Thomas Cooper and David J. McCord, eds., *The Statutes at Large of South Carolina*, 10 vols. (Columbia, S.C., 1836–1841), VII, 345, 352, 365; Cushing, comp., *The First Laws of the State of South Carolina*, 2 vols. (Wilmington, Del., 1981), pt. 1, 162–166; Michael Stephen Hindus, *Prison and Plantation: Crime, Justice, and Authority in Massachusetts and South Carolina, 1767–1878* (Chapel Hill, N.C., 1980), 61; Allen D. Candler, ed., *The Colonial Records of the State of Georgia*, 25 vols. (New York, 1970), XVIII, 102–112; Oliver H. Prince, comp., *A Digest of the Laws of Georgia . . .* (Milledgeville, Ga., 1822), 446, 461. Unlike other southern and mid-Atlantic colonies, Maryland retained jury trials for enslaved men. See James Bisset, comp., *Abridgment and Collection of the Acts of Assembly of the Province of Maryland, at Present in Force* (Philadelphia, 1759), 143–145.

See also Philip D. Morgan, *Slave Counterpoint: Black Culture in the Eighteenth-Century Chesapeake and Lowcountry* (Chapel Hill, N.C., 1998), 264; A. Leon Higginbotham and Anne F. Jacobs, "The 'Law Only as an Enemy': The Legitimization of Racial Powerlessness through the Colonial and Antebellum Criminal Laws of Virginia," *North Carolina Law Review*, LXX (1992), 992–993; Daniel J. Flanigan, "Criminal Procedure in Slave Trials in the Antebellum South," *JSH*, XL (1974), 537–564.

9. For Pennsylvania: John D. Cushing, ed., *The Earliest Printed Laws of Pennsylvania, 1681–1713* (Wilmington, Del., 1978), 68; Cushing, comp., *The First Laws of the Commonwealth of Pennsylvania* (Wilmington, Del., 1984), 284. See also William H. Loyd, Jr., "The Courts of Pennsylvania in the Eighteenth Century prior to the Revolution," *University of Pennsylvania Law Review*, LVI (1908), 42–43. For New York: *The Colonial Laws of New York*

New England colonies, however, tried free and enslaved African American men in the same judicial system as other men. Connecticut, Rhode Island, Massachusetts, and New Hampshire tried all rape cases at superior courts, requiring both a grand jury presentment and a petit jury trial for slave and free, white and black. Perhaps with far fewer African Americans and no slave uprisings that might have promoted stricter criminal treatment of enslaved defendants (New York instituted separate slave courts months after its 1712 slave revolt), New England colonies did not see the need to create a separate criminal trial system for blacks or slaves. Or perhaps New England's court systems, with some of the highest conviction rates in the colonies, seemed suitable for maintaining racial order. No single reason explains New England's departure from its southern neighbors, but we should not assume that a more liberal racial attitude was responsible for these colonies' unsegregated court systems: New Englanders still embraced slavery throughout most of the eighteenth century and still disproportionately convicted black men of sexual assaults.[10]

Separate slave courts provided procedural rights to accused slaves, but, as Philip Morgan writes, they provided "a rapid, harsh, and singular justice." They deprived black men of opportunities to end a prosecution that superior courts afforded to white men. Close to 20 percent of rape cases involving white defendants ended in an ignoramus ("we do not know") verdict from the grand jury—a possibility unavailable to the hundreds of black men tried for rape in slave courts. Mainstream criminal courts required a jury's unanimous decision for a guilty verdict, but many slave courts needed only a majority of justices and slave owners to convict a defendant.[11]

------

from the Year 1664 to the Revolution . . . , 5 vols. (Albany, N.Y., 1894–1896), I, 765–766; The Colonial Laws of New York, II, 684–685. For New Jersey: Bernard Bush, comp. and ed., Laws of the Royal Colony of New Jersey, II, 1703–1745, New Jersey Archives, 3d Ser. (Trenton, N.J., 1977), 28–30; John D. Cushing, ed., The Earliest Printed Laws of New Jersey, 1703–1722 (Wilmington, Del., 1978), 19–20. This act was overturned in 1768 by An Act to Repeal the Trial of Slaves . . . ; see Bush, comp., Laws of the Royal Colony of New Jersey, IV, 1760–1769, New Jersey Archives, 3d Ser. (Trenton, N.J., 1982), 480.

10. On the comparative efficiency of New England's colonial court systems, see Douglas Greenberg, "Crime, Law Enforcement, and Social Control in Colonial America," American Journal of Legal History, XXVI (1982), 293–325. On New England's racial ideologies, see Sweet, Bodies Politic; Melish, Disowning Slavery.

11. Morgan, Slave Counterpoint, 264. For the traditional view that emphasizes slaves' procedural rights, see A. E. Keir Nash, "A More Equitable Past? Southern Supreme Courts and the Protection of the Antebellum Negro," NCLR, XLVIII (1970), 197–242; Flanigan, "Criminal Procedure in Slave Trials," JSH, XL (1974), esp. 538; Sommerville, "The Rape

The specific charges leveled against black and white defendants also differed greatly. Black men accounted for 46 percent of known rape charges, far more than their proportion of the early American population between 1700 and 1820. Broken down another way, 48 percent of white men's prosecutions for sexual assault included rape charges, compared to 69 percent of black men's prosecutions. Separate trial systems were not the sole cause of more severe charges against blacks: blacks were more likely overall targets of rape prosecutions even in New England's unsegregated court system. Connecticut's nearly complete superior court records show that blacks were prosecuted for rapes at a rate higher than their proportion of the population. Black men accounted for more than one-third of known Connecticut rape charges from 1700 to 1820, even though they never averaged more than 3 percent of Connecticut's population. Maryland, the only southern colony without a separate trial system for slaves or African Americans, also charged black men at much higher rates than whites; black men accounted for two-thirds of the known rape charges. Unfortunately, no southern colony with separate court systems has complete trial records for both blacks and whites, but fragmentary evidence suggests that black men were charged disproportionately. North Carolina's relatively complete superior court records show that between 1700 and 1820, at least fourteen white men were charged with rape. The records of North Carolina's magistrates and freeholders slave court are fragmentary, but they include at least twenty-three rape prosecutions against black men, even though black men were always less than 40 percent of the population. Black men, whether in the North or South or in separate or shared courts, were far more likely to face a rape charge than were white men.[12]

─────

Myth in the Old South Reconsidered," *JSH,* LXI (1995), 515. Thomas Morris argues that, despite all the procedural developments, "slave justice could not be a truly rational system," because "no trial form really had much significance" under the oppression of slavery (Morris, *Southern Slavery and the Law,* 220, 228, 247). See also Higginbotham and Jacobs, "The 'Law Only as an Enemy,'" *NCLR,* LXX (1992), 984–1004.

The verdict is known in 179 charges of rape against white men. Less than 1 percent of 179 rape prosecutions against black defendants ended with a verdict of *ignoramus. Ignoramus* rates also appear to have been higher for rape than for other crimes. See Jack Marietta and G. S. Rowe, "Rape, Law, Courts, and Custom in Pennsylvania, 1682–1800," in Merril D. Smith, ed., *Sex without Consent: Rape and Sexual Coercion in America* (New York, 2001), 87.

12. I have identified 412 rape charges for which the defendant's identity is known. Sexual assaults involving white defendants accounted for 442 charges; black defendants appeared in 274 cases. Thanks in large part to Cornelia Dayton's assistance, I have located

These higher numbers of rape charges against black men depended not only on increased attention to black men's sexual crimes but also on minimization of white men's sexual misdeeds. As discussed earlier, white men could commit sexual assaults in ways that black men could not — ways that might seem less forceful to a court. Consequently, black men were charged with rape more than twice as often as for lesser crimes, but white men were charged with lesser crimes as often as they were charged with rape. Some justices might believe a lesser charge was the most they could bring against community members for sexual assault, and communities' unwillingness to convict any of their members of capital offenses undoubtedly contributed to this downgrading of white men's sexual crimes. Some evidence of this is apparent in the refiling of lesser charges after rape prosecutions against white men failed. In 1745, a Georgia court charged a white man with attempted rape when a grand jury did not indict the defendant on a rape charge; in 1768, John Adams defended a Massachusetts man tried for attempted rape after a rape prosecution failed; and, in 1787, a New Jersey court quashed a rape indictment and replaced it with a second indictment for assault and abuse.[13]

---

29 cases of rape in the Connecticut superior courts from 1700 to 1820. For Connecticut population estimates through 1780, see U.S. Bureau of the Census, *Historical Statistics of the United States,* 756. By the 1820 census, 97 percent of the Connecticut population was identified as white. See http://fisher.lib.virginia.edu/census/. I have located 38 Maryland rape charges: 24 against blacks and 14 against whites. In colonial America, blacks accounted for up to 30 percent of the population, and by 1820 still made up less than 40 percent of the population. On colonial populations, see Jim Potter, "Demographic Development and Family Structure," in Jack P. Greene and J. R. Pole, eds., *Colonial British America: Essays in the New History of the Early Modern Era* (Baltimore, 1984), table 5.2, 138; http://fisher.lib.virginia.edu/census/.

13. Because I have not conducted systematic studies of the reams of lower court records where white men might be prosecuted for lesser crimes, the number of white men's less-than-rape prosecutions is undoubtedly even higher. On magistrates' role in "downgrading" or otherwise limiting sexual assault prosecutions in eighteenth-century London, see Antony E. Simpson, "Popular Perceptions of Rape as a Capital Crime in Eighteenth-Century England: The Press and the Trial of Francis Charteris in the Old Bailey, February 1730," *Law and History Review,* XXII (2004), 60–62; Dayton, *Women before the Bar,* 261; Candler, ed., *Colonial Records of the State of Georgia,* XXV, 20, 31, 110, 120, 244, 268; L. H. Butterfield, ed., *The Diary and Autobiography of John Adams,* 4 vols. (Cambridge, Mass., 1961), I, 353–354; L. Kinvin Wroth and Hiller B. Zobel, eds., *The Legal Papers of John Adams,* 3 vols. (Cambridge, Mass., 1965), I, li; *State v Charles Meloy,* December 1786, New Jersey Supreme Court Actions-at-Law, no. 36933, NJSL.

Black and enslaved men were less enmeshed in the white community and likely had few powerful supporters at court. Owners of accused slaves might stand to lose a valuable asset upon conviction, but they could generally expect reimbursement for the value of an executed slave. Slave owner jurors also had a vested interest in controlling and punishing defiant enslaved men. Furthermore, black men faced more serious charges than whites even for sexual assaults that merited charges less than rape. Courts charged black men with crimes of sexual violence such as attempted rape while white men might be charged with a variety of less serious crimes that addressed *either* sex or violence (such as lewd behavior and fornication or assault and breach of the peace), rather than both. Thirteen percent of white men's total criminal prosecutions involved a charge other than rape or attempted rape, compared to only 2 percent of black men's prosecutions. Masters might have dealt informally with enslaved men's lesser sexual threats. In 1775, one Virginia planter threatened to hang any slave who tried to have sex with his sixteen-year-old house slave. But the few less-than-attempted-rape charges against blacks suggest that courts were hypervigilant at prosecuting black men for sexual infractions toward whites. In 1714, a Massachusetts court bound a free black man for fifty pounds after a white woman "found him on her Bed." In 1754, a thirteen-year-old South Carolina slave was charged with carnally knowing a ten-year-old white girl "in consequence of her own consent." Black men were not only charged with crimes for which white men would likely not have been charged, but any clear black-on-white sexual aggression was also likely to merit at least an attempted rape charge.[14]

14. Statistics are based on 442 criminally charged white defendants and 274 criminally charged black defendants. On payment for executed slaves, see Marvin L. Michael Kay and Lorin Lee Cary, "'The Planters Suffer Little or Nothing': North Carolina Compensations for Executed Slaves, 1748–1772," *Science and Society,* XL (1976), 288–306. For examples of payment for executed slaves, see Caroline County Order Book, May 28, 1736, reel 13, 349–350, LOV; claim of Roger Ormond and Wyrnot Ormond, Sept. 3, 1765, Treasurer and Comptroller Papers, Miscellaneous Group, 1738–1909, box 8, NCSA; case of Negro Jack Durham, 1786, in Negley K. Teeters, "Public Executions in Pennsylvania: 1682–1834," in Eric Monkkonen, ed., *The Colonies and Early Republic,* vol. II of Crime and Justice in American History (Westport, Conn., 1991), 806; Spotsylvania County Order Book, May 12, 1792, reel 47, 646–647, LOV; Hunter Dickinson Farish, ed., *Journal and Letters of Philip Vickers Fithian, 1773–1774: A Plantation Tutor of the Old Dominion* (Williamsburg, Va., 1957), 185. See also Flanigan, "Criminal Procedure in Slave Trials," *JSH,* XL (1974), 540; case of Tully, a free negro, Nov. 11, 1714, Miscellaneous Bound Manuscripts Collection, 1629–1908, MHS; *State v Caesar Parker,* October 1805, Hillsborough County Superior

White men, on the other hand, were repeatedly charged with lesser criminal sexual offenses that did not require proof of force for a conviction, even though the incident might have warranted an attempted rape charge. As the 1730s Chester County court of quarter sessions records showed, courts could purposefully reduce rape charges against white men to charges of nonforced sexual acts. In 1769, a Connecticut court charged James Benton only with lewdness for exposing his private parts to his daughter "with many aggravating circumstances." In 1789, a Pennsylvania court charged David Robb with adultery with his servant, even though the grand jury questioned the servant about the degree of force David had used. Such charges turned white men's sexual assaults into consensual, illicit sex, emphasizing the notion that white men's sexual misdeeds stopped short of attempts at rape.[15]

Courts charged other white men with noncapital crimes of violence (such as assault or breach of the peace) for a sexual assault. In 1702, a New Jersey court bound Samuel Coates forty pounds for good behavior toward Elizabeth Brown and Elizabeth White specifically because the women were afraid that Samuel would "abuse or ravish them." A 1754 New York court charged four men with assaulting Mary Anderson when they dragged her into a dark hall and tried to rape her. In 1780, a Maryland court charged Henry Gray with breach of the peace for pulling up a woman's clothes in an "indecent manner" and "otherways abusing her." In 1793, a New Hampshire court charged Elisha Thomas with assault for grabbing a woman by the throat, throwing her on the ground, and punching her in the face while he tried to force her into sexual relations. Courts probably brought such charges out of practical concerns: assault rather than attempted rape was undoubtedly an easier charge to prosecute against white men. But, in so doing, they lessened both white men's criminal responsibility and the public image of white men as rapists.[16]

Court Judgments, April 1805–April 1807, box 606113, 190–191, NHA; *South Carolina Ar Council Journal*, XXIII, Apr. 16, 1754, 192–193, SCDAH.

15. *D. v James Benton, Jr.,* January 1769, New Haven County Court Book, VII, 164, CSL, and New Haven County Court Files, drawer 45, CSL; *Respublica v David Robb,* Yeates Legal Papers, March–April 1789, fol. 2, HSP. See also *Rex v James (John?) Logan,* February 1717, New Haven County Court Files, drawer 3, CSL, cited in Cornelia Hughes Dayton, "Women before the Bar: Gender, Law, and Society in Connecticut, 1710–1790 (Ph.D. diss., Princeton University, 1986), 116.

16. Charges against Samuel Coates, February, May 1702, in H. Clay Reed and George J. Miller, eds., *The Burlington Court Book of West New Jersey, 1680–1709,* American Legal Records, V (Washington, D.C., 1944), 265–267; *King v John Lawrence et al.,* Aug. 1, 1754, Su-

In contrast, courts repeatedly charged black men with other crimes in addition to rape or attempted rape. Black men comprised more than three-quarters of the defendants tried on a dual charge of rape or attempted rape and another crime. The majority of these prosecutions (thirty-seven out of forty-three total) involved a charge of burglary. Northern colonies and states might occasionally charge a black man with a simultaneous burglary and rape, but such charges were overwhelmingly a southern phenomenon; southern courts filed twenty-five of the thirty dual charges against black men. A lone southern woman whose house was robbed by an enslaved man seemed likely to see the robbery also as an attempted rape. A slave named Jack was charged with a burglary and rape against Elizabeth Brown in 1742, but the Virginia court ultimately convicted him of burglary and assault instead. In 1791, a Virginia court accused a slave named Abraham of, on one night, stealing blankets, bacon, and hay and trying to rape one woman and murder another. Southern courts seemed willing to charge — if not convict — enslaved men who breached white women's domestic space with rape. The "typical southern style" of charging black robbers of white households with attempted rape in the post–Civil War period was already underway in early America. In a race-based slave labor system, blacks' trespasses on the social and economic spaces of whites might easily slide into sexual trespasses. By breaking into whites' homes, slaves wrongly entered their masters' domains, and those domains included sexual access to their masters' women. As with laws that set rape by slaves alongside other forms of rebellion, slaves' economic transgressions could also be read as a sexual threat to the white establishment.[17]

preme Court Pleadings, reels 48–49, K–501, K–650, NYHR, and New York City Supreme Court Minute Book, 1754–1757, 53, 145–146, NYHR; petitions for Henry Gray, 1780, Governor and Council, Pardon Papers, box 1, folder 60, MdSA; *State v Elisha Thomas,* April 1793, Rockingham County Superior Court Cases, no. 13253, NHA. See also recognizance of Kearns et al., July 19, 1766, Miscellaneous Documents, no. 2351, HHR; trial of Timothy Spillman, Dec. 26, 1775, WO 71/82, 250–256, TNA:PRO. See also *D. v Daniel Patterson,* March 1734, Chester County Quarter Sessions Court Docket, 44, 49, and Chester County Quarter Sessions File Papers, CCA; *D. v Thomas Culling,* February 1731, Chester County Quarter Sessions Court Docket, 213, 215, 223, and Chester County Quarter Sessions File Papers, CCA.

17. Trial of Jack, Jan. 7, 1741/2, Elizabeth City County Order Book, reel 17, 265, LOV; case of Abraham, 1791, Auditor of Public Accounts, no. 756, Condemned Slaves, 1791, 1795, box 1966, LOV. See also trial of Fern, May 12, 1792, Spotsylvania County Order Book, reel 47, 646–647, LOV; trial of Billy, a.k.a. William, Sept. 24, 1793, Northumberland

Conversely, a theft charge against a white man might replace a charge of sexual coercion. As previously discussed, in 1734, a Pennsylvania court charged Thomas Beckett with theft when he stole an array of goods from Mindwell Fulfourd after trying to force her to have sex with him. In 1800, a burglary charge against William Newberry was filed, as the judge later wrote, in lieu of "the attempt to commit a Rape, the true Crime." Such economic prosecutions could replace prosecutions for white men's sexual coercion because white men's sexual assaults did not carry the same racial threat as black-on-white attacks. Charges against white defendants were a remedy for individual misdeeds, not a means to reaffirm racial order.[18]

Enslaved men were also punished extralegally without trials or despite legally determined innocence. Untold numbers of black men suffered punishments for sexual infractions when masters chose to personally punish their property. In Massachusetts, a slave owner asked for a commuted sentence for his slave because he had already beaten the man "much more" than the court-ordered four sets of thirty-nine stripes. Also unlike white men, black men might occasionally be punished when found *not* guilty. In 1767, a Virginia court acquitted a slave named Prince of rape but still sentenced him to thirty-nine lashes. In 1784, a Virginia court found Demus not guilty of attempted

---

County Order Book, reel 59, LOV; Lou Falkner Williams, "Federal Enforcement of Black Rights in the Post-Redemption South: The Ellenton Riot Case," in Christopher Waldrep and Donald G. Nieman, eds., *Local Matters: Race, Crime, and Justice in the Nineteenth-Century South* (Athens, Ga., 2001), 176–177. For an exceptional northern dual-charged case, see *State v Pompey*, June 1783, New Jersey Supreme Court Actions-at-Law, no. 37216, NJSL. For southern cases, see *State v Dick*, Sept. 14, 1782, Goochland County Order Book, reel 26, 140, LOV. For other cases, see case of Dick, December 1810, Virginia Executive Papers, box 169a, Dec. 21–30 folder, LOV; trial of Sip, Feb. 2, 1775, New Bern District Superior Court Miscellaneous Records, 1758–1806, NCSA; trial of Toney, Apr. 7, 1759, Fairfax County Order Book, reel 38, 331–332, LOV; trial of Glasgow, Sept. 2, 1767, Accomack County Order Book, reel 84, 253–254, LOV; trial of Sam, Prince Edward County Order Book, June 27, 1780, reel 22, 80, LOV (2d part of docket); trial of Jem, July 26, 1783, in Helen S. Stinson, comp., *Greenbrier Co., W. Va. Orders, 1780–1850* (Moorpark, Calif., 1988); trial of Jemmy, June 4, 1752, York County Order Book, reel 29, pt. 2, 36, LOV; *State v Toney*, April, May 1814, Salisbury District State Appearance and Trial Docket, NCSA.

18. *D. v Thomas Beckett*, August 1734, Chester County Quarter Sessions Court Docket, and Chester County Quarter Sessions File Papers, CCA; Justice Powell's Report from Mt. Dorchester, Sept. 22, 1800, Civil Secretary, Correspondence, Upper Canada and West Upper Canadian Sundries, RG–5, 443–445, NAC.

rape but gave him thirty-nine lashes for the newly invented crime of intending to attempt to rape.[19]

This treatment of black and white defendants paralleled an inverse treatment of black and white victims. Black women's racial identity virtually barred them from seeking redress in early American courts. Ironically, the few pre-Revolutionary sexual assault charges brought on behalf of black women occurred in Massachusetts—a colony with one of the lowest percentages of African Americans. In 1717, the Plymouth court charged a white man named Zebulon Thorp with raping an "Ethiopian" woman. However, the case never went to trial because Zebulon, a "very debauch'd man," fell off his horse while riding drunk and died. In 1758, this same court convicted James Studley of throwing himself on a mulatto woman and trying to have sex with her in a public place. Perhaps the Puritan heritage that demanded strict moral accountability for all sexual sins encouraged Massachusetts courts to hold white men accountable for their sexual misdeeds even with black women. In both cases, extenuating factors might have made the courts more willing to punish the sexual assault of a nonwhite woman: Zebulon was a known drunkard, and James committed public indecency, both acts independently worthy of punishment. Whatever the reasons, cases involving African American victims were exceptionally uncommon in colonial America.[20]

The post-Revolutionary court records reveal a small number of black victims of sexual assaults. Many of these cases involved assaults by African American men. Some southern states accused enslaved men of sexual assaults on

19. Sentence of Bristol, 1721, Domestic Relations, 1643–1774, IX, 178–179 (page numbers illegible), MA; trial of Prince, Sept. 18, 1767, Fauquier County Minute Book, reel 42, 311–312, LOV; trial of Demus, Aug. 3, 1784, Brunswick County Order Book, reel 27, 469–470, LOV. See also trial of Will, Apr. 10, 1769, Bedford County Order Book, reel 39, 516 in printed page numbers (92 in originals), LOV. For a possible attempted lynching of a Native American man accused of raping a white woman, see case of Tuskegu Tuslenegaw, 1798, "Indians—Creeks—Outrages," group 4–2–46, loc. no. 1543–02, box 76, folder 7, GA. On southern plantation justice, see Higginbotham and Jacobs, "The 'Law Only as an Enemy,'" *NCLR*, LXX (1992), 1062–1067; Flanigan, "Criminal Procedure in Slave Trials," *JSH*, XL (1974), 540; Charles William Janson, *The Stranger in America* . . . (London, 1807), 386–387.

20. M. Halsey Thomas, *The Diary of Samuel Sewall, 1674–1729* (New York, 1973), II, 853; case of James Studley, in David Thomas Konig, ed., *Plymouth Court Records, 1686–1859* (Wilmington, Del., 1978–1981), III, *1748–1751*, 97. See also Newhall indicted in Salem, Essex, Nov. 7, 1786, Massachusetts Superior Court of Judicature Records, Suffolk Files, no. 133633, MA; Henry M. Brooks, *Some Strange and Curious Punishments* (Boston, 1886), 49.

enslaved women, though few of these cases ever went to trial. Without the kind of community pressure for legal punishment that might result from a slave's rape of a white woman, slave owners likely settled disputes arising from slave-on-slave rapes outside of the courtroom. Northern states prosecuted several free and enslaved black men for assaulting black women. Early-nineteenth-century New York City, with one of the largest free black populations at the time, seemed most willing to hold men accountable for sexual assaults on black and mulatto women. In June 1810, a New York City court convicted a black man of raping a six-year-old "yellow girl" and a second man of attempting to rape a "little Black girl." In 1818, the same court acquitted Charles Carpenter of attempting to rape Ellen Larsen, a seventeen-year-old woman described alternately as mulatto or black. The extremely young age of nonwhite victims minimized the relevance of Anglo-American beliefs in black women's general lack of chastity. In the nineteenth century, free black (especially young) victims could at least bring sexual assault complaints to legal authorities, yet New Yorkers still gave comparatively little attention to the rape of black women.[21]

Part of this uncertainty likely related to increasing northern fears about free blacks' social and sexual behavior. In 1808, one New York City case that resulted in a published trial transcript charged a white man with an assault with intent to seduce a black woman. This unique charge (forwarded by a civil court after the case had been withdrawn from criminal prosecution) of a forceful *seduction* avoided the question of whether a black woman's claim of rape was

21. For slave-on-slave rapes that did not go to trial, see case of Sam, Jan. 18, 1773, York County Judgments and Orders, reel 210, LOV; trial of Kitt, July 29, 1783, Westmoreland County Order Book, 148, LOV; trial of Toby, Dec. 2, 1783, Norfolk County Minute Book, reel 62a, 222, LOV; trial of Ned, July 20, 1790, Essex County Order Book, 298, LOV; petitions for Jerry, 1814, Governor and Council, Pardon Papers, box 16, folder 36, MdSA. For rare cases of enslaved men charged with raping free mulatto women, see case of Peter, September 1797, Virginia Executive Papers, Sept. 11–20 folder, LOV; case of Tom, Jan. 22, 1810, Virginia Executive Papers, box 164, LOV. For northern slave-on–free black assaults, see case of Pompey, November 1796, indictments, no. 3376 and unnumbered doc., HHR; *State v James Irvine*, September 1810, Windham County Superior Court Records, I, pt. 3, 342, CSL; *The People v William Jersey*, June 14, 1810, New York County Court of General Sessions Indictment Papers, NYMA. Several cases involving black victims had defendants of unidentified racial identity. See, for instance, *The People v Christopher Basketdore*, Dec. 8, 1807, *The People v George Turpintine*, June 11, 1810, and *The People v Charles Carpenter*, Nov. 13, 1818, all in New York County Court of General Sessions Indictment Papers, NYMA; *The People v Charles Carpenter*, December 1818, in D[avid] Bacon, ed., *The New-York Judicial Repository*, 6 vols. (New York, 1818–1819), I, IV, 165–173.

worth pursuing. The verdict in this case still gave a clear message about the value of a black woman's sexual integrity and a white man's sexual license: the black victim won the suit but was awarded only one dollar in damages. Although purposefully dismissive of black women's sexual rights, such a case reflected a slight increase in black women's opportunities for legal redress after the northern abolition of slavery. In the South, however, only enslaved men were tried for sexual assaults on women of color. As the South became more of a slave society and the North became a society with fewer slaves, the legal possibilities for African American victims diverged.[22]

Thus, race structured legal action even before courts adjudicated the merits of a sexual assault charge. First and foremost, white women were the only regular, legitimate victims of sexual attacks. Second, women and the communities who influenced them seemed far more ready to see punishable sexual force in a black man's behavior than in a white man's. Courts charged black defendants with the most serious crimes and white defendants with a variety of lesser charges that might focus on *either* the force *or* the sex involved in the incident but often not the two together that mandated a rape charge. Even before adjudication of a case, rape began with a default image of a black attacker and a white victim. Criminal trials refined and intensified this race-based picture.

PROVING THE CASE: DEFENDANTS, VICTIMS, AND EVIDENCE

Criminal trials were meant to determine the guilt or innocence of the defendant: did he commit the sexual assault of which he was accused? In many ways, however, both accuser and accused were on trial—he for a sexual assault and she for being a potentially willing participant in illicit sexual activity. Because

22. *The Trial of Captain James Dunn, for an Assault, with Intent to Seduce Sylvia Patterson, a Black Woman* (New York, 1809), NYHS. For a historian's assumption that this case was a "confidence game" involving consensual sex, rather than a sexual assault, see Graham Russell Hodges, *Root and Branch: African Americans in New York and East Jersey, 1613–1863* (Chapel Hill, N.C., 1999), 210–211. On increasing concern over free blacks' behavior in northern cities and black women's chastity in particular, see Sweet, *Bodies Politic*, 288, 368–378; Melish, *Disowning Slavery*, 123–128. On the distinction between slave societies and societies with slaves, see Ira Berlin, *Many Thousands Gone: The First Two Centuries of Slavery in North America* (Cambridge, Mass., 1998), 7–13. On general shifts resulting from northern abolition of slavery, see Melish, *Disowning Slavery*. For a legalistic account, see the classic, Arthur Zilversmit, *The First Emancipation: The Abolition of Slavery in the North* (Chicago, 1967).

most cases did not have ready witnesses who could testify to seeing the physical interaction between accused and accuser, judges and juries adjudicated sexual assaults by weighing factors outside the individual incident. In addition to the standards of circumstantial evidence laid out by Sir Matthew Hale, they most commonly looked at the reputation of the victim and the motive behind the accusation. Judges and juries evaluated a woman's reputation and dissected any other motives she might have had for making an accusation. Race again framed these evaluations. First, white women were somewhat more believable accusers than black women, especially when they accused black men of rape, because Anglo-Americans assumed that respectable white women would be far less likely to have voluntary sexual relations with black men than with white men. Second, black defendants' racial identity was used against them as convincing evidence of unlikely innocence, while white men's racial identity more likely allowed their individual actions to indicate probable guilt or innocence. Together, these factors made convicting a black man of raping a white woman a far more frequent occurrence than convicting a white man for raping any woman.

Black and white defendants did have one thing in common: they both overwhelmingly pleaded not guilty. Because a man charged with the crime of rape could not do much worse than the likely death sentence or lengthy prison term that could result from a guilty plea, 99 percent of white defendants and 95 percent of black defendants pleaded not guilty to rape charges. Even slaves, the men most vulnerable to coerced confessions, might have been encouraged to plead not guilty to most sexual assault charges by the lawyers that their masters hired to defend them. Still, the rare guilty plea to rape might have been more proof of the will of others than of the crime of the accused: in a Revolutionary-era Maryland case, the victim asked for the commutation of her black rapist's death sentence because he was "Convicted upon (as I believe) a Confession extorted from him upon a whipping inflicted on him by his said Master," so she could not swear that he was the attacker. Aside from such exceptional cases, most men accused of a sexual attack had their legal guilt determined by a court's verdict.[23]

23. White defendants' pleas are known in 111 cases, black defendants in 115 cases. James D. Rice found that guilty pleas in Maryland criminal cases averaged about 6 percent and became less common after 1780 (Rice, "Crime and Punishment in Frederick County and Maryland, 1748–1837: A Study in Culture, Society, and Law" [Ph.D. diss., University of Maryland at College Park, 1994], 251, 259). For cases against slaves that mention a defense lawyer's involvement, see *Rex v Cuff*, March 1743, Newport County Superior Court of Judicature Docket, C, 127–128, RIJRC; case of Dick, December 1810, Virginia Executive

Part of the court's ultimate determination hinged on the jury's opinion of the accused. As one judge in an 1812 case in Pennsylvania summarized, a defendant's good character, "which tho of no avail when the fact [of a sexual assault] is proven, is of consequence in a doubtful case." For white men, juries and communities saw a man's lifelong actions as indicative of his likely guilt or innocence. So in 1758, a Massachusetts court called a white man convicted of attempted rape "a person of ill fame and conversation." In South Carolina in 1797, witnesses testified that a man accused of attempted rape was of "suspicious Carrector and Evil." In pronouncing their guilty judgment against another white rapist in 1806, Kentucky judges concluded that "the defendant appears to be a man of worthless character."[24]

In contrast, black men were more likely to be described via their racial identity, even beyond their automatic classification as "negro" or "mulatto." In 1743, the husband of one Connecticut rape victim called her attacker "an Inhuman Negro Slave." Some defenses of black defendants were likewise set in the context of racial identity. In 1817, one witness testified at the rape trial of a Connecticut man that his character was, "for a black man, uncommonly good," and another inverted that dubious compliment to proclaim the defendant's character "as good as that of a white man." Despite the defendant's having a character that was deemed exceptional for his race, the judge in the trial reminded the grand jury that blacks came from a savage nation and a race full of "insolence and rapacity." Even a lifetime of positive behavior did not negate a black man's membership in a race of slaves, while the invisibility of whiteness allowed evaluations of white defendants' individual characters.[25]

Papers, box 169a, Dec. 21–30 folder, LOV; *Trial of Amos Adams* (New Haven, Conn., 1817), AAS; case of Billy Scott, Feb. 4, 1805, Virginia Executive Papers, box 133, LOV. For a case where the court appointed a lawyer for the accused slave, see case of Abraham, Aug. 3, 1799, Virginia Executive Papers, box 109, LOV. See also Flanigan, "Criminal Procedure in Slave Trials," *JSH*, XL (1974), 560–564; Higginbotham and Jacobs, "The 'Law Only as an Enemy,'" *NCLR*, LXX (1992), 1011–1016; case of Abraham, June 1770, in *Archives of Maryland*, 72 vols. (Baltimore, 1883–1972), XXXII, 368–370.

24. *Commonwealth v Taylor*, Jan. 8, 1812, Pennsylvania Court Papers, HSP; case of James Studley, April 1758, in Konig, ed., *Plymouth Court Records*, III, *1748–1751*, 97; *State v John Mitchell*, April 1797, Pinckney District General Sessions Court, Sessions Rolls, no. 88, SCDAH; *Commonwealth v John Morrow*, October 1806, Warren County Circuit Court File Papers, KLA.

25. Memorial of Ephraim Andrews, 1743, Connecticut Archives, Crimes and Misdemeanors, 1st Ser., IV, 71–73, CSL; *Trial of Amos Adams*, 8, 21, 22. See also indictment of Lenass Brawn, April 1792, Dockets of Cases and Notes of Evidence Taken by Hon. In-

A victim's perceived character was even more crucial to the outcome of a rape trial, and sexual chastity was the most important component of a woman's reputation. Despite the British legal consensus that a "common Strumpet" was as protected by rape law as any other woman, a woman's previous sexual relationships would quickly undermine support for a claim that she had been forced into sex. If a woman were known to willingly have had illicit sex on other occasions, a court would likely doubt that she had refused on this one. Thus, court testimonies were filled with commentaries on women's sexual habits.[26]

Prosecutors, judges, and clerks made virginity a crucial piece of evidence in rape cases, using it to suggest that girls and women who had always refused sexual relationships would be likely to have refused in the incident before the court. Indictments specified when young white women had been virgins. Chief Justice Thomas McKean characterized the white victim in one Pennsylvania rape case as an eighteen-year-old woman with virginal innocence. Some victims would go to great lengths to prove their chastity: after accusing a man of trying to rape her in 1738 in Pennsylvania, Isabella Gibson produced a certificate from her Quaker meeting stating that she was not a whore.[27]

---

crease Sumner, 1782–1797, 159–161, MHS; *State v Thomas Farrell,* Sept. 7, 1789, Camden County General Sessions Court, Sessions Rolls, SCDAH; *King v Jannean,* 1738, New York County Quarter Sessions, Manuscript Minutes, 348–350, NYHR; case of Edmund Fortis, 1795, Robert Treat Paine Papers, Charges to Grand Juries, reel 17 (near the end of the reel), MHS. For rape by Native Americans described in similar terms, see letter of Alexander Steele, Sept. 12, 1792, East Florida Papers, bundle 122E10, no. 323, reel 47, pt. 2, Library of Congress MSS, Washington, D.C.

26. William Hawkins, *A Treatise of the Pleas of the Crown* . . . (London, 1724–1726; rpt. New York, 1972), I, 108; James Parker, comp., *Conductor Generalis* . . . (Woodbridge, N.J., 1764), 360; John E. Hall, *The Office and Authority of a Justice of the Peace in the State of Maryland* (Baltimore, 1815); [Richard Burn], *Burn's Abridgment; or, the American Justice,* 2d ed. (Dover, N.H., 1792); William Simpson, *The Practical Justice of the Peace of South-Carolina* (Charleston, S.C., 1761).

27. For specifications of virginity, see John Ward indicted, Mar. 11, 1766, Massachusetts Superior Court of Judicature Records, Suffolk Files, nos. 100811, 100815, MA; case of James Corbit, February 1756, Massachusetts Superior Court of Judicature Records, Suffolk Files, no. 75329, MA; *D. v Daniel Patterson,* March 1734, Chester County Quarter Sessions File Papers, CCA; *Rex v Vanskelly Mully,* 1760, Connecticut Superior Court Record Book, XVII, 44, CSL; notes of charges delivered to grand juries by Chief Justice Thomas McKean, 1779, Thomas McKean Papers, 1759–1847, HSP; *D. v John West,* August 1738, Chester County Quarter Sessions File Papers, CCA. On the historic importance of

Because enslaved women could not legally marry and have legitimate sexual relations, all of their sexual behavior appeared illicit. Early Americans' association of blackness with slavery meant that all African American women's sexual reputations were suspect, thus undermining their believability as rape victims. When a black woman named Sylvia Patterson accused a white man, James Dunn, of attempted rape in early-nineteenth-century New York City, her sexual reputation came under repeated attack. Witnesses claimed that she was not only married to a man who had six other wives but also that she was hospitalized for a venereal disease, associated with prostitutes, and improperly bared her legs in public. Even Sylvia's attorney implicitly degraded Sylvia's character on account of her race, arguing that James had tried to have sex with Sylvia because "no white woman that had the least regard for herself would have any thing to do with him." Even the frontispiece for the published trial remade what Sylvia called a sexual assault into an image of prostitution. During the trial James was described as trying to bribe Sylvia's *husband* with a pocket watch so that he and Sylvia would not prosecute James, but the frontispiece pictured James offering Sylvia a watch while pulling up her dress. For black women especially, early Americans often saw little distinction between their consent and a white man's coercion. All women might be subject to a maligned sexual reputation, but the few nonwhite women who claimed a sexual assault could be summarily disgraced by racial associations to sexual impurity.[28]

White women might avoid automatic assumptions of sexual dishonor, but those who accused white men had to pass a barrage of questions that sought to discover any hidden motives for a rape accusation. Thomas Jefferson, like many early Americans, believed that women could use rape charges for personal revenge: he criticized harsh punishment for rape "on account of the temptation women would be under to make it the instrument of vengeance against an inconstant lover, and of disappointment to a rival." Similar fears arose at trials. In 1764 in North Carolina, a witness in one attempted rape case testified that the victim had *"Said that she would be Revenged"* of the defendant. In 1803 in New York, Mathias Hays defended himself from his servant's rape

---

virginity, see Keith Thomas, "The Double Standard," *Journal of the History of Ideas,* XX (1959), 195–216.

28. *The Trial of Captain James Dunn,* 5, 16. On images of black women as sexually voracious and unchaste, see Jennifer L. Morgan, "'Some Could Suckle over Their Shoulder': Male Travelers, Female Bodies, and the Gendering of Racial Ideology, 1500–1770," *WMQ,* 3d Ser., LIV (1997), 167–192; Fischer, *Suspect Relations,* 28, 151; Richard Godbeer, *Sexual Revolution in Early America* (Baltimore, 2002), 201.

TRIAL

OF

CAPTAIN JAMES DUNN.

Then vain is thy sweet power
To soothe my pained breast.

PLATE 2. *Frontispiece to* The Trial of Captain James Dunn, for an Assault, with Intent to Seduce Sylvia Patterson, a Black Woman *(New York, 1809).* Collection of The New-York Historical Society

accusation by claiming that she accused him only after he fired her. Trial transcripts in the early Republic frequently contained defense lawyers' suggestions that victims claimed rape as revenge. In 1789 in Pennsylvania, Rebecca McCarter specified under cross-examination that "[never] did I say I could have Revenge" on the man who had impregnated her. The defendant's lawyer in a New York case claimed that a thirteen-year-old girl had charged her stepfather with rape only so that her mother could get rid of a disagreeable husband. Another New York defense attorney reminded the jury, "You all know how strong the passion of revenge exists in a female breast." Because fears of false rape charges were widespread, lawyers could defend their clients by suggesting a victim's ulterior motive for making her accusation.[29]

Women's sexual reputations could be a hurdle to any claim of rape — even, occasionally, ones that involved black defendants. In a 1792 case in Maryland, petitioners to the governor asked for commutation for one enslaved rapist on the grounds that the white victim "had no character to lose" and that there was the "strong appearance of intimacy subsisting between her and the Said Negro for sometime before the prosecution." As explanation of this intimate relationship, petitioners recounted, in part, that "she confessed he had given her fish"

29. Thomas Jefferson to James Madison, Dec. 16, 1786, in Julian P. Boyd et al., eds., *The Papers of Thomas Jefferson*, 31 vols. (Princeton, N.J., 1950-), X, 604; Robert J. Cain, ed., *Records of the Executive Council, 1755-1775*, Colonial Records of North Carolina, 2d Ser., IX (Raleigh, N.C., 1994), 467, emphasis in original; *The People v Matthias Hays*, Dec. 17, 1803, New York County Court of General Sessions Indictment Papers, NYMA; *Republica v David Robb*, Yeates Legal Papers, March–April 1789, fol. 2, HSP; *Report of the Trial of Richard D. Croucher, on an Indictment for a Rape on Margaret Miller; on Tuesday, the 8th Day of July, 1800* (New York, 1800), 8, 9; *Report of the Trial of Henry Bedlow, for Committing a Rape on Lanah Sawyer* (New York, 1793), 32, 60–61. See also William Alexander, *The History of Women: From the Earliest Antiquity, to the Present Time* (Philadelphia, 1796), 322; *Commonwealth v John Morrow*, October 1806, Warren County Circuit Court File Papers. For an exceptional case of a black man claiming that a woman's grudge against him led legal officials to wrongly charge him with rape, see *Life of William Grimes, the Runaway Slave* (New York, 1825), in Arna Bontemps, comp., *Five Black Lives* (Middletown, Conn., 1971), 109–110. On fear of malicious prosecutions, see Laurie Edelstein, "An Accusation Easily to be Made? Rape and Malicious Prosecution in Eighteenth-Century England," *Am. Jour. of Legal Hist.*, XLII (1998), 351–390; Antony E. Simpson, "The 'Blackmail Myth' and the Prosecution of Rape and Its Attempt in Eighteenth-Century London: The Creation of a Legal Tradition," *Journal of Criminal Law and Criminology*, LXXVII (1986), 101–150. On the intransigency of this belief, see Susan Estrich, "Palm Beach Stories," *Law and Philosophy: Philosophical Issues in Rape Law*, XI (1992), 11.

and sold her a chicken, from which the petitioners surmised they must have had a quarrel about payment. In 1812, a Virginia slave named George might have been pardoned because his white victim was known to spend late nights in the kitchen, presumably engaging in inappropriate socialization with people of color. White women's reputations mattered even when black slaves were the ones accused, because early Americans evaluated character and motive to determine guilt and innocence. But the reputations that would derail a white man's *prosecution* would more likely (as in these cases) be an issue in deciding a black man's *punishment*. A white woman's sexual or social improprieties did not seem to occasion the same degree of disbelief in her rape accusation against a black man as it would against a white man.[30]

Beyond race-based reputations and suppositions of dishonorable motives, courts depended on evidence of the actual assault. Yet court listeners' perceptions about race influenced their interpretations of this evidence as well. Women who charged enslaved men with rape were often formulaic and nonspecific in their descriptions of what had been done to them. A particularly detailed collection of early-nineteenth-century Virginia court papers exemplifies this pattern. Phebe Pool gave few specifics when she testified about Mulatto Jesse's rape of her in 1804. She did not explain whether she screamed, whether people were nearby, whether she was injured, or how soon afterward she told others about the attack. Instead, Phebe formulaically stated that Jesse pulled her off her horse, "threw her down and ravished her by actual penetration and emission." In 1806, a court convicted a black man whose victim testified only that he had thrown her down and "effected his purpose." In 1818, Robert Parkinson testified that Parthena Rucks told him "with tears in her eyes, that she had been beaten and misused by a negroe." When questioned further, Parthena never mentioned rape explicitly, and Robert did not feel the need to press for more details or to have any women examine Parthena for signs of a sexual attack. Instead, being told that a slave had thrown a white woman down, Robert would testify, "satisfied him with regard [to the slave's] mad scheme" of rape. To a modern reader, what actually happened to Parthena might be unclear. But, in the early nineteenth century, Parthena's vagueness might have made her all the more believable, indicating her modesty and respectability: her rapist was convicted and executed. Because black men were

30. Petitions for Jack, 1793, Governor and Council, Pardon Papers, box 6, folder 50, MdSA; case of George, Oct. 24, 1812, Virginia Executive Papers, LOV. Diane Sommerville points to the importance of women's class status in southern black-on-white rape prosecutions in "The Rape Myth in the Old South Reconsidered," *JSH,* LXI (1995), 481–518.

more easily imagined as rapists of white women than as consensual sexual partners, black-on-white assaults did not require specific details to result in convictions.[31]

Black men might be convicted even when the victim's statements were easily impeachable. In 1756, Hannah Beebe accused a Connecticut slave of a rape that she recanted after his conviction. Hannah made up a story that she had fallen into fits when he had "rumaged her private parts" but nevertheless knew she had been raped. Despite the lack of details in her false claim, the slave was convicted of the crime. When Elizabeth Truax accused John Morris, a free black man, of raping her in 1792 in Delaware, she testified that even though she passed out during the attack, she believed "from the hurts received during the struggle and what she felt and discovered after she recovered from the insensible state she was reduced to, that he had carnal knowledge of her." Even though Elizabeth could not testify to the actual act performed, the court convicted and hanged John for the crime. A case prosecuted in Virginia in 1819 provides one of the most blatant examples of the minimal evidence required to convict black men of rape. Elizabeth Smith accused Dennis of raping her, but, when questioned at court, she denied that he had entered her body, despite her claim that he had "rogered her." Although her confusion about (if not denial of) penetration should have excluded a rape conviction, the court convicted Dennis. These white women faced little scrutiny when they accused black men (enslaved or free) because the presumption of an unwelcome black man's sexual intent was evidence of his guilt, and because the community had a stake in maintaining racial hierarchies.[32]

31. Case of Mulatto Jesse, Aug. 6, 1804, Virginia Executive Papers, box 131, LOV; case of Peter Twine, 1806, Auditor of Public Accounts, no. 756, Condemned Slaves, box 1967, LOV; case of Lewis, Aug. 1, 1818, Virginia Executive Papers, box 248, LOV. See also *D. v Joe,* n.d., Kent County Oyer and Terminer File Papers, DPA; case of Luke, Mar. 7, 1804, Virginia Executive Papers, box 129, LOV. On the nineteenth-century legal argument that white women would not consent to black men, see A. Leon Higginbotham, Jr., and Barbara K. Kopytoff, "Racial Purity and Interracial Sex in the Law of Colonial and Antebellum Virginia," in Werner Sollors, ed., *Interracialism: Black-White Intermarriage in American History, Literature, and Law* (Oxford, 2000), 124–128. On early colonial societal allowance for black men's sexual relations with white women, see Hodes, *White Women, Black Men,* 19–38.

32. Case of Bristo, January 1757, Connecticut Archives, Crimes and Misdemeanors, 1st Ser., V, 47–53, CSL; *State v John Morris,* December 1792, Kent County Oyer and Terminer Docket, microfilm p. 0075, DPA; case of Dennis, June 1819, Virginia Executive Papers, box 254, June 24–30 folder, LOV. See also case of Archy, 1805, Auditor of Public Accounts, no.

The formulaic descriptions of rape and the few specifications of how the attacker forced his victim to have sex may seem to show early Americans' recognition of the difficulties women might have in talking about violent sex. But all of these rules changed when a white man was the accused: white women who charged white men with rape had to provide substantial specifics about the attack. When Rachel Davis testified to a Pennsylvania court in 1808 about being raped by a white man, she explained how he had pulled up her clothes, pressed her mouth into his body, and bruised her arms, why she could not push him off, at what point he had pulled his breeches down, and she even quoted his exact statement, "You dear creature, I must fuck you." Rachel's detailed testimony apparently helped convince the court to convict her attacker. However, when Christiana Waggoner claimed in 1783 that a white man had assaulted her, the Pennsylvania court was not satisfied with her detailed discussion of exactly how the sexual act took place. Christiana repeatedly explained how the man had held her with her feet nearly off the ground, where both of his hands were, where her hands were, how he had strangled her, and how he had kept her petticoat up and her legs apart with his knee during the attack. But, ultimately, the justice of the peace to whom she reported the crime doubted her claim, because, as he told the court, "I never could have done it" in the way that she described. Despite all of Christiana's descriptive powers, this justice defended the accused by verbally putting himself in the white man's position.[33]

Lawyers and community members rigorously cross-examined white women who testified against white men about the physical details of the attack. Mary Jinkins claimed that she "fell into a fitte" during a rape in her northern New England home in 1710. But her neighbor told the court that she had grilled Mary about her claims, asking Mary how she knew he had raped her if she had been unconscious. When Mary could not provide a convincing answer, the neighbor concluded: "Hee Never lay with you atole. for you sd hee did not Ly

756, Condemned Slaves, box 1967, LOV. On the different evidence necessary to convict black and white rapists, see Donna J. Spindel, *Crime and Society in North Carolina, 1663–1776* (Baton Rouge, La., 1989), 108–109.

33. *Commonwealth v William Cress,* February 1808, Pennsylvania Court Papers, HSP; notes of evidence in *Respublica v Abraham Moses,* May 21, 1783, Yeates Legal Papers, April–May 1783, fol. 7, HSP. For a case where a lawyer declared that a man could not force a woman to have sex unless he used his right hand, see *Report of the Trial of Henry Bedlow,* 41. See also *King v John Lawrence et al.,* Aug. 1, 1754, Supreme Court Pleadings, reels 48–49, K–501, K–650, NYHR, and New York City Supreme Court Minute Book, 1754–1757, 53, 145–146, NYHR.

with you before your fitte Nor after your fitte and in your fitte you whare not Sencebel hee laid with you." Such purposeful effort at disbelief directly contrasted with a community's acceptance of a white woman's claims of being unconscious during a black man's rape. Similarly, in 1729, neighbors questioned Abigail Kindall about her claim that a white neighbor had raped her. One ultimately concluded "that she had been distracted, and she might be mistaken and therefore might think that he did that which he did not." Community members were less likely to accept white women's claims against white men without explicit details. By the nineteenth century, early Americans would have been quite familiar with the image of the sensitive woman who might faint at such depredations on her chastity. But I have seen no successful rape prosecutions against white men where women claimed a loss of consciousness as a substitute for detailed testimony about the attack.[34]

Colonists' careful attention to the details of white men's sexual attacks continued in the early Republic. In her testimony at a 1783 trial in Pennsylvania, Jane Mathers had to provide just such convincing details of her attack. She specified that James Paxton had torn her away from the tree to which she clung, "threw me down, pulled up my petticoats and put it into me — He put his hand on my mouth when I was screaming — I hallowed out — He swore he would do it and choaked me a little." Despite this fairly detailed testimony, Jane also had to provide further specifications under cross-examination before the court was satisfied with the truth of her testimony. Under such scrutiny, many women were not able to prove their cases against white men. When Rebecca Fay testified about the assault made on her by a white man in 1810, she explained how she had loudly told her attacker to stop, how he had shut the door and covered her mouth with his chest to muffle her screams, and how he was ultimately able to sexually assault her on a dining room table. Under cross-examination, Rebecca further explained how he had raised her skirts, how the buttons on the knees of his breeches had rubbed off her skin, how her thigh was bruised, and how he had used his hands in the attack. Still, her white attacker was acquitted.[35]

---

34. Case of John White and Mary, the wife of Rowland Jinkins, July 1710, in Neal W. Allen, Jr., ed., *Province and Court Records of Maine,* IV (Portland, Maine, 1958), 378–381; case of Thomas Procter, July 29, 1729, Massachusetts Superior Court of Judicature Records, Suffolk Files, no. 23157, MA.

35. Notes of evidence in *Respublic v James Paxton,* May 27, 1783, Yeates Legal Papers, April–May 1783, fol. 7, HSP; *Trial of Charles Wakely, for a Rape on Mrs. Rebecca Fay* (New York, 1810), 5–9.

Differing evidentiary expectations remind us that racial prejudice is too simplistic an explanation for the multiple ways in which race operated at early American courts. Courts did not simply assume guilt and convict and execute all African American men, but from the moment that a victim appeared at the courtroom doors, courts uniformly privileged whiteness. White men appeared to be less likely rapists because they had far more opportunities than black men to avoid rape convictions. Courts in all regions made racially based judgments that led to large numbers of convictions of black men and virtually no convictions for the sexual assault of black women. These practices led to starkly different images of early American black and white rapists.

CONVICTION AND PUNISHMENT

Not surprisingly, black men were convicted at higher rates than were white defendants. Whites were more likely to have charges dropped or extralegally settled, were more likely to be convicted of lesser crimes than those originally charged, and were far more likely to be acquitted when a case did go to trial. We might expect southern courts to have high conviction rates for enslaved men. They did. But black men — free and enslaved — were convicted of rape more frequently than white defendants in all regions. Even the abolition of slavery in the North seemed to have no discernible effect: mid-Atlantic and New England conviction rates hovered at about the same levels in the colonial era and in the early Republic.[36]

Sentencing practices, however, reveal regional and chronological differences. Although all regions punished blacks much more severely than whites, southern courts punished blacks in ways that explicitly set them apart from free whites. With excessive whippings, castrations, and physical mutilations, southern courts ordered slave rapists to be visibly marked at the very time that white men were being exempted from most forms of corporal punishment. By the early Republic, white men were rarely capitally punished, making the continuation of harsh sentences against blacks a public lesson about the supposed danger posed by blacks. These final judgments sealed the image of black men as dangerous rapists and white men as occasional sexual transgressors.

36. Although the numbers are too small for valid statistical conclusions, six out of the eight New England rape trials of black men from 1700 to 1776 resulted in a guilty verdict, compared to eight out of ten guilty verdicts from 1777 to 1820. The four known mid-Atlantic trials of black rapists before 1777 resulted in three guilty verdicts, as did seven out of the ten trials from 1777 to 1820.

White men had multiple means beyond that of a not guilty verdict to avoid a conviction. Some ended prosecutions with economic settlements. In mid-eighteenth-century Georgia, one woman complained that several soldiers raped her, but before she could be officially sworn about the matter, she was given ten pounds in return for a promise never to prosecute the men who had assaulted her. In 1783, Pennsylvanian John Waggoner unsuccessfully tried to settle Abraham Moses's assault on his wife without a trial. John testified that he "offered to make up the matter and so did my Wife if I recd £300 or £400 if he gave me with a Certificate of his having used [her] against her will." But Abraham would not agree to these terms and facetiously countered with an offer of "5 or 6 dollar if she would stand Certified a Whore."[37]

Slaves, who rarely had their own funds, were dependent on their masters' desire to settle a case out of court and on communities that might be far less likely to let a black rapist avoid public punishment. In one of the few known cases where a white victim purposefully avoided prosecution of a black rapist, Deborah Metcalfe went to the master of the Massachusetts slave who had raped her in 1768, and "she being unwilling to have me hanged, proposed making the Matter up for a proper Consideration, provided my Master would send me out of the Country; to which he agreed." Unlike monetary settlements with white attackers, this settlement included a provision to exile the attacker—a punishment that might be identical to a court's eventual sentence. But, before this plan could proceed, a constable showed up with a warrant for the slave; apparently, community members were intent on criminally prosecuting him.[38]

Partly because of extralegal settlements, trials of whites ended at earlier stages more often than did those of blacks. Nearly one-third of white men's rape charges either were dropped by the prosecutor or ended without an indictment, compared to only a small percentage of those of black rape de-

37. John Terry to the Trustees of Georgia, in Candler, ed., *Colonial Records of the State of Georgia*, XXIV, 254; notes of evidence in *Respublica v Abraham Moses*, May 21, 1783, Yeates Legal Papers, April–May 1783, fol. 7, HSP. See also *King v John Williams*, July 1757, Minutes of Monmouth County, cited in Henry Clay Reed, "Chapters in a History of Crime and Punishment in New Jersey" (Ph.D. diss., Princeton University, 1939), 340; *Penn. Gaz.*, Nov. 10–13, 1729; *Commonwealth v Hutchinson*, 10 Mass. 225 (1813); petitions for William James Holmes, 1790, Governor and Council, Pardon Papers, box 5, folder 11, MdSA; testimony in *Commonwealth v John Walker*, January 1815, Pennsylvania Court Papers, box for 1807–1809, HSP; *Commonwealth v Murphy*, 14 Mass. 387–388 (1817). On the impact of class on one's ability to "make up" a rape accusation out of court, see Simpson, "Popular Perceptions of Rape," *LHR*, XXII (2004), 48.

38. *The Life and Dying Speech of Arthur, a Negro Man* . . . (Boston, 1768).

fendants. To put it another way, of all of the cases that were dropped, more than three-quarters of the defendants were white men. (Here, again, the victim's race was especially relevant: charges involving a nonwhite victim were dropped at a rate three times higher than in prosecuted sexual assault cases generally.) Slave courts, without the benefit of a grand jury hearing, could not end a trial at the indictment stage. Even those colonies with identical trial procedures for black and white men were less willing to question the evidence against a black man. New England courts either did not indict or dropped sexual assault charges against white men twice as often as they did against black men. Overall, courts convicted 35 percent of white defendants and 84 percent of black defendants charged with rape. With the abolishment of capital punishment for most white defendants in the 1790s, white conviction rates for rape rose somewhat but still remained at about one-half the rate of black convictions.[39]

There is no doubt that criminal courts convicted blacks of sexual assaults at much higher rates than whites, but comparing blacks' conviction rates for rape to their conviction rates for other crimes is more difficult. Most studies of the criminal treatment of blacks focus on the nineteenth-century South, and systematic statistics on black crime throughout early America do not exist. However, by piecing together various early American criminal studies, it seems that enslaved men were convicted of rape at higher rates than for other crimes. From 1706 to 1785, Virginia courts convicted slaves of crimes against persons 69 percent of the time, compared to more than an 80 percent conviction rate for rape charges specifically. From 1691 to 1776, slaves in colonial New York accused of economic, violent, or master-directed crimes averaged about a two-thirds conviction rate. Of the four black men known to have been accused of a sexual assault in colonial New York, three were convicted. If we compare

39. Statistics are based on 179 white and 179 black defendants' rape prosecutions for which the verdict is known. The black and white percentages are less dramatically different for verdicts in lesser charges, but white defendants' percentage of dropped cases is still at least two times higher than blacks'. New England convictions are based on 36 New England black defendants and 108 New England white defendants. Similar rate differences apply to rape charges alone.

The pre-1800 white conviction rate hovered at 31 percent, whereas the post-1800 rate rose as high as 42 percent (114 pre-1800 white defendants and 65 post-1800 white defendants compared to 127 pre-1800 black defendants and 52 post-1800 black defendants). On overall historical averages in the mid–30 percent range for rape prosecutions, see Sean T. Moore, "'Justifiable Provocation': Violence against Women in Essex County, New York, 1799–1860," *Journal of Social History*, XXXV (2002), 902, table 3.

general prosecution of blacks in New York to all mid-Atlantic colonial prosecutions against black men for sexual assaults from 1700 to 1776, it again appears that mid-Atlantic colonies more harshly punished African American men's sexual crimes: ten of the eleven black men charged with a sexual assault were convicted (one of a lesser charge). Similarly, seventeen out of the nineteen black men charged with sexual assaults in New England were found guilty. Furthermore, there was no discernible difference in the conviction rates for free and enslaved black men in either northern or southern courts. Not only were black men more frequently convicted of rape than of other crimes, but it appears that shared Anglo-American racial ideologies, as much as any specific race-based slave judicial system, structured the differential treatment of white and black sexual assault defendants.[40]

A guilty verdict led inexorably to the final step of a criminal prosecution: sentencing. Nearly two-thirds of all sexual assaults prosecuted against black men ended with a death sentence. White men, however, were likely to receive a more diverse array of punishments: only slightly more than 10 percent of their prosecutions resulted in a death sentence. Both southern and northern judges sentenced black men to death far more often than they did whites. Roughly one-half of the death sentences in the New England and mid-Atlantic re-

---

40. On nineteenth-century southern black or enslaved crime, see Michael S. Hindus, "Black Justice under White Law: Criminal Prosecutions of Blacks in Antebellum South Carolina," *Journal of American History,* LXIII (1976), 575–599; Christopher Waldrep, *Roots of Disorder: Race and Criminal Justice in the American South, 1817–80* (Urbana, Ill., 1998).

For Virginia statistics, see Schwarz, *Twice Condemned,* 39, 74. The eighty-nine black men accused of rape in Virginia from 1700 to 1820 averaged an 83 percent conviction rate, with another 9 percent convicted of a lesser crime. Similarly, from 1818 to 1860, Michael Hindus found a 67 percent general conviction rate for blacks in South Carolina; see Hindus, "Black Justice under White Law," *JAH,* LXIII (1976), 590.

For New York statistics, see Douglas Greenberg, *Crime and Law Enforcement in the Colony of New York, 1691–1776* (Ithaca, N.Y., 1976), 74. I have calculated this number from the raw data on serious crimes provided by Greenberg: 38/69 thefts, 149/214 crimes against masters, and 13/16 violent crimes (of which some might have been rape) resulted in conviction. In an antebellum New York county, Sean T. Moore has estimated a conviction rate for rape and attempted rape at 35 percent (Moore, "'Justifiable Provocation,'" *Jour. Soc. Hist.,* XXXV [2002], 897).

Ninety percent of the 199 slaves and 91 percent of the 23 free blacks charged with a sexual assault received a guilty verdict (including for lesser charges). In the South, all six free blacks were convicted (compared to 91 percent of the 164 slaves tried), but I am hesitant to draw definite conclusions from such small numbers.

gions were pronounced against black men—a number far higher than blacks' presence in the general population. Southern courts pronounced more than 90 percent of their recorded death sentences against black men. This number, although undoubtedly inflated by the dearth of extant criminal records on white rapists, still indicates southern courts' readiness to capitally punish black men for sexual crimes.[41]

Southerners also institutionalized a postmortem dismemberment and display of executed black rapists. In 1701, a Virginia court ordered that an enslaved man who had raped a white woman be executed and his severed head be displayed on a pole close to the James River "to Deter Negroes and other Slaves from Committing the Like Crymes." In Maryland in 1739, a slave convicted of rape was hung in chains after being executed, presumably as an example to others. North Carolinians regularly stuck the heads of convicted black rapists on poles at frequently traveled crossroads. These punishments literally tore apart black rapists and physically excised any threat they might have posed to the white community. This visible display of slaves' severance from civilized society both warned other black men and made visible the violence that colonists used to maintain racial order.[42]

41. Cases in which white men's prosecuted sexual assaults resulted in a known sentence numbered 188; black men's prosecuted sexual assaults that resulted in a known sentence numbered 217. Courts pronounced at least 22 death sentences in New England and 23 in the mid-Atlantic. Southern courts pronounced at least 137 known death sentences. These ratios are comparable for rape prosecutions alone: blacks received 114 of the 123 known southern death sentences in rape prosecutions.

42. Governor Nicholson to Board of Trade, Dec. 1, 1701, CO, class 5, 1312, pt. 2, folder 22–23, Virginia Colonial Records Project, cited in Schwarz, *Twice Condemned,* 72; case of Robin, August 1739, *Archives of Maryland,* XXVIII, 181. For other Chesapeake slaves hung in chains, see the case of Sharper, 1751, Governor and Council, Commission Records, 1726–1786, 117 (97 of transcript), MdSA; trial of Toney, Apr. 7, 1759, Fairfax County Order Book, reel 38, 331–332, LOV. For North Carolina rapists' bodies on display, see *Crown v George,* May 1770, Secretary of State, Court Records, Magistrates and Freeholders Courts, NCSA; *Crown v Ben,* September 1775, Treasurer and Comptroller Papers, Miscellaneous Group, 1738–1909, box 8, NCSA; *Crown v Jem,* April 1775, New Bern District Superior Court Miscellaneous Records, 1758–1806, "Slave Records 1766, 1778, 1775" folder, 177, NCSA; *State v Liberty,* Dec. 16, 1801, Rutherford County Court Minutes, NCSA. For an order to burn a slave rapist's body, see *Crown v Titus,* Aug. 25, 1777, Onslow County Miscellaneous Records, box 10, "Criminal Action Papers concerning Slaves" folder, NCSA. See also Fischer, *Suspect Relations,* 185–190; *National Register,* VI (1818), 301.

Northerners did not institutionalize these macabre displays, but mob violence did seem to be directed primarily against black rapists. In 1744, rumors circulated that a New Jersey black man convicted of rape would be set on fire. In 1763, when a black man was executed for attempting to rape a child, his body was pelted with "a shower of Snow-Balls, Stones, etc" by an incensed mob of New Yorkers. In 1770, Bostonians so pelted a black attempted rapist that he could scarcely stand when he was released from the pillory. These punishments, whether legally ordered or spontaneously enacted, taught a very public lesson. As a New York newspaper described the execution scene of one black rapist, many "of the Black Tribe" attended, and the editors hoped that "it may be a Means to deter others from attempting such wicked Crimes for the future."[43]

After the American Revolution, shifts in early national penal codes influenced the racialized image of rape. As incarceration became the standard punishment for former capital crimes, fewer whites were executed for rape. In northern states, a few black men also benefited from the abolition of capital punishment. In 1807, for example, Eli Holbrook, "a black man or man of colour," was sentenced to five years in a Connecticut prison for attempted rape, much as a white rapist would have been. But white men were the overwhelming beneficiaries of capital punishment reform. Before 1800, approximately one-half of white men convicted of rape received a death sentence, compared to about 85 percent of black men. After 1800, black sentencing rates for rape remained the same, but fewer than one-quarter of white men were sentenced to death for the same crime. Thus, penal reform primarily left black men as publicly irredeemable rapists. Although white men incarcerated for rape might return to their communities and live out their lives, the continued capital punishment of most black men emphasized their inherently dangerous nature.[44]

Punishments for attempted rape also increasingly emphasized the disparate treatment of black and white convicts. Over the course of the eighteenth cen-

43. *Penn. Gaz.*, Dec. 14, 1744; *Newport Mercury* (R.I.), Dec. 5, 1763. For similar southern cases, see *Virginia Gazette* (Williamsburg), Aug. 19–26, 1737; *Providence Gazette* (R.I.), Jan. 27, 1770; *Boston Gazette*, Jan. 15, 1770; *New-York Gazette*, Jan. 28, 1734. On the significance of public punishments, see Michael Meranze, *Laboratories of Virtue: Punishment, Revolution, and Authority in Philadelphia, 1760–1835* (Chapel Hill, N.C., 1996), 19–54.

44. *State v Eli Holbrook*, August 1807, New Haven Superior Court Criminal Files, box 598, CSL. Before 1800, 47 white convicted rapists had known sentences; from 1800 to 1820, 29 did. Before 1800, 115 black rapists had known sentences, and between 1800 and 1820, 44 black rapists did.

tury, courts began to turn away from corporal punishment for white men. In colonial America, corporal punishment accounted for one-half of white men's attempted rape sentences. After the Revolution, however, only one-fifth of white men convicted of attempted rape received corporal sentences. In contrast, black convicts' punishments for attempted rape remained particularly harsh. More than one-quarter of black men convicted of attempted rape faced a death penalty, and, in contrast to the trend for whites, these numbers did not decrease over time: some southern states made attempted rape a capital crime for enslaved men in the early Republic. Enslaved men also received far harsher corporal punishments than did whites. In 1775, a Virginia slave convicted of attempted rape had his ears nailed to the pillory and then cut off, was branded on the cheek with a hot iron, and was given thirty-nine lashes. Other slaves were castrated for attempted rapes. Though most common in southern courts, northern colonies occasionally applied equally severe corporal punishments to slaves. In 1770, a Pennsylvania slave convicted of attempted rape was sentenced to thirty-nine lashes, had an R branded on his forehead, and was put in prison until his master could sell him out of the state. In contrast, the corporal sentences of white men convicted of attempted rape generally consisted of whippings rather than purposeful, permanent mutilation. Bodily mutilation and castration emphasized the difference between black and white men: by the American Revolution, only blacks were regularly mutilated as a punishment for their crimes. The visible punishment of many enslaved rapists further emphasized the racial boundaries between black and white sexual transgressions.[45]

45. Trial of Tom, Lancaster County Order Book, Sept. 14, 1775, XVI, 1778–1783 (despite the mismatched dates), 8 (upper left), 14 (lower right), LOV; trial of Daniel, June 12, 1774, Accomack County Order Book, reel 85, 214, LOV; trial of Dick, Sept. 14, 1782, Goochland County Order Book, reel 26, 140, LOV; Henry Graham Ashmead, *History of Delaware County, Pennsylvania* (Philadelphia, 1884), 160. See also trial of Will, June 12, 1769, Loudon County Order Book, reel 71, 221–222, LOV; trial of Ned, July 20, 1790, Essex County Order Book, 298, LOV; trial of Peter, Jan. 5, 1782, Northampton Minute Book, reel 50, 334–335, 339, LOV.

Between 1700 and 1776, 35 white men were sentenced for attempted rape, compared to 44 from 1777 to 1820. The rate of death sentences for attempted rape by black men doubled in the early Republic and occurred largely in southern courts. From 1700 to 1776, only 4 out of 23 black attempted rapists were sentenced to death, compared to 11 out of 32 black men who were sentenced to death for attempted rape from 1777 to 1820.

For an exceptional case of a white man asking that his death sentence be commuted to castration for a rape, see case of James Gibson, March 1783, Connecticut Archives, Crimes and Misdemeanors, 1st Ser., VI, 220–222, CSL. On the nineteenth-century corporal pun-

Punishment might have been the ultimate goal of an accusation, but sentencing was often not the final legal move. Many convicted rapists appealed their sentences, especially in capital cases. Some scholars have pointed to black men's ability to get sentences commuted as evidence of less concern over black men's rapes. Yet a comparison of whites' and blacks' abilities to get sentences commuted again underscores the leniency toward white rapists. The circumstances that might have acquitted a white man would more likely just have reduced a black man's sentence. In 1752, the justice in a Maryland rape case petitioned for commutation of a slave's death sentence because he believed there had not been enough evidence to convict him. The victim in a 1770 rape case petitioned for commutation because she could not swear to her black rapist's identity, and she believed his confession had been coerced. In 1783, fourteen men petitioned the Maryland governor to commute Harry's sentence because "the Prosecution might have been malicious." In an 1803 Virginia case, the white victim was known to have three mixed-race children and said to be "a woman of the worst fame," and the enslaved man she accused of rape received a commuted death sentence. The reasons given in all of these successful petitions — lack of proof, mistaken identity, malicious prosecution, a victim's promiscuity — were the rationales used to successfully defend white men from rape *convictions*. But doubt about a black man's guilt apparently carried weight after his conviction, not during his trial. And, even so, black men were still only half as likely as white men to have their death sentences commuted.[46]

ishment of enslaved criminals, see Daniel John Flanigan, "The Criminal Law of Slavery and Freedom, 1800–1868" (Ph.D. diss., Rice University, 1973), 12–16. On the social and racial meanings of mutilated black bodies, see Fischer, *Suspect Relations,* 175–181; Walter Johnson, *Soul by Soul: Life inside the Antebellum Slave Market* (Cambridge, Mass., 1999), 145.

For examples of white men's corporal sentences for attempted rape convictions, see John Murphy (twenty lashes), July 20, 1756, Massachusetts Superior Court of Judicature Records, Suffolk Files, no. 75839, MA; Philip Stone (twenty-one lashes), Pennsylvania Court of Oyer and Terminer Court Papers, RG–33, boxes 6, 7, PSA; John Kelly (twenty-five lashes), June 1749, New Castle Oyer and Terminer Docket, RG–2825, 34, 35, DPA.

46. Diane Sommerville calls white citizens' petition for a black rapist's pardon "astonishing" (Sommerville, "The Rape Myth in the Old South Reconsidered," *JSH,* LXI [1995], 481–482). Martha Hodes theorizes her evaluation of antebellum attitudes by distinguishing between "tolerance" and "toleration" (Hodes, *White Women, Black Men,* 3). Case of Negro Harry, November 1752, in *Archives of Maryland,* XXVIII, 577; case of Abraham, June 1770, ibid., XXXII, 368–370; petitions for Harry, 1783, Governor and Council, Pardon Papers, box 2, folder 57, MdSA; case of Carter, May 9, 1803, Virginia Executive Papers, cited in James Hugo Johnston, *Race Relations in Virginia and Miscegenation in the South,*

The reasons for the differences in commutation rates might have had much to do with racialized perceptions of black and white defendants. A series of Maryland petitions from black and white men in the early Republic reflects the different identities used to defend white and black men. Most petitions for commutation of enslaved men's sexual assault sentences focused on a mistaken conviction; only a few petitions argued that the convicted slave's good reputation should lead to a commutation. Those few petitioners who referred to black men's identity often used descriptions related to the men's status as slave laborers: Adam was "orderly and well behaved," Andrew was "faithful, orderly, and valuable," and Jacob was said to be "a negro of Good Character."[47]

In contrast, white men could draw on multiple features of their individual identities, and almost every white man's petition focused on his good character. One defendant had "an unimpeachable Reputation," an "uprite Caracter," and a "proper Deacent manner"; others were "sober, Industrious" and "Steady, pun[c]tual." Some white men's petitions drew on family reputation: one was from "a large family of Good Citizens," and another was "of Reputable parents and connections." In this post-Revolutionary period, white men also claimed their citizenship as a defense to a rape. One white defendant was an "honest and industrious Citizen" and another a "respectable Citizen of Mary-

---

1776–1860 (Amherst, Mass., 1970), 260. For other black men's petitions involving issues that might have derailed their conviction, see case of Ben, April 1769, *Archives of Maryland*, XXXII, 270–271; case of Jeremiah Hamilton, Oct. 22, 1796, Virginia Executive Papers, box 97, LOV; *Raleigh Register, and North-Carolina Weekly Advertiser,* Oct. 22, 1804; case of Ben, Aug. 7, 1810, Virginia Executive Papers, box 168, 2 docs., LOV; case of Roz Norman, Apr. 15, 1797, ibid., box 99; petitions for Jack, 1793, ibid., box 6, folder 50; case of Greenock, June 20, 1801, ibid., box 117; case of Peter, Oct. 13, 1808, ibid., box 157.

Of 33 white men sentenced to death, at least 4 men had their sentences commuted, whereas only 10 of the 152 black men sentenced to death are known to have had their sentences commuted. For statistics on southern black men's commutations, see Sommerville, "The Rape Myth in the Old South Reconsidered," *JSH,* LXI (1995), 509.

47. Petitions for Andrew, 1793, Governor and Council, Pardon Papers, box 6, folder 54, MdSA; petitions for Adam, 1787, ibid., box 3, folder 96; petitions for Jacob, 1789, ibid., box 4, folder 65.

I have identified 37 of these petitions from 1778 to 1818, 17 from black defendants and 20 from white. For an overview of such petitions, see Rice, "Crime and Punishment in Frederick County and Maryland," 330. For black men's petitions focusing on wrongful conviction, see petitions for Harry, 1783, Governor and Council, Pardon Papers, box 2, folder 57, MdSA; petitions for Adam, 1787, ibid., box 3, folder 96; petitions for Dick Munse, 1815, ibid., box 17, folder 21.

land." This multifaceted masculinity, based on social, economic, political, or family reputation, was a privilege of whiteness. In contrast, black men were more likely to be defended, if at all, with the single identity of their enslavement, which contained within it the belief that black men were permanently part of a potentially dangerous and subservient race.[48]

Black men's convictions and the resulting harsh punishments meted out to them were the constant in sexual assault trials. At every stage of criminal justice, individual prosecutorial choices that might not have seemed explicitly racist combined to lead to profound racial differences in the handling of rape throughout early America. By the early Republic, changes in the punishment of many white rapists allowed slaves' corporal and capital sentences to reinforce a public image of the mutilated black rapist against a backdrop of unmarked white bodies. As we shall see, this image of rape as a crime committed by black men on white women reached far beyond the courtroom doors.

PUBLICITY AND SHIFTING PRESENTATIONS OF WHITENESS

Early Americans regularly learned of rape trials in their local communities through word of mouth, but much of this oral communication is lost to the historian. We may see hints of the numbers of people who attended trials or hangings, but we depend largely on the printed commentaries such events generated to provide a picture of the public image of rape prosecutions. Numerous scholars have relied on northern (largely New England) criminal narrative publications on rape. These trial transcripts and last words that began to appear in the Revolutionary era have been used to analyze the late-eighteenth-century print discourse of black-on-white rape. Here I expand the focus to

48. The following sources are in Governor and Council, Pardon Papers, MdSA: petitions for Thomas Potter, 1814, box 16, folder 64; petitions for John Gibson, 1816, box 17, folders 87, 91; petitions for Richard Burket, 1815, box 17, folder 16; petitions for Samuel Phillips, 1803, box 10, folder 54; petitions for George Hartsough, Jr., 1785, box 3, folder 11. For an argument that avoiding prison would make a convicted white man a better citizen, see petitions for Thomas Potter, 1814, box 16, folder 64. For similar statements about white defendants in other regions, see *Penn. Gaz.*, Nov. 10–13, 1729; *Commonwealth v John Walker*, January 1815, Pennsylvania Court Papers, HSP; petitions for James Paxton, May 29, 1783, Clemency Papers, RG–27, reel 38, 255–256, PSA. On the importance of citizenship to white men accused of sexual assaults, see Marybeth Hamilton Arnold, "'The Life of a Citizen in the Hands of a Woman': Sexual Assault in New York City, 1790–1820," in Kathy Peiss and Christina Simmons, eds., *Passion and Power: Sexuality in History* (Philadelphia, 1989), 35–56.

compare published criminal narratives of white-on-white and black-on-white rape prosecutions. To examine the print culture of rape in the colonial era, I turn to shorter commentaries on rapes that appeared in newspapers throughout the eighteenth century. Newspaper reports of rape prosecutions from 1728 to 1776 reinforced the legal system's racialized treatment of rape by highlighting it as a black-on-white crime and presenting white-on-white rapes as attacks by single, misguided individuals. Newspaper reports of rape show that Americans had already developed associations between African American men and rape in the colonial period. The more extensive criminal narratives of the Revolutionary and post-Revolutionary eras suggest that a growing public minimization of white-on-white rapes contributed to an intensification of the image of black men as rapists.[49]

Since an entire issue of a colonial newspaper was usually only a few pages long, most rapes were reported in one or two sentences that confirmed the occurrence of the rape or the outcome of the prosecution. However, we can learn much about the colonial attitudes toward rape — especially the intersection of race and rape — from these brief reports. As in criminal prosecutions, newspapers reported higher numbers of incidents involving African American defendants in proportion to their numbers in the general population. Of thirty-nine reports of rape in the *Pennsylvania Gazette* between 1728 and 1776, fourteen (more than one-third) involved black rapists. The *Gazette*

---

49. On trials or executions, see Louis B. Wright and Marion Tinling, *The Secret Diary of William Byrd of Westover, 1709–1712* (Richmond, Va., 1941), 95; *The Life and Confession of Daniel Wilson . . .* ([Providence, R.I., 1774]); *New-York Gaz.,* Jan. 28, 1734. On print culture scholarship, see Slotkin, "Narratives of Negro Crime in New England," *AQ,* XXV (1973), 18–28; Cohen, "Social Injustice, Sexual Violence, Spiritual Transcendence," *WMQ,* 3d Ser., LVI (1999), 481–526.

Between 1728 (the founding date of the *Pennsylvania Gazette)* and 1776, I have located nearly one hundred newspaper reports of rape or attempted rape prosecutions in twenty-one different newspapers published in nine different colonies. Besides serendipitous findings of prosecutions, I have done a comprehensive study of two major colonial newspapers, the *Pennsylvania Gazette* and the *Virginia Gazette.* As this book was in press, I searched Readex's Early American Newspapers online (http://infoweb.newsbank.com/) for additional newspaper discussions of rape, and these results matched my previous findings.

On colonial newspapers, see Charles E. Clark, "Early American Journalism: News and Opinion in the Popular Press," esp. 358–359, and James N. Green, "English Books and Printing in the Age of Franklin," esp. 221, 248, 255–257, both in Hugh Amory and David D. Hall, eds., *The Colonial Book in the Atlantic World,* vol. I of A History of the Book in America (Cambridge, 2000).

repeatedly reported on rape trials of black men beyond its own geographical boundaries: it told readers about a black man who had attempted to rape a white woman in Braintree, Massachusetts, in 1764, about slaves who had raped white women in Maryland in 1751 and 1754, and about a slave who had been executed for the attempted rape of a white girl in Jamaica in 1767. Even in New England, where few blacks lived, residents could read in the *Boston Post-Boy* about the conviction of a black man who had attempted to rape a white girl in Philadelphia in 1735 and in Rhode Island's *Newport Mercury* about the execution of a black man for rape in New York in 1763.[50]

Despite their brevity, newspapers conveyed racial interpretations of rape. First, reports of white-on-white rape regularly listed the name but not the race of the defendant and reports of black-on-white rape usually referred to the defendant simply as a "Negro." In the first half of the eighteenth century, the *Pennsylvania Gazette* referred to one accused rapist as a "Negro Man" but specified that a white rapist, "a likely young Fellow," was named William Coulter. In the 1750s and 1760s, New England newspapers reported that a Quaker named Daniel King attacked a young girl and that a mariner named James Corbit was accused of attacking a seventeen-year-old woman but reported just that a "negro fellow" had been sentenced to death for rape. The invisibility of whiteness allowed white sexual attackers to be seen as individuals in categories other than race. Second, newspapers referred to a white woman attacked by a white man without racial identifiers, as just a "woman" or a "young woman." However, when accusing an African American man, newspapers specified that the victim was a "white woman" or a "white child," further emphasizing the image of rape as a crime committed by blacks against whites.[51]

50. *Penn. Gaz.,* Apr. 11, 1751, May 16, 1754, Dec. 13, 1764, Jan. 1, 1767, June 29, 1769; *Boston Post-Boy,* Aug. 4, 1735 (thanks to David Copeland for this citation); *Newport Mercury,* Dec. 5, 1763. Although I have not conducted systematic studies of postcolonial newspapers, they appear to follow similar patterns. Of fourteen rape prosecutions that I have found in newspapers from 1777 to 1820, half involved black-on-white rapes. Estimates of overall African American population ranged from 10 to 18 percent of the American population between 1700 and 1800. See U.S. Bureau of the Census, *Historical Statistics of the United States,* 9, 756. In northern colonies, where most newspapers were published, the African American population was even lower. Blacks never averaged more than 2–3 percent of the New England population and 7–8 percent of the mid-Atlantic population through the eighteenth century.

51. *Penn. Gaz.,* July 24, 1735, Sept. 29, 1743; *Boston Evening-Post,* Nov. 12, 1750, Mar. 15, 1756; *Boston Chronicle,* Oct. 3, 1768; see also *Connecticut Journal* (New Haven), Oct. 7, 1768. For lack of black defendants' names, see *Maryland Gazette,* Dec. 9, 1747; *Penn. Gaz.,*

Reports of black-on-white rape generally provided few specifics about the attacks. The *Pennsylvania Gazette* reported, "We hear that a dead warrant is issued for the execution of a Negroe fellow, condemned at last Calvert county court for a rape," without mentioning any other information about the assault. A Maryland newspaper told of the conviction and pending execution of a black man named Sharper for the rape of a white woman but provided no particulars about the incident. In contrast, reports of sexual attacks by white men included shocking details. In 1750, a New England paper reported a Pennsylvania rape where a white man had assaulted a four-year-old girl, "torn open the poor Creature with his Fingers, and most vilely used her." In 1753, a story of white soldiers' rape of a woman claimed that the "two unnatural villains had carnal knowledge of her after she was dead." The four-man gang rape of a young woman received newspaper coverage in 1772. Four New England newspapers detailed how an ex-soldier had raped and tried to kidnap a woman who was seven months pregnant at knifepoint in Falmouth, New Hampshire, in 1774.[52]

Such details made reports of white-on-white rape noteworthy as extraordinarily horrific attacks. Readers were asked to share in the outrage at such an unquestionably uncivilized act by an individual, not in any condemnation of

July 7, 1743; *Penn. Gaz.,* Nov. 28–Dec. 5, 1734; *Penn. Gaz.,* May 16, 1754; *Vir. Gaz.,* Aug. 19–26, 1737; *New-York Gaz.,* July 28–Aug. 4, 1735; *Boston Post-Boy,* Aug. 4, 1735; *South-Carolina Gazette,* Mar. 17, 1746. For one of the few reports without the name of a white defendant, see the report on a "transient" accused of rape in *Conn. Jour.,* July 6, 1770. For an exceptional use of a black man's name, see *Vir. Gaz.,* Sept. 17, 1767. For examples of victims identified just as women, see *Penn. Gaz.,* Oct. 7–14, 1736, Mar. 25, 1756; *Prov. Gaz.,* Nov. 4–11, 1769; *Newport Mercury,* Nov. 9, 1772. For victims identified as white, see *Rhode-Island Gazette,* Oct. 11, 1732; *Boston Gaz.,* Aug. 4, 1735; *Md. Gaz.,* Feb. 20, Apr. 17, 1751; *Penn. Gaz.,* Sept. 17, 1761.

52. *Penn. Gaz.,* Jan. 9, 1750; *Md. Gaz.,* Apr. 17, 1751; *Boston Evening Post,* Nov. 12, 1750, Apr. 5, 1753; *Penn. Gaz.,* May 7, 1772. See also *Rhode-Island Gaz.,* Oct. 11, 1732; *South-Carolina Gaz.,* Mar. 17, 1746; *Massachusetts Spy* (Boston), Sept. 8, 1774; *Essex Journal* (Newburyport, Mass.), Sept. 14, 1774; *Essex Gazette* (Salem, Mass.), Sept. 20, 1774; *Boston Evening Post,* Sept. 26, 1774. For an exception to the pattern of little information about black-on-white rapes, see *Penn. Gaz.,* July 7, 1743. For multiple newspapers reporting a white man's rape and murder of a nine-year-old girl, see *Conn. Jour.,* Sept. 14, 1770; *Penn. Gaz.,* Sept. 6, 1770; *Boston Evening Post,* Sept. 17, 1770. For reports of white men's rapes on particularly vulnerable victims, see *Penn. Gaz.,* Aug. 25, Sept. 29, 1743. On the increasing eighteenth-century eroticism of criminal narratives, see Karen Halttunen, *Murder Most Foul: The Killer and the American Gothic Imagination* (Cambridge, Mass., 1998), 33–90.

white men's general depravity. We might expect that colonial newspaper editors would emphasize the details of black-on-white rapes to show the horrors of black men's sexual misdeeds. But the interracial nature of these attacks meant that, unlike in white-on-white rapes, editors did not need to do more than identify the black attacker to distinguish the rape from potentially consensual sex. Furthermore, racial tensions and fears might have made the details of black-on-white attacks too transgressive to write about.

Instead of the horrors of the attack, reports of black-on-white rapes focused on the punishment that would be meted out to the black attacker. In 1744, the *Pennsylvania Gazette* reported that a Maryland slave convicted of raping a white girl "will be burnt alive." A decade later, the *Gazette* reported that an enslaved man had been found guilty of the rape and murder of a twelve-year-old girl but apologetically told its readers that "what Death he is to suffer we have not yet heard." And in 1761 it reported on a South Carolina rape prosecution where "a Negroe fellow, about 17 years old, was burnt alive, at a stake on the green." The conviction of a black man for attempted rape of a white girl in New York occasioned multiple newspaper reports of the scene of his execution, where they "dragged his Body through some of the streets." In one of the most detailed (and possibly apocryphal) descriptions of a black-on-white rape, the *Boston News-Letter* in 1718 told the story of a man, who, upon seeing a "Negro" having "accosted to lye with" an "English" woman, promptly "cut off . . . [the black man's] unruly parts smack and smooth." As in other newspaper reports of rape, the (white) man ended the "unruly" activity by reimposing his authority over the black man — in this instance, through physical mutilation. And, in case the message that black men were not allowed to have sex with white women was unclear, the editor explicitly stated that he had printed this story "as a caveat for a Negroes medling for the future with any white Woman." By focusing on the punishment of black men rather than the shocking nature of their crimes, newspapers emphasized not only the absolute guilt of blacks but also the importance of colonial racial hierarchies. The stark image of burning or mutilated black bodies separated them from *individual* white offenders, marking African Americans in general as a danger to colonial society and preempting any public discussion of black and white sexual acts.[53]

53. *Penn. Gaz.*, May 16, 1754 (had the publishers waited for more information, they might have told their public that the slave was eventually executed and hung in chains on a public road [*Archives of Maryland*, Apr. 24, 1754, XXXI, 31–32]); *Newport Mercury*, Dec. 5, 1763; *New-York Gazette*, Nov. 28, 1763; *Penn. Gaz.*, Dec. 14, 1744, Jan. 9, 1750, Sept. 17, 1761; *Boston News-Letter*, Feb. 24–Mar. 3, 1718. See also *Vir. Gaz.*, Aug. 19–26, 1737.

A direct comparison of two newspaper reports of the prosecution of a black man and a white man for rape shows the total effect of race-based differences in reporting. In 1736, the *Pennsylvania Gazette* reported: "Saturday last was tried here a Negro Man for Ravishing a White Woman near Derby, and is condemnd to be hangd. Tis said that Saturday next is appointed for his Execution." In 1754, the *Gazette* reported, "Last Thursday Night, one James Gale, a Taylor, was sent to our Goal, for committing a Rape on the Body of a Child about six Years old." At first glance, these reports may seem similar in their dispassionate reporting, but even these few sentences emphasized racialized meanings of rape. Accused rapist James Gale was identified by both name and occupation, not just as a white man. The distinguishing characteristic of James's victim was her young age rather than her race. Further, the report detailed only James's arrest, not his conviction or punishment. In contrast, the unnamed "Negro man" was convicted of raping a "White Woman," and half of the report focused on his upcoming execution. Such differences were repeated in scores of rape reports in colonial American newspapers. Instead of overt statements of racial discrimination, colonial newspapers subtly inscribed racial differences in their reports of rape. Even in regions that did not prosecute many blacks for rape, people could read about black rapists in their local papers. Although abolition, new print genres, and the expansion of the plantation system might have led to increased nineteenth-century commentary on racialized rape, white colonial Americans had already been taught that rapes were repeatedly committed by black men on white women.[54]

The growing numbers of criminal narrative publications in the second half of the eighteenth century greatly contributed to this image of black-on-white rapes. These publications included trial transcripts, condemned rapists' last words and confessions, and occasional commentary and sermons. Of the sixteen rape trials that occasioned such stand-alone publications from 1768 (when the first one appeared) through 1820, seven involved African American defendants—a fairly high number, considering that all of the crimes with African American defendants occurred in New England, where relatively few blacks resided. Further, New Englanders could read more about black-on-white rapes than any other crimes committed by black men. For instance, of the more than thirty American publications from 1768 to 1800 that related to the conviction or execution of murderers, only two appear to have involved black or mulatto defendants.[55]

54. *Penn. Gaz.*, July 22–Aug. 2, 1736, Dec. 5, 1754.

55. Richard Slotkin has reached similar conclusions about the overemphasis on publica-

In the post-Revolutionary era, the Puritan tradition of publishing of execution sermons and last words shifted to a more secular and more broadly northern criminal genre of trial transcripts. This print culture transformation enhanced the disparate portrayal of white and black rape defendants. Rather than religious publications meant to warn all sinners on the occasion of one sinner's execution, newly popular trial transcripts focused on defendants who were convicted *or* acquitted of rape. When we look at the racial breakdown of these publications, we again see an emphasis on black rapists: Of the twelve rape *convictions* that led to publications (out of a total of sixteen publications of rape trials), seven involved black defendants. In contrast, the four published rape trials that led to *acquittals* all involved white-on-white rape charges. These publications presented the possibility that white men might not be rapists but only publicized those black-on-white rapes that led to conviction and execution.

The Revolutionary-era cases involving African American defendants that were chosen for publication repeatedly focused on the ruined innocence of young white victims. In 1791, the published version of a black man's description of the thirteen-year-old Connecticut girl he had raped called her "an innocent girl," and a newspaper report called her a "harmless and innocent maid." In 1795, an ex-slave reportedly called his rape and murder of a white girl in Massachusetts a "crime against innocence" in his last words. In 1804, John Battus's final words focused extensively on his victim's innocence. She was an "innocent Daughter" whom he, a mulatto man, had "disrobed . . . of that virgin purity." Despite this growing public attention to nonwhite men's attacks on innocent young women and girls, white and black men had actually been convicted of sexually assaulting young victims (under age ten) at about the same rate over the course of the eighteenth century—the only instance in which the conviction rate of whites even came close to that of black defendants. Yet, in one of the few post-Revolutionary publications related to the conviction of a white man for raping a white girl, the trial transcript and the defendant's last words contained significant discussion about the thirteen-year-old's possible consent to the rape. Unlike this document, repeated publications on black men's crimes against virginal white girls and young women gave public emphasis to rape as a crime of black attacks on white innocence.[56]

---

tions involving black rapists. See Slotkin, "Narratives of Negro Crime in New England," *AQ*, XXV (1973), 17–18.

56. *The Life and Adventures of Joseph Mountain, a Negro Highwayman* (Bennington, Vt., 1791), 13; *Conn. Jour.*, Aug. 18, 1790, cited in Daniel E. Williams, *Pillars of Salt: An Anthology of Early American Criminal Narratives* (Madison, Wis., 1993), 305; *The Last*

In contrast, white women — especially young, unmarried women in cities — who accused white men of rape in the early Republic were portrayed as unchaste in crime genre publications. When Lanah Sawyer charged a New York white man with rape in 1793, a defense lawyer told the jury that she "had abandoned the outerworks of her chastity." Thus, the lawyer could argue that his client "may have seduced this girl; yet he did not force her." Nearly a dozen witnesses told a Massachusetts court that Rebecca Day, Jr., was a prostitute and a common strumpet when she charged two men with raping her in 1817. Both Lanah's and Rebecca's attackers were acquitted, showing how working-class socializing and courting practices were used to raise objections to a woman's claim that she had refused sex. Publications also forwarded an image of white men's sexual transgressions as somewhat less than rape. Northern printers began publishing trial pamphlets on a variety of white men's sexual crimes that fell short of rape. A New York trial transcript about a breach of promise case against a man for seducing and impregnating a woman through promises of marriage appeared in 1798, and a trial for assault and battery involving another seduction appeared in 1811. Thus, by the early Republic, published images of white men's criminalized sexual transgressions increasingly focused on noncapital cases or cases where the defendants were acquitted.[57]

Words and Dying Speech of Edmund Fortis, a Negro Man (Exeter, N.H., 1795); *The Confession of John Battus . . .* (n.p., [1804]), 10, 11, 20; *Report of the Trial of Ephraim Wheeler for a Rape Committed on the Body of Betsy Wheeler, His Daughter, a Girl Thirteen Years of Age . . .* (Stockbridge, Mass., 1805), 20, 26, 33; *A Narrative of the Life of Ephraim Wheeler . . .* (Stockbridge, Mass., 1806), 7; Samuel Shepard, *A Sermon, Delivered at Lenox, (Massachusetts), February 20th, 1806 . . .* (Stockbridge, Mass., 1806), 11–12. For similar comments about an Irish rapist's victim, see *The Dying Criminal: A Poem* (New London, Conn., 1779). Although my overall conclusions differ from Daniel Cohen's, see Cohen, "Social Injustice, Sexual Violence, Spiritual Transcendence," *WMQ*, 3d Ser., LVI (1999), 499.

Ten of the fifteen black men charged with sexually assaulting a girl under ten years old were convicted. Of thirty-five white men, twenty-five were convicted. Sixty out of seventy-one prosecutions against white men for sexual assaults on girls up to thirteen years old led to a guilty verdict (including for lesser charges), compared to twenty out of twenty-three prosecutions against black men. The youth of the victims undercut white men's standard defense that the sex was consensual. Despite its legal irrelevance, several white men still claimed that young girls were the sexual aggressors. For example, see trial of John Fisher, Feb. 24, 1778, WO 71/149, no. 8, 16, TNA:PRO.

57. *Report of the Trial of Henry Bedlow*, 19, 41, 44–61; *Report of the Trials of Stephen Murphy and John Doyle, before the Supreme Judicial Court at Dedham, Oct. 23, 1817* (Boston, 1817), 8–13; *The Hypocrite Unmask'd, Trial and Conviction of John Baker . . .* ([New York], 1798);

The colonial publications that began as a means for New Englanders to teach lessons about the sin of rape turned into lessons on the dangers of black-on-white attacks in a society that had newly and uneasily embraced abolition. To be sure, the disproportionate emphasis on black-on-white rape had existed throughout colonial America, but the growing *de*emphasis on white men as rapists left black men as the sole image of sexual predators. Thus, in the years before the Revolution, early Americans might have read about the conviction and execution of a mulatto man named Arthur for raping a widow in Massachusetts and about the execution of a white man named Bryan Sheehen for raping a married woman from Marblehead. Yet, in 1817, for instance, early Americans looking at published rape trials would have the option of reading about the trial and execution of Connecticut slave Amos Adams for raping a married white woman, or about the Massachusetts trial and acquittal of two white men for the rape of a fifteen-year-old unmarried factory worker. Shifting presentations of white men's crimes as much as intensified concerns about black behavior highlighted what a century of prosecutions had already been enacting: rape was undoubtedly a black-on-white crime, and the belief in black men's proclivity to rape was on its way to becoming the myth of black men's hypersexuality.[58]

The index to a 1765 publication of the *Laws of Maryland* contained the following entry: "Rape. See *Negroes*." Although the volume's editor probably did not intend that directive literally, it encapsulates the end product of a legal system where racial ideologies structured every stage of the criminal process: when early Americans thought about rape, they saw "Negroes." Still, the outcome of sexual assault cases cannot be ascribed to any single moment of racism. From accusation to execution, blacks and whites received substantially different

---

William Sampson, *Trial of Mr William Parkinson . . . on an Indictment for Assault and Battery . . .* (New York, 1811). See also *The People v Matthias Hays*, Dec. 17, 1803, New York County Court of General Sessions Indictment Papers, NYMA; *Report of the Trial of Richard D. Croucher,* 19. For a case where allegations of the victim's promiscuity were effectively rebutted, see ibid., 9–11. For a case where a married woman's sexual reputation derailed a prosecution, see *Trial of Charles Wakely,* 39–44. On the growing nineteenth-century interest in sexual licentiousness, see Patricia Cline Cohen, "The Helen Jewett Murder: Violence, Gender, and Sexual Licentiousness in Antebellum America," *NWSA Journal,* II (1990), 374–389.

58. *The Life and Dying Speech of Arthur; An Account of the Life of Bryan Sheehen, This Day Executed in Salem . . .* (Portsmouth, N.H., 1772). On the fears about free blacks in the North, see Melish, *Disowning Slavery,* 123–134; Sweet, *Bodies Politic,* 167, 169, 368–378.

forms of justice. White men were offered innumerable options from which blacks were excluded by custom or law. Whites were guaranteed the protection of a trial by jury. Whites were more likely to have lesser charges filed against them. Whites were more likely to have those charges dropped. Whites were more likely to be found not guilty. Whites were more likely to be convicted of a lesser charge. Whites who were convicted of a rape were less likely to receive capital punishment or to have that sentence carried out. Blacks, on the other hand, were trapped in the vicious cycle of being more easily convicted because of an image of black rapists — an image supported by the numerous convictions it helped to assure.[59]

These racial ideologies structured prosecutions of rape throughout eighteenth- and early-nineteenth-century America, whether in northern communities with few black residents or on southern plantations where black slaves threatened to outnumber white freemen. Through court trials and published reports of those trials, early Americans learned to associate race with certain sexual behaviors: black men had a proclivity to rape, and white men did not. White women were legitimate victims of rape, and black women were not. Unfortunately, there is little to document in courts' treatment of black victims because, above all else, courts viewed whiteness as the essential attribute of a raped woman. In punishing black-on-white rapes far more severely than white-on-any-woman rapes, criminal courts helped create a society where all blacks had a permanent mark of sexual suspicion upon them; this mark laid the foundation for rising fears about black men's sexuality in the nineteenth century. The "myth of the black rapist" that scholars have sought to establish, qualify, or discredit may more accurately (though perhaps less gracefully) be called the "myth of the black-on-white rapist."

Some scholars have argued that black men were not seen as particularly likely rapists until the mid-to-late nineteenth century. As one writes of the antebellum period, "There is no evidence, however, to suggest that white southerners were apprehensive or anxious about their slaves raping white women." Yet how, then, do we explain the overwhelming consistency in the prosecutorial results across time and region in cases of black-on-white rapes? For early America, we might want to consider that an absence of expressed fear does not negate the presence of the belief that black men were much more likely to rape than were white men. Instead of manifesting their anxiety in lynchings or polemical attacks, early American courts charged, convicted, and punished black sexual attackers at a much higher rate than whites. Every time a black

59. Thomas Bacon, comp., *Laws of Maryland at Large* . . . (Annapolis, Md., 1765), n.p.

man was convicted of rape and a white man was not, the image of black sexual danger was reinforced. Even a slight rise in conviction rates for white-on-white rapes after many states eliminated capital punishment was contradicted by both the increasing public emphasis on white men's innocence in rape cases and the rising interest in white men's participation in *consensual* sexual misdeeds. In contrast, the many successful rape prosecutions against black men allowed their convictions to be paraded through newspapers, town squares, and early American memories. With shifting notions of race in the early Republic — in the meanings of both whiteness and blackness — white men began to fit the public and published image of dangerous rapists even less than they had in the colonial period. The prosecution of rape took individual lives. The publicity of rape created a society that made rape a political tool in the creation of white American citizenship.[60]

60. Sommerville, "The Rape Myth in the Old South Reconsidered," *JSH,* LXI (1995), 486, 490.

CHAPTER SIX

NEW WORLDS OF RAPE:
MASCULINITY, MYTH, AND
REVOLUTION

In 1676, Nathaniel Saltonstall's account of the Algonquians' "in-humane Barbarities" during King Philip's War included their deliberate rape of English women. "If they were Women," he wrote, the Indians "forced them to satisfie their filthy Lusts" before murdering them. In a New York conspiracy trial of rebellious slaves in 1741, a prosecuting attorney claimed that the slaves had planned on *"killing the Gentlemen, and taking their Wives to themselves."* In her early-nineteenth-century history of the American Revolution, Mercy Otis Warren railed against "the indiscriminate ravages of the Hessian and British soldiery" who raped "wives and daughters" while "many unfortunate fathers, in the stupor of grief, beheld the misery of their female connexions, without being able to relieve them."[1]

These commentators used rape to condemn a New World enemy. Whether Indian warrior, African slave, or British soldier, the willingness to rape could label each one as savage. Such associations of rape were not new: for thousands of years, rape has been a sign of political and military domination, a means for soldiers to solidify victory by claiming patriarchal rights over women of the vanquished. Charges of rape were adjudicated in courts, but political discussions of rape took the facts of the sexual attack as a given. Making such purport-

---

1. Nathaniel Saltonstall, *New and Further Narrative,* 98–99, cited in Jill Lepore, *The Name of War: King Philip's War and the Origins of American Identity* (New York, 1998), 71–72; [Daniel Horsmanden], *A Journal of . . . the Detection of the Conspiracy Formed by Some White People, in Conjunction with Negro and Other Slaves, for Burning the City of New-York . . .* (New York, 1744), 41, 42, emphasis in original; Mercy Otis Warren, *History of the Rise, Progress, and Termination of the American Revolution: Interspersed with Biographical, Political, and Moral Observations,* ed. Lester H. Cohen, 2 vols. (1805; Indianapolis, 1988), I, 191.

edly factual rapes believable required the adoption of particular narrative forms and settings.[2]

Americans could make the very personal sexual interaction of rape publicly useful in multiple ways. In the post-Revolutionary period, the focus on women's bodies as a signifier of national anxieties increased interest in using rape to condemn America's challengers. But to do so effectively, writers relied on particular narrative constructions of rape's gendered dynamics that had transatlantic origins. Most frequently in discussions of political, moral, or social enemies, writers removed women from rape's retelling. When men were not the central figures in narratives of rape, the rapes were portrayed as either avoidable or questionable. By making unquestioned rapes an occasion for men to speak to other men about a range of male prerogatives, print discourse cast rape as a symbolic threat to legitimate masculinity. Focusing attention on men's protection of women's virtue allowed authors to minimize the thorny issue of women's role in safeguarding their own morality. Thus unencumbered by the concern about women's sexual desires put forth in stories of seduction or in false rape charges, transatlantic novels and adventure stories set illegitimate patriarch-rapists against legitimate patriarch-saviors, allowing for tales of undisputed rapes.

With this ready-made iconography of heroes and villains, rape could be deployed in political battles. Because men believed themselves harmed by the rape of their dependent women, rape narratives could affirm the extent of proper patriarchal protection, mark lines of social authority, or, increasingly in the Revolutionary era, define privileges of American citizenship. After exploring various transatlantic narrative settings for rape, I turn to three sets of New

2. For early American discussions of rape in history, see William Alexander, *The History of Women: From the Earliest Antiquity to the Present Time* (Philadelphia, 1796), 145–146, 255–257; *The Rape: A Poem, Humbly Inscribed to the Ladies* . . . (London, 1768), 12–15; Nathaniel Morton, *New-Englands Memoriall* . . . (Cambridge, 1669), 17. On the long-term association of rape and war, see Lois G. Schwoerer, *"No Standing Armies!": The Antiarmy Ideology in Seventeenth-Century England* (Baltimore, 1974), 62; Nicoletta F. Gullace, "Sexual Violence and Family Honor: British Propaganda and International Law during the First World War," *American Historical Review,* CII (1997), 714–747; Ruth Harris, "The 'Child of the Barbarian': Rape, Race, and Nationalism in France during the First World War," *Past and Present,* no. 141 (November 1993), 170–206; Atina Grossmann, "A Question of Silence: The Rape of German Women by Occupation Soldiers," in Robert G. Moeller, ed., *West Germany under Construction: Politics, Society, and Culture in the Adenauer Era* (Ann Arbor, Mich., 1997), 33–52; Susan Jeffords, "Rape and the New World Order," *Cultural Critique,* no. 19 (Autumn 1991), 203–215.

World conflicts that occasioned repeated rape-related commentaries. The first two conflicts related to early Americans' perceived sexual threats from rebelling Africans and enemy Indians. The myths that African Americans and Native Americans wanted to rape white women followed divergent trajectories in the eighteenth century. Early images of enslaved black rapists grew into a long-lasting myth of black men's hypersexuality. In contrast, seventeenth-century colonists expected savage Indians to rape white women during military conflicts, but by the eighteenth century Indians no longer appeared to be likely rapists. These differing paths reaffirm rape's relation to early American understandings of sex and of sexual natures. White colonists' predisposition to see nonwhite men as rapists needed supporting beliefs and experiences to ultimately lead to the widespread belief that African American men innately sought to rape white women.

The third set of conflicts involved British soldiers' rape of American women. In the short term, the American Revolution focused the rhetorical power of rape on that political crisis to a degree unparalleled in early American history. Rape-related stories pitted upstanding American male citizenry against corrupt British rule and made rape a powerful rallying cry for a new American nation. Rape resonated as a means to disgrace and dismiss the British imperial system by transforming attacks on individual bodies into attacks on the American body politic. As American soldiers fought for their own rights as independent men, rape stories rallied supporters around the moral and political condemnation of the British Empire. The enemy of America was now the dominant villain in politicized stories of rape.

None of these public uses of rape were possible without particular understandings of rape. The differential staying power of the myths that African Americans and Native Americans wanted to rape white women reminds us that we need to understand both the meaning of rape and women's place in its discourse to fully make sense of the political uses of rape. Ultimately, the longest-standing narratives were those in which rapes could be read as assaults on white freedom and citizenship in the new American nation.

THE TRANSATLANTIC FICTIONS OF RAPE

In 1769, the *Virginia Gazette* reprinted a story about a man who planned to kidnap a young woman so that he could forcibly marry and rape her. When the woman's brother discovered the plot, he dressed up in his sister's clothes and let himself be kidnapped instead. After the kidnapper brought the "pretended female" to his family home, he put "her" to bed with his own sister until a priest could arrive to perform the marriage ceremony. The supposed bride-to-be then raped and impregnated the kidnapper's sister before escaping. The *Gazette* reported that this turn of events caused "great mortification and disappointment of the intended bridegroom," and the story ended by explaining that "the hero of the farce"—the bride-to-be/rapist—was "honourably acquitted" of a rape.[3]

This apocryphal anecdote typifies many fictionalized stories of rape. Rather than focusing on the women's experiences, its plot revolves around the men's conduct: a man raped a woman to punish her brother's planned rape of his sister. The story emphasized the two brothers as the victims of the rape. Like his pregnant sister, the kidnapper lost his marital prospects, and the rapist-brother's "honorable" acquittal of rape paralleled his sister's close escape from rape-induced dishonor. As attacker, savior, and victim, men filled all roles in this retelling, which transformed an account of rape into a story about men's relations with other men. Moreover, the story made rape seem, if not honorable, then at least comprehensible under the right circumstances. Men who violated the norms of civilized masculine behavior forfeited the right to protect their female dependents from other men's retributive justice.

More scholarship has focused on the mid-eighteenth-century rise of seduction novels than on stories of rape. But seduction stories filled a very different purpose than did those of rape: seduction stories hinged on questions of women's desires, actions, and malleability. Because I am exploring how early Americans used *rape* in popular discourse, I focus primarily on those stories that viewed a given sexual interaction as an unquestionable rape, not those seductions often appearing in sentimental fiction that may be classified as sexual force by modern standards. Fictionalized rape could avoid the angst about a woman's own contribution to her moral downfall by bypassing her narrative role. By providing infallible (male) witnesses to the facts of the rape, readers did not need to adjudge the woman's version of the attack. Her husband or father had already established her nonconsent, thus setting the scene as far from that of a seduction narrative (where a woman might have been convinced to consent) as possible.[4]

3. Purdie and Dixon's *Virginia Gazette* (Williamsburg), June 29, 1769; *Connecticut Journal* (New Haven), June 30, 1769.

4. On rape in eighteenth-century British fiction, see Frances Ferguson, "Rape and the Rise of the Novel," *Representations*, XX (1987), 88–112; Susan Staves, "Fielding and the Comedy of Attempted Rape," in Beth Fowkes Tobin, ed., *History, Gender, and Eighteenth-Century Literature* (Athens, Ga., 1994), 86–112; John Valdimir Price, "Patterns of Sexual

Samuel Richardson's *Clarissa; or, the History of a Young Lady* provides an excellent example of the blurring of the boundaries of sexual consent and force when male witnesses did not authorize the reality of a rape. As discussed in Chapter 1, contemporaries and scholars have classified Lovelace's tricking and drugging of Clarissa as both seduction and rape. Even within the novel, friends encouraged Clarissa to prosecute Lovelace, but she shunned court proceedings (what she called "pursuing a doubtful event"), in part because she feared that her encouragement of Lovelace's attentions and his subsequent offer of marriage would make their interaction look less like a criminal rape. Contrary to the typical rape prosecution, where women's testimony established the facts of a sexual assault, fictional sexual encounters became unequivocal rape through *male* voices. And once women moved to the margins, men's emotions and grievances could be the focal point of rape narratives.[5]

Several episodes in a popular adventure story first published in America in 1793 show how rape could be figured to represent and resolve conflicts between men and to define the bounds of honorable patriarchy. *The Remarkable History of Miss Villars* was originally part of *The Voyages and Adventures of Captain Robert Boyle,* a British heroic tale that went through at least ten editions after its first publication in 1726. *The Remarkable History of Miss Villars* detailed a young British woman's repeated encounters with lascivious suitors and sailors. Miss Villars was an orphan and "a woman of business" with "no inclination to marry." The story began when one of her rejected suitors, Captain Bourne, bribed a maid to hide him in Miss Villars's bedroom closet so that he could later rape her. Just as Miss Villars was "so faint with struggling that he was very near accomplishing his barbarous design," a "former suitor and guardian" leapt out of another closet to fight off her attacker. Later in the story, when a kidnapped Miss Villars refused to submit to a forced marriage to Captain Bourne, he then threatened to rape Miss Villars's servant Susan as punishment. The captain told Susan that after "I have had the first cut of you,

Behaviour in Some Eighteenth-Century Novels," in Paul-Gabriel Boucé, ed., *Sexuality in Eighteenth-Century Britain* (Totowa, N.J., 1982), 159–175; Elizabeth Sungeun Kim, "Exploiting Rape: Women's Literary Representations of Rape in Early Eighteenth-Century Prose Fictions" (Ph.D. diss, University of Michigan, 1995). William Beatty Warner points out that, "while there are many seductions in [canonical] literature, there are few rapes outside of romance" (Warner, "Reading Rape: Marxist-Feminist Figurations of the Literal," *Diacritics,* XIII, no. 4 [Winter 1983], 13). For scholarship on seduction, see Chapter 1, n. 48.

5. Samuel Richardson, *Clarissa; or, The History of a Young Lady,* ed. Angus Ross (1747–1748; New York, 1985), 1251–1257 (quote on 1255).

I'll let my sailors go to dinner," and he promised a reward to the sailor who "should prove the greatest rogue" with her. Suspecting "there is some reason of the Captain's liberality," the sailors hesitated. One specifically objected, "I love a woman well enough, but don't care to have her forced upon me; it's like eating against one's stomach." During this exchange, the first mate fortuitously recognized Miss Villars and eagerly swore to protect her because he had been "put in . . . [his position as first mate] by your honorable father; and had been Captain, if it had not been for the tricks of that rascal." The first mate captured the captain, and Miss Villars rewarded the first mate by naming him the new captain of the ship.[6]

Both *The Remarkable History of Miss Villars* and *The Voyages and Adventures of Captain Robert Boyle* abound with the literary devices, dramatic deliverances, and clear messages about status, loyalty, love, and betrayal that were common in eighteenth-century adventure tales. The stand-alone American publication of *Miss Villars* in the early Republic reflects not only the increasing American interest in fictional stories of women's endangerment through tests of their virtue but also the transatlantic rape discourses of legitimate and illegitimate masculine identities. We have a near rape of a fatherless (and therefore sexually vulnerable) woman who refused to accept the protection of marriage. That rape was averted by a man who could claim a patriarchal relation to her as her guardian. Later, the illegitimately powerful Captain Bourne substituted one woman's body for another's by threatening Miss Villars's servant as leverage to force Miss Villars's consent. We then see other men's reactions to an offer of rape: they would not be forced into a sexual act on another man's orders, for to do so would make them unnaturally subservient to another man's undeserved authority. The first mate, a man originally placed *in loco patriarchae* by Miss Villars's father, then used an attempted rape to encourage a mutiny and resolve his own conflicts with the captain's authority. In each of these incidents, legitimate patriarchs prevented rape, and illegitimate patriarchs tried to commit rape. In fiction, women's bodies were the means through which men performed their masculine identities. And this emphasis on the dangers of independent women was a particularly common theme in popular post-Revolutionary stories.

6. [W. R. Chetwood], *The Remarkable History of Miss Villars* (Keene, N.H., 1795), 2–4, 6, 13–16. Editions of W. R. Chetwood's *Voyages and Adventures of Captain Robert Boyle* that included the Miss Villars story were published in America at Boston in 1792; Greenfield, Massachusetts, 1794; Cooperstown, New York, 1796; Walpole, New Hampshire, 1799 and 1812; and New York, 1805.

Other novels in post-Revolutionary America set similar scenes where men could save the women that they would often later marry from sexual attacks. In the popular 1795 novel *The Man of the World,* both "Miss Lucy's" brother and future husband saved her from a rapist, aptly named Sir Sindall. To emphasize his patriarchal illegitimacy, Sir Sindall was, unbeknownst to Lucy, her biological father as a result of his rape of Lucy's mother. In Rinallo D'Elville's 1813 novel, *The Rescue; or, The Villain Unmasked,* the virtuous Rosalia's long-lost love saved her from rape, and their marriage soon followed. In such highly stylized stories, writers built on a pattern that identified men who prevented rapes as patriarchal figures. By saving a woman (often fatherless) from rape, a man visibly demonstrated his qualifications as a husband; these narratives of rape contrasted acceptable and unacceptable masculine behavior, stressing the danger of patriarchal failure.[7]

In the post-Revolutionary era, where individual rather than parental marital choice was increasingly privileged, and romantic and companionate marital unions were emphasized, men who tried to force women into marriage through rape (a practice that dated back centuries) became prime examples of illegitimate masculinity. In some tales that were a twist on both rape stories and seduction narratives, attackers tried to force virtuous English women to agree to sexual relations under physically coercive circumstances. This was the case in the *Very Surprising Narrative of a Young Woman, Who Was Discovered in the Gloomy Mansion of a Rocky Cave!* in which a beautiful, young, American woman hacked to death the giant in a cave who ordered her to either be his sexual partner or be killed. Similarly, the *History of the Captivity and Sufferings of Mrs. Maria Martin, Who Was Six Years a Slave in Algiers* was a popular adventure tale that was published in a dozen editions in the first decades of the nineteenth century. In this story, the English Mrs. Martin protected her sexual virtue against her Turkish captor's "lustful passion" and repeated attempts to force her into marriage (apparently, his country's laws would have him beheaded if he physically raped her), even when "like a mad-man, drawing his dirk, he threatened me with instant death." Mrs. Martin chose to be starved and imprisoned for years rather than consent, and she ultimately escaped with the

7. Rinallo D'Elville, *The Rescue; or, The Villain Unmasked* (New York, 1813), 39–44; [Henry Mackenzie], *Man of the World* (Boston, 1795), 317–319. On incest in early American novels, see Anne Dalke, "Original Vice: The Political Implications of Incest in the Early American Novel," *Early American Literature,* XXIII (1988), 188–201. For an early-eighteenth-century novel with a similar plot, see Jane Barker, "Exilius," in *The Entertaining Novels of Mrs. Jane Barker* (London, 1719).

help of a Christian man and was reunited with Mr. Martin. Such stories created a fiction that women could choose whether to consent to rape and made their ability to resist rape a sign of their — and ultimately, their nation's — virtue.[8]

It was no accident that the men failing to force the unnamed young woman and Mrs. Martin into sexual relationships were not Englishmen. When rape was a mark of men's illegitimate power over other men, attempts at rape could condemn adversaries in a variety of transatlantic political and religious contexts. As in the story of Mrs. Maria Martin, multiple publications in the early Republic on Muslim societies emphasized the connections between unrestrained sexual and political lust. Although the attention to such types of stories increased in the early Republic (where women's morality was regular fodder in a variety of political forums), the connections between illegitimate patriarchs and rape were not new. Catholics had been a similarly favored subject of sexual indecency throughout the eighteenth century. In a 1740 drama about the evils of Catholic Spaniards, Don Pedrillo tried to force himself on a virtuous English wife, assuredly claiming that "my good Father Confessor will absolve me." *The French Convert,* a novel published more than a dozen times throughout the eighteenth century, described a Franciscan friar's sexual assault on the "fair and beautiful *Deidama*" that convinced her (and was meant to convince the readers) of the evils of Catholicism. Such rhetoric had self-reinforcing functions: the obvious uncivilized nature of the attackers signified believable rape attempts without requiring women's potentially dubious claims, and the attackers' attempts at sexual force not only confirmed the malevolence of one's enemies but also emphasized the virtue of British Protestantism.[9]

By validating rape as an act committed, prevented, and determined by men,

8. Abraham Panther, pseud., *A Very Surprising Narrative of a Young Woman, Who Was Discovered in the Gloomy Mansion of a Rocky Cave! . . .* , 3d ed. (Windsor, Vt., 1796), 5–11; Maria Martin, *History of the Captivity and Sufferings of Mrs. Maria Martin, Who Was Six Years a Slave in Algiers . . .* (Boston, 1807), 64–66. On this shift after the American Revolution, see Jan Lewis, "The Republican Wife: Virtue and Seduction in the Early Republic," *William and Mary Quarterly,* 3d Ser., XLIV (1987), 694–696. On the rise of companionate marriage in eighteenth-century England, see Lawrence Stone, *The Family, Sex, and Marriage in England, 1500–1800* (New York, 1977), 187–191.

9. *The Bravo Turn'd Bully; or, The Depredators* (London, 1740), 17; [A. D'Auborn], *The French Convert . . .* (New Haven, Conn., 1798), 20; see also *Popish Cruelty Displayed: Being a True Account of the Bloody and Hellish Massacre in Ireland . . . in the Year 1641 . . .* (Boston, [1753]), 17, 22, 23. On the early Republic connections between the sexual and political tyranny of the Muslim world, see Robert J. Allison, *The Crescent Obscured: The United States and the Muslim World, 1776–1815* (New York, 1995), 61–85.

rape discourse provided a forum through which men's worth could be evaluated and displayed. Eighteenth-century British condemnations of heretical Catholics paralleled the use of rape in New World conflicts, where African American and Native American men, both potential enemies to Anglo-American colonial power, were prime targets for public tales of rape. Yet all enemies did not necessarily make equally believable rapists; the myths surrounding African American and Native American sexual offenses would follow distinct paths, based on Anglo-Americans' expectations, experiences, and understandings of rape.

RAPE AND NEW WORLD RESIDENTS

Those who wrote about early America regularly used rape to mark the illegitimacy of competing racial and political groups. Imperial rivals gleefully claimed moral superiority by reporting each other's rape and pillaging. A British publication claimed that Indians had destroyed Fort Hispaniola in 1493 because the Spanish had committed *"inhuman* Acts of Violence" that included using the Indians' "Wives and Daughters, to satisfy their lustful Desires." A British traveler reported that a group of Spanish and allied Indians attacked a community of southeastern Indians: "They satisfied their Lusts with the women, and that one of them being so abused as not any longer to be capable of it, they ript her up with a Knife, and not long after finished her Murder."[10]

But the most consistent stories of Anglo-American women's vulnerability to rapes focused on attacks by nonwhite New World residents. As potential enemies, African American and Indian men might have seemed like ready-made rapists: both groups were considered savage, and both repeatedly threatened to overwhelm British colonies. Indeed, seventeenth-century colonists believed African American and Native American men were equally likely to use rape against white Europeans. But, by the eighteenth century, black men took

10. *The British Sailor's Discovery; or, The Spanish Pretensions Confuted* . . . (London, 1739), 10; Francis Moore, *A Voyage to Georgia, Begun in the Year 1735,* ed. Trevor R. Reese ([1744]; rpt. Savannah, Ga., 1974), 154. See also Jennifer L. Morgan, "'Some Could Suckle over Their Shoulder': Male Travelers, Female Bodies, and the Gendering of Racial Ideology, 1500–1770," *WMQ,* 3d Ser., LIV (1997), 174–175. For anti-French rape stories, see *Boston Gazette,* Mar. 26, 1754; *Connecticut Courant* (Hartford), Sept. 20, 1800; and [Anthony Aufrer], *The Cannibals' Progress; or, The Dreadful Horrors of French Invasion* (Albany, N.Y., [1798]), 9.

center stage as the most likely rapists, even though Indians' continued capture of white women might have made them equally vulnerable to such accusations. These divergent images resulted from colonists' views of rape, of sexual ideologies, and of the public emphasis on the prosecution of black rapists.

The first known published association of rebelling slaves with the rape of white women referred to the Caribbean islands where widespread enslavement of Africans first took hold. The 1676 account of the Barbados slave rebellion claimed that the revolting slaves "intended, to spare the lives of the fairest and Hansomest Women (their Mistresses and Daughters) to be Converted to their [the slaves'] own use." John Oldmixon's 1708 history, *The British Empire in America,* told of a 1687 conspiracy in the West Indies where "all the Planters were to be killed, their Wives to be kept for the chief of the Conspirators." Such accusations continued through the eighteenth century: in 1774, a history of Jamaica claimed that the leader of the Maron rebels had planned to obtain "(among other fruits of victory) the Lieutenant Governor's lady for his concubine."[11]

By the mid-eighteenth century, mainland North American slave rebellions occasioned similar commentaries. The "monstrous" scheme of the New York slave revolt of 1741 included "that the White Men should be all killed, and the Women become a Prey to the rapacious Lust of these Villains." A Hessian soldier fighting in the American Revolution retold a rumor about a slave uprising that had occurred nearly half a century earlier. He had heard that "the entire Negro population . . . had conspired to assault masters on a certain night," making the widows "either their slaves or us[ing] them to gratify their desires." Such formulaic claims continued to be widespread in the nineteenth century. In September of 1800, Philadelphia Quaker Thomas Cope reported hearing of the aborted Richmond, Virginia, slave rebellion: "All the male whites were to have been massacred. The females were to have been spared and given up to their conquerors." In a South Carolina slave uprising in 1816, one woman told her cousin that the slaves had planned to "murder the men but the women they intended to reserve for their own purposes."

11. *Great Newes from the Barbadoes . . .* (London, 1676), 6; [John Oldmixon], *The British Empire in America . . . ,* 2 vols. (1708; rpt. New York, 1969), II, 42; [Edward Long], *The History of Jamaica . . . ,* 3 vols. (London, 1774), II, 457n (see also 449). On New World associations of sexual threat and slave rebellions, see Winthrop D. Jordan, *Tumult and Silence at Second Creek: An Inquiry into a Civil War Slave Conspiracy* (Baton Rouge, La., 1993), 149–160.

From the sixteenth through the nineteenth centuries, Anglo-Americans assumed that rebellious slaves would exercise their freedom through the physical destruction of their masters and the sexual destruction of their mistresses.[12]

However, there is no evidence that slaves attempted to rape white women during any slave rebellions. Regardless, commentators retold such accusations because raping white masters' women neatly symbolized the fear that white patriarchs would be replaced with rebelling ex-slaves. Rape was the utmost rejection of the fundamental unit of patriarchal control: legitimate marriage. Rape was publicly figured as a means to attack, affront, or access patriarchal prerogatives. Slaves who sought to turn the political order upside down with their rebellion were likely to disrupt the patriarchal order of white men's protection of their dependent women. This displacement of rape from an attack on *a* woman into an affront on a racialized patriarchy made it a useful discursive emblem in a New World that was increasingly dependent on a racially divided labor system. Whites feared that rebelling slaves would "take" white men's wives and daughters as a sign of their newfound supremacy over white men, and white men condemned these actions, linking rape and rebellion to emphasize the need for their own race-based hierarchy. Thus, Anglo-Americans interpreted black men's rapes of white women as part of their resistance to enslavement.[13]

Some modern historians, too, have implicitly endorsed the association between black men's rape of white women and their resistance to slavery. Graham Hodges reiterates early American views that enslaved men used rape as a means of rebellion. He argues that slaves' sometimes violent "desires for freedom" created some "angry slaves [who] raped their mistresses, burned their homes, and attacked and murdered their masters." Rape, murder, and pillaging were the longtime hallmarks of an enemy attack, and African American slaves readily

12. [Horsmanden], *A Journal of the Detection of the Conspiracy,* 42; diary of Captain Johann Hinrichs, in Bernhard A. Uhlendorf, ed. and trans., *The Siege of Charleston . . . Diaries and Letters of Hessian Officers* (Ann Arbor, Mich., 1938), 322–323; Eliza Cope Harrison, ed., *Philadelphia Merchant: The Diary of Thomas P. Cope, 1800–1851* (South Bend, Ind., 1978), 22; R. Blanding to her cousin, July 4, 25, 1816, William Blanding Papers, South Caroliniana Library, University of South Carolina, Columbia, S.C., cited in Jordan, *Tumult and Silence at Second Creek,* 153. See also Herbert Alan Johnson, ed., *South Carolina Legal History: Proceedings of the Reynolds Conference . . .* (Spartanburg, S.C., 1980), 212.

13. On the lack of evidence of rape during slave rebellions, see Jordan, *Tumult and Silence at Second Creek,* 149. For an exceptional case involving the rape of a mulatto woman in a Jamaica rebellion in 1760, see Michael Craton, *Testing the Chains: Resistance to Slavery in the British West Indies* (Ithaca, N.Y., 1982), 129.

fitted the bill of potentially dangerous assailants. Thus, enslaved black men's rape of white women was the perfect symbol for the sexual legitimacy and patriarchal power denied to enslaved men.[14]

Discussion of Native American rapists began at virtually the same moment as did the commentaries on rapacious, rebelling slaves. Most of these comments forwarded the same hyperbolic claims of rape, murder, and pillaging that had long characterized New and Old World conflicts. In 1675, the governor of the Leeward Islands complained about "Caribbee Indians, who have murdered on Antigua the King's subjects of both sexes, ravished women, carried away men, women, and children, kept them slaves, burned houses, and committed other enormities." By the time New England and Indian relations had disintegrated to the flash point of King Philip's War in the 1670s, some New Englanders assumed that Indians would express their savagery sexually. Nathaniel Saltonstall reiterated his opinion of Indians' "filthy lusts" in an anonymous British publication, claiming that Algonquians burned houses, corn, and hay, killed people, stole livestock, and "any Woman they take alive, they Defile." In a similar vein, Benjamin Thompson's epic poem on the war condemned the Indians' "unbridled lust" that led them to "strip . . . bind . . . ravish, flay and roast." These seventeenth-century writers assumed Indians' sexual savagery as part of the panoply of Indian atrocities.[15]

Yet other seventeenth-century commentators were less likely to include rape among the Indians' wrongdoings. William Hubbard's narrative of King Philip's War claimed that Indians had not offered "any uncivil Carriage to any of the Females, nor ever attempted the chastity of any of them." Mary Rowlandson's captivity narrative, first published in 1682, also claimed, "Not one of them ever offered me the least abuse of unchastity to me in word or action." Like William, Mary credited the Indians' sexual restraint to "the presence of God, and to his glory." In 1706, Cotton Mather agreed, "Tis a wonderful

14. Graham Russell Hodges, *Root and Branch: African Americans in New York and East Jersey, 1613–1863* (Chapel Hill, N.C., 1999), 134. See also Philip J. Schwarz, *Twice Condemned: Slaves and the Criminal Laws of Virginia, 1705–1865* (Baton Rouge, La., 1988), 82.

15. "Col. Stapleton, Governor of the Leeward Islands, to the Committee of Council for Plantations," Dec. 20, 1675, in Karen Ordahl Kupperman, John C. Appleby, and Mandy Banton, eds., *Calendar of State Papers, Colonial: North America and the West Indies, 1574–1739* (CD-ROM, 2000), IX, item 748, 319–320; N. S., *The Present State of New-England with respect to the Indian War,* in Charles H. Lincoln, ed., *Narratives of the Indian Wars, 1675–1699* (New York, 1913), 30; Benjamin Thompson, "New England's Crisis," in Richard Slotkin and James K. Folsom, eds., *So Dreadfull a Judgment: Puritan Responses to King Philip's War, 1676–1677* (Middletown, Conn., 1978), 219.

Restraint from God upon the Bruitish Salvages, that no *English Woman* was ever known to have any Violence offered unto her *Chastity*, by any of them." Because these colonists still assumed that Indians were savages, they believed that a Christian God, not the inner restraint of heathen tribes, had saved English women.[16]

Seventeenth-century writers' mixed opinions of Indians' propensity to rape English women gave way to a fairly uniform eighteenth-century belief that English women were safe from Indians' sexual attacks. In place of New Englanders' emphasis on God's salvation, eighteenth-century commentators began crediting Indians for the sexual safety of captive women. In his history of the British colonies published in 1749, William Douglass concluded that the Indians "never offer Violence to our Women Captives." "Bad as the savages are," concurred General James Clinton during the American Revolution, "they never violate the chastity of any women, their prisoners." William Martin, the son of Virginia's Indian agent to the Cherokees, Joseph Martin, recalled a story of a "mighty warrior" in the Revolutionary era who had once attempted "some rudeness" with a female war captive. The warrior was stopped by his comrades, and Martin ended his story with the proclamation, "This, I believe is the only instance I have ever heard of an Indian's treating a female captive immodestly." These commentators had varied levels of interaction with and firsthand knowledge of Native American groups, but they all endorsed the belief that Indians would not rape white captives.[17]

Even captivity narratives denied Indians' sexual aggression toward English women. In Elizabeth Hanson's story of captivity, first published in 1728, Elizabeth held that Indians were generally "very civil toward their captive

16. William Hubbard, *The Present State of New-England; Being a Narrative of the Troubles with the Indians, 1677* (Bainbridge, N.Y., 1972), 61 (see also 78), in Hubbard, *A Narrative of the Indian Wars in New-England . . .* (Boston, 1775), 117; *The Narrative of the Captivity and Restoration of Mrs. Mary Rowlandson* (Boston, 1930), 70–71 (see also 33); Cotton Mather, *Good Fetch'd out of Evil* (Boston, 1706), 33–34.

17. William Douglass, *A Summary, Historical and Political, of the First Planting, Progressive Improvements, and Present State of the British Settlements in North-America* (Boston, 1749), I, 175; *Public Papers of George Clinton, First Governor of New York,* 10 vols. (New York, 1899–1914), IV, 702–703, cited in Barbara Graymont, *The Iroquois in the American Revolution* (Syracuse, N.Y., 1972), 196; William Martin to Lyman C. Draper, Dec. 1, 1842, Draper MSS, King's Mountain Papers, 14DD113, State Historical Society of Wisconsin, Madison (thanks to Nathaniel Sheidley for this quotation and for biographic details on William Martin). See also Martin to Draper, July 7, 1842, Draper MSS, Tennessee Papers, 3XX4, 2, State Historical Society of Wisconsin.

Women . . . which is commendable in them so far." A 1756 narrative recounted Indians who told captive William Fleming "not to be afraid that they should abuse [his] Wife, for they would not do it, for fear of offending their God." After her captivity by Shawnee and Seneca Indians in the 1780s, Mary Jemison described Indians as loyal, moderate, honorable people for whom "chastity was held in high veneration, and a violation of it was considered sacrilege."[18]

By the post-Revolutionary era, captivity narratives had begun their transformation into nineteenth-century pulp thrillers. But even as captivity tales became increasingly eroticized, discussions of Indians still did not mention outright rapes of white women. White women were dragged from their homes "almost destitute of clothing" or "almost naked" but were not explicitly sexually assaulted. Post-Revolutionary writers were certainly not afraid to write about darkly erotic atrocities. In *A Selection, of Some of the Most Interesting Narratives of Outrages, Committed by the Indians in Their Wars with the White People*, an 1808 collection of graphically violent captivity narratives, Indians gruesomely murdered husbands, slashed children's throats, tomahawked scalps, and tore infants from mothers' arms. A list of Indians' barbarities during the War of 1812 included the accusation that they had captured a pregnant woman, whom they "immediately tomahawked, stripped naked, her womb ripped open, and the child taken out." Rape would have fit perfectly with these symbolic destructions of American families and futures, but writers still did not attribute this crime to their Indian enemies.[19]

18. Samuel Bownas, ed., *An Account of the Captivity of Elizabeth Hanson,* vol. VI of Garland Library of Narratives of North American Indian Captives (1728; New York, 1977), 35. Hanson's narrative was republished in 1754, 1760, 1780, 1782, 1787, and 1791 in at least three separate editions. For a slightly different version of this statement, see the 1760 London-published version in Richard VanDerBeets, ed., *Held Captive by Indians: Selected Narratives, 1642–1836* (Knoxville, Tenn., 1973), 147. See also William Fleming, *A Narrative of the Sufferings and Surprising Deliverances of William and Elizabeth Fleming . . .* (1756; New York, 1978), 16. For an exceptional British-published (Edinburgh, York, Glasgow through 1812) captivity narrative that included explicit torture and alluded to rape, see Peter Williamson, *French and Indian Cruelty, 1757,* vol. IX of Garland Library of Narratives of North American Captives (New York, 1978), 45–48. See also James E. Seaver, *A Narrative of the Life of Mrs. Mary Jemison . . .*, ed. Allen W. Trelease (1824; New York, 1961), 72–73. See also Varnum Lansing Collins, ed., *A Brief Narrative of the Ravages of the British and Hessians at Princeton in 1776–1777* (1906; rpt. New York, 1968), 15. On use of captivity narratives as historical evidence, see Linda Colley, *Captives* (New York, 2002), 12–17.

19. *The War; Being a Faithful Record of the Transactions of the War between the United States*

Unlike the seventeenth-century writers who portrayed English captives as narrowly escaping rape by the grace of God, eighteenth- and early-nineteenth-century Euro-American commentators had apparently concluded that Native American cultural beliefs prevented rape. In the 1750s, an anonymous French soldier traveling in New France contended, "Generally, savages have scruples about molesting a woman prisoner, and look upon it as a crime, even when she gives her consent." James Adair, who spent decades trading with southeastern Indians, wrote of the "religious war custom" that "Indians will not cohabit with women while they are out at war." In his report of his 1820 trip to the Sauk, Jedidiah Morse noted that "an Indian intending to go to war" would "refrain from all intercourse with the other sex." Even *A Selection, of Some of the Most Interesting Narratives of Outrages* explained that Indian beliefs precluded the rape of captured women: "If a young man were. . . . to indulge himself with a captive taken in war, and much more were he to offer violence in order to gratify his lust, he would incur indelible disgrace." These writers did not just deny that Native Americans would rape captives; they believed that Indian warriors would not have *any* sexual relations with women. Native American prohibitions of any kind of sexual interactions (rather, perhaps, than Indians' respect for women's consent) seemed to be at the heart of Europeans' belief that Indians would not sexually attack female prisoners.[20]

------

of America . . . and the United Kingdom of Great Britain and Ireland . . . , 3 vols. (New York, 1813–1817), II, 122; "A Narrative of the Captivity and Escape of Mrs. Frances Scott," in Archibald Loudon, ed., *A Selection, of Some of the Most Interesting Narratives of Outrages, Committed by the Indians . . .* , 2 vols. (Carlisle, Pa., 1808), I, 33, 35; *An Affecting Narrative of the Captivity and Sufferings of Mrs Mary Smith* (1818), in James Levernier and Hennig Cohen, eds., *Indians and Their Captives* (Westport, Conn., 1977), 66. The Mary Smith narrative contains an eroticized phallic torture of "helpless virgins" (65–68, 71–72) that originally appeared in the "Affecting History of the Dreadful Distresses of Frederic Manheim's Family," in Loudon, ed., *A Selection, of Some of the Most Interesting Narratives,* I, 58–59.

On captivity narratives, see David Haberly, "Women and Indians: *The Last of the Mohicans* and the Captivity Tradition," *American Quarterly,* XXVIII (1976), 431; June Namias, *White Captives: Gender and Ethnicity on the American Frontier* (Chapel Hill, N.C., 1993). On eroticization, see Karen Halttunen, *Murder Most Foul: The Killer and the American Gothic Imagination* (Cambridge, Mass., 1998), 33–90. On clothing and nakedness in colonial cultural contact, see Ann M. Little, " 'Shoot That Rogue, for He Hath an Englishman's Coat On!' Cultural Cross-Dressing on the New England Frontier, 1620–1760," *New England Quarterly,* LXXIV (2001), 238–273.

20. Sylvester K. Stevens et al., eds., *Travels in New France by J. C. B.* (Harrisburg, Pa., 1941), 69; James Adair, *Adair's The History of the American Indians,* ed. Samuel Cole Wil-

When myths of savage rapists had had so much staying power, when rape was a consummate example of the danger posed to civilization by one's enemies, and when rape had been used by victorious armies since classical civilizations, why was there comparatively so little emphasis on rape by Indians? Scholars have argued that Indians did not rape because many Native American nations had strict proscriptions against mixing sex and war. Ramón Gutiérrez has pointed out that some Native American cultures drew a dividing line between life-taking war and life-giving sexual acts, and James Axtell has suggested that Eastern Woodland Indians' strong incest taboos prohibited sexual relations with a woman who might be adopted later as a sister or cousin.[21]

Although uncovering Native American sexual mores from Europeans' observations is a daunting task, scholars may be correct in their assertions that rape occurred less frequently in eastern Native American societies than in European societies. Very few reports document Native American men's rape of Native American women. In an exceptional case, James Adair reported that Cherokee and Choctaw men punished female adulterers with a purposeful gang rape. The claim of George Croghan, an eighteenth-century Indian trader and Indian agent, that Native American men would "be putt to Death for Committing Rapes, wh[ich] is a Crime they Despise" suggests that, at least by the eighteenth century, rape was not unknown in Native American com-

liams (1775; rpt. Johnson City, Tenn., 1930), 171; Jedidiah Morse, *A Report to the Secretary of War of the United States, on Indian Affairs: Comprising a Narrative of a Tour Performed in the Summer of 1820* (New York, 1970), 130; Loudon, ed., *A Selection, of Some of the Most Interesting Narratives,* II, 220. See also "Charles Thomson's Commentaries," in Thomas Jefferson, *Notes on the State of Virginia* (1787), ed. William Peden (Chapel Hill, N.C., 1955), 200; Elias Johnson, *Legends, Traditions, and Laws, of the Iroquois, or Six Nations, and History of the Tuscarora Indians* (1881; New York, 1978), 22–23. For an exceptional example that included rape alongside other Indian barbarities, albeit instigated by the French, see *Boston Gaz.,* Mar. 26, 1754.

21. Ramón Gutiérrez, *When Jesus Came, the Corn Mothers Went Away: Marriage, Sexuality, and Power in New Mexico, 1500–1846* (Stanford, Calif., 1991), 19–20, 26; James Axtell, *The European and the Indian: Essays in the Ethnohistory of Colonial North America* (New York, 1981), 182. See also John E. Ferling, *A Wilderness of Miseries: War and Warriors in Early America* (Westport, Conn., 1980), 47; Gregory Evans Dowd, *A Spirited Resistance: The North American Indian Struggle for Unity, 1745–1815* (Baltimore, 1992), 9–10; Alden T. Vaughan, *Roots of American Racism: Essays on the Colonial Experience* (New York, 1995), 339 n. 129; Namias, *White Captives,* 89; Alice Nash, "'None of the Women Were Abused': Indigenous Contexts for the Treatment of Women Captives in the Northeast," in Merril D. Smith, ed., *Sex without Consent: Rape and Sexual Coercion in America* (New York, 2001), 26.

munities. And men from Native American communities—often under the influence of alcohol—occasionally were charged with raping colonial women. Yet whether Indians did or did not rape may be largely irrelevant to how colonists perceived the sexual danger from their native neighbors: the dearth of actual rapes by rebelling slaves did not deter rumors that successful slave revolts would lead to mass rape of white women. Instead, the ways that Anglo-Americans understood rape and viewed Native American sexual mores crucially influenced their growing surety that Indians would not rape white women.[22]

As discussed in Chapter 1, early Americans generally believed that rape occurred because a man's natural sexual passions spun out of his control, not because he had planned an act of violence. This belief that rape was an outgrowth of consensual sex undergirded many of the commentaries on Native Americans. Many of the observations previously mentioned stated that Indians would not rape captives because Indians frowned upon *all* sexual relations during war (Indians "will not cohabit with women while they are out at war," and they "refrain from all intercourse with the other sex"). Other commentators took this a step further to consequently label Indian men as less sexually passionate than Anglo-American men. As mentioned previously, William Douglass's explanation that Indians would not rape claimed that Indians "are not so LASCIVIOUS as *Europeans*." For Douglass, lack of innate sexual desire explained the absence of rape. In an 1802 travel narrative, William Priest spent

22. Adair, *Adair's The History of the American Indians,* 145 in original; George Croghan, "The Opinions of George Croghan on the American Indian," *Pennsylvania Magazine of History and Biography,* LXXI (1947), 157. For a rape involving alcohol, see Proclamation Book AAA, 1782–1823, Mar. 23, 1798, microfilm 40–41, 167–170, GA; Conrad Weiser Papers, call no. 700, I, 25, HSP. Scholars have surmised that Native American cultural beliefs about the rape of captives might have varied among native groups and might have shifted after contact with Europeans. See Albert L. Hurtado, *Intimate Frontiers: Sex, Gender, and Culture in Old California* (Albuquerque, N.Mex., 1999). For example, the few East Coast documented cases of Indian-on-white rapes during military conflicts involved East Florida Indian groups. See John McQueen to Enrique White, Feb. 9, 1802, East Florida Papers, bundle 137G11, reel 56, pt. 2, 137–139, Library of Congress MSS, Washington, D.C.; letter of Alexander Steele, Sept. 12, 1792, ibid., bundle 122E10, reel 47, pt. 2, 323; Richard Lang to governor of Saint Augustine, Dec. 8, 1790, ibid., bundle 195M15, reel 82, 381–383.

On the (lack of a) relationship of actual to perceived risk, see Daniel Scott Smith and J. David Hacker, "Cultural Demography: New England Deaths and the Puritan Perception of Risk," *Journal of Interdisciplinary History,* XXVI (1996), 367–392.

two pages discussing Indian men's sexual habits toward European women. Although warriors might "frequently tomahawk and scalp the most beautiful women. . . . they are never known to take the slightest liberty with them *bordering on indecency.*" He concluded that such restrained behavior either "proceeds from education or what the french call temperment." In an often-cited paragraph that likewise explained Indians' proclivity not to rape captives, Charles Thomson agreed, "It is true, they do not indulge those [sexual] excesses, nor discover that fondness which is customary in Europe." In early American minds, Indian men did not rape because they were sexually uninterested in (European) women. Even some historians have assumed this connection between sexual desire and wartime rape: James Axtell argues that Indians might not have raped English women because they found white women unattractive.[23]

Native American sexual customs might provide another explanation for why Indians did not seem to be interested in rape. Anglo-American colonists frequently commented on the sexual availability of Native American women. In his narrative of southern backcountry travels, William Byrd repeatedly recalled occasions when Indian women "put on all their Ornaments to charm us." In his Revolutionary-era travels, Nicholas Cresswell wrote of continually being "obliged to accept" Native American women's sexual companionship. "If I do not take a Squaw to myself," he wrote, he would "often meet with" unrelenting sexual overtures from Native American women. English men might have read sexual willingness from Indian women far more readily than these women intended, but the colonists believed that because Native American women seemed sexually available, and because rape was seen as an outgrowth of men's sexual needs, Native American men seemed less likely to "need" to rape.[24]

23. Douglass, *A Summary, Historical and Political, of the First Planting,* I, 175; William Priest, *Travels in the United States of America* (London, 1802), 96–97, emphasis in original; "Charles Thomson's Commentaries," in Jefferson, *Notes on the State of Virginia,* ed. Peden, 200; Axtell, *The European and the Indian,* 181–182. For an exceptional comment that likely grew out of his lack of distinction between fornication and rape, see William Bartram, *Travels of William Bartram,* ed. Mark Van Doren (New York, 1928), 183–184.

24. William Byrd, *Histories of the Dividing Line betwixt Virginia and North Carolina,* ed. William K. Boyd (New York, 1967), 115, 116; *The Journal of Nicholas Cresswell, 1774–1777* (New York, 1924), 105, 108, 113. See also Nancy Shoemaker, "How Indians Got to Be Red," *AHR,* CII (1997), 633. On divergent English and Algonquian meanings given to Algonquian women's seeming sexual willingness, see Kathleen M. Brown, "The Anglo-Algonquian Gender Frontier," in Nancy Shoemaker, ed., *Negotiators of Change: Historical Perspectives on Native American Women* (New York, 1995), 26–48. See also Gary B. Nash,

Some eastern Native Americans' matrilineal and matrilocal social systems might have also confirmed to European men that Native American men were effeminate and undersexed. Eastern Woodland Indian women might perform agricultural duties, control community property, and play a larger role in political decisions than European women. Socially feminized and without obvious sexual control over "their" women, Indian men appeared to be sexually emasculated. Indeed, a Choctaw chief complained in 1765 that traders "often call . . . [Choctaw warriors] Eunuchs." Men who did not fulfill European notions of proper patriarchal social roles were also seen as unable to fill patriarchal sexual roles.[25]

Finally, because rape occupied one small end of the Anglo-American continuum of coerced and consensual sexual interactions, European commentators did not read many forced sexual interactions as rape. With no notion of rape within marriage, early Americans did not view captive white women's eventual forced adoption as wives as rape. One early-nineteenth-century story told of a woman's fear that she was being married to an Indian in an adoption ceremony that she did not understand, suggesting her lack of ability to give meaningful

Red, White, and Black: The Peoples of Early North America, 3d ed. (Englewood Cliffs, N.J., 1992), 281. For Indians' complaining about male colonists' unwelcome sexual overtures, see William Stephens, The Journal of William Stephens, 1741–1743, ed. E. Murton Coulter (Athens, Ga., 1958), 223; Oakchoy King, speech [to Gov. Boone and John Stuart], Little Halsey, Apr. 10, 1764, enclosed in John Stuart to Thomas Gage, May 20, 1764, Thomas Gage Papers, American Ser., XVIII, Clements Library, Ann Arbor, Mich.; Dunbar Rowland, comp. and ed., Mississippi Provincial Archives . . . 1763–1766, I (Nashville, Tenn., 1911), 238–239, 241.

25. Rowland, comp. and ed., Mississippi Provincial Archives, I, 238. On European interpretations of Indian bodies, see Karen Ordahl Kupperman, Indians and English: Facing Off in Early America (Ithaca, N.Y., 2000), 41–76. On the gendered structure of Native American social systems, see Brown, "The Anglo-Algonquian Gender Frontier," in Shoemaker, ed., Negotiators of Change, 26–48; Lucy Eldersveld Murphy, "Autonomy and the Economic Roles of Indian Women of the Fox-Wisconsin Riverway Region, 1763–1832," in Shoemaker, ed., Negotiators of Change, 72–89; Eleanor Burke Leacock, "Women in Egalitarian Society: The Montagnais-Naskapi of Canada," pt. 1 of Leacock, Myths of Male Dominance: Collected Articles on Women Cross-Culturally (New York, 1981), 31–81; Martha W. McCartney, "Cockacoeske, Queen of Pamunkey: Diplomat and Suzeraine," in Peter H. Wood et al., eds., Powhatan's Mantle: Indians in the Colonial Southeast (Lincoln, Neb., 1989), 173–195; Elisabeth Tooker, "Women in Iroquois Society," in Michael K. Foster et al., eds., Extending the Rafters: Interdisciplinary Approaches to Iroquoian Studies (Albany, N.Y., 1984), 109–123.

consent. A 1790s recollection of a "Mrs. Howe's" captivity during the Seven Years' War recalled her horror that Indians had "selected a couple of their young men to marry her daughters," but she did not appear to have considered these marriages equivalent to rape. In another narrative, an Anglo-American woman who had had a child with an Indian claimed "that before she had consented, they had tied her to a stake in order to burn her." Even though we may ask whether such forced adoption ceremonies should be considered rape, such women did not — being tied to a stake did not negate consent. For early Americans, rape was generally a onetime event that was accomplished with immediate physical force, not a continuing marriage that began with coercion. White women's marriages to Indian men might have caused great concern to Europeans, but not because they considered these relationships to be rapes.[26]

Thus, Indians did not meet all of Europeans' criteria for likely rapists. Yes, Indians were heathen savages; yes, as the American residents who literally stood in the way of expansion, Indians were the ultimate outsiders to colonization. This certainly made them seem probable perpetrators of a variety of horrific acts. But Indian men were not sexually aggressive, and Indian women were sexually available — two strong deterrents to rape in early American minds. Because rape was seen as a threat by and against patriarchal control, feminized Native Americans seemed less threatening than the enslaved men who produced white men's wealth. Black men who lived within white society were a constant potential threat to all colonists, unlike those Indians living on the fringes of colonization (we could imagine that a mid-eighteenth-century New Yorker would view the likelihood of rape by an Iroquois as a very distant possibility but might perceive a rape by the slave living down the road as a very real risk). Because whites were accustomed not only to reading about rape as a threat to legitimate patriarchy but also to hearing about black men's prosecutions for rape, the image of rape by rebelling slaves struck chords in the early American imagination that rape by Native Americans did not.

If the damage of rape had been an overthrow of women's will, Indians' forced adoption and forced sex through marriage might have made Indians seem like rapists. But the real harm of rape — the harm threatened by rebelling

26. *A Narrative of the Captivity and Sufferings of Benjamin Gilbert and His Family,* in Loudon, ed., *A Selection, of Some of the Most Interesting Narratives,* II, 110; David Humphreys, *An Essay on the Life of the Honorable Major-General Israel Putnam . . .* (New York, 1790), 241 (contrast this with the classic description of attempted rape by a French Canadian later on 242–243); *The Account of the Captivity of Richard Baird,* in Loudon, ed., *A Selection, of Some of the Most Interesting Narratives,* II, 52.

slaves — was a complete overthrow of British colonial, and later American, society. Indians adopted women into their social structure; they did not turn to rape to remake Anglo-American society. Thus, by the eighteenth century, Americans were as sure that Indians would not rape captive women as they were that rebelling slaves planned to usurp white men's patriarchal power by immediately claiming white women as their sexual property. With the coming of revolution, Americans found a new predatory enemy: invading British forces became a prominent target for rape accusations in America's fight for self-determination.

RAPE AND REVOLUTION

When British troops fought against the colonists during the Revolution and again against American citizens in the War of 1812, tales of rape provided a forum for the creation of a national community of aggrieved American citizens. Wartime propaganda during the American Revolution foregrounded men's injuries from rape. Such stories were particularly useful against the British because rape illuminated their perversion of power and their betrayal of patriarchal protection. There is little surprise that the Revolution, like many other wars, occasioned rape accusations; war and rape have been linked throughout European history. Yet the extensive Revolutionary-era rhetoric on British rapes easily dwarfed the New World political rhetoric against Africans or Indians. Rape by British soldiers became a propaganda tool of proportions unmatched in early American history. American patriots proved the need for their independence from Britain through their raped women and, in so doing, gave rape a new prominence as a marker of threats to the American nation.

The following story, published in a 1776 Pennsylvania broadside and subsequently reprinted in other colonies, typified the discourse of rape in the American Revolution:

> WILLIAM SMITH, of *Smith's* Farm, near *Woodbridge*, hearing the cries of his daughter, rushed into the room, and found a *Hessian* Officer attempting to ravish her, in an agony of rage and resentment, he instantly killed him; but the Officer's party soon came upon him, and he now lays mortally wounded at his ruined, plundered dwelling.[27]

27. *Bucks County, December 14, 1776* (Philadelphia, 1776). See also Dixon and Hunter's *Vir. Gaz.*, Dec. 27, 1776. For a more detailed exploration of Revolutionary rhetoric on rape, see Sharon Block, "Rape without Women: Print Culture and the Politicization of Rape, 1765–1815," *Journal of American History*, LXXXIX (2003), 849–868.

Rather than emphasize the damage done to his characteristically unnamed daughter, this story begins and ends with William Smith: we learn about his agony, his mortal wounds, and his plundered dwelling. It is possible that Smith's physical injuries were worse than his daughter's, but the story allows the reader little consideration of her pain. The father's suffering took center stage, and the daughter was relegated to being a sign of his ruin. Another newspaper's report of Revolutionary rape similarly showcased a father's grief to evoke readers' sympathy: "One man had the cruel mortification to have his wife and only daughter . . . ravished; this he himself, almost choaked with grief, uttered in lamentations to his friend." During the War of 1812, several publications repeated rumors that British soldiers had raped Virginia women. One told how the "infamous and inhuman conduct at Hampton" by the British had raised "a storm of indignation and horror, of pity for the sufferers." But the author's sole example of "sufferers" was "the father, as he clasped his daughter to his breast, [who] bethought himself of the females of Hampton — their fate might, perhaps, be the fate of his own child." Men would either be saviors of their wives and daughters or victims of the damage done to their dependent women. Regardless, public discussion of rape that emphasized men's injuries particularly suited war propaganda. Wrongly abused patriarchs — whether abused by British soldiers or the Hessians the British army had hired — were a powerful symbol in a battle for the privileges of political rule.[28]

Throughout the Revolution, propagandists directly told men that their support for the patriot cause would protect them from British attacks on their property and their wives, thereby tying political success to personal preservation. In 1776, a letter from the Philadelphia Council of Safety warned American men of the need "to secure your property from being plundered, and to protect the innocence of your wives and children." A 1780 Massachusetts call to arms, reprinted in a Pennsylvania newspaper, urged men to think about those who had "their farms laid desolate; — their property plundered; — their virgins *ravished*." A later commentator on the Revolution condemned the British soldiers for mistreating their own supporters: "The elegant houses of some of [the Britons'] own most devoted partisans were burnt: their wives and daughters pursued and ravished." Even enemies of the British expected that support for the British state would ensure the protection of those supporters' depen-

28. *Pennsylvania Packet* (Philadelphia), Dec. 27, 1776, in *Archives of the State of New Jersey*, 2d Ser., 5 vols. (Trenton, N.J., 1901), I, 245; *Pennsylvania Evening Post* (Philadelphia), Dec. 28, 1776; *The War*, II, 4. On the intersection of familial and political metaphors, see Lewis, "The Republican Wife," *WMQ*, 3d Ser., XLIV (1987), 689–693.

dents and property. The violation of these shared codes of honorable masculinity further delegitimized British rule.[29]

Rather than treating dependent women *as* property, these reports presented ownership *and* sexual control as joint constituents of patriarchal prerogative. To say that women were viewed as property neglects the problematic instability caused by women's agency: although there could be no question as to whether one's house wished to be burned, a man might fear that his wife or daughter had invited a sexual encounter that she now labeled a rape. Placing rape in the setting of other visible offenses was a way to negate the need for a woman's version of the sexual encounter and to provide believable grounds for condemnation of an enemy. Uncivilized marauders were likely rapists, despite the details of the encounter that a victimized woman might provide.

Such narratives of rape validated American independence in both the Revolution and the War of 1812. Congregationalist minister Samuel Phillips Payson rhetorically asked a Boston audience in 1778 whether it was possible "to hear the cries and screeches of our ravished matrons and virgins that had the misfortune to fall into the enemies' hands, and think of returning to that cruel and bloody power which has done all these things?" Likewise, pamphlets detailing British rapes in Virginia in 1812 used rape in a call to arms against the British. Stories of rape were "enough to fire every manly bosom with the irrepressible desire of revenge . . . against the enemy wherever he dares to show his face." One published letter detailed the rapes of various women and concluded by pleading: "Men of Virginia! will you permit all this? — Fathers, and Brothers, and Husbands, will you fold your arms in apathy, and only curse your despoilers?" The appeals to men's protective roles toward women translated the sexual attacks on women into the despoiling of men, verbally bypassing the damage done to women in favor of the offense committed against their fathers, brothers, and husbands. Rape by soldiers symbolized British misappropriation of power and justified war against America's former king.[30]

29. *Penn. Evening Post,* Dec. 28, 1776; *Pennsylvania Gazette* (Philadelphia), Aug. 2, 1780 (rpt. from *Boston Journal,* July 13, 1780); Warren, *History of the Rise, Progress, and Termination of the American Revolution,* I, 191, 256, 324. See also *Bucks County, December 14, 1776;* "Oration Delivered in Boston, March 5, 1772, by Dr. Joseph Warren," in *An American Selection of Lessons in Reading and Speaking* (Boston, 1799), 138–139.

30. Samuel Phillips Payson, "A Sermon: Boston, 1778," in Charles S. Hyneman and Donald S. Lutz, eds., *American Political Writing during the Founding Era, 1760–1805,* 2 vols. (Indianapolis, 1983), I, 535; *Documents Demonstrating beyond the Possibility of Doubt, the Brutal Violence and Cruelty Practised by the British, on Private and Unarmed Citizens, and on Helpless American Females* . . . (n.p., [1813?]), 18. See also United States Congress, House

Such appeals portrayed American men's action as the solution to British rape. Stories of rape were meant to encourage American men to rise up and defeat the British. Just as English law justified one man's avenging the rape of his wife or daughter, social rhetoric encouraged the men of a new nation to avenge the rape of its women. Defense against rape thus became a means to define the privileges and responsibilities of American citizenship. Citizens protected their women just as they protected their country from a British tyranny that sought to destroy virtue and liberty. As one soldier complained to Thomas Jefferson in 1776, the British "to the disgrace of a Civilisd Nation Ravish the fair Sex." Assaults on women's bodies became publicly noteworthy as assaults on the body politic.[31]

Several political commentators made these connections between rape and illegitimate political rule explicit. One letter writer asked his "dear countrymen and fellow citizens" to avoid the horrors that had befallen other formerly free countries, now subject to "merciless depredations upon the chastity, property, liberty and happiness of their vassals." In 1777, a published list of misbehavior by British soldiers compared the soldiers' propensity to rape innocent women to the appalling behavior of "persons and bodies of the highest rank in Britain . . . King and Parliament." In 1779, a reprinted letter reported that several daughters of a gentleman "became victims to the lust of those monsters of Hell," the British soldiers, and warned readers, "If these things don't rouse America, we ought to be forever slaves." Building on the association between wrongful enslavement and British tyranny, one writer in 1813 even blamed British soldiers for encouraging African Americans to rape. A Major Crutchfield claimed that Hampton's (white) women were not only abused by the British army and its hired Hessians but also "by the infatuated Blacks who

---

of Representatives, Committee, *Barbarities of the Enemy, Exposed in a Report of the Committee of the House of Representatives of the United States . . .* (Troy, N.Y., 1813), 117–119; general orders, Jan. 1, 1777, in John C. Fitzpatrick, ed., *The Writings of George Washington from the Original Manuscript Sources, 1745–1799,* 39 vols. (Washington, D.C., 1931–1944), VI, 466; *Penn. Packet,* Jan. 4, 1777, Aug. 4, 1778. For a tongue-in-cheek exception that encouraged women to rise up like Joan of Arc and defend themselves from rape, see [Thomas Paine], *The American Crisis Number I* (Norwich, Conn., [1776]), 2–3.

31. Adam Stephen to Thomas Jefferson, Dec. 20, 1776, in Julian P. Boyd et al., eds., *The Papers of Thomas Jefferson,* 31 vols. (Princeton, N.J., 1950–), I, 659. On the legal doctrine that men could avenge the rape of their wives or daughters, see William Blackstone, *Commentaries on the Laws of England,* 4 vols. (1765–1769; rpt. Chicago, 1979), IV, 181; and John G. Bellamy, *Criminal Law and Society in Late Medieval and Tudor England* (New York, 1984), 159.

were encouraged by them in their excesses." The British were so corrupt as to encourage the sexual anarchy Anglo-Americans long believed could result from slave rebellion. From the American perspective, the British perverted the empire with their oppressive tyranny just as they perverted the most sacred of bodily interactions with their rapes of unwilling American women. Rape proved the illegitimacy of British rule because legitimate patriarchs, whether as individuals or as fathers of the nation, did not encourage rape. Stories of rape affirmed the righteousness of American rebellion and rhetorically created a collective body of male resisters to British imperial rule.[32]

Rape provided such a powerful rallying cry in the Revolutionary era because it set American innocence at the mercy of improperly seized power and made formerly British citizens in America the ultimate victims of the rapes by British soldiers. Rape — as the consummate evidence of men's uncontrolled lust for power or sex — was particularly poised to serve as a signifier of power wrongly claimed. Rape combined the image of unrestrained, illegitimate power with images of innocent, helpless, female victims who needed to be saved by righteous American men. But, to do so, rape was transformed from a personal contest between men's and women's words into a public portrayal of men incontrovertibly wronged. The specific details of rape were both unnecessary to and potentially destabilizing of rape's public functions.

To be sure, accusations of rapes by British soldiers were not pulled out of thin air. The Continental Congress collected a handful of women's depositions about such rapes during the Revolution, and dozens more women undoubtedly resisted speaking so publicly about the sexual attacks they suffered. When the Continental Congress ordered William Livingston to procure affidavits of rapes committed by British soldiers, he found this "more difficult to prove than any of the rest [of soldiers' abuses], as the Person abused, as well as the Relations are generally reluctant against bringing matters of this kind into public Notice." Testimonies of the women who did come forward reiterated the distance between women's stories of rape and the popular discourse that employed rape in a political forum. They also show the importance of the setting (war or peace, rebellion or cultural incorporation) in determining the meaning of the sexual act. In 1779, Connecticut resident Christiana Gatter described British soldiers' attempts to rape her to the Continental Congress.

32. *Penn. Gaz.*, Feb. 22, 1775, May 26, 1779; *Penn. Evening Post,* Apr. 24, 1777, in Frank Moore, ed., *The Diary of the American Revolution: From Newspapers and Original Documents* (New York, 1967), 217–218; *Documents Demonstrating beyond the Possibility of Doubt,* 10. See also *Penn. Gaz.*, Aug. 2, 1780.

PLATE 3. Boston Cannonaded. *1775. In response to the Boston Port Bill, this woodcut depicts the colonies' political endangerment from Lord North through an image of a sexually endangered America. Reprint from the title-page woodcut of Edmund Freebetter,* New England Almanac . . . 1776 *(New London, Conn., 1775). This item is reproduced by permission of* The Huntington Library, San Marino, Calif., *RB–24572*

Unlike most women who gave personal testimonies about rape, Christiana was not testifying in a judicial setting; her deposition was intended to provide a sympathetic Congress with details of British atrocities. As such, it belongs neither squarely in the category of print discourse (it was never published, just collected as a handwritten report) nor legal discourse (though it was taken as a deposition, no cross-examination, trial, or formal charges appear to have been considered). As such, it provides an alternative narrative to the many printed versions of Revolutionary rapes by British soldiers that did widespread political service.[33]

Christiana explained that a British soldier had appeared in her garden and "presented his Gun at her . . . [and] told her to Lye down." Thinking quickly, she suggested that it would be better to "go into the House." When the soldier ordered that "he would have me go into the Cellar, I told him that place was not good, [so] he asked me to go up Stairs. I pretended to Comply, went into the Entry and told him we had better go out the fore door into the Green where I flattered him along till we came in sight of" a neighbor, and Christiana called for help. Unfortunately, several soldiers returned later that night. While Christiana's "husband made his Escape thro the back door" and, by his own admission, "hid in a Corn Field till Morning," two soldiers raped her.[34]

Christiana's story focused on her own ingenuity in resisting the soldiers' rape attempts: by pretending to acquiesce to the first soldier's wishes, she managed to lead him into a public area where she could call for help. Her husband appeared in the story primarily to explain his absence rather than to save and protect his wife. Unlike examples of wartime propaganda, her story neither foregrounded men's conflicts nor explicitly presented rape as a means to define American privilege or to display masculine prowess. Instead, Christiana's self-centrality throughout the narrative made this quasi-public recording of a rape exceptional. She focused on the mechanics of the rape instead of the meanings of rape to the wider community or polity.

If Christiana's attacker had not been an enemy soldier, her evasiveness and

33. "Papers and Affidavits relating to the Plunderings, Burnings, and Ravages Committed by the British, 1775–1784," Papers of the Continental Congress, reel 66, item 53, U.S. National Archives and Records Administration, College Park, Md.

34. Depositions of Christiana Gatter and Martin Gatter, July 26, 1779, ibid., 236–238, punctuation added; George Herbert Ryden, ed., *Letters to and from Caesar Rodney, 1756–1784* (Philadelphia, 1933), 181. For comparison with printed versions of rape accounts in the Revolution, see discussions above as well as Francis Alexander's deposition on British rapes, *Penn. Gaz.,* Sept. 3, 1777.

pretended acquiescence might have made her appear to be a willing sexual partner. To avoid such possibilities, printed versions of such rapes turned attacks on women into a call to arms that paralleled national hostilities and focused on men's role in preventing or avenging rapes. In public discourse, narratives of rapes by British soldiers became wartime propaganda — stories told by men about men who committed attacks on other men. They were stories that encouraged the reader to draw conclusions about the legitimacy of each group's claims to political power. The rhetorical power of stories of British rapes of American women lay in their stark portrayal of villains and victims, a portrayal that paralleled American belief in the British Empire's betrayal of its American subjects.

Reducing women's role in rape stories could surmount the problem of women's credibility that characterized early American courtroom discourse. Bypassing the need to determine a woman's truthfulness allowed men to claim the rape on her behalf. The convincing male witness to rape, so rare in courtrooms, became a stock figure in rape publications, and that literary convention allowed patriarchal figures to reaffirm masculine identities through the male witness's classification of rape. Rape was unequivocal when men stood at the center of the story; when women remained central figures, rape was either resistible or nonexistent.

By substituting witnessed women for testifying women, writers found a way to resolve a fundamental instability of rape, providing a standard of proof most actual rapes could not attain. Such "real" rapes could then be prisms through which other sets of power relationships could be viewed. Without women's public voices, rape was a metaphor for a multitude of masculine conflicts, and men's sexual assaults on women could be seen as symbols of power and identity vis-à-vis other men and other bodies politic. This politicization of rape was part of what Lynn Hunt has called Americans' gendered "imagination of power" and what Cathy Davidson has called the nationalization of female sexuality in Revolutionary America.[35]

By the time of the Revolution, rape provided a means for Americans to display the consequences of British tyranny through the combination of the gendered significance of sexual attacks and the ideologies of revolution. American allegations of rape by British soldiers were an ironic inversion of their

35. Linda K. Kerber et al., "Forum: Beyond Roles, Beyond Spheres: Thinking about Gender in the Early Republic," *WMQ*, 3d Ser., XLVI (1989), 577; Cathy N. Davidson, *Revolution and the Word: The Rise of the Novel in America* (New York, 1986), 46.

longtime fears of rape by black slave revolutionaries. British and African American challenges to Anglo-American rule earned both groups the label of dangerous rapists. In contrast, early Americans' reluctant conclusion that Indians would not rape white women grew not only out of Anglo-Americans' understanding of rape, sex, and Native American sexual ideologies but out of the knowledge that, although Indians might be enemies, they did not plan to replace white men in Anglo-American society.

The trajectories of each of these myths was integrally tied to the meaning afforded to women's sexual behavior. The extensive circulation of stories of British rape among American readers fitted into the kinds of early national print entertainment that already focused on women's bodies as signifiers of larger political anxieties. Rape had always been a sign of power improperly claimed. But, in the early Republic, the public emphasis on white women's sexual morality alongside shifting punishments of white citizens and black slaves gave rape particularly powerful racial meanings that gained momentum through the nineteenth century. Transforming an individual woman's claim into a shared cultural truth inextricably tied rape, race, and gender to the American body politic.

CONCLUSION

In her 1808 testimony about how her master, William Cress, sexually coerced her, Rachel Davis repeatedly used versions of the phrase "He said I must." Rachel recalled William using these words to force her to have sex with him on multiple occasions. Once, Rachel remembered, "he caught hold of me and said, I must go sleep with him." Another time, William insisted that Rachel accompany him alone to the dark field where he would rape her: "He said . . . I must come." The phrase "He said I must" reminds us that sexual coercion was utterly enmeshed in social standing, racial privilege, and household authority. Contrary to the typical image of rape as irresistible physical force, William's position of mastery allowed him to coerce Rachel into situations where she was sexually vulnerable. By using orders rather than immediate violence, William reshaped his use of force into an appearance of her consent.[1]

But William did not always use incarnations of the phrase "he said I must" only as direct orders to Rachel. Rachel also recalled that, while raping her, "he said, Nate you dear creature, I must fuck you." In this statement, the "I" who "must" fulfill the master's orders was William, not Rachel. William's verbal narrative of his own lack of self-control neatly summarized the conflicting logic of rape: from William's perspective, the act was a fulfillment of his sexual passions; he needed sex. From Rachel's standpoint, William's pursuit of his own pleasure led to her experience of sexual force. At the intersection of these two uses of "must" — a man's compulsion to have sex and his forcing a woman to fulfill that need — was much of the conundrum of rape. A woman's response marked the division between consensual sex and rape, but, as in William's comments, men could erase or minimize women's ability to express their view of a sexual encounter. Thus, "He said: 'I must!'" is the verbal reenactment of rape — the subsumption of a woman's will under a man's desires.[2]

How, then, did early Americans know when sexual coercion moved from a man's acceptable pursuit of his own sexual fulfillment to the unacceptable

1. *Commonwealth v William Cress*, February 1808, Pennsylvania Court Papers, HSP.
2. Ibid. Nate was a family nickname for Rachel.

erasure of a woman's will by force? This was a problem that continually vexed early Americans: the fundamental inability to know whether a woman who claimed rape had truly resisted to her utmost or had secretly consented to the encounter. Protection and betrayal were flip sides of the same patriarchal structure. On one side, powerful men were supposed to protect their women from the predatory overtures of other men; on the other lay the danger that a woman would deny a patriarch his role as protector by sexually offering herself to an inappropriate man. In a society built around the central pillar of marriage, sex was crucial to the appearance of social order. Sexual relations used wrongly could profoundly threaten the very social structures that they were meant to confirm.

Still, rape was never an attack committed through monolithic gender binaries: A Man assaulting A Woman. The process of the attack, an individual's response to the incident, and the range of available institutional redress all depended on social identities and status relations. William's ability to coerce Rachel with words relied on the power early American society afforded to his position of mastery and on Rachel's dependency as his servant. Yet, early Americans saw rape's connection to patriarchy in very different terms than those I suggest here. For them, rape was a direct affront that challenged the fundamental right of patriarchs to control sexual access to their wives and daughters. Early Americans built a society that depended on the appropriate use of husbands' and fathers' power to determine dependent women's sexual interactions. This was what made rape seem so threatening and what made it nearly impossible to see the ways that powerful men could coerce sex, often with near impunity. Beyond the literal bounds of the family, men's political, racial, and social powers meant that legitimate patriarchs did not need to rape. They were expected to control themselves just as they controlled their dependents.

In a society where male-to-female sexual aggression could be an acceptable part of sexual relations, the meaning of force was largely determined by the identities of those who participated in the act. Early Americans set their evaluations of sexual acts within a framework that used race as a fundamental dividing line for status, power, and authority. By racially segregating rape defendants and victims, rape could be cordoned off from the murky grounds of women's possible consent and dubious claims of coercion. Rather than policing rape as a moral offense to which all sinners might fall victim, rape could be treated as a violent offense against a racial or social hierarchy. Black men's rape of white women was the perfect sign of the inappropriate desires for sexual legitimacy and patriarchal power denied to enslaved men.

But sexual coercion was not just about those acts that would be classified as rape. Existing relationships between men and women allowed for forms of sexual coercion that deviated from the sudden, violent rape by a stranger. In a race-based slave labor system that denied the privilege of legal marriage and encouraged reproduction as a profitable venture, sexual assaults on enslaved women by black or white attackers went largely unrecorded, unremarked, and unremedied. Women of color, often the most socially vulnerable members of society, were the most sexually vulnerable to rape and public sexual humiliation — and the least likely to appear in the historical record. Rape was part of the architecture of early American racial and gender hierarchies that used women's bodies to delineate its rules and its boundaries.

This work has emphasized the ways that power was created, exercised, and maintained in early American society. Studying *how* sex could be coerced reveals that sexual power was inextricable from social power. I have striven to uncover how daily interactions created and gave meaning to visible racial differences via gendered interactions. Treating rape as a series of continual formulations, rather than a singular act summed up by a seven-word definition ("carnal knowledge, by force, against her will"), reveals the profound imbrications of race, gender, and sexuality.[3]

My interests in individual women's experiences and the process of sexual coercion raise a tension that I have navigated throughout this project. Much about sexual coercion seems profoundly transhistoric, yet, as a historian, I have been trained to mark the exceptionality of an era, region, or cultural group. Certainly there were variations across early American regions and time periods. But I have found — despite persistent efforts to sort my sources chronologically and regionally — that the sections that deal with the most intimate, one-on-one interactions between people are those that seem often startlingly reminiscent of sexual coercion in other times and places. Although I have been careful to avoid ahistoricism or essentialism, I have also not ignored some of the obvious continuities related to rape: the blurred boundaries of sexual coercion and consent, the expression of social power through sexual power, the sexual vulnerability that accompanied social vulnerability, the intimacy of women's communities, and the ongoing distrust of many women's claims of rape. All of these generalities are important to my study. Accordingly, my historically specific narrative does not necessarily focus only on the particularities of a given time and place. Rather than limit my analysis to that which is, for example, indicative

3. William Blackstone, *Commentaries on the Laws of England*, 4 vols. (1765–1769; rpt. Chicago, 1979), IV, 210; Richard Starke, *The Office and Authority of a Justice of Peace, Explained and Digested, under Proper Titles* (Williamsburg, Va., 1774).

of the transition from the early to late colonial period, or of the regionalism of mid-Atlantic versus New England print culture, I maintain that those interactions that do not so easily illustrate historical changes are still crucial to understanding how power operated in daily life.

A second challenge has been to show women's daily experiences with sexual coercion without replicating the gendered divisions of power that erased or minimized women's role in rape. Despite the public image of rape, early American women actively negotiated the terms of sexual relationships even under the most unequal systems of power; they mediated other women's claims of assault and tried to shape their stories for all-male juries. Maintaining women's perspectives while documenting the structural and institutional systems that depended on the silencing of particular forms (and therefore particular victims) of sexual coercion can be difficult. I have been influenced by literary scholars, such as Lynn Higgins and Brenda Silver, who caution that understanding rape "involves listening not only to who speaks and in what circumstances, but who does *not* speak and why." I have tried to give voice to those who might not have had the words or the opportunities to speak for posterity. Beyond just documenting agency or recovering voices, however, I have argued that these silences were crucial to sustaining the meanings of rape in early America.[4]

Ultimately, in the hopes of finding a middle ground between structure and process, continuity and change, and specificity and generalities, I have turned to multiple methodological approaches: a chronological narrative of statutory law, a social history of women's reactions to sexual coercion, a quantitative and qualitative study of the criminalization of rape, an intellectual history of widespread beliefs about sexual relations, and a cultural history of the shifting myths of rape. Each approach adds a different piece to the puzzle of sexuality in early America but also complicates my attempts to provide a single narrative about the history of sexual coercion. Should I focus on the enduring double standard, or the increasing sentimentalization of heterosexual relations? Should I emphasize the clear shifts in sentencing practices or the kinds of extralegal coercion that persisted largely unchallenged and unchanged? Should I give priority to the prosecution of rape, or to the process of sexual coercion? These kinds of questions are fundamental to histories of sexuality: how do we combine the microhistories of individual interactions with the macrohistories of institutional or cultural views on sexual behavior? One answer may be in a multiplicity

4. Lynn A. Higgins and Brenda R. Silver, "Introduction: Rereading Rape," in Higgins and Silver, eds., *Rape and Representation* (New York, 1991), 3.

of approaches and sources — even if the results provide a messier story than we may prefer.

When I began this project, my most pressing concern was that I would be unable to unearth enough historical evidence. A decade later, I find that material related to sexual coercion is virtually unavoidable. I am thrilled that my original fears were unfounded, but the bounty of evidence led to other theoretical and conceptual difficulties. As I tried to reconstruct the many perspectives on rape — individual women's experiences, community reactions, institutional mandates, courtroom practices, print culture, and mainstream ideologies — I struggled to balance continuity and widely shared beliefs with change over time and regional specificities. By emphasizing the big picture and taking a thematic approach to rape, I have continually run the danger of underplaying local distinctions. To some degree, writing a monograph on a topic that covers thousands of miles and more than a century inevitably faces the problem of dissatisfying some readers with my lack of attention to the particularities of specific regions or time periods.

Because discussions of various chronologic and regional specificities appear at separate moments in the text, I now want to suggest how these moments may fit together. I see two major chronological shifts, climaxing interdependently after the Revolution. The first shift relates to the racialization of rape, and the second to rape discourse. Regional specificities, although less easily identified because of variations in source availability (New England is notable for its extensive criminal genre print culture; the mid-Atlantic for its prominent and accessible *Pennsylvania Gazette* newspaper; the South for many documents on slave executions but far fewer on white rape defendants), also can be teased out from the many commonalities I have traced.

The first chronological shift relates to the racialization of rape. By the early eighteenth century, multiple colonies had set up separate trial courts for black or enslaved defendants and had begun to pass statutes that targeted black-on-white rape. Once a defendant entered the criminal justice system, men of color, often the least powerful members of American society, experienced a slew of further disadvantages in legal and print forums that enacted racial meaning without relying on a single moment of racist action. Black men were the unabated targets of the overwhelming number of prosecutions, convictions, and executions through the eighteenth and early nineteenth centuries. The hundreds of public trials of black (usually enslaved) men for rape in early America laid the foundation for the increasing fears of black rapists of white women in the nineteenth century.

The continuity in the criminalization of black rapists was also marked by the diminution of white men's culpability for rape. As my study of a decade of a Pennsylvania county's court records suggests, local courts' and justices' flexibility minimized the criminality of white men's sexual assaults. By the early Republic, several other trends magnified this distancing of white men from rape. The post-Revolutionary move toward abolition of capital punishment for free men eliminated the death penalty for most white rapists but few black rapists. Thus enslaved men increasingly accounted for the majority of defendants publicly executed for rape. At the same time, the popularity of seduction literature emphasized a view of white men as reprehensible rakes rather than irredeemable rapists. In a young nation that needed to pride itself on its citizenry, white men appeared as less likely rapists than black men. To be sure, this was not yet the myth of the hypersexual rapist that would be leveled at black men in the later decades of the nineteenth century. It was an important stepping-stone to that eventuality, but early Americans did not yet have the vocabulary of Foucaultian identities to label anyone a "rapist" — the Oxford English Dictionary traces the original use of "rapist" to the last quarter of the nineteenth century, when a United States newspaper referred to a "'nigger' rapist."[5]

The second major shift related to rape discourse. The explosion of print and political commentary in the last quarter of the eighteenth century gave rape extensive public significance. Rape had long been used as a signifier for various societal transgressions: American religious writers' concerns over rape as part of a panoply of sexual sins continued into the nineteenth century; transatlantic writers used rape to condemn other New and Old World powers; and rebellious slaves were regularly rumored to have designs on white men's white wives. In the American Revolutionary era, allegations of the rape of American women by British soldiers signified an attack on liberty and the rights of Americans. Even after the British imperial threat dissipated in the first decades of the nineteenth century, rape continued to be transformed from an intimate sexual act into a public symbol. The rise of a transatlantic sentimental print culture that centered on women's bodies, actions, and sexual choices simultaneously foregrounded stories of rape that marginalized women to symbolize an array of growing national tensions. Rape's damage to the very fabric of a

5. *Oxford English Dictionary*, 2d ed., s.v. "rapist." On one nineteenth-century "frenzy" of Indian hatred that extended to widely publicized rape accusations against Dakota Indians, see June Namias, *White Captives: Gender and Ethnicity on the American Frontier* (Chapel Hill, N.C., 1993), 225, 231.

world organized along gender hierarchies was a ready prism through which to define other power relationships. Rather than an example of a sin to which all might fall victim, hardening racial divisions increasingly made attacks on individual bodies into attacks on the (white) American body politic. The accepted politicization of rape in late-eighteenth- and early-nineteenth-century print culture opened the door for distinctly American meanings of rape that eventually culminated in racial myths of savage rapists.

Such chronological cultural shifts reveal the role of gender, race, and sexuality in colonial state formation, yet there were also noteworthy regional particulars to rape. In several ways, New England was the most exceptional of the British mainland settlements. New England was the only region that generally did not specifically criminalize and separately try enslaved men for rape. New England's Puritan heritage and its religiously oriented colonial print culture meant that public concern about sinfulness held sway even after other colonies began to embrace more secular concerns about rape. In the early eighteenth century, especially, we can see clear remnants of the Puritan emphasis on rape as a moral crime. Overall, however, the New England record of prosecutions, convictions, and executions matches its southern neighbors' emphasis on race in the legal handling of rape. Blacks tried in New England courts uniformly faced a far higher conviction rate than whites, and, as in other colonies, nonwhite women had precious few opportunities to prosecute sexual assaults in New England courts.

As abolition took hold in the North, statutes expressly segregating white and black or free and enslaved defendants disappeared from the mid-Atlantic states. As in New England, mid-Atlantic records nevertheless suggest continuing criminal emphasis on black-on-white rapes. Mid-Atlantic court records also reveal the influence of the growing urbanization of port cities toward the end of the eighteenth century. The increasing numbers of free people of color in northern cities, such as New York, led local courts to consider the slight possibility that nonwhite victims could make charges of sexual assault (often against nonwhite men). At the same time, increasing numbers of unmarried, white women in cities (in the mid-Atlantic and, to a lesser degree, in New England) appeared as victims of possible rapes by young men with whom they had socialized — often in incidents that courts dismissed as postcoitally regretted seductions. The increased mobility of young women and the decreased parental control over children's heterosexual socializing created new social dynamics through which sex could be coerced. Both of these developments reflect the rising attention to racial and class divisions in these growing cities.

Southern slave systems continued to grow apart from northern societies following the American Revolution, even though, as John Wood Sweet has written, "the everyday realities of race continued to unite the new nation long after the politics of slavery began to divide it." Certainly, many more black (overwhelmingly enslaved) men were prosecuted for the rapes of white women in the South than in the North. Although blacks' conviction rates dramatically outstripped whites' in all regions, black-on-white attacks—especially in the nineteenth-century South—might have been brought more frequently before courts. Unfortunately, the lack of surviving records makes any attempts at determining the numbers of rape prosecutions per capita exceedingly sketchy. We also know that while northerners were inching toward the courtroom admittance of nonwhite victims of rape, southerners were moving toward a legal denial of the possibility of the rape of enslaved women. Nevertheless, the heightened role of race in southern slave societies continued to be informed by widely held ideologies that made sexual power a matter of national significance throughout early America.[6]

The patriarchal and racial significance of rape is epitomized by the statement of one man writing from the Florida frontier in 1792. In trying to persuade another man not to commit a rape, Alexander Steele made the patently false claim "that White men did not offer any such insults to their Women." White men did rape "their" women. White men raped women and girls of all racial and cultural backgrounds. Such statements reflected the political service rape could do by transforming an attack on a woman into an expression of social ideals. By seeing rape as an attack on public order, early Americans gave rape a potent legacy extending beyond an individual assault.[7]

This study has explored the profound power of rape in early American society and culture. Far beyond the level of scattered prosecutions or individual assaults, the cultural scripts of sexual coercion created daily enactments of racial ideologies, labor relations, and gender hierarchies. The criminal handling of sexual assaults institutionalized privileges of whiteness. The public discourse of rape gave religious, political, and fictional commentaries a means to differentiate good from evil. Through these mediums, the racialized practices of

6. John Wood Sweet, *Bodies Politic: Negotiating Race in the American North, 1730–1830* (Baltimore, 2003), 11.

7. Letter of Alexander Steele, Sept. 12, 1792, East Florida Papers, bundle 122E10, reel 47, pt. 2, 323.

rape that began in colonial America formed the infrastructure of sexual politics for at least the duration of the nineteenth century. Only by attending to the micro and the macro, to individuals and institutions, to daily life and discourse, can we recreate the role of sexual coercion in the creation of an American New World.

KNOWN SEXUAL COERCION INCIDENTS DIVIDED
CHRONOLOGICALLY AND GEOGRAPHICALLY, 1700–1820

This is a tabulation of all sexual coercion incidents found in the available court and legal records, newspapers, almanacs, other print materials, and manuscript sources consulted for the period. Rather than a statement on the frequency of sexual coercion in a given time and place, the variation in these numbers largely reflects source availability and other idiosyncrasies of the historical record.

	1700–1720	1721–1740	1741–1760	1761–1780	1781–1800	1801–1820	No Date	Total
New Hampshire	0	1	1	3	4	4	0	13
Massachusetts	10	14	7	17	17	25	0	90
Rhode Island	1	2	3	8	0	2	0	16
Connecticut	5	11	9	16	11	33	0	85
New York	1	4	5	17	13	45	1	86
New Jersey	10	6	13	27	13	1	1	71
Pennsylvania	4	19	19	22	44	34	0	142
Delaware	0	1	4	4	1	7	1	18
Maryland	1	2	12	12	21	18	0	66
Virginia	6	12	15	41	41	52	3	170
North Carolina	1	6	4	19	5	20	0	55
South Carolina	2	0	4	8	4	27	0	45
Georgia		1	7	0	1	4	0	13
Other	2	0	1	9	11	18	1	42
Total	43	79	104	203	186	290	7	912

APPENDIX B
LEGAL RECORDS CONSULTED

PUBLISHED AND MANUSCRIPT LEGAL RECORDS

Beyond tracking individual citations gathered from published works and provided by kind colleagues, I looked through the following legal records for cases
of sexual coercion. When collections extend past the dates of my study or dates
are not listed, I examined available records pertaining to the years between
1700 and 1820. This appendix does not include non-legal sources in which I
located incidents of sexual coercion.

Connecticut

Farrell, John T., ed. *The Superior Court Diary of William Samuel Johnson, 1772–
1773....* Washington, D.C., 1942.

Trial of Amos Adams, for a Rape, Committed on the Body of Lelea Thorp. New
Haven, 1817. AAS.

Trumbull, J. Hammond, and Charles J. Hoadly, eds. *The Public Records of the
Colony of Connecticut, [1636–1776].* 15 vols. Hartford, 1850–1890.

Connecticut State Library, Hartford

Connecticut Archives. Crimes and Misdemeanors: Series 1, 2.

New Haven Superior Court Criminal Files, box 598.

New Haven Superior Court Trials, box 1.

New London Superior Court Records, Trials 1798–1820.

Superior Court Files for Fairfield County (boxes 53, 84, 625, 626),
Hartford County (boxes 44, 45), Litchfield County (boxes 193, 194),
New Haven County (boxes 339–341), New London County (box 30,
38, 41, 133), Tolland County (boxes 2, 4, 7).

Superior Court Records, 1798–1820, for Hartford County, Windham
County.

Delaware

Horle, Craig W., ed. *Records of the Courts of Sussex County, Delaware.* Vol. II,
1690–1710. Philadelphia, 1991.

Delaware Public Archives, Dover

Oyer and Terminer Dockets for Kent County, New Castle County, Sussex
County.

Oyer and Terminer Papers for Kent County, New Castle County, Sussex
County.

Georgia

Candler, Allen D., ed. *The Colonial Records of the State of Georgia.* 25 vols. 1904–1915; New York, 1970.

Georgia Archives, Morrow
Franklin County Superior Court Case Files.
Franklin County Unbound Superior Court Records.
Greene County Superior Court Miscellaneous Records.
Hancock County Civil and Criminal Case Files.
Jackson County Miscellaneous Bound Superior Court Records.
Jackson County Superior Court Minutes, 1796–1802.
Lincoln County Docket of Slaves Indicted for Capital Crimes, 1814–1838.
Miscellaneous Records for Baldwin County, Montgomery County.
Superior Court Cases, Criminal, boxes 24–28.
Superior Court Cases, Criminal, "Indictments and Bonds."
Superior Court Docket Books for Jasper County, Jones County.
Trial of Slaves for Baldwin County, Putnam County.
Wilkes County Grand Jury Docket, 1788–1790.
Wilkes County Superior Court Subpoena Docket, 1793–1797.
Wilkes County Unbound Minutes, 1782–1787.

Kentucky

Cook, Michael L., and Bettie A. Cummings Cook, eds. *Jefferson County, Kentucky Records.* Vol. I. Evansville, Ind., 1987.

Kentucky Department for Libraries and Archives, Frankfort
Fleming Circuit Court, Order Book, 1798–1803.
Jessamine County Circuit Court, 1800–1811.
Madison County Circuit Court, Loose Criminal Papers, 1787–1807.
Warren County Circuit Court, 1803–1806.
Whitley County Circuit Court, Commonwealth Indictments.

Maryland

Archives of Maryland. 72 vols. Baltimore, 1883–1972.

Maryland State Archives, Annapolis
Baltimore Oyer and Terminer Docket, 1789–1816.
Charles County Court Record.
Governor and Council. Pardon Papers, boxes 1–20.
Harford County Court Criminal Docket, 1774–1788.
Queen Anne's County Court Criminal Record, 1751–1831.

Massachusetts

Allen, W. Neal. *Province and Court Records of Maine*. Vol. IV. Portland, Maine, 1958.

Commonwealth v Battis. 1 Mass. 95 (1804).

Commonwealth v Hutchinson. 10 Mass. 225 (1813).

Commonwealth v Murphy. 14 Mass. 387 (1817).

Konig, David Thomas, ed. *Plymouth Court Records, 1686–1859*. 16 vols. Wilmington, Del., 1978–1981.

Report of the Trial of Ephraim Wheeler for a Rape Committed on the Body of Betsy Wheeler, His Daughter, a Girl Thirteen Years of Age. . . . Stockbridge, 1805.

Report of the Trials of Stephen Murphy and John Doyle before the Supreme Judicial Court at Dedham, Oct. 23, 1817. Boston, 1817.

Rice, Franklin P., ed. *Records of the Court of General Sessions of the Peace for the County of Worcester, Massachusetts, from 1731 to 1737*. Worcester, 1882.

Wroth, L. Kinvin, and Hiller B. Zobel. *Legal Papers of John Adams*. 3 vols. Cambridge, 1965.

Massachusetts Archives, Boston

Entries of Convicts in the State Prison, Charlestown, 1805–1818.

Superior Court Judicial Dockets, 1798–1820.

Superior Court Papers, Suffolk Files.

Massachusetts Historical Society, Boston

Dockets of Cases and Notes of Evidence Taken by Hon. Increase Sumner.

New Hampshire

New Hampshire Division of Archives and Records Management, Concord

Hillsborough County Superior Court Judgments.

Rockingham County Superior Court Record Books.

Superior Court Minute Book, 1699–1738.

New Jersey

New Jersey Archives. Trenton, 1901–.

Reed, H. Clay, and George T. Miller, eds. *The Burlington Court Book: A Record of Quaker Jurisprudence in West New Jersey*. Washington, D.C., 1944.

Votes and Proceedings of the General Assembly of the Province of New-Jersey. Woodbridge, 1769.

Princeton University Library, Rare Books and Special Collections

New Jersey Court of Oyer and Terminer and Gaol Delivery, 1749–1762.

New Jersey State Library, Trenton
Court of Oyer and Terminer Minutes for Bergen County, Cape May
County, Cumberland County.
Supreme Court Actions-at-Law Papers.

Hunterdon Hall of Records, Flemington
Hunterdon County Circuit Court Docket Books, 1810–1820.

New York

*The Commissioners of the Alms-House, vs. Alexander Whistelo, a Black Man; Being
a Remarkable Case of Bastardy. . . .* New York, 1808.

[Horsmanden, Daniel]. *A Journal of the . . . Detection of the Conspiracy Formed
by Some White People, in Conjunction with Negro and Other Slaves, for Burning
the City of New-York in America. . . .* New York, 1744.

New-York Judicial Repository. 6 nos. New York, 1818–1819.

Report of the Trial of Ann Saffen versus Edward Seaman for Seduction. New York,
1818. NYHS.

Report of the Trial of Henry Bedlow, for Committing a Rape on Lanah Sawyer.
New York, 1793.

*Report of the Trial of Richard D. Croucher, on an Indictment for a Rape on
Margaret Miller; on Tuesday, the 8th Day of July, 1800.* New York, 1800.

*The Trial of Captain James Dunn, for an Assault, with Intent to Seduce Sylvia
Patterson, a Black Woman.* New York, 1809. NYHS.

Trial of Charles Wakely, for a Rape on Mrs. Rebecca Fay. New York, 1810.

*The Trial of Nathaniel Price: For Committing a Rape on the Body of Unice
Williamson, a Child between 10 and 11 Years of Age, at Brooklyn in King's
County, in May 1797. . . .* New York, [1797].

Wheeler, Jacob D. *Reports of Criminal Law Cases Decided at the City-Hall of the
City of New York.* New York, 1823.

Municipal Archives, Hall of Records, New York City
New York County Court of General Sessions Indictment Papers.

New-York Historical Society, New York City
John Tabor Kempe Papers, Lawsuits.

North Carolina

Parker, Erma Edwards, et al. *The Colonial Records of North Carolina.* 2d Ser.
Vols. III–VIII. Raleigh, 1971–1988.

Saunders, William L., et al., eds. *The State Records of North Carolina:*

Published under the Supervision of the Trustees of the Public Libraries, by Order of the General Assembly. 30 vols. New York, 1968–1978.

North Carolina Division of Archives and History, Raleigh

Criminal Action Papers for Edgecomb County, Rowan County, Wake County.

Edenton District Court Papers, 1751–1787.

Edenton District Execution Docket, 1801–1813.

Governor Richard Caswell Letter Book, 1776–1786.

Governor's Office. Proclamations Offering Rewards for Apprehension of Criminals.

Governors' Papers. Vols. XXIV–XXX, XXXV–XXXIX, XLVIII–L.

Miscellaneous Collection. Slavery Papers.

New Bern District Superior Court Miscellaneous Records, 1758–1806.

Onslow County. Miscellaneous Records, box 10, folder: Criminal Acts.

Secretary of State. Court of Oyer and Terminer.

Secretary of State. Court Records. Magistrates and Freeholders Courts.

Superior Court Appearance and Trial Dockets for Pasquotank County, New Bern District, Salisbury District.

Superior Court Minute Dockets for Edenton District, Rutherford County.

Superior Court State Dockets for Craven County, Cumberland County, Edgecomb County, Fayetteville District, Gates County, Granville County, Hyde County, Nash County, Pasquotank County, Person County, Rockingham County, Rowan County, Salisbury County, Surry County, Tyrrell County.

Treasurer and Comptroller. Miscellaneous Group, box 8, 1738–1798.

Wake County Superior Court Criminal Book.

Pennsylvania

L[ogan], J[ames]. *The Charge Delivered from the Bench to the Grand-Jury, at the Court of Quarter Sessions, Held for the County of Philadelphia, the Second Day of September, 1723.* Philadelphia, 1723.

Minutes of the Provincial Council of Pennsylvania. 10 vols. Philadelphia, 1851–1852.

Minutes of the Supreme Executive Council of Pennsylvania. 6 vols. Harrisburg, 1852–1853.

Pennsylvania Archives. 119 vols. Philadelphia, 1852–1935.

Chester County Archives, West Chester

Chester County Oyer and Terminer Docket.

Chester County Quarter Sessions Court Docket, 1730–1739.

Chester County Quarter Sessions File Papers, 1730–1739.
Chester County Quarter Sessions Index to All Cases.

Lancaster County Historical Society, Lancaster
Lancaster County Oyer and Terminer Docket.
Lancaster County Quarter Sessions Docket, 1797–1803.

Historical Society of Pennsylvania, Philadelphia
Criminals and Their Victims. Box 39, case 13, of the Simon Gratz
   Collection.
Pennsylvania Court Papers.
Thomas McKean Papers.
Yeates Legal Papers.
York County Docket.

Pennsylvania State Archives, Harrisburg
Clemency Papers.
Coroner's Inquisitions (select records).
Miscellaneous: 1704–1713 Oyer and Terminer Court Records.
Pardon Books.
Pennsylvania Court of Oyer and Terminer, Court Papers.
Pennsylvania Court of Oyer and Terminer, Dockets.
Pennsylvania Supreme Court, Eastern District, Divorce Papers (select
   records).
Records of Pennsylvania's Revolutionary Government, 1775–1790.
   Clemency Reels, 37–40.
Records of the Supreme Court (Eastern District).

Rhode Island

Rhode Island Supreme Court Judicial Records Center, Pawtucket
Superior Court Dockets for Bristol County, Kent County, Newport
   County, Providence County, Washington County.

South Carolina
State v LeBlanc. 1 Treadway SC 354 (1813).

South Carolina Department of Archives and History, Columbia
General Sessions Court Journals for Barnwell County, Camden County,
   Chester County, Darlington County, Edgefield County, Fairfield County,
   Greenville County, Horry County, Laurens County, Union County, York
   County.

General Sessions Court Sessions Rolls for Darlington County, Fairfield County, Greenville County, Marlboro County, Pinckney County, Spartanburg County, Union County.

Magistrates and Freeholders Court for Camden County, Kershaw County.

Virginia

Barton, Robert T., ed. *Virginia Colonial Decisions. . . . The Reports by Sir John Randolph and by Edward Baradall of Decisions of the General Court of Virginia, 1728–1741.* 2 vols. Boston, 1909.

Cook, Michael L., ed. *Virginia Supreme Court: District of Kentucky: Order Books, 1783–1792.* Evansville, Ind., 1988.

Dorman, John Frederick, comp. *Caroline County, Virginia, Order Book, [1732–1754].* 10 vols. Washington, D.C., 1965–1973.

Goochland County, Virginia, Court Order Books: An Every-Name Index, [1728–1735]. Miami Beach, Fla., 1992.

Jefferson, Thomas. *Reports of Cases Determined in the General Court of Virginia, from 1730 to 1740; and from 1768 to 1772.* Charlottesville, 1829.

McIlwaine, H. R., ed. *Minutes of the Council and General Court of Colonial Virginia.* 2d ed. Richmond, 1979.

McIlwaine, H. R., and John Pendleton Kennedy, eds. *Journals of the House of Burgesses of Virginia, [1619–1776].* 13 vols. Richmond, 1905–1915.

Palmer, Wm. P., et al., eds. *Calendar of Virginia State Papers . . . , IX, January 1, 1799–December 31, 1807.* Richmond, 1890.

Quarrier, Alex. *Abstract of Prisoners Received into the Jail and Penitentiary House.* [Virginia, 1805?]. LOV.

Rankin, Hugh F. *Criminal Trial Proceedings in the General Court of Colonial Virginia.* Charlottesville, [1965].

Sparacio, Ruth, and Sam Sparacio, comps. *Minute Book Abstracts of Fauquier County, Virginia.* Vols. I–III. McLean, 1993–.

Sparacio, Ruth, and Sam Sparacio, comps. *Order Book Abstracts of Caroline County, Virginia.* Vols. III–XV. McLean, 1989–1995.

Stinson, Helen S., comp. *Greenbriar Co., W.Va, Court Orders, 1780–1850.* Moorpark, Calif., 1988.

Library of Virginia, Richmond

Auditor of Public Accounts. Condemned Slaves.

Auditor of Public Accounts. Criminal Charges. Jurors' and Witnesses' Certificates, 1784–1817.

County Court Records for Caroline County, Chesterfield County, Fluvanna County, Franklin County, Orange County, Pittsylvania County.

Fluvanna Supreme Court of Law Minute Book, 1809–1820.

Legislative Petitions.

Richmond Criminal Trials, 1710–1754.

Surrey County Record of Criminal Trials, 1797.

Town of Alexandria Oyer and Terminer Court, Record of Trials and
Examination of Criminals, 1794–1800.

Virginia Executive Papers.

Miscellaneous

*The American Digest: A Complete Digest of All Reported American Cases from the
Earliest Times [1658] to 1896.* Century Edition. 50 vols. St. Paul, Minn., 1897–
1904.

Catterall, Helen Tunnicliff, ed. *Judicial Cases concerning American Slavery and
the Negro.* 5 vols. Washington, D.C., 1926–1937.

Russell, J[ohn]. *An Authentic History of the Vermont State Prison.* . . . Windsor,
Vt., 1812.

United States v Dickinson. Federal Cases (US) No. 14, 957a (Hempstead
[US] 1), 1820.

Wallace v Clark. 2 Tenn. (2 Overt.) 93–94 (1807).

Public Record Office, Kew Gardens, London
WO 71/82, 83, 84, 86, 88, 89, 91–97, 148, 149, 150a, 150b.

LEGAL TREATISES AND STATUTES

Connecticut

Acts and Laws, of His Majesties Colony of Connecticut in New-England. Boston,
1702.

Acts and Laws . . . of His Majesty's English Colony of Connecticut. . . . New
London, 1750.

Acts and Laws of the State of Connecticut in America. Hartford, 1805.

Cushing, John D., comp. *The First Laws of the State of Connecticut.*
Wilmington, Del., 1982.

Cushing, John D., ed. *The Earliest Laws of the New Haven and Connecticut
Colonies, 1639–1673.* Wilmington, Del., 1977.

Hoadly, Charles J., et al., comps. *Public Records of the State of Connecticut,
[1776–1803].* 11 vols. Hartford, 1894–1967.

The Public Statute Laws of the State of Connecticut. Hartford, 1808.

The Public Statutes of the State of Connecticut . . . . Hartford, 1821.

Delaware

Cushing, John D., comp. *The First Laws of the State of Delaware*. 2 vols. Wilmington, 1981.

Cushing, John D., ed. *The Earliest Printed Laws of Delaware, 1704–1741*. Wilmington, 1978.

Laws of the Government of New-Castle, Kent, and Sussex, upon Delaware. Philadelphia, 1752.

Laws of the State of Delaware . . . [1798]. New Castle, 1798.

Laws of the State of Delaware . . . [1798–1805]. Wilmington, 1816.

Florida

Duval, John P. *Compilation of the Public Acts . . . of the Territory of Florida Passed prior to 1840*. Tallahassee, 1839.

Rea, Robert R., and Milo B. Howard, eds. *The Minutes, Journals, and Acts of the General Assembly of British West Florida*. University, Ala., 1979.

Georgia

Lamar, Lucius Q. C., comp. *A Compilation of the Laws of the State of Georgia, [1810–1819]*. Augusta, 1821.

Marbury, Horatio, and William H. Crawford, comps. *Digest of the Laws of the State of Georgia: From Its Settlement as a British Province, in 1775, to the Session of the General Assembly in 1800, Inclusive*. Savannah, 1802.

Prince, Oliver H., comp. *A Digest of the Laws of Georgia . . . [to 1820]*. Milledgeville, 1822.

Watkins, Robert, and George Watkins, comps. *Digest of the Laws of Georgia*. Philadelphia, 1800.

Illinois

Philbrick, Francis S., ed. *The Laws of Illinois Territory, 1809–1818*. Springfield, 1950.

Pope, Nathaniel, ed. *Laws of the Territory of Illinois. . . .* Kaskaskia, 1815.

Indiana

Laws of the Indiana Territory. . . . Vincennes, 1807.

Philbrick, Francis S. *The Laws of the Indiana Territory, 1801–1809*. Springfield, 1930.

Thornbrough, Gayle, and Dorothy Riker, eds. *Journals of the General Assembly of Indiana Territory, 1805–1815*. Indianapolis, 1950.

Kentucky

Bradford, John. *The General Instructor; or, The Office, Duty, and Authority of Justices of the Peace, Sheriffs, Coroners, and Constables, in the State of Kentucky.* Lexington, 1800.

Toulmin, Harry, and James Blair. *A Review of the Criminal Law of the Commonwealth of Kentucky.* 1804; Holmes Beach, Fla., 1983.

Louisiana

Kerr, Lewis. *An Exposition of the Criminal Laws of the Territory of Orleans.* . . . New Orleans, 1806.

Maryland

Bacon, Thomas, comp. *Laws of Maryland at Large.* . . . Annapolis, 1765.

Bisset, James, comp. *Abridgment and Collection of the Acts of Assembly of the Province of Maryland, at Present in Force.* Philadelphia, 1759.

Colvin, John B. *A Magistrate's Guide; and Citizen's Counsellor.* . . . Fredericktown, Md., 1805.

Hall, John E. *The Office and Authority of a Justice of the Peace in the State of Maryland.* Baltimore, 1815.

Herty, Thomas. *A Digest of the Laws of Maryland.* . . . Baltimore, 1799.

The Laws of Maryland . . . [1799–1810]. Annapolis, 1811.

Maxcy, Virgil, comp. *The Laws of Maryland, with the Charter, the Bill of Rights, the Constitution of the State, and Its Alterations, the Declaration of Independence, and the Constitution of the United States, and Its Amendments.* 3 vols. Baltimore, 1811.

Votes and Proceedings of the House of Delegates of the State of Maryland, March Session, 1778. [Annapolis], 1778.

Massachusetts

Acts and Laws. . . . Boston, 1697.

The Book of the General Lawes and Libertyes concerning the Inhabitants of the Massachusets. 1648; Pasadena, Calif., 1975.

The Charters and General Laws of the Colony and Province of Massachusetts Bay. . . . Boston, 1814.

Davis, Daniel. *A Practical Treatise upon the Authority and Duty of Justices of the Peace in Criminal Prosecutions.* Boston, 1824.

Dickinson, Rodolphus. *A Digest of the Common Law, the Statute Laws of Massachusetts, and of the United States, and the Decisions of the Supreme Judicial*

Court of Massachusetts relative to the Powers and Duties of Justices of the Peace. Deerfield, [Mass.], 1818.

Freeman, Samuel. *The Massachusetts Justice.* . . . Boston, 1795.

Freeman, Samuel. *The Massachusetts Justice.* . . . Boston, 1802.

Mississippi

Toulmin, Harry, comp. *The Magistrates' Assistant . . . Compiled for the Use of Justices of the Peace in the Mississippi Territory.* Natchez, 1807.

Missouri

Geyer, Henry S. *Digest of the Laws of Missouri Territory.* St. Louis, 1818.

New Hampshire

Batchellor, Albert Stillman, ed. *Laws of New Hampshire, Including Public and Private Acts and Resolves and the Royal Commissions and Instructions, with Historical and Descriptive Notes, and an Appendix.* 10 vols. Manchester, 1904–1922.

Cushing, John D., comp. *The First Laws of the State of New Hampshire.* Wilmington, Del., 1981.

Cushing, John D., ed. *Acts and Laws of New Hampshire, 1680–1726.* Wilmington, Del., 1978.

The General Laws and Liberties of the Province of New Hampshire, 1681. Calendar of State Papers, Colonial Series, *America and West Indies, 1574–1739.* Vol. XI. CD-ROM, 2000.

Hodgdon, Moses. *The Complete Justice of the Peace: Containing Extracts from Burn's Justice, and Other Justiciary Productions.* Dover, N.H., 1806.

New Jersey

Bush, Bernard, comp. and ed. *Laws of the Royal Colony of New Jersey.* New Jersey Archives, 3d Ser. 5 vols. Trenton, 1977–1986.

Cushing, John D., comp. *The First Laws of the State of New Jersey.* Wilmington, Del., 1981.

Cushing, John D., ed. *The Earliest Printed Laws of New Jersey, 1703–1722.* Wilmington, Del., 1978.

Parker, James. *Conductor Generalis; or, The Office, Duty, and Authority of Justices of the Peace.* . . . Woodbridge, N.J., 1764.

Pennington, William S., comp. *Laws of the State of New-Jersey.* Trenton, 1821.

New York

Acts of Assembly Passed in the Province of New-York from 1691 to 1725. New York, 1726.

The Colonial Laws of New York, from the Year 1664 to the Revolution. 5 vols. Albany, 1894.

Cushing, John D., comp. *The First Laws of the State of New York.* Wilmington, Del., 1984.

Cushing, John D., ed. *The Earliest Printed Laws of New York, 1665–1693.* Wilmington, Del., 1978.

Dunlap, John A. *The New-York Justice; or, A Digest of the Law relative to Justices of the Peace in the State of New-York.* New York, 1815.

Gentleman of the Law. *A New Conductor Generalis.* . . . Albany, N.Y., 1803.

Gentlemen of the Bar. *A New Conductor Generalis.* . . . Albany, N.Y., 1819.

Laws of the State of New York Passed at the Sessions of the Legislature, [1777–1801]. 5 vols. Albany, 1886–1887.

Laws of the State of New-York, Passed at the Thirty-sixth Session of the Legislature. Albany, 1813.

Parker, James. *Conductor Generalis.* . . . New York, 1788.

North Carolina

Clark, Walter, ed. *The State Records of North Carolina.* 14 vols. Goldsboro, Winston, 1895–1904.

A Complete Revisal of All the Acts of Assembly of the Province of North-Carolina, Now in Force and Use. New Bern, 1773.

Cushing, John D., ed. *The Earliest Printed Laws of North Carolina, 1669–1751.* 2 vols. Wilmington, Del., 1977.

Davis, James. *The Office and Authority of a Justice of Peace.* New Bern, 1774.

Haywood, John. *The Duty and Office of Justices of Peace, and of Sheriffs, Coroners, Constables, etc., according to the Laws of the State of North Carolina.* Halifax, 1800.

Haywood, John. *A Manual of the Laws of North-Carolina.* Raleigh, 1814.

Iredell, James, comp. *Laws of the State of North-Carolina.* Edenton, 1791.

Iredell, James, and François-Xavier Martin, comp. *The Public Acts of the General Assembly of North-Carolina.* New Bern, 1804.

Martin, François X. *The Office and Authority of a Justice of the Peace . . . of North Carolina.* New Bern, 1804.

Ohio

Swan, Gustavus, comp. *A Compilation of Laws, Treaties, Resolutions, and Ordinances, of the General and State Governments Which Relate to Lands in the State of Ohio [to 1815–1816]*. Columbus, 1825.

Pennsylvania

Bache, Richard. *The Manual of a Pennsylvania Justice of the Peace*. . . . Philadelphia, 1810.

Cable, Robert L., comp. *The Statutes at Large of Pennsylvania from 1682 to 1700*. Vol. I. Harrisburg, 2001. http://www.palrb.us/stlarge/index.asp

A Collection of All the Laws of the Province of Pennsylvania, Now in Force. Philadelphia, 1742.

Cushing, John D., comp. *The First Laws of the Commonwealth of Pennsylvania*. Wilmington, Del., 1984.

Cushing, John D., ed. *The Earliest Printed Laws of Pennsylvania, 1681–1713*. Wilmington, Del., 1978.

Dunlop, J., comp. *The General Laws of Pennsylvania, from the Year 1700 to April 22, 1846*. Philadelphia, 1847.

George, Staughton, et al., comps. and eds. *Charter to William Penn, and Laws of the Province of Pennsylvania, Passed between the Years 1682 and 1700*. . . . Harrisburg, 1879.

Graydon, William. *The Justices and Constables Assistant*. . . . Harrisburg, Pa., 1805.

Mitchell, James T., and Henry Flanders, comps. *The Statutes at Large of Pennsylvania from 1682 to 1801*. Vol. XV. Harrisburg, 1911.

Read, Collinson. *Precedents in the Office of a Justice of Peace*. Philadelphia, 1794.

Rhode Island

Acts and Laws of the English Colony of Rhode-Island and Providence Plantations. . . . Newport, 1767.

Bartlett, John Russell, ed. *Records of the Colony of Rhode Island and Providence Plantations in New England*. 10 vols. Providence, 1856–1860.

Cushing, John D., comp. *The First Laws of the State of Rhode Island*. 2 vols. Wilmington, Del., 1983.

Cushing, John D., ed. *The Earliest Acts and Laws of the Colony of Rhode Island and Providence Plantations, 1647–1719*. Wilmington, Del., 1977.

South Carolina

Cooper, Thomas, and David J. McCord, eds. *The Statutes at Large of South Carolina*. 10 vols. Columbia, 1836–1841.

Cushing, John D., comp. *The First Laws of the State of South Carolina*. 2 vols. Wilmington, Del., 1981.

Cushing, John D., ed. *The Earliest Printed Laws of South Carolina, 1692–1734*. 2 vols. Wilmington, Del., 1978.

[Grimké, John Faucheraud]. *The South-Carolina Justice of Peace*. . . . Philadelphia, 1796.

Grimké, John Faucheraud, comp. *The Public Laws of the State of South-Carolina*. Philadelphia, 1790.

O'Neall, John Belton. *The Negro Law of South Carolina*. Columbia, 1848.

Simpson, William. *The Practical Justice of the Peace of South-Carolina*. Charleston, 1761.

Tennessee

Haywood, John. *The Duty and Authority of Justices of the Peace in the State of Tennessee*. Nashville, 1810.

A Revisal of All the Public Acts of the State of North Carolina and of the State of Tennessee Now in Force in the State of Tennessee. Nashville, 1809.

Vermont

The Laws of the State of Vermont. . . . 2 vols. Randolph, 1808.

Slade, William, comp. *The Laws [of Vermont] . . . to . . . 1824*. Windsor, 1825.

Soule, Allen, and John A. Williams, eds. *Laws of Vermont, [1777–1795]*. State Papers of Vermont, XII–XV. Montpelier, 1964–1967.

Virginia

Hening, William Waller. *The New Virginia Justice*. . . . Richmond, 1795.

Hening, William Waller, comp. *The Statutes at Large, Being a Collection of All the Laws of Virginia*. . . . 13 vols. Richmond, Philadelphia, 1809–1823.

Shepherd, Samuel. *The Statutes at Large of Virginia, from October Session 1792, to December Session 1806, Inclusive*. Richmond, 1835.

Starke, Richard. *The Office and Authority of a Justice of Peace, Explained and Digested, under Proper Titles*. Williamsburg, Va., 1774.

Tate, Joseph, comp. *Digest of the Laws of Virginia*. . . . Richmond, 1823.

Tate, Joseph, comp. *Digest of the Laws of Virginia*. . . . Richmond, 1841.

Webb, George. *The Office and Authority of a Justice of Peace*. . . . Williamsburg, Va., 1736.

Miscellaneous

[Auckland, William Eden]. *Principles of Penal Law.* 2d ed. London, 1771.

Blackstone, William. *Commentaries on the Laws of England.* 4 vols. 1765–1769; Chicago, 1979.

Blackstone, William. *Commentaries on the Laws of England: With Notes of Reference to . . . the United States. . . .* Edited by St. George Tucker. 5 vols. Philadelphia, 1803.

[Burn, Richard]. *Burn's Abridgment; or, The American Justice.* 2d ed. Dover, N.H., 1792.

Chambers, Robert. *A Course of Lectures on the English Law Delivered at the University of Oxford, 1767–1773.* Edited by Thomas M. Curley. Madison, Wis., 1986.

Conductor Generalis; or, The Office, Duty, and Authority of Justices of the Peace. . . . Philadelphia, 1722.

Dagge, Henry. *Considerations on Criminal Law.* London, 1772.

East, Sir Edward Hyde. *A Treatise of the Pleas of the Crown.* Vol. I. Philadelphia, 1806.

Hale, Matthew. *Historia Placitorum Coronae: The History of the Pleas of the Crown.* 2 vols. London, 1736.

Hale, Matthew. *Pleas of the Crown: A Methodical Summary.* 1678; London, 1972.

Hawkins, William. *A Treatise of the Pleas of the Crown. . . . 1724–1726.* 2d ed. New York, 1972.

Jacob, Giles. *The Modern Justice. . . .* London, 1720.

Lambert, Sheila, comp. *House of Commons Sessional Papers of the Eighteenth Century.* 14 vols. Wilmington, Del., 1975.

M'Dougal, John. *The Farmer's Assistant; or, Every Man His Own Lawyer.* Chillicothe, Ohio, 1813.

Nelson, W[illia]m. *The Office and Authority of a Justice of Peace. . . .* 5th ed. London, 1715.

INDEX

Dick (Va., 1782), 176n, 196n

Dick (Va., 1808), 100n, 103n, 112n, 118n, 138n

Dick (Va., 1810), 176n, 180n

Dickinson (Ark., 1820), 141n

Divorce, 57n, 66, 75n, 98n, 105n, 114, 134n

Doctors: and examination of rape victims, 103–104, 112–113

Dolbe, John, 134

Domaine, John, 93n, 102, 117n, 119n, 146n

Douglass, William, 31, 222, 226

Downs, Hannah, 104

Dudley, Joseph, 132

Duffy, Sarah, 102, 117

Dunn, Capt. James, 30n, 121, 179n, 183–184

Dunn, John, 82n, 126

Durham, Jack, 173n

Dwight, Margaret Van Horn, 94–95

Dwight, Theodore, 77n

Eastworthy, Anne, 44

Ellis, Mary, 59

Ely, John, 75n, 96n, 98, 134n, 147n

Emission, 135–139

Enslaved women: sexual coercion of, 64–74, 100–101, 116, 118n, 178n, 246

Equiano, Olaudah, 1

Evans, Celia, 53, 86

Evans, Foster, 120

Extralegal punishment, 119–120, 176–177

Extralegal settlement, 121–122, 183, 191–192

Farr, Samuel, 111, 140

Farrell, Thomas, 182n

Fay, Rebecca, 119, 132, 189

Feminist scholarship, 9, 10, 51, 80; criticism of, 56

Fern, 175n

Fish, 185

Fisher, John, 93n, 104n, 206n

Fithian, Philip Vickers, 100, 173n

Fleming, William, 223

Fogg, John, Sr., 75n, 105n, 123n

Fogg, Ursula, 75, 105

Force: and consent, 16–18, 68, 73–74, 77, 86, 94–95, 239–240

Fornication, 1, 30, 32–34, 37, 51, 227n; prosecution for, 43, 64, 141, 153–158, 167, 173; statutes on, 149

Forshee, Maria, 70, 114

Fortis, Edmund, 26, 33n, 45n, 182n, 206n

Foster, Hannah Webster, 34n, 35n, 36, 46

Foster, Rebecca, 122

Fox, Sarah, 99

France, 44, 83n, 217, 218n, 224–225n, 229n

Franklin, Benjamin, 1, 19, 37

Free blacks, 78, 168–170, 190n, 193; and coerced sex incidents, 85, 124, 173, 178–179, 187

Fryley, Mary, 93

Fulfourd, Mindwell, 24, 156, 158, 176

Gale, James, 204

Galvin, Peter, 98

Gates, Mary, 98

Gates, Silas, 75

Gatter, Christiana, 234, 236

Gatton, James, 98

Genner, William, 98

George (N.C.), 194n

George (Va.), 62n, 186

Georgia: coerced sex incidents in, 1, 102, 121n, 144, 172, 177n, 191, 226n, 249; statutes in, 144n, 146, 149–150, 168

Gibson, Isabella, 156–157, 182

Gibson, James, 108n, 151n, 196n

Gibson, John, 36n, 199n

Gilbert, Benjamin, 8

Girls (twelve and under), sexual coercion

McVaugh, John, 108n, 112n

Maine: coerced sex incidents in, 38, 58, 61n, 92, 122, 189

Major, 2n

Mallery, Joseph, 92n, 107n, 133n

Marony, Thomas, 110n, 124n

Marriage, 30, 220; sex within, 17–19, 40, 183, 240; changes in, 38, 216; rape within, 44, 78–80, 213–216, 228–229; promises of, 64; protection of, 123, 206, 215–216, 241

Marsh, Mary Ann, 121

Martin, Jesse, 150n

Martin, Joseph, 222

Marvin, David, 134n

Maryland: coerced sex incidents in, 28n, 30n, 36, 56, 62n, 66n, 85, 101, 131n, 143n, 146–147, 151, 172n, 174, 178n, 180–181n, 185, 191n, 194, 197–199, 201–203, 249; statutes in, 146–150, 169n, 207

Massachusetts: coerced sex incidents in, 1, 22, 25, 29n, 30–34, 43, 45n, 55–56, 59, 61n, 63, 65n, 76, 81, 96–98, 102–105, 108, 122, 131n, 136, 141, 145, 159n, 172–173, 175–177, 181–182n, 189, 191, 195, 197n, 201–202, 205–207, 225n, 249; statutes in, 129, 133n, 142–143, 146, 148–149

Mastery, 10, 54–55, 77–78; and sexual coercion, 23–24, 63–74, 97, 100–101, 239–240; and mistresses, 93, 114–116. *See also* Coerced sex; Race.

Mather, Cotton, 1, 30, 221–222

Mathers, Jane, 61, 108, 116–117, 189

Mathers, Mary, 116–117

Matrons' juries, 106, 109

Matthewson, Patience, 131

Medical jurisprudence, 111, 137, 140

Meloy, Charles, 173n

Men: superiority of, 19–23; and sexual pursuit, 20–23; and women's consent,

40–43; and path to court, 116–124; and evidence, 119–120; in rape narratives, 211–218

Metcalfe, Deborah, 191

Mid-Atlantic: slave courts in, 168–169, 245; conviction rates in, 190, 193–194; population of, 201n; and regionalism, 242–243; and race, 245; cities in, 245. *See also individual colonies and states*

Midwife, 108

Miller, Anne, 117

Miller, Margaret, 106, 131n, 185n

Mills, Robert, 25, 156–157

Mitchell, Ann, 1

Mitchell, John, 181n

Mittelberger, Gottlieb, 41, 66n, 105n, 132n, 154n

Modesty, 88, 90–91, 105, 125

Montgomery, Elizabeth, 66

Mooklar, 118

Morgan, Lydia, 64n

Morony, Thomas, 110n, 124n

Morris, John, 45n, 109n, 187

Morrow, John, 121, 181n, 185n

Morse, Jedidiah, 224

Moses, Abraham, 25, 27, 34n, 60n, 109n, 120n, 122n, 124n, 188n, 191

Mountain, Joseph, 26

Mully, Vanskelly, 111n, 138n, 143n, 182n

Munse, Dick, 198n

Murder, 26, 28n, 33, 53–54, 57, 83–84, 88, 175, 202n, 203–205; of men, 47, 120, 230; threat of, 53, 57, 76–77, 96, 98, 100, 126, 216; punishment for, 144; laws on, 149–150, 169; and Native Americans, 210, 218, 221, 223; and slave revolts, 210, 219–221

Murphy, John, 22, 197n

Murphy, Mary, 56

Murphy, Stephen, 28n, 63n, 107n, 122n, 131n, 191n, 206n

Muslims, 217

Native Americans, 58, 148, 153; Creek, 3; sexual coercion of, 3, 53, 80–84n, 164n; sexual mores of, 31, 225–229; as rapists, 177, 182, 210, 212, 218, 221–224, 244n; Cherokee, 222, 225; Choctaw, 225, 228

Ned, 178n, 196n

Newberry, William, 176

New England, 164–165; morality in, 5, 28, 35, 60, 81, 92, 177; crime literature in, 32–33, 199, 205, 207, 242–243; and race-based laws, 128, 147–148, 152, 168, 170; capital punishment in, 143; sentencing in, 146; African Americans in, 171, 204; conviction rates in, 190–194; newspaper reports in, 201–202; and Native American relations, 221–222; exceptionalism of, 245; cities in, 245. *See also individual colonies and states*

Newhall, Calvin, 177n

New Hampshire: coerced sex incidents in, 75–76, 96, 107, 109, 115, 140–141, 146, 159, 170, 174, 202, 270; statutes in, 129, 149

New Jersey: coerced sex incidents in, 1, 25, 27–28, 53, 62, 65n, 82, 93, 98, 138, 145, 159, 172, 174–176n, 178n, 191n, 195n, 230–231, 249; statutes in, 129, 143, 148–151, 169

Newspapers, 8, 200–204

New York: coerced sex incidents in, 20, 29, 31, 45–46, 59, 62, 70, 77n, 82n, 88, 93–94n, 97–99, 102, 104n, 106, 112, 114n, 117–123, 126, 131n, 132–134, 138, 141, 144–149, 159n, 174, 178, 182–185, 188n, 189n, 195, 201–203n, 206, 207n, 249; statutes in, 146–148, 169–170

Nichols, Maria, 93

Noble, Mary, 25

Noel, Taylor, 105

Nolan, Gabriel, 45n, 56, 158n

Norcum, James, 69–73

Norcum, Mary, 71

Norman, Roz, 29n, 111n, 198n

North: and African American defendants, 118, 178, 195–196; and South, 128, 151–152, 175, 208, 245–246; capital punishment in, 143; abolition of slavery in, 179, 190, 245; conviction rates in, 190, 193; population of, 201n; criminal print genre in, 205–207

North Carolina: coerced sex incidents in, 2, 30, 66, 68–73, 93, 116, 120, 138n, 147, 151n, 173n, 176n, 183, 194n, 198n, 249; statutes in, 168

Oakchoy King, 3n, 228n

O'Hara, Patrick, 110n, 124n

Ohio: coerced sex incidents in, 94–95

Opperman, Andrew, 146n

Orgasm, 139–140

Osborn, Hester, 1

Packard, Mary, 104

Paine, Thomas, 1, 233n

Painter, Elizabeth, 27, 44

Parish, Diana, 111–112

Parker, Caesar, 141n, 159n, 173n

Parkinson, Robert, 186

Parkinson, William, 207n

Parkman, Ebenezer, 100n, 121

Parry, Catherine, 25, 93, 156–157

Passions, 17–19, 28, 34–37, 46, 48–51, 62, 77, 216, 226, 239; shifting views on, 35–37, 48–49, 95

Patriarchy, 4, 11, 56n, 125, 214, 220, 229, 240

Patterson, Daniel, 155–156, 175n, 182n

Patterson, Sylvia, 30n, 121, 179n, 183

Patton, Ann, 159

Paxton, James, 34n, 61, 108n, 116–117n, 120n, 189, 199n

Peaches, 61

Pearls, Margaret, 24, 27

Pears, Elizabeth, 25

Penetration, 69, 110, 112, 135–139, 186–187

Penn, William, 90

Pennington, James, 101

Pennsylvania: coerced sex incidents in, 8, 16, 23–27, 34, 44–45, 53, 57, 59–61, 63–64, 68–74, 79, 83, 93, 97, 99, 102–105, 107–110, 112–117, 120, 122–124, 131n, 132–133, 136, 138n, 139, 141, 144–147, 152–160, 163, 174–176, 181–182, 185, 188–189, 191, 196–197n, 199n, 201–202, 204, 206n, 226n, 239, 249; statutes in, 129, 142, 144, 147–148, 169

Penross, Amos, 112n, 117n

Perkins, John, Jr., 53n, 75–76, 92n, 96n, 102

Perkins, Sarah, 53, 75–76, 86, 92n

Peter (Va., 1782), 196n

Peter (Va., 1797), 178n

Peter (Va., 1808), 198n

Petitions, 36, 85, 134, 141, 143n, 150, 176, 180, 185–186, 196–199

Pettigrew, John, 85

Pettit, Eleanor, 79

Pettit, Samuel, 79

Phalet, Mary, 137

Pherill, Joseph, 151n

Phillips, Samuel, 30, 199n

Phillis, 70

Pompey, 26–27, 62

Pool, Phebe, 99, 186

Potter, Thomas, 199n

Poverty, 42, 104; and coerced sex, 12; and rape charges, 114, 122

Power of Sympathy, The, 34, 36, 49

Pregnancy: premarital, 18, 43–44, 46, 57, 64, 135, 206; after coerced sex, 41n, 57, 75, 92, 105, 123, 185, 213; and enslaved women, 65, 77; sickness from, 79; of rape victim, 84, 202, 223; and criminal charges, 104–106, 158; and proof of rape, 139–141

Price, Nathaniel, 70n, 97, 99n, 103n, 113n, 133n, 144n

Pridham, Christopher, 24n, 64n, 97n, 159

Prince, 176

Proctor, Thomas, 189n

Propaganda, 230–235, 237

Property, rape as offense against, 11, 232

Prostitution, 24, 27, 28n, 40, 183, 206

Pryor, Thomas, 83

Race, 86, 163–167; and stranger rape, 56–57; and neighbor rape, 61; and charges, 160, 171–176; in early Republic, 166, 243–244; and courts, 167–170; and extralegal punishment, 176–177; and pleas, 180; and character, 181–186; and evidence, 186–190; and conviction, 190–193; and sentencing, 193–199; and commutation, 197–199; and publicity, 199–207; and criminal justice, 207–209. *See also* Mastery

Ransom, Joshua, 81n, 136n

Rape: versus coerced sex, 2–4; legal definition of, 16, 29, 128–129; proof of, 17; sinfulness of, 30–33; archetypal, 54–57, 63, 77, 164; false charges of, 57, 187; as punishment, 80; criteria for, 130–139, 142; punishments for, 144; publicity of, 199–207; public uses of, 210–237; discourse of, 243–245. *See also* Coerced sex

Rape law: history of, 29; racialization of, 127–128, 162; Americanization of, 142–152

Rape myth of black men, 10, 14, 212, 218, 244; historiography of, 164–166; reframing of, 165–167, 207–209

Ravishment. *See* Coerced sex; Rape

Rawdon-Hastings, Francis, Lord, 41

Religion, 17, 28, 30–35, 93, 205, 224, 244

Remarkable History of Miss Villars, The, 214–215

Reuben, 99

Revenge: rape as, 183, 185; for rape, 232–233, 247

Reynolds, Mary, 22

Rhode Island: coerced sex incidents in, 22, 64n, 65–66, 81, 124n, 131, 134–135n, 137, 145, 148, 159, 180; statutes in, 142, 148, 170

Rice, David, 65

Richardson, Abraham, 156, 158, 161n

Richardson, Samuel, 45, 214

Robb, David, 16, 44n, 70n, 97n, 105n, 141n, 174, 185n

Robin, 194n

Rockefeller, Christopher, 145n

Rood, Hannah, 76, 92, 96, 123

Rook, James, 27n, 28n, 138n

Rowlandson, Mary, 221

Rucks, Parthena, 119, 186

Sadism, 55, 80, 83–85

Saltonstall, Nathaniel, 210, 221

Sam (Conn.), 113n, 118n

Sam (Va., 1773), 178n

Sam (Va., 1780), 176n

Sanders, William, 104n, 112n

Sanford, Peter, 46

Saub, George, 120

Sawyer, Lanah, 62, 93, 206

Scandlin, Terry, 120n

Scott, Billy, 118n, 181n

Seduction, 6, 24–26, 28–29, 32–34, 37, 68n, 123, 178, 206; in literature, 17–18, 34, 40, 45–52, 211–214, 216, 244–245

Sell, Moses, 120

Seller, Mary, 22

Sentimentalism, 28, 242

Sentimental literature, 17, 34–36, 45–46, 90, 213, 244

Sermons, 30–33, 204–205, 232

Servants: coerced sex of, 64, 66–74, 97, 114–116

Seventeenth century: images of women in, 28, 30, 35n, 38, 46; sex crimes in, 30, 92n, 124n; matrons' juries in, 106n; images of black men in, 164, 218–219; images of Native Americans in, 212, 221–223

Sexual coercion. *See* Coerced sex

Sexual double standard, 18, 38, 51, 91, 105–106, 242

Sexually transmitted disease, 103–104, 112, 183

Sexual relations: as continuum, 16–52; medical views on, 19; as aggressive, 20–25; as negotiation, 68–69, 71–73, 242; knowledge of, 107

Sharper, 194n, 202

Sheehen, Bryan, 34n, 207

Sip, 176n

Slave rebellion, 127, 149, 162, 170, 175, 210, 219–221, 226, 229–230, 244

Slavery: and criminal justice, 163, 167–171, 243; laws on, 147–152

Slaves. *See* Enslaved women: sexual coercion of; Race; Slave rebellion; Slavery

Smith, Benjamin, 132n

Smith, Elizabeth, 110, 187

Smith, Mary, 156, 160

Smith, William, 230–231

Social status, 3–4, 12, 25, 27, 63–74, 80–83, 118, 240

Sodomy, 11, 31, 79, 135, 149

Sources, 8–9

South: and planter gentry, 21–22; and seventeenth-century morality, 92; and regionalism, 118, 128, 151–152, 243, 245–246; sentencing in, 146–147, 150–151, 194; rape myth in, 165, 208; slave courts in, 168–171; dual charges in, 175; black-on-black prosecutions in, 178–179; and conviction rates for slaves, 190, 193; postmortem displays in, 194, 195n; sentencing in, 196; commutations in, 198; Native Americans in, 227